Great Wall of China

BEIJING & NORTHERN CHINA

the Bradt Travel Guide

Thammy Evans

谭美

edition
1

www.bradtguides.com

Bradt Travel Guides Ltd, UK
The Globe Pequot Press Inc, USA

Faces of the Great Wall...

Shanhaiguan
— the Old Dragon's Head —
where the Great Wall enters
the sea
(GR) page 121

Simatai
Great Wall at sunset,
Beijing province
(LG) page 169

Qingshankou
Hebei province
(GR) page 123

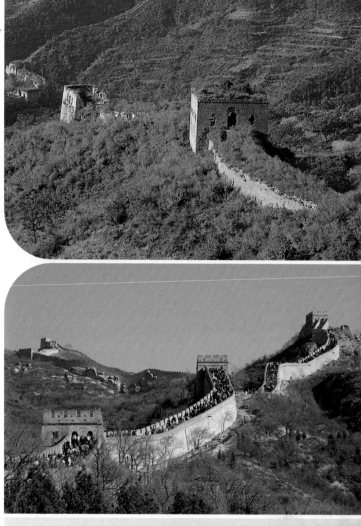

Crowded Badaling
Great Wall
(GR) page 177

Simatai
Great Wall in winter
(LG) page 169

Author

Born in London of Welsh and Malay Chinese parents, Thammy Evans has travelled, lived and worked abroad for over 15 years, mostly in China and southeast Europe. Her first trip overseas was to Malaysia at age eight, and she has been dabbling in numerous foreign languages ever since. Amongst many other travels her most memorable are the Trans-Siberian railway from Tianjin to Moscow in 1991, mountaineering in Bolivia in the summer of 1999, and the field research for this guidebook. Her professional career has ranged from travel-guide author to new business development in hydrogen fuel-cell cars in China to political analyst in Macedonia. Her articles and Master's thesis on China have appeared in various media including *Modern Asian Studies*, *Whole Earth*, *Automobility* and *Forum*. *Macedonia: The Bradt Travel Guide* was Thammy's first book. This is her second.

DEDICATION

To my husband, Victor Peter Ullom, who learnt to cook while I wrote this book.

FEEDBACK REQUEST

At Bradt Travel Guides we're aware that guidebooks start to go out of date on the day they're published – and that you, our readers, are out there in the field doing research of your own. You'll find out before us when a fine new family-run hotel opens or a favourite restaurant changes hands and goes downhill. So why not write to us and tell us about your experiences, for the next edition? We'll include you in the acknowledgements of the next edition of *Great Wall of China* if we use your feedback. So write to us – we'll look forward to hearing from you!
bradtgreatwall@yahoo.co.uk

Hilary Bradt

The first Bradt travel guide was written in 1974 by George and Hilary Bradt on a river barge floating down a tributary of the Amazon. In the 1980s and '90s the focus shifted away from hiking to broader-based guides covering new destinations – usually the first to be published about these places. In the 21st century Bradt continues to publish such ground-breaking guides, as well as others to established holiday destinations, incorporating in-depth information on culture and natural history with the nuts and bolts of where to stay and what to see.

Bradt authors support responsible travel, and provide advice not only on minimum impact but also on how to give something back through local charities. In this way a true synergy is achieved between the traveller and local communities.

I faced Thammy Evans's latest manuscript with some trepidation. I knew virtually nothing about China and the only fact I could dredge up about the wall was that it was the only manmade object visible from space. Within a few pages Thammy disabused me of that notion and drew me into the intoxicating possibilities and heartening realities of travel in northern China. This is a reassuring book, as much for what it tells you is impossible (hiking the full length of the wall) as for what is possible. I particularly appreciated the insider knowledge, calming common anxieties on how to get from the airport, choosing from a menu, using public transport and so on. With this book anyone could face China with confidence.

First published May 2006
Bradt Travel Guides Ltd
23 High Street, Chalfont St Peter, Bucks SL9 9QE, England; www.bradtguides.com
Published in the USA by The Globe Pequot Press Inc,
246 Goose Lane, PO Box 480, Guilford, Connecticut 06437-0480

Text copyright © 2006 Thammy Evans
Maps copyright © 2006 Bradt Travel Guides Ltd
Illustrations © 2006 individual photographers and artists (see below)

The author and publisher have made every effort to ensure the accuracy of the information in this book at the time of going to press. However, they cannot accept any responsibility for any loss, injury or inconvenience resulting from the use of information contained in this guide.

British Library Cataloguing in Publication Data
A catalogue record for this book is available from the British Library

ISBN-10: 1 84162 158 7
ISBN-13: 978 1 84162 158 6

Photographs
Front cover Fairy Tower, Simatai (Li Guicheng)
Back cover Dragon relief, Beijing (HS/TIPS)
Title page Street decoration, Beijing (LC/TIPS), Man dressed as Ming dynasty soldier (DS), Great Wall at sunset, Simatai (LG)
Text Thammy Evans (TE), Li Guicheng (LG), Chris Page (CP), Geoffrey Roy (GR), Victor Ullom (VU), Dave Saunders (DS), Martin Scheel (MS), TIPS: Luis Castaneda (LC/TIPS), Haral Sind (HS/TIPS)

Illustrations Thammy Evans
Maps Alan Whitaker with Thammy Evans

Typeset from the author's disc by Asian Absolute, London
Printed and bound in Italy by Legoprint SpA, Trento

KEY TO STANDARD SYMBOLS

Bradt

—·—·—	International boundary	🇪	Embassy
·········	District boundary	(PSB)	Public security bureau
⌶⌶⌶⌶	National park	⊠	Post office
✈	International airport	✚	Pharmacy
✈	Other airport	$	Bank
▬▬▬	Railway	🅿	Car parking
▬▬▬	Metro (underground)	🛺	Rickshaw hire
═══	Main road dual carriageway	🚲	Cycle hire
═══	Main road	Ⓔ	Internet access
═══	Minor road	♩	Telephone
=======	Track (4x4 etc)	♣	Buddhist temple
·············	Featured path/trek etc	☯	Daoist temple
·············	Other footpath	🏯	Drum tower
■	Capital city	⼤	Pavilion
●	Main town or city	🌲	Pagoda
○	Small town or village	➤	Gateway
▙▙▙▙	Ming Great Wall	🏠	Qing tomb
▪▪▪▪	Other walls (inc city walls)	†	Cathedral/church
🚌	Bus station	Ç	Mosque
☐	Railway station	⼁	Statue
Ⓜ	Metro terminus	❀	Garden
M	Metro station	∴	Archaeological/historic site
⛴	Ferry	※	View point
ℹ	Tourist information	●	Other place of interest (town plan)
⌂	Hotel/accommodation	•	Other place of interest (regional)
Λ	Campsite	⛽	Garage/fuel station
♟	Bar	|||||||||	Steps (town plan)
✗	Restaurant	🚠	Cable car/ropeway/slideway
☕	Café	◉	Cave/grotto
🎭	Theatre/cinema	▲	Hilltop/summit (height in metres)
⚱	Museum/art gallery	⌇⌇10km	Distance between broken road cases
🏛	Important/historic building	▨	Open water
🏰	Castle/fortification	▨	Town plan background
✚	Hospital/clinic/health centre	▨	Urban park
🏃	Stadium	⧄⧄	Urban market area

III

Contents

LIST OF MAPS

Acknowledgements

Where do I start with all the thanks, gratitude and acknowledgements for the help given to me to write this book? Of course, I must start with Hilary Bradt for thinking of me to take it on. A big thanks goes to all those at Bradt Travel Guides for their subsequent help with editing, preparation, pointing out glaringly obvious errors after I could no longer comprehend the text for all the words, and other book-publishing-type things. Then, I must thank Geoffrey Roy for letting me take his infant book and run with it in my own way. I think that puts us (me and the book) about age two now: rambunctious with much more to learn! Alan Whitaker, cartographer extraordinaire, has been extremely helpful in my attempt to take short cuts on compiling the maps electronically – it's been a painstaking cartographical ride, and I could not have done it without you – and I think I still saved some time!

Researching the Ming Great Wall in China was greatly assisted and smoothed by the China network extended to me by the UK-based tour operator, Explore! It is inspiring to realise the depth of knowledge and back-up that Explore! has behind its tours in China, which can only be heartily recommended. I would specifically like to thank: Nick Anstead for suggesting that Explore! could help; Nicola Waller for approving that Explore! would help; Caroline Phillips for introducing me to Zhanghua; Zhanghua for telling his contacts that they should help. His ground contacts, who have been my forward-planning eyes and ears and who have been invaluable: my heartfelt thanks and appreciation go to them all – Peter Cheng Haijian, Mrs Shenfeng, Mr Yang, Gao Shangjie, Bai Feng, Billy Huang Jihui and Fan Xinzhi.

My field research would have been utterly miserable without my travel partners. Firstly YM, who is my mother and my travel partner of old. We first travelled in China for a month in April 1991. Fourteen years later and another five weeks of travel together in China has been just as much fun – thanks Mum. Then came Chris Page – thanks for keeping up with the programme, lending me your iPod, and listening to my incessant frustrations with China – I look forward to our next trip together. Then we were four, with Vanessa Gray and Anne Sieger – a bar-hopping, massage-parlouring, yoghurt-slurping, Mongolian-trekking, invincible foursome: thank you. Thank you Vanessa also for your contributions to the sections on economy, telecommunications, smoking and spitting! Finally, my husband, Victor Ullom, who came for the grande finale and to whom this book is dedicated. He has supported this book in many more ways than travelling and cooking.

Special mention must go to two sets of people in China. Firstly, China's leading Great Wall experts, who offered me their valuable time and insights: Luo Zhewen, Cheng Dalin and William Lindesay. Thanks also to UNESCO China's Director of World Heritage, Beatrice Kaplan. Secondly, my thanks must go to all those hapless people who helped me on my way: Lei Haili, for the audacity to drag us off our bus early and then show us the Beijing wall; Li Guicheng for showing us around Simatai and providing some fantastic photography (see front cover); Zhou at Huangyaguan for giving me Sellotape to mend my notebook; Nicolas from France for reintroducing me to the value of 'thank you'; the Daoist teachers at Erlangshan for giving us an apple; Louisa Lim for her valuable insights and recommendations; Calvin Quek for advice on driving in China; Fong for fish and chips and French wine on a veranda over Beihai; Brian Wallace for tea on a cold day.

Outside of China I must thank: Li Ruru and Panyuan for helping me with translations; Bill Browning, green architect guru, for introducing me to The Commune – one day I hope to have the money to stay there; Damian Howells for help with the language section and reminding me of long hard lessons in tones; Henry Clough of Asian Absolute for PC to Mac interpretation in accented pinyin and catching all my pǔtōnghuà cuòwù before Ruru saw them in print; Martin Walters for flora and fauna advice; Daniel Dillon for his contribution to the topography section on the loess plateau; the US State Department for their press release on Capt Troy 'Gordie' Cope; Stephen Mansfield for his textbox on Zheng He; Gao Hongwei of UNICEF Macedonia for helping me put my China experiences in some context and helping me with yet more mapping; Zhang Wei for providing me with Chinese food when my salivation over the food chapter could be contained no more. I would also like to note here the significant contribution by Richard Willoughby (see pages 111-118) from his Bradt Guide to North Korea. The borders of this guide have been extended – thank you.

Finally, I must particularly thank my work colleagues at NATO HQ Skopje: Brigadier Dennis Blease for letting me take my two months' leave all together to do the field research for the book; Dr Glenn Kelly and Art Shemwell III for man-handling the office in my absence; Mimi, Lari, Zoran and Artan for coping with my bad moods when the deadline was getting precariously close and for providing me with much tea.

Introduction

I first went to China in 1990 to study for a year. It was a love–hate relationship then, and I think I can safely generalise that it continues to be a love–hate relationship for most visitors to China even today, especially if you go beyond the dazzling lights of can-do Beijing. Travelling outside the capital can be so frustrating. Perhaps, because I am half Chinese, it is even more frustrating for me: I can blend in where most visitors cannot, and what I see is a population that knows it was once great, and strives almost without realising it to regain that greatness. Yet so often, the Chinese shoot themselves in the foot by continuing at the same time to promote what they hate most about themselves and/or the West: corruption, a widening gap between the rich and the poor, senseless bureaucracy, destruction of natural riches in the name of progress, jumping ahead of the queue, squalid latrines (or none), and spitting.

So, if outside the comforts of the capital can be so frustrating, why do I love it so much and why should you or I persevere? It is in part because every time I master one of those frustrations, or learn how to get something done, the sense of victory is immense. And it is also because the rewards of travelling into the interior are enormous. Beyond Beijing is still a land little visited. You will come across people who might these days have seen a foreigner on TV, but will not have seen one in flesh and blood. There are literally millions of places and things in the interior of China, off the beaten path, that are famous or sacred or peculiar to the Chinese but not covered in Western guidebooks. And the food is fantastic everywhere - if you know what to ask for. Hopefully, this guidebook will help you with the food, the travel and the frustrations.

And what about the Great Wall – the title and main theme of this guide? This book covers the best sections of the fourth and most famous Great Wall of China built by the Ming dynasty. The image that most non-Chinese have of the Great Wall is of endless stretches of magnificent stonework snaking their way over mountain tops as far as the eye can see. In fact, I reckon that around 70% of the Great Wall, if not more, is made of rammed earth and meanders through semi-arid desert. It is this mud wall, much more so than its stone counterpart, which has forged the path of China's expansion to the borders of Turkmenistan through harsh and inhospitable terrain, leaving garrison and trading towns behind it. This is the wall that has protected the Silk Road. It is the Great Wall that protects the life of the Yellow River and the beginnings of the Chinese civilisation we know today.

It is also the wall that is the most vulnerable to erosion, both natural and manmade. I implore you, therefore, while visiting the mighty Great Wall, to respect this great monument and not be the cause of its further destruction. This means not walking on unmanaged wall and certainly not taking pieces of it back home.

As you read this book, I hope that you will get a sense of the magnitude of the work that is the Great Wall. China in and of itself is enormous - approximately the same size as the USA with over four times as many people. For most travellers to China, it is impossible to visit the whole country, yet few people are going to visit just the Great Wall on a first – or even subsequent – visit. Some may take the Great Wall as a theme for a visit that will also encompass Beijing, while others may be focusing on the broader spectrum of northern China. It is for this reason that I have included some of the most famous and worthwhile attractions along the wall, including ten of the best sites in Beijing; the Yungang Grottoes (housing some of the most magnificent Buddhist stone carvings in the world); the sacred mountain monastery complex of Wutaishan; and the little-known and extremely worthwhile Daoist temple complex, Erlangshan. There is much more to northern China, of course; this is just a start. In addition, this guide offers some insights into China, and how the Chinese tend to see themselves. Most importantly, there are also extensive menu translations in the book so that you too can enjoy the delights of hotpot, the latest Chinese fusion cuisine and many other Chinese culinary delights. And to guide you around, almost a dozen of the guide's 38 maps are a first in English – and all the main maps are bilingual.

Which brings us back to the Great Wall. Long just a frontier barrier, detested by forced labourers who met their death there, and incessantly breached by barbarians, it has only recently come to symbolise China itself: a long-standing civilisation, enduring, tolerant of change and built on hard work; but also ingenious, economic, dynamic and rightly proud.

And, no, it cannot be seen from space.

A NOTE ON SPELLING

Pinyin, the present world standard for transliteration of Chinese characters into Roman letters, is used throughout this book with the notable exception of people and place names, such as Sun Yatsen (Sun Zhongshan in *pinyin*), that have become more established in their Wade–Giles rendition.

The Wade–Giles system of spelling was introduced by Thomas Wade and Herbert Giles in the 19th century. It is best suited to Cantonese, but was gradually applied to Mandarin or pǔtōnghuà. Essentially, hard consonants followed by an apostrophe (eg: p'e k'ing) are indeed pronounced as hard consonants. Without the apostrophe such consonants are misleadingly pronounced as soft consonants. Over time, these all important apostrophes have been dropped out of typographical laziness. 'Peking' is, therefore, in fact pronounced even in the Wade-Giles system as 'Beijing' – which is why there is the confusion between the amateur pronunciation of the capital of China as 'Peking' when in fact it was always pronounced by the China hand (the in-house term for an expert on China) as 'Beijing'. The BBC adopted the Beijing pronunciation of the capital of China in 1997. Many older texts, such as *Response to the West*, and some modern authors wanting to recapture the mood of the time, such as Anchee Min's *Empress Orchid*, use the Wade–Giles system, which is confusing for those unfamiliar with both systems. For the pronunciation of pinyin see the *Language* appendix at the end of this guide.

Part One

General Information

Length of all Chinese defence walls built over last 2,000 years 50,000km

Circumference of the Earth 40,000km (just under 25,000 miles)

Definition of a Great Wall At least 10,000 *li* in length (just over 5,000km)

First Great Wall Built by the Qin dynasty 221–207BC, Liaodong to Lintao, 5,000km

Second Great Wall Built by the Han dynasty to reinforce the Qin Great Wall and add a primary defence line in present Inner Mongolia 205–127BC, 5,000km

Third Great Wall Built by the Jin dynasty AD1200, also known as the Great Ditch Wall, built mostly in Inner Mongolia 5,000km

Fourth Great Wall Built by the Ming dynasty 1367–1644, Yalu River to Jiayuguan 6,700km (7,300km including branches and offshoots)

Estimated number of visitors per year 10 million to Badaling alone (including Chinese visitors)

Estimated number of foreign visitors to China per year 41.8m in 2004 (World Tourism Organisation)

Listed as a World Cultural Heritage Site 1987

Can it be seen from space? No

Lowest point Sea level at Laolongtou

Highest point in Beijing 1,534m at Heita Mountain

Largest tower Zhenbeitai in Shaanxi province

Composition 70% of its length is made of rammed earth or adobe; the remainder is made of stone or brick face over a composite mud and rock interior

Terrain type along the Great Wall Ranging from temperate, coastal and mountainous, to semi-arid and desert

Background on the Great Wall of China

The wall was erected at ruinous expense to protect China's northern frontiers from attack, but over the following 1,600 years it had been allowed to crumble into disrepair. [Ming Emperor] Zhu Di began a programme of rebuilding and strengthening, adding watchtowers and turrets along the wall's existing 5,000 kilometres and extending it by a further 1,400. It ran from the Pacific as far west as the Heavenly Mountains in central Asia.

Gavin Menzies, 2002

HISTORY OF THE GREAT WALL

A 'great wall' as defined by the Chinese must be at least 10,000 *li* (5,000km) in length. The order for the first Great Wall was given by the first unifier of China, Emperor Qin Shi in 221BC. He wanted a great wall built to protect the unification he had fought so long to secure. This wall, however, joined and fortified a number of shorter walls already built by the smaller kingdoms within the new empire.

PRE THE FIRST GREAT WALL The oldest of the pre-Great Wall sections dates back to 685–645BC when the Kingdoms of Qi and Chu (in present-day Shandong province) built a wall between their lands. This wall already set the trend of incorporating natural features in the terrain to extend the defensive intentions of the wall. The Chu/Qi wall was built right up to the river Han, which then extended as a natural border and barrier between the two kingdoms. The river Han was considered a 'great wall of water' (shuǐ chángchéng).

It was another two centuries before the next section of pre-Great Wall was built by the Kingdom of Qin from 461BC to 409BC in what is now southern Shaanxi province in order to keep out the State of Jin to the north and west of the Yellow River. Over the course of the next two centuries, wall building as a defensive measure became more common all over China between the various kingdoms of the Warring States period.

Significantly for the first Great Wall of China, the Kingdom of Qin decided in the mid 3rd century BC to extend its northern border walls in order to keep out the marauding Eastern Hu nomads. This brought the Qin kingdom's northern wall to over 4,000 *li* (2,000km) extending from today's Gansu province in the west, past Yulin city to the northernmost bend on the Yellow River in the east. At almost the same time, some 20 years later, and for the same reason of keeping out the Eastern Hu nomads, the Kingdom of Yan also built a northern border of some 2,400 *li* (1,200km). The Yan wall extended from the Yellow River in the west past today's Zhangjiakou city into Liaoning province in the east. The new and improved northern defensive front stood at almost 7,000 *li* in length.

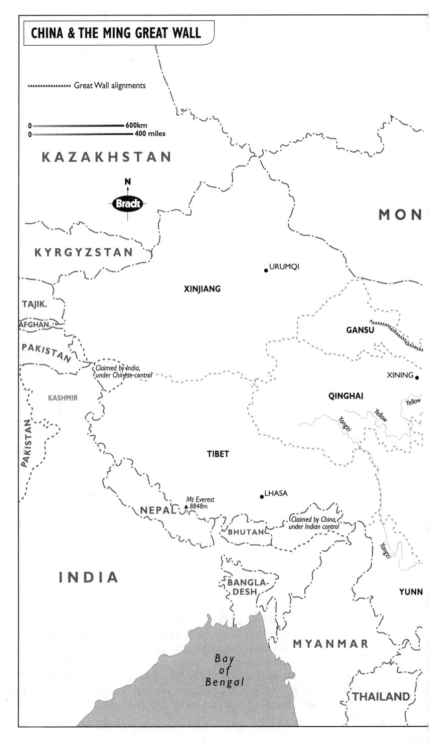

CHINA & THE MING GREAT WALL

.... Great Wall alignments

0 ——————— 600km
0 ——————— 400 miles

KAZAKHSTAN

N

Bradt

MON

KYRGYZSTAN

• URUMQI

XINJIANG

GANSU

TAJIK.

AFGHAN.

XINING •

PAKISTAN

*Claimed by India,
under Chinese control*

QINGHAI

Yellow

KASHMIR

Yellow

Yangzi

PAKISTAN

TIBET

Mt Everest
▲ *8848m*

• LHASA

NEPAL

*Claimed by China,
under Indian control*

BHUTAN

Yangzi

INDIA

**BANGLA-
DESH**

YUNN

MYANMAR

*Bay
of
Bengal*

THAILAND

4

wall was built from Jingle, just northeast of today's Taiyuan – the capital of Shanxi province – past what would later become Women's Pass (Niangziguan) and on to Daixian, thus connecting it up with the inner wall built in 446.

The Wei kingdom and the ensuing unifying Sui kingdom continued the tradition of wall building and reinforcement for almost the next two centuries, until the Sui was overthrown by the Tang dynasty in AD618. The ensuing Tang dynasty pursued a policy of engagement, and trade with the nomads to the north began. As a result the Great Wall became a means of regulating trade and levying customs taxes. By the beginning of the 10th century the Qidan nomads of the northeast had settled and become an accepted part of northern China. A period of turmoil ensued after the fall of the Tang dynasty, until the Liao and the Song dynasties emerged to divide China. The Liao dynasty, established in 937, controlled the north, while the Song dynasty, founded in 960, regrouped and shifted the Chinese heartland as they retreated into the south. Having incorporated the Qidan into their dynasty, midway through the 11th century the Liao were troubled by another tribe from further north, the Nuzhen (known as Manchu in Mandarin). In 1058, the Liao tried to curb their incursions by building the northernmost defensive walls of China on the rivers Heilong and Songhua in today's Harbin province. These walls were not wholly successful, however, and just over half a century later the Nuzhen destroyed both the Liao and the Song dynasties.

THE THIRD GREAT WALL OF DITCHES OF THE JIN DYNASTY In 1115, the Nuzhen established the Jin dynasty over the largest territory of China ever ruled by a single emperor. Coming from the north themselves, the Nuzhen fully understood that incursions from the northern Mongols would be forthcoming. So in 1148, the Jin dynasty emperor ordered the fortification of their northern frontier. Walls were built and reinforced in today's Heilongjiang province, and another inner wall was built through today's Inner Mongolia. Many of these walls were characterised by the incorporation of ditches running alongside the Jin walls. These additional fortification measures were designed to make scaling the wall even more difficult. While very few of these ditches remain visible today, well-kept records and archaeological digs record their existence.

Despite the new and improved fortified walls the Mongols, led by the infamous Kublai Khan, overthrew the Jin in 1276 and established the Yuan dynasty. Ruling over the largest extension of borders ever known to China, the Yuan had no need for the Great Wall. As a result they let it fall to rack and ruin throughout their reign until 1368, when the indigenous Chinese Ming dynasty retook control of China.

THE FINAL GREAT WALL OF THE MING DYNASTY After finally succeeding in ousting the Mongols from China, the Ming dynasty was determined to ensure that neither the Mongols, nor any other non-Chinese, such as the Manchu, would rule over China again. This was approached in different ways at first. Hongwu, the first emperor, re-established manning on the Great Wall by deploying a double line of defence. The first line consisted of fortresses, beacons and passes along the remains of the old ruined Great Wall. This included the building of Jiayuguan fort in 1372 at the westernmost end of the Ming wall. Then, set back a few days' march from the wall and evenly spaced along its length, eight garrisons were set up as a second line of defence to reinforce the Great Wall if it came under siege.

The second Ming emperor, Yongle (1403–25), took a very different tack for dealing with potential threats. He embarked upon a programme of engagement with and exploration of the lands and peoples beyond the inner circle of the Middle Kingdom. He re-established the capital at Beijing, where he built the magnificent Imperial Palace (commonly known as the Forbidden City), and sent ships as far as Africa, America, the Antarctic and Siberia. (For a well-written account of this, read Menzies's *1421*, see *Appendix 3*.) By the end of his reign though, bad omens turned the emperor against such pricey explorations, which had cost much in lives and money. The Great Wall once again took on renewed importance.

It took, however, until 1449 and a vicious defeat at the hands of the Mongols in the Battle of Tumu before reinforcement of the Great Wall was really taken seriously. Juyong Pass itself was fortified and further walls were built to the north (Badaling started in 1539, and Shangmen) and to the south (Nankou). While the Mongols had moved into the long-abandoned Ordos loop of the Yellow River bend, the Ming built walls in the southern Ordos across today's Ningxia province to the Helan Mountains.

Between 1569 and 1583, the commander of Jizhou garrison, General Qi Jiguang, embarked upon the most well-known reinforcements of the Ming Great Wall. These are the famous walls north of Beijing that symbolise the Great Wall to most of the world. General Qi's reinforcements, making extensive use of rock and stone, took the lives of thousands of men and took many times longer than previous efforts at wall building had taken. They were built to take ten armoured men abreast or five mounted horses abreast. It was during this period that a branch of the Great Wall was built down to the Yellow Sea's Bohai Gulf at Shanhaiguan. Shanhaiguan soon became a separate garrison, the ninth. The emperor, however, disappointed at the slow progress of the wall, had General Qi put to death for wasting time and resources. Later when General Qi's reinforced walls at Badaling succeeded in repelling the Mongols, the emperor had the name of the general reinstated and his statue stands today at Taipingzhai on the Tianjin wall.

THE POST-MING PERIOD UNTIL THE PRESENT DAY The Manchu retook China in 1644 and formed the Qing dynasty. Again, having no use for the Great Wall as a defensive barrier, it was abandoned to the rigours of natural enemies – the sun, wind and rain. The last battle fought at the Great Wall was in 1938, when the Japanese broke through the ranks of the Eighth Army at Gubeikou to march on Beijing. Bullet marks from the infantry battle can still be seen in the wall at Gubeikou.

Over the last century, and especially during the Cultural Revolution, much of the Great Wall was robbed of rocks and stones either by local people who have used the materials for building their own houses or by local governments for more ambitious projects, such as the dam at Huanghuacheng. Other sections of the Great Wall have been dismantled to make way for highways or enlarging towns.

In 1984, President Deng Xiaoping, recognising the great cultural value and national symbolism of the Great Wall, embarked upon its restoration and protection. A few years later in 1987, Badaling, the closest section of the Great Wall to Beijing, was declared a World Cultural Heritage Site by UNESCO. This was the first section of the Great Wall to be administered by the state and opened to the public for an entrance fee. Since then, protection of the wall has become an increasingly elusive issue (see *Conservation and development,* pages 18-21).

CHRONOLOGY OF BUILDING THE GREAT WALL

685–645BC	Construction of the first pre-Great Walls between the Kingdom of Qi and the Kingdom of Chu (now Shandong Province) of the Spring and Autumn (Zuozhuan) Period.
461–409BC	Walls are built by the Kingdom of Qin during the Warring States (Zhanguo) in what is now

southern Shaanxi southeast of the Yellow River. More defensive walls are built throughout the Warring States period by different kingdoms all over China.

272BC	The Kingdom of Qin extends its northern walls to over 4,000 *li* (2,000km), from what is now Gansu province past Yulin in present-day Shaanxi province to the most northern bend in the Yellow River.
254BC	The Kingdom of Yan extends the northern defensive wall concept another 2,400 *li* (1,200km) even further to the east past what is now the town of Zhangjiakou in Hebei province all the way to today's Liaoning province.
214–210BC	Emperor Qin Shi orders the construction of the first Great Wall of 10,000 *li*, joining previous sections of border walls to extend from Min Xian (Lin Tao in today's Gansu province) to what is now Pyongyang in North Korea.
204BC	The first emperor of the Han dynasty has the Great Wall extended further west to help keep out the Xiongnu nomads.
130BC	Emperor Wudi rebuilds much of the Qin Great Wall, which had been breached by the Xiongnu nomads, and extends an outer wall from Zhangjiakou to Hohhot in Inner Mongolia.
127BC	General Huo Qubing sets up command posts in Wuwei and Jiuquan and extends the Qin Great Wall in order to protect the new outposts.
111BC	Further command posts are established at Zhangye and Dunhuang and the Great Wall is extended from Jiuquan to Yumenguan.
102BC	The Han Great Wall is extended to Lopnor in Xinjiang and external walls are added behind it.
AD423	The Northern Wei kingdom builds an outer wall of almost 2,000 *li* from Chifeng to Wuyuan in today's Inner Mongolia.
AD446	Emperor Tai of the Northern Wei kingdom drafts 100,000 labourers to build 1,000 *li* of inner wall from Juyongguan to the Yellow River at Heqi.
AD543	The Eastern Wei builds another inner wall of 150 *li* from Jingle, northeast of Taiyuan, the capital of today's Shanxi province, to join the previous inner wall at Daixian.
AD618–917	The Tang dynasty embraces the nomadic tribes north of the Great Wall and pursues a policy of trade and engagement.
AD900	The Qidan nomads start to settle and are incorporated in northern China.
AD937	The Liao dynasty establishes its rule over northern China and becomes the keeper of the Great Wall (the Song dynasty controls southern China as of AD960).
1058	The Liao dynasty builds the northernmost defensive walls of China in today's Harbin province at Heilong and Songhua (Soungari) rivers in order to keep out the Nuzhen (Manchu) tribe.
1148–99	The Jin dynasty of the Nuzhen fortify their northern frontier against the Mongols, and build a further inner wall through Inner Mongolia.
1276–1368	The Great Wall falls into ruin during the Mongolian Yuan dynasty whose borders extended well beyond the Great Wall.
1372	Jiayuguan fort is built at the westernmost end of the renewed wall.
1376	The first Ming emperor, Hongwu, orders the establishment of eight garrisons along the Great Wall and reinforces the passes of Juyong, Gubeikou, Xifengkou and Songjing.
1449	The Battle of Tumu brings the Mongols within a day's march of the capital, Beijing.
1539	Fortifications at Badaling are started.
1569–83	General Qi Jiguang builds the Ming wall from Juyong Pass to Shanghaiguan.
1644	The Ming dynasty is overthrown by the Qing dynasty of the Manchus and the Great Wall falls into disrepair.
1900	The British destroy part of the Great Wall at the sea near Shanhaiguan as part of an offensive against the Boxer Rebellion.
1932	Ripley's *Believe It or Not* asserts that the Great Wall 'would be visible from the moon'.
1938	The Japanese break through the Great Wall at Gubeikou to march on China during World War II.
1953	Restoration begins on some of the most damaged sections of the Great Wall.
1956	The city walls of Beijing are dismantled under protest to make way for modern highways and rail tracks.
1966–75	Hundreds of kilometres of the Great Wall are damaged during the Cultural Revolution.

1972	US President Richard Nixon visits the Great Wall.
1987	The Great Wall of China is listed as a World Cultural Heritage Site.
2003, October	China's first man in space confirms that the Great Wall cannot be seen from space.

MYTHS

Myths about the Great Wall are numerous, most having developed as a result of the distinct lack of regard that most Chinese had for the Great Wall. Records and folk tales show that the first Great Wall built by Emperor Qin Shi was in fact seen as a symbol of the despotism of the first emperor of all China. The Han dynasty which followed the Qin were keen to promote this version of events and so legitimise their own rule, even though they themselves went on to build another Great Wall.

Most Chinese throughout the centuries have had very little idea – if any at all – of the Great Wall, and it was not accorded any significance as a national symbol until the 20th century. During the Yuan dynasty (1267–1386) and the Qing dynasty (1644–1911), prior and post the Ming dynasty, the Great Wall was abandoned altogether and disappeared into memorial oblivion, as neither of these northern tribes (the Mongols and the Manchu respectively) had a need for a wall between the south and the expanded northern territories. For those few in the know, the 'Great Wall' (chángchéng) was that wall first ordered by Emperor Qin Shi in 214BC, and all other walls after that were merely border walls – bian as they were called, even by the Ming rulers.

By the 20th century, the Ming wall was simply known as the 'old frontier' (lăobiān). For instance, when Frederick Clapp of the *Geographical Review* reached the Ming wall at Shenmu, Shaanxi, in 1920, he wrote in his article of the trip that 'the natives said: "This is not the 'Great Wall'; this is the 'First Frontier Wall', built only 400 years ago; the 'Great Wall' is further north."'

At the beginning of the 20th century, Sun Yatsen, who established the Republic of China in 1912, wrote for the first time about the first Great Wall of Emperor Qin Shi as a protector of the Chinese race. He asserted that although Qin Shi had clearly been a despot, the Great Wall ordered by him, and for which many thousands of people died, had prevented the annihilation of the Chinese by the nomads of the north, and thus helped to preserve the Chinese up until the modern day.

Later, during the 1940s and early 1950s, even the communist leader Mao Zedong alluded to the greatness of the Great Wall in some of his famous poems. Reconstruction of the worst section was even undertaken. By the crazed years of the Cultural Revolution, however, the Great Wall was again reviled for its association with despotism and old cultural values. Hundreds of kilometres of the Great Wall were destroyed.

Only in the last 20 years of the Great Wall's 2,220-year history has it really taken on meaning as a national icon symbolising the greatness of the Chinese nation itself. Before that it was regarded by the few Chinese who even knew about it as an accursed pile of mud and stones.

CAN THE GREAT WALL BE SEEN FROM SPACE? The biggest living myth about the Great Wall of China is that it can be seen from space. This is not in fact true, and was confirmed by the first Chinese astronaut on his maiden voyage in October 2003. Nobody has actually seen the wall from anything higher than an aeroplane. Some claim that it might be visible from within Earth's orbit (up to 300km from the ground) but not from outer space (at least 400km from Earth) and certainly not from the moon (384,500km from Earth).

The original myth seems to have first taken root when the American-published magazine *The Century* asserted in 1893 that the Great Wall was 'the only work of man of sufficient magnitude to arrest attention in a hasty survey of the earth's surface'. By 1932, Robert Ripley, the 20th-century Marco Polo, was claiming in his illustrated magazine *Believe It or Not* that the Great Wall was the 'mightiest work of man' and 'the only one that would be visible to the human eye from the moon!' This claim, made long before space flight was even possible, continued all the way up to the 1950s, and it is easy to see how the supposition 'could be seen from the moon' becomes 'can be seen from space'.

The myth has become so widespread that, when evaluating the Great Wall of China for listing as one of UNESCO's World Heritage Sites, the International Council on Monuments and Sites (ICOMOS) stated in their evaluation report that the Great Wall of China is 'the only work built by human hands on this planet that can be seen from the moon'!

WERE ONE MILLION MEN BURIED IN THE GREAT WALL? The same illustration plate in Ripley's *Believe It or Not*, mentioned above, also claims that 'one million men were buried in the walls to make them strong'. To date, however, no bones, human or otherwise, have ever been found in the wall, nor are there official records that humans, alive or dead, were deliberately or accidentally buried in the wall. There are, however, several poems and tales that lament the number of men who were conscripted to work on the wall and died doing so, never to return to their families or home towns. One such poem, possibly dating from as early as the last few decades BC goes:

> Don't you just see below the Long Wall
>
> Dead men's skeletons prop each other up?

These common lines developed into one of the most famous tales in China of the Great Wall, that of weeping Meng Jiangnü (see page 131 below), who travelled hundreds of miles to see her husband, only to find him eventually buried in the wall. This tale has led to the modern-day Western variant that men were buried alive in the Great Wall in order to help protect the wall and the people of China from incursion and dominance by foreign nomads. Such burials were not, however, true, although the number of people who died building the wall is certainly in the millions.

IS THE MORTAR IN THE GREAT WALL MADE FROM GROUND HUMAN BONES? There is a popular myth that the mortar used to bind stones and bricks together in the Great Wall is in part made of crushed human bones. In actual fact, the bonding agent in Ming Chinese mortar is rice flour. This unique bonding agent is what helps to identify other constructions found around the world that are believed to have been made by the Ming Chinese. When the Ming dynasty embarked upon its frenzy of wall building, the use of rice as a bonding agent, the confiscation of rice from the south to feed conscripted labour on the wall, the conscription of labour itself, as well as many other draconian measures helped to keep wall building a source of resentment among the population.

CONSTRUCTION OF THE GREAT WALL

The Great Wall of China, like many military constructions since, was at the forefront of design for its time. Repeatedly, no expense was spared on its construction, and millions of people were forced to build it. By the Ming dynasty, almost one million soldiers were stationed in nine garrisons along the wall. In addition to these men, prisoners were sent to do hard labour on the Great Wall, and, if more labour was

Originally published in 1932 in the magazine Believe It or Not, Robert Ripley's panel is the likely source of the myth that the Great Wall can be seen from space. Reproduced from Arthur Waldron's The Great Wall of China: From History to Myth

needed, men from all over China were conscripted. The variety of architectural designs, innovations and defence measures used in creating the Great Wall is testimony to the genius of humankind. The Great Wall Museum at Jiayuguan has an excellent display in both English and Chinese explaining the architecture of the Great Wall. If you can't start there, then the following should serve as an introduction to the variety of what you might come across.

TYPES OF WALL CONSTRUCTION There are five types of wall construction used in building the Great Wall: rammed earth, adobe, stone, brick and cliff. By the Ming dynasty, walls were graded into three levels. Grade one was the most superior of the three categories and indicated a wall made of a foundation of stone slabs, a brick inner and outer wall filled with rubble or stone, and fortifications and surfaces made of brick. Grade one walls were built at the most important passes, such as Shanhaiguan, Gubeikou, Jinshanling and Mutianyu. Grade two walls used brick on the outer wall but local small stone on the inner wall, such as at Jiumenkou Water Pass (see page 119). Grade three walls consisted mostly of stone or cliff walls or single brick wall constructions, such as Huangyaguan (page 133) and Simatai (page 169). Most of the stone and brick Great Wall of the Ming dynasty was also made as horse ways (the forerunner of motorways), ie: wide enough and strong enough to take up to five mounted armoured men abreast.

Rammed earth The earliest type of construction used in the Qin and Han walls is tamped or rammed earth. This type of construction was mostly used in the loess plateau from Datong to Jiayuguan and in Inner Mongolia. Moulds were constructed from wooden planks, into which loess and or clay was filled to a depth of seven cùn (inches or 18cm) and packed in using a sledgehammer-like weight to a depth of five cùn (13cm). Once tamped, the next layer was added and tamped. Overall, the wall had to taper towards the top as vertical sides were not stable. Reeds were often laid in the construction to help bind the sand together and add strength. These walls, some of which are over 2,000 years old, can still be found at Wulate in Inner Mongolia, and at Yangguan in Gansu province.

Adobe Adobe wall, which was much more versatile in its use, overtook rammed earth walls upon the spread of adobe brick-making methods in the 2nd century AD. Adobe bricks were made of packed clay and, after drying hard in the sun, were cemented together using clay as a mortar. Adobe walls were easier to make wide enough to carry men atop them or even mounted horses. They did not wear well though and could erode easily under heavy rain or friction. As a result, a coating of loess plaster was applied to the outside of adobe walls, which were mostly built in the dry regions of the northwest. Despite later inventions of brick or the obvious superiority of stone, the Ming continued to use adobe in the western regions as this made use of easily available local materials. The Jiayuguan and the Gansu province wall is made almost entirely of adobe.

Stone Stone walls have been in existence for several millennia in China. Many early stone walls are simple drystone piles of unworked or rough hewn local rocks. Later, especially, after the Qin and Han periods, larger walls were constructed using smooth worked rocks on the outer wall, rough hewn rock on the inner wall with rammed earth and rubble filling the interior. By the Ming dynasty stone walls often used large hewn stone slabs at the bottom of the wall and kiln-fired bricks might complete the tops, surface and battlements. Stone walls were used extensively throughout the mountainous regions of Beijing and Hebei provinces. The superior durability of stone made these walls enduring and almost impenetrable to enemy onslaught. Badaling, Mutianyu and Jiankou are fine examples of grade one, superior stone wall (see diagram page 14 overleaf).

Brick Brick walls were at the height of their design in the Ming dynasty. Having mastered how to make kiln-fired bricks of intense durability, the Ming set about constructing great swathes of brick wall throughout the northeast from the Yalu River to Datong and beyond. The durability of kiln-fired bricks, coupled with the

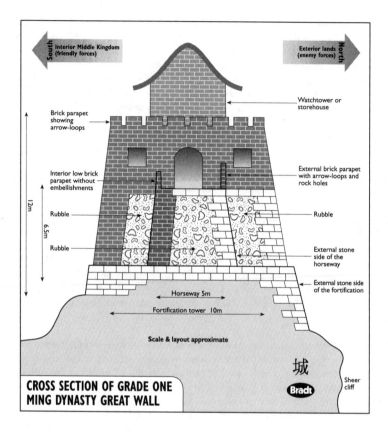

Interior Middle Kingdom (friendly forces) — South

Exterior lands (enemy forces) — North

Watchtower or storehouse

Brick parapet showing arrow-loops

Interior low brick parapet without embellishments

External brick parapet with arrow-loops and rock holes

Rubble

Rubble

Rubble

External stone side of the horseway

12m

6.5m

Horseway 5m

Fortification tower 10m

External stone side of the fortification

Scale & layout approximate

城

Bradt

Sheer cliff

CROSS SECTION OF GRADE ONE MING DYNASTY GREAT WALL

use of a superior mortar made of lime and rice water, made brick walls almost impervious to the rains of the northeast. They were also easy to transport, easily formed into different shapes, and made very smooth-sided walls, which were difficult for the enemy to scale. When needed, bricks were used to face both the inner and outer wall and the interior filled with rubble. Fortifications, battlements and surfaces were completely made of brick. Jinshan wall in Beijing province, Xifengkou at Panjiakou Reservoir, and Shanhaiguan on the seafront are some of the best examples of grade one brick walls.

Cliff Cliff walls consisted of naturally occurring cliffs, which were incorporated into the construction of the Great Wall. Sometimes wall building would stop at the cliff edge and continue on the other side. Cliffs were common alongside rivers and where passes in the Great Wall occurred. Later, mountainsides were even hewn to create smooth-sided cliffs which were not easily scaled by the enemy. A good example of the use of cliffs in the Great Wall is at Huangyaguan in Tianjin province.

Passes and gates Archways built into the wall to allow passage of traders and troops were called gates or kǒu (口), such as Gubeikou, Zhangjiakou and Jiankou. A simple structure usually consisted of double wooden doors reinforced with metal sheet plating and large copper nails. These openings had to be protected by troops and inevitably barrack quarters and even small towns would build up alongside the gate.

Many openings were required at passes (guān 关) through mountain ranges, such as at Juyongguan, Huangyaguan and Niangziguan. Later the word ' guān ' was used for troop garrison towns through which travellers or traders had to register on their way in and out of the wall, such as Shanhaiguan and Jiayuguan, despite the fact that these were built in fairly flat areas.

Owing to the strategic importance of these passes, the gate itself was usually reinforced by outer cordon walls and significant defence in depth (see page 16). Passes could be either dry passes or water passes. Dry passes, such as Shanhaiguan and Jiayuguan, had no river running through them. Water passes, such as Jiumenkou and Huangyaguan, built sophisticated sluice gates, dams and other water breakers to control the flow of water out to the 'barbarians' beyond the wall.

Towers, platforms and beacons A variety of towers, platforms and beacons were built into and around the wall in order to fortify it and hold or call for reinforcements. Basic open-topped square platform towers were built into the wall at frequent intervals, some as close as a couple of hundred metres apart. They were used to fortify long stretches of wall, especially corners, and troops would gather there from which to fight invaders. Platform towers, or wall terraces (qiáng tái 墙台) as they were called, might also be topped with a watchtower which could house stationed troops. Most passes usually had a pass tower atop the main gate that served as an administrative structure and watchtower.

The largest fortification tower along the Great Wall is Zhenbeitai, north of Yulin in Shaanxi province (see page 215).

Beacon towers or fire signal towers (fēnghuǒtái 烽火台) could be found along the wall itself as well as on their own, far out in front of the wall or many miles behind the wall. They were designed to use fire or smoke signals to send messages from the lookout posts back to the wall and garrison commanders in the interior. This type of line of sight communication was much faster and safer than a runner or rider and was later supplemented by the use of gunshots. One fire and one gunshot signified a small enemy force of fewer than 100 men; two fires and two gunshots for up to 500 enemy troops; three fires and three gunshots for a battalion of 1,000; four of each for a division of 5,000; and five of each for an army of 10,000.

A few of the larger and strategic passes also had inspection terraces built into them. These were large open platforms where the generals would gather to inspect assembled troops. Inspection terraces can still be seen at Huanghuacheng and Jiumenkou.

Battlements Many different battlements topped the wall itself. For the most part, this consisted of a crenellated (also known as arrow loop) wall on the exterior side and a shorter straight-topped parapet on the interior side. The crenellated exterior wall, as well as the outer walls of beacon and pass towers, often had embrasures at waist level for firing arrows through, as well as rock holes at the foot of the upper walls through which to throw heavy projectiles. These holes in the upper defence walls were often built to slope downwards in order to aid with firing arrows and missiles.

On steep sections of wall, where soldiers were easily exposed to enemy fire, barrier walls were built perpendicular to the crenellated side of the wall. This allowed troops regular protection from the enemy whilst they passed up or down the wall. The barrier walls usually contained embrasures so that soldiers could give covering fire for the movement of friendly forces whilst they pepper-potted up or down the wall. Original barrier wall can still be seen at Jiaoshan, Jinshanling, and reconstructions at Hushan.

Defence in depth By the Ming dynasty an amazing array of ingenious obstacles and security measures were employed to provide defence in depth, ie: layers of security to prevent the enemy from approaching and to prevent the army's own troops from deserting (see diagram on facing page).

Moats were one of the simplest constructions, initially a simple by-product of digging up earth to build the wall itself or make bricks for the wall. Sometimes these were filled with water, or merely left as ditches. The third Great Wall of the Jin dynasty made extensive use of this defensive measure.

In front of the pass gate a defensive wall called wèngchéng often built to prevent the enemy getting direct access to the gate. This wall was usually built in a square formation with entrances on the short side walls. Once this far, the enemy was easily trapped and slaughtered from the parapets above. A smaller wengcheng was sometimes built on the inside of the pass gate. At Shanhaiguan only the eastern wengcheng facing toward the sea is still in existence.

Luòchéng were the next line of defence usually consisting of a circular wall ahead of the wengcheng. Luocheng still exist outside the eastern gate at Shanhaiguan as well as on the southern gate of Juyonguan. Watchtowers were often added to these outer walls.

Fighting walls created smaller secondary walls some 40–50m ahead of the main wall from which soldiers would ward off the enemy before retreating to the main defence. If enemy cavalry were involved (which was characteristic of the Mongols and northern nomads) then Hǔluò were set out. Huluo were large areas in front of the wall set with short and sharp wooden spikes to deter the advance of the cavalry – simple but very effective. In combination with these measures, mǎniúshǐ (dried horse or cow dung) was thrown with the wind to blind oncoming invaders.

Another ploy used to detect and help prevent the desertion of troops or detect the advancement of spies, was the use of tiántián areas. These were areas of smoothly raked sand in which it was easy to see the footprints of anyone approaching or leaving.

Outlying support buildings With a military structure as large as the Great Wall needing a million soldiers to patrol it, there were a great many outlying buildings constructed to support the wall and its defence of the Middle Kingdom. Barrack castles (yíngbǎo) for the staging of troops through to the Great Wall were dotted throughout the north of China. They were all built with city walls, usually of adobe, and some were even connected to the Great Wall with branch horse way walls. This was the case with Shahukou and the interior barrack castles or towns that can still be seen today. Even after the Qing took over from the Ming and the wall was no longer patrolled, these barrack castles continued as small villages. They remain obvious today by their names and their adobe town walls, although most are almost completely abandoned save a few old folk.

Storehouses or block houses for grain, guns and ammunition were dotted along the Great Wall itself as well as in many villages. Sometimes these were simple, round one-storey constructions such as the one at Huangyaguan, or they would have a second storey for sheltering soldiers upstairs, and maybe a command post storey such as the one at Jinshanling.

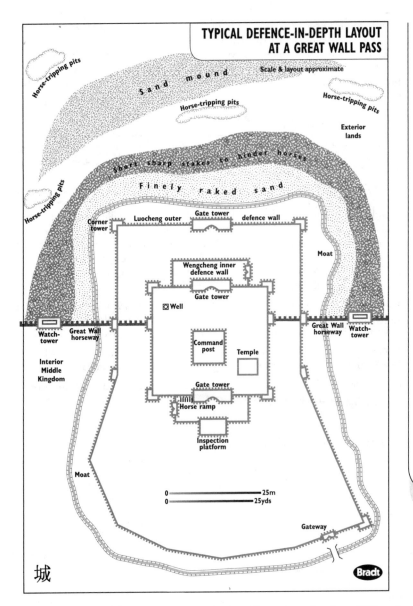

TYPICAL DEFENCE-IN-DEPTH LAYOUT AT A GREAT WALL PASS

Scale & layout approximate

Horse-tripping pits

Sand mound

Horse-tripping pits

Horse-tripping pits

Exterior lands

Short sharp stakes to hinder horses

Finely raked sand

Horse-tripping pits

Corner tower

Luocheng outer

Gate tower

defence wall

Moat

Wengcheng inner defence wall

Gate tower

Well

Great Wall horseway

Watch-tower

Watch-tower

Great Wall horseway

Command post

Temple

Interior Middle Kingdom

Gate tower

Horse ramp

Inspection platform

Moat

0 ——— 25m
0 ——— 25yds

Gateway

城

Bradt

Brick and mortar kilns were numerous in the villages along the Great Wall, and the significance of their role in the superior brick construction of the Ming dynasty has still to be fully researched. Kilns can be found near Zhenbeitai and in Qingquan.

Finally, temples were an integral part of any section of the Great Wall that had soldiers, a command post or a pass. Sometimes temples were built on a small offshoot of the Great Wall itself, such as at Badaling and Juyongguan, although the temples themselves no longer exist. More often, however, the temple to a local god or figure was in a nearby village. This is the case with the Yungang Buddha

Grottoes near Datong (see page 183), the Eight Spirit Temple at Huangyaguan and the Dule Temple in the nearby town of Ji in Tianjin province. Undoubtedly, the most famous temple connected with the Great Wall is that of the Temple of Weeping Meng Jiangnü, whose wailing broke open part of the Great Wall at Jiumenkou when she could not find her conscripted husband at the wall (see box, page 131).

CONSERVATION AND DEVELOPMENT

With the adoption of the Great Wall of China as a national symbol and the recognition of it as a world-renowned heritage site, conservation and development of the Great Wall have been taken up apace in the last 20 years. Unfortunately, the two (conservation and development) do not necessarily go hand in hand in China.

Although China does have a history of extremely skilled and outstanding craftsmanship, of which the Great Wall is also an example, such craftsmanship, especially in restoration, in today's Chinese climate of cheap and fast manmade disposables is sorely lacking. Before delving into the broad arguments of conservation versus development, the reader should note the following definitions used throughout this guidebook:

Restoration: to put something back to its former condition. With regards to building work, this would involve the use of original building materials and techniques in order to maintain the originality and integrity of the piece of work.

Renovation: to renew something in keeping with its original intent but usually with some additions and improvements and use of more modern materials.

Reconstruction: to build something again from scratch to look like the original but using modern techniques and materials. The reconstructed object is not considered original.

Destruction of the Great Wall The Great Wall had survived remarkably well until the beginning of the 20th century. Even sections of the first Great Wall of the Qin dynasty, built in 214BC, can still be seen in Wulate in Inner Mongolia. Broadly speaking, the Great Wall has suffered two types of damage: environmental and human. The severity of the natural elements, sun, wind and rain has taken some toll on the Great Wall, especially the older sections made purely of rammed earth or reed constructions. For the most part, the solid interior of these walls remains, and it is the battlement, steps and other smaller features that have weathered away.

Far greater damage, however, has been wreaked on the Great Wall by humankind. People have undoubtedly destroyed more of the Great Wall in the last century than the environment has managed in the past two millennia. Human damage to the Great Wall falls into three main categories.

In the name of modernisation The first is that of literally and deliberately dismantling the wall in the name of modernisation and urbanisation. Considerable stretches of the Great Wall have been taken down to make way for high-rise blocks, motorways, railways, dams and oil and gas pipelines. This is the case with the dam at Huanghuacheng in Beijing province, where the road cuts through the Great Wall into Inner Mongolia at Sandaoguan, and where the Xinjiang to Shanghai gas pipeline cuts through the Great Wall at Shapatou. Hundreds of kilometres of the Great Wall were dismantled by Red Guards during the Cultural

Revolution, especially in Beijing and Hebei. Lots of the wall has also been robbed of its facing bricks or stones in order to build local homes. The exposure of the unprotected interior to the weather has then hastened the destruction of even more of the wall.

Inadvertent wear and tear The second type of damage is that of inadvertent wear and tear. There have been over 150 million visitors to the Great Wall since it was opened to tourists some 50 years ago. That is very possibly more than the number of invaders who have ever breached it over the last two millennia. Many millions more go in search of the wild wall, untouched by local government and where there is no entry fee. Most people going here do not think that they might be damaging the wall. But as you may have seen on hiking paths around the world, it does not take long for a few people hiking every few days to start an irreversible track of soil erosion. When this happens the elements can take an even greater toll. In many other countries around the world, popular hiking paths are maintained by local grants or community projects at no direct cost to the visitor. Instead, a percentage of their money spent in local shops and facilities is ploughed back into a maintenance fund. This type of management has yet to take hold along most of the wall. In the mean time, the best you can do if you do decide to go to the wild wall is to try to minimise your impact (for more on this see the box on page 61).

Cheap and nasty tourist development In an attempt to cater for mass Chinese tourism, much of the Great Wall is being completely reconstructed, often damaging or completely destroying what was left of the original. This raises the question of whether the Great Wall you are visiting is really the Great Wall any more or merely a movie set reconstruction, such as in a lot of Zhenbeibao Film City (see page 231). As if this is not bad enough, the entertainment being constructed around the most popular sites such as Badaling and Mutianyu certainly detracts from the authenticity and integrity of the original site. Many visitors, and the Chinese particularly, really do just go for the T-shirt, the obligatory photo, maybe a video of them on a flying carpet above the Great Wall (sometimes without even having actually set foot on the Great Wall) and to get the 'tick in the box'. Is this really experiencing the real Great Wall? Whilst it might not be the Great Wall of the Ming era or earlier, the hustle and bustle, hawkers and food stalls at places like Badaling could be seen as reminiscent of the days when previous dynasties did use the wall passes as a place for trade between the inner circle and the barbarians on the outside. Keeping this in mind might help you get through the throngs of visitors in the couple of hours you have on your package tour to one of the greatest wonders of the world.

The dilemma of protecting the Great Wall It is easy to lament the human destruction of the Great Wall and to feel that humans are raping the very integrity of one of the greatest manmade constructions on earth. But humans will be humans. So much of the Great Wall is already so damaged and robbed of its protective facing bricks and battlements, that it can now be argued that it is better to restore, renovate or reconstruct the Great Wall to its original glory than to see it in the dilapidated and sorry state that will only get worse with time. Moreover, if managed well by local communities, the revival of a local economy in some of the poorest and most abandoned parts of western China can only benefit local people's lives and the overall stability of China.

Conservation and development of the Great Wall started in 1953 at Badaling, which was opened for the first time to tourists in 1959. Back in the 1950s, the Great Wall was repaired by hand, using modern mortar but traditional bricks. In 1987, Badaling was listed as a World Heritage Site by UNESCO (see box below). Since those days, however, visitors to Badaling alone have topped five million a year. Other sites, such as Shanhaiguan, Laolongtou, Mutianyu, Simatai, Jinshanling and Jiayuguan in the west, have since come under state administration in an effort to cope with the crowding at popular sites of the Great Wall and to capitalise on the money to be made from Great Wall-crazed visitors.

It is nevertheless very debatable how much of the money made from the Great Wall goes back into restoring the remainder of the wall in a way that preserves its integrity and originality. Increasingly, for instance at Shahukou (see page 192) and the Overhanging Castle (xuánbìlóu page 253), in the interest of speed and saving money, metal girders and pre-formed concrete sections are used to reconstruct the basic frame of the Great Wall. Then, often, grey plaster is applied to the structure and a brick façade is inlaid to make it look as if the entire wall is faced with real bricks like the original. Even when real bricks have been used, they are generally the cheap variety. Many of the original bricks used at the Great Wall were of such outstanding kiln work that their density and durability remains even today almost unrivalled. Reconstruction of the Great Wall in most places uses inferior bricks, which wear away easily. Whilst this might help to make the reconstruction look old in a very short period of time through the wear and tear of mass tourism, in the long run constant repairs will probably outweigh the cost of doing it right in the first place. And, at the end of the day, you are no longer really experiencing the original Great Wall, but a folly and a cheap façade.

The conservation movement The destruction and cheap mass development of the Great Wall is of serious concern to the Chinese ancient architecture and archaeology community, which includes Beijing and Qinghua universities, UNESCO, leading experts on the Great Wall and several noted societies. This community fears the loss of thousands of years of ancient history, but knowing that development in China is unstoppable at this stage, they struggle with how to manage and protect the Great Wall while restricting mass-market development of it. Two societies dedicated to this difficult mission are the China Great Wall Society and the International Friends of the Great Wall.

China Great Wall Society 5th Building, No 106 Beisihuan East Rd, Chaoyang District, Beijing; ✆ 010 6449 9913; ✉ cgws@public2.bta.net.cn; www.chinagreatwall.org or http://my.clubhi.com/bbs/661298. This society is run purely by Chinese and funded by the State Administration of Cultural Heritage (SACH, www.sach.gov.cn). Its honorary presidents include China's leading Great Wall expert, Luo Zhewen. The younger Dong Yaohui is the society's secretary general. Both have produced excellent photographic and literary works on the Great Wall, some of which are available in English (see Appendix 3, Further Information). Unfortunately, the society does not have an English-language website nor an English speaker to provide information on the details of their work.

International Friends of the Great Wall ✉ wuqi@friendsofgreatwall.org; www.friendsofgreatwall.org/English. Based in Beijing, this society is run by the Englishman William Lindesay and is funded by a number of sponsors including Shell Oil. Lindsay has written several books on the Great Wall and through the society is carrying out some outstanding work on documentation of, and education about, the Great Wall. His latest project has been to re-photograph the wall from the same location and angle as old photographs of the wall in order to document how the Great Wall has changed over time. An exhibition of his works should go public in 2006. The society runs a number of clean-up days on the wall, which you may be able to join if you arrange so beforehand. It also works with the local community around the Great Wall in Beijing to promote concepts of environmental management. The society's mission aims to stop further mass tourism

WHAT IS A WORLD CULTURAL HERITAGE SITE?

Since the adoption of the *Convention concerning the Protection of World Cultural and Natural Heritage* by the United Nations Educational, Scientific and Cultural Organization (UNESCO) in 1972, over 800 sites have been listed as World Heritage Sites. To be included on the World Heritage List a site must be of outstanding universal value and meet at least one of ten criteria. These criteria include being a masterpiece of human creative genius, an important interchange of human values, an exceptional testimony to a civilisation, or an outstanding example of an architectural ensemble. It is not enough, however, for sites to merely meet these criteria. The authenticity and integrity of a site and its protection and management are as important.

The World Heritage Fund was created in 1972 by the World Heritage Convention to assist in identifying, preserving and promoting World Heritage Sites. The fund manages some US$4 million a year towards five clearly defined categories: the preparation of nominations (preparatory assistance), as well as training, technical, emergency, educational and promotional assistance for existing sites. Most of the funding for site protection and management, however, has to come from the state parties or countries themselves.

The Great Wall of China in its entirety was enscribed as a World Cultural Heritage Site in 1987 for meeting five of the ten criteria, and most notably for being the world's largest military structure and for its historic, strategic and architectural significance. As with most World Heritage Sites, the management, and in particular the management of the impact of tourism on the long-term preservation of a site is an enormous challenge. It can prove a time-consuming process that requires applying policies that are often disliked by both tourists and the tourist industry. UNESCO has launched various actions such as the World Heritage Sustainable Tourism Programme and constructive dialogue with the tourism industry to join forces in safeguarding World Heritage properties such as the Great Wall of China. For more literature on the Great Wall of China as a World Heritage Site and periodic reporting on management of the wall, especially at Badaling, go to http://whc.unesco.org/en/list/438.

Other World Heritage Sites in northern China include the Imperial Palaces of the Ming and Qing dynasties in Beijing (page 160) and Shenyang, the Yungang Grottoes (page 190) and the Imperial Tombs of the Ming and Qing dynasties (page 166; page 131).

development of the Great Wall while managing and protecting those areas not already turned into a veritable circus. The society has a difficult and worthy task ahead of it and is making slow but steady progress.

2

History and Politics in China

At the end of two days' journey you reach, once more, the great river Kara-moran [Yellow River] … It is a mile wide and of vast depth, and upon its waters great ships freely sail with their full loading.

The Travels of Marco Polo

HISTORY OF NORTHERN CHINA

MYTHIC ORIGINS Pan Ku, a monkey-like figure born from an enormous egg of chaos, is believed according to Chinese legend to be the father of Earth as we know it. Pan Ku allegedly lived for 18,000 years between Earth (Yin) and Heaven (Yang). During this time he shaped the Earth into mountains and seas with the help of a dragon, a phoenix, a tortoise and a unicorn. Upon his eventual death, his body was transformed into the soil of the earth, his blood became the rain and filled the rivers, and his eyes became the sun and the moon. The fleas from his coat became humans. From these humans a series of demigods became successive rulers. The demigods discovered fire, farming, silk, and how to measure time throughout the year. Silk clothing, and pottery made in fire kilns have been found in northern China dating back to 5000BC.

THE YELLOW RIVER CRADLE Often in the West, traditional Chinese history is believed to be centred around what is today's southern China, and around symbols like rice, junks and hot humid weather. This may be due to the recent focus on Hong Kong as the portal to mainland China, and an emphasis of Hong Kong historians on the southern dynasties. In fact, the first recorded beginnings of Chinese civilisation started around the Yellow River in northern China, some four millennia before Emperor Qin unified the warring states and conquered the south.

These records document what is known now as Yangshao culture due to its proximity to the village of Yangshao, just west of Luoyang near the Yellow River. Ancient graves dating back to 4000BC and historical records indicate that the society was matriarchal. Rice was cultivated by the Yangshao, but was essentially a crop of the south. The northern Chinese cultivated wheat, which was used to make noodles, the predecessor of spaghetti.

Legend claims that the demigods ruled during this time, one of whom was the Yellow Sovereign, Huang Di, of the 27th century BC. Huang Di took his name from his rule of part of the Yellow River, which in turn took its name from the colour of the river, which was made yellow by the high content of loess sand in it. Yellow has long been considered the colour of the earth and the right to rule it. Thus Chinese emperors through the millennia have worn the colour yellow. In legend, the discovery of silk is attributed to Huang Di's wife, Empress Xiling Shi, even though evidence suggests it was already in use some 2,000 years earlier. Nevertheless, silk became a closely guarded imperial secret and a form of money for the next 3,000 years.

Country name People's Republic of China (PRC)

Country name in Chinese Full name: Zhōnghuá Rénmín Gònghéguó 中华人民共和国; short name: Zhōngguó 中国

Status Independent and unified since 210BC; communist republic (minus Taiwan) since 1949

Language Mandarin pǔtōnghuà 普通话, or guóyǔ 国语, known as huáyǔ 华语 among the overseas Chinese

Alphabet No alphabet; uses pictogram characters

Population 1,306,313,812 (estimated as at July 2005): 92% Han

Ethnic minorities 55 making up 8% of the population

Adult literacy 84% (UNICEF)

Life expectancy 72.27 years

Religion Officially aethiest; some Buddhism, Daoism, Islam 2%, Christianity 4%

Government Communist one-party state

Executive cabinet State Council appointed by the legislative branch

Legislative branch National People's Congress (single chamber of 2,985 seats)

Political parties Chinese Communist Party (CCP) and eight small parties

President Hu Jintao (15 March 2003)

Next presidential elections March 2008

Prime Minister Wen Jiabao (16 March 2003)

Capital Beijing

Other major towns Shanghai, Tianjin, Guangzhou, Xian, Chongqing, Wuhan, Nanjing

Border countries to the north Afghanistan, Tajikistan, Kyrgizstan, Kazakhstan, Mongolia, Russia, North Korea

Area Total: 9,596,960km^2; land (minus inland water): 9,326,410km^2; inland water: 270,550km^2

National parks 119

UNESCO protected areas 30 sites among which are the Great Wall, the Forbidden City and the Temple of Heaven

Total length of roads 1,402,698km

Total surfaced roads 314,204km, including 17,000km of motorway

Total length of railway 70,058km

Airports 507

Highest point Mount Everest (Qolompoqi) on border with Nepal, at 8,850m

Lowest point Turpan Pendi in Xinjiang province, at -154m

Time China keeps Beijing time (GMT + 8) throughout its provinces

Climate Average temperature northern China in summer 29 °C, autumn 19 °C, winter -5 °C, spring 20 °C.

Currency Yuán (¥) 元, kuài 块 or rénmínbì (RMB) 人民币

Exchange rate US$1 = ¥8.01, £1 = ¥14.60, €1 = ¥10.10 (May 2006)

Average annual income US$1,290 (World Bank, 2004)

International telephone code +86

Electricity 220 volts AC, using a variety of two- and three-pin plugs

Flag Five golden stars in the top left of a red background

The last demigod, King Yu, founded the Xia dynasty of 2205–1766BC. He began what would become a long Chinese tradition of building dykes and irrigation ditches to control the frequent flooding of both the Yellow and the Yangtze rivers. The increase in arable land through irrigation brought with it the desire by the emperors to extend China's border to include land suitable for cultivation.

By the Shang dynasty of 1766–1122BC, the Chinese controlled the Yellow River areas from the Ordos loop to the coast. During this bronze age, the advent of Chinese writing on oracle bones is seen as the birth of Chinese civilisation and recorded history, even though the Chinese may have had a writing system up to 1,000 years earlier. The Shang domesticated horses to plough the land and pull carriages.

XIAN FIRST BECOMES CAPITAL OF A UNITED CHINA
In 1122BC, the Zhou dynasty overthrew the Shang and established its capital at Chang An (later known as Xian). The Zhou compiled the first dictionary of the Chinese language. Although Confucius was born in 551BC during the Zhou dynasty, his teachings did not become an established part of Chinese rule until over 400 years later. The Zhou dynasty eventually disintegrated into the Warring States period between the 5th and 3rd centuries BC.

Then, in 221BC, the Warring States were unified under King Qin. He awarded himself the title of First Emperor Shi Huangdi. It is from his name, Qin (pronounced 'chin') that China gets its present Latin name, although it was known from this period on as the Middle Kingdom Zhōngguó 中国. Emperor Qin did much to unite the Chinese people and traditions. Weights and measures were standardised, as were road widths by standardising the width of wagon axles. Writing styles were also standardised and a single currency was introduced.

Aside from the giddy acknowledgement of being the first to unite China and commission the first Great Wall, First Emperor Qin is mostly known as a tyrant. In order to solidify his rule, he had 460 scholars buried alive. (Mao Zedong is accredited later in 1958 to have claimed to be a hundred times better than Qin Shi Huangdi for having buried 46,000 scholars alive.) Essentially a hard labour camp, building the first Great Wall also cost up to a million lives and left a bitter memory of Great Wall building in the eyes of the Chinese until very recently.

When Emperor Qin died in 209BC, he was buried with some 8,000 terracotta soldiers in a tomb just outside the capital, which lay undiscovered until 1974. He had expanded Chinese rule all through the Ordos loop and down to Guangzhou (Canton) in the south.

THE HAN DYNASTY, ANCESTORS OF THE MAJORITY HAN RACE OF CHINA
In 202BC, the Han overthrew the Qin and started the expansion of Chinese influence through the Hexi corridor into the Turkic-speaking lands of today's Xinjiang, as well as into the Korean peninsula and the Mekong valley. By the 1st century BC, General Ban Chao had established the Silk Road all the way to the Caspian Sea and the Roman Empire. The Han extended the Great Wall by another 5,000 *li* into Korea and along the north of the Hexi corridor as a means of protecting the Silk Road.

It is since this Han-dominated period that the spoken Chinese language is known as hànyǔ 汉语, Chinese characters are known as hànzì 汉字 (also the Japanese word *kanji* meaning Chinese characters) and the majority ethnicity in China is known as hànrén 汉人.

BARBARIANS RULE THE NORTH
The Han dynasty disintegrated in AD220 and the north was essentially ruled from Luoyang by the Wei dynasty until the Xiongnu nomads overran the capital in 311. There is still some debate as to whether the Xiongnu

were the Huns, who, when finally ousted by the Sui dynasty some two centuries later were already on their way to invade India and much of Europe.

Until the Sui dynasty finally reunited southern and northern China in 589, the north was variously ruled by five competing nomad races each of whom became increasingly sinified over their almost three centuries of ruling northern China. These five races were: the Xiongnu, or Huns, who spoke a variation of Mongolian; the Xianbei who spoke ancient Turkish; the Jie or Nuzhen who spoke Manchu and came from the far northeast; the Qiang and finally the Di, both of whom were part of the Tangut (early Tibetan) people. These races, who ruled northern China before the advent of Islam, intermarried with the ethnic Han and assimilated much of Chinese culture and traditions.

The Sui dynasty was short lived, lasting only from 589 to 618, but during this short period the printing press was invented and Emperor Yang ordered the repair and improvement of the entire Grand Canal which linked the Yangtze to the Yellow River and to Beijing. He died in 618 trying to retake Korea.

THE GOLDEN AGE OF THE TANG AND THE TIBETAN TAKEOVER OF THE NORTHWEST Upon
Yang's death, the Tang dynasty took over the core of China for the next three centuries. In central China, Tang rule was so steadfast that even today the Cantonese word for Chinese is *tongyen* 唐人, meaning Tang people. During this period Chinese culture excelled. Typeset printing presses were invented and eventually the world's first book, the *Diamond Sutra*, was printed in China in 868. Poetry and literature flourished. Buddhism became the official religion of the Middle Kingdom in 624 and gunpowder was also invented around this time (used initially for celebratory fireworks). By 900, fine bone china or porcelain was being churned out of the imperial kilns.

Early in their reign, the Tang pushed Chinese borders all the way out to the Turkistans, but were later repelled by Arab invasions. By 763, Tibetans had driven the Tang out of today's Xinjiang and even briefly occupied the Tang capital at Xian. Despite being driven back from the Tang capital, the Tibetans consolidated their occupation of the west and by 791 had a firm hold of all Gansu. Trade along the Silk Road continued, with the Tibetans taking concessions for that portion of the journey. It is during this period that Muslims started to move into the northwest region. These immigrants are the distant ancestors of the Chinese Muslim minority, the Hui (see page 41).

THE WESTERN XIA AND THE LIAO RULE THE NORTH By 907, the Tang dynasty was in
decline and, after a period of fighting, the Middle Kingdom was divided into the Song dynasty in the south, the western Xia in the northwest, and the Liao in the northeast. The western Xia and the Liao were nomadic and, as their original homelands extended beyond the Great Wall, they did little to maintain it.

The western Xia or Tangut were descendants of the Tibetans. They gradually took over rule of the northwest from 933 until, as a minority ruling elite over the Turkic-speaking Xianbei people of the region, they established the Xi Xia Empire in 1032. During their 200-year control of the Hexi corridor, the Tangut fought off repeated Tibetan re-encroachment and profited from the trade along the Silk Road. They adapted Chinese characters to form their own script, which was also related to the Tibetan script – samples of their writing can still be found around China today, including inside the original Ming gateway at Juyongguan. Their rule lasted until they became a vassal state under Genghis Khan from 1207–27, after which they were practically exterminated by the Khan's son and first emperor of the Yuan dynasty, Unfortunately, much of Xi Xia history was destroyed with this brutal extermination. As a result of Kublai Khan's orders, the Xi Xia kingdom became known as Ningxia, meaning 'subjugation of the Xia', which is still the name of the province today. Despite the effective genocide of the Tangut, a few escaped to the Qinghai Plateau where they can still be found today.

The Liao were descendants of the Turkic Xianbei and were given the rule of the northeast of China in exchange for peace with the Song dynasty in the south. They ruled from 907–1127, during which time these nomadic people assimilated much of the settled Chinese customs of the north. By 1127, they had become so settled and weak that the Song took advantage of an alliance with the Jin to try to oust them from the northeast. Coupled with invasions from the north by the Nuzhen (Manchu), the Liao picked up and retreated along their original route into China and ended up to the west of the Xi Xia. They remained there until 1227, when they too were overrun by the Mongols.

The Song dynasty ruled in the south, which is still often seen as the heart of Chinese culture, even if the dynasty did in fact originate around the Yellow River in the north. It was the Song who took on the peculiar practice of foot binding, which was to prevail for the next millennium, as a sign of beauty and freedom from labour.

THE RULE OF GENGHIS KHAN AND THE YUAN DYNASTY OF KUBLAI KHAN Genghis Khan came to power in Mongolia in 1207. He quickly conquered the western Xia and the western Liao and, on his death in 1227, the lands were divided among his sons. By 1234, the Mongol Khans had conquered the Jin and the Manchu all the way from the Great Wall to Korea and western Russia. In 1260, Kublai Khan ascended the throne of the Mongol Empire. He moved his capital from Mongolia to Dadu, the precursor to Beijing. It was during this time that the Venetian traveller Marco Polo came to Dadu and served in the court of Kublai Khan for 17 years.

Kublai Khan conquered all of southern China in 1279, at which point he took on a Chinese name. He named the dynasty Yuán 元, meaning 'beginning' and this indeed started the trend in the following two dynasties of naming a conquering dynasty by its proposed character as opposed to by a regional or ethnic name. The Yuan dynasty ruled China for just under a century until 1368, when the Ming of southern China rose up against the Yuan and pushed them back to their homelands in Mongolia.

MING RETURN TO ISOLATIONISM The Míng 明, meaning 'bright', rode the wave of their victory in the first few decades of their rule and the Chinese began an open-door policy, which expanded trade and improved livelihoods. By 1421, the third Ming emperor, Yongle, had sent his Muslim eunuch, Zheng He, to explore the oceans with huge Chinese treasure ships. Zheng He succeeded in rounding the Cape of Good Hope and reached the Americas and the Antarctic. Yongle, meanwhile, moved the capital from the Ming's traditional cultural centre of Nanjing back to Beijing, where the emperor felt he would have greater control over the marauding northern nomads. Enormous effort and resources went into constructing the treasure ships and what became known as the Forbidden City, built on the foundations of Kublai Khan's own palace. But the drain, both on resources and on the goodwill of the people, brought discontent. When a bad omen appeared to the emperor, he reversed his open-door policy and recalled Zheng He. When Zheng He returned to Beijing with the stories of his success, he found an introverted

2

emperor who had put a stop to all expeditionary voyages and all building work, save the complete renovation and extension of the Great Wall of China.

Successive Ming emperors, all the way till their decline at the beginning of the 17th century, had millions of men toil over improving the Great Wall defences to the north. This was the greatest period of wall fortification and extension, much of which can still be seen today. And over these next 250 years, the wall was effective in keeping out the Mongols and the Manchu. In the south, culture and traditional crafts flourished, including porcelain. Trade continued along the Silk Road, but also with early European seafarers. The Portuguese settled in Macao in 1557, and the Dutch took Taiwan in 1635 while the British settled into Canton. By now the Ming were corrupted and blind to the outside world behind the walls of the Forbidden City. Money for the Great Wall was siphoned off by corrupt officials and, left in disrepair after constant raiding from the Manchu, the wall was eventually breached.

MANCHU INVASION AND THE QING DYNASTY In 1644, a peasant uprising against the corrupt Ming toppled the dynasty. This was quickly taken advantage of by the northern Manchu, who swept away the peasant king and installed themselves in the Forbidden City as the Qing 清 (meaning 'clear') dynasty. The Qing, coming from the north, had no need for the Great Wall defences and so left them to rack and ruin. The Manchu expanded the empire, soon conquering Mongolia by 1697 and Tibet by 1724. The Manchu forbade foot binding among their women, but it was continued among the Han Chinese, many of whom were taken as concubines (but never as wives or the princess regent). Even some theatre actors (who were permitted to be only men or eunuchs) had their feet bound in order to facilitate their role-playing of women.

Resting on its laurels from here on in, the Qing, like every other dynasty before it, fell into corrupt decline. Retreating into the Forbidden City and scared of the encroachment of the foreign devils from over the seas, the Ming tried to keep the Europeans at bay whilst conniving officials encouraged back-door trade.

THE MOTHER OF CAPITALISM Despite the efforts of the Qing to keep out the Europeans, both their merchants and their missionaries, the Europeans were making big money from the triangular trade between Indian colonies, China and home nations in Europe. Opium produced in India and Pakistan was shipped to China and traded for silk, porcelain, lacquerware, jade and other goods. These were sold back in Europe, which financed the whole deal. Pirating on the seas during these heady days of trade was rampant, and in order to minimise the risk of losing a ship to pirates, merchants would take, for instance, a one-tenth stock in ten ships rather than finance one whole ship of goods. This was the start of modern-day capitalism as we know it – stocks and shares bought and sold in the East India docks of east London and similar ports around Europe.

With the Europeans sick and tired of the limitations on trading imposed by the Qing house, and the Qing incensed by European barbarity of feeding the opium addiction created among the Chinese, the situation was bound to lead to an almighty confrontation. In 1839, Commissioner Lin sent a letter to Queen Victoria, imploring her to stop the 'illegal' trade, but this letter was returned the following year with an envoy, who refused to kowtow to the emperor on account of the queen being equal to the emperor. The Qing and the majority of the Chinese at the time still believed that the Middle Kingdom really was the centre of the universe and the emperor really was the son of heaven, therefore nobody was equal to him. The emperor, now doubly insulted, ordered a British merchant ship full of opium to be burnt. The British took this as an act of war and responded with cannon shots and explosives, flattening Chinese coastal forts and war junks. What became known as the First Opium War ensued, which the British won three years later in 1842. The concessions to the British at the end of the war included Hong Kong and five other trading ports where the British would enjoy extra territoriality (ie: the freedom to run the port under British and not Chinese law). A series of similarly 'unequal treaties', as they became known, were pursued by other trading nations.

INTERNAL STRIFE BRINGS EXTERNAL CALAMITY 内乱外患 nèi luàn wài huàn By the end of the 19th century, corruption was so rife and the abuse of the peasantry by the Mandarins was so high that rebellions and uprisings were abundant, both against the Qing house and against foreigners. In 1900, the famous Boxer Rebellion against foreigners for their unequal treaties and their damage to the heavens by church steeples only brought further humiliation to the Chinese. Believing that their 'boxing' or *gongfu* had supernatural powers, impenetrable to the foreign rifle bullet, Chinese peasants surrounded the foreign embassies and churches, only to be mown down by sprays of rifle fire. In the ensuing retaliation of the Eight Allies (Britain, France, Germany, America, Austro-Hungary, Italy, Russia and Japan) the summer palace was ransacked, thoroughly looted and razed – predominantly by British forces.

The Empress Dowager Cixi, the regent and the court fled to the summer residence at Chengde. Although they managed to return some months later, clearly the Qing days were numbered. The Empress Dowager, renowned for her ruthlessness, died at the age of 73 on 15 November 1908. Her successor, Puyi, only three years old at the time, ascended the throne in 1909 to become the last emperor of the Middle Kingdom. His reign lasted only two years before he was forced to abdicate in favour of establishing the Republic of China under Dr Sun Yatsen.

THE REPUBLIC, WARLORDS AND THE ANTI-JAPANESE WAR OF RESISTANCE After the 10/10 rebellion on 10 October 1911, rule by the Qing dynasty was brought to an end. On 1 January 1912, Dr Sun Yatsen was declared president, but he was forced to resign three months later to allow the former Beijing army commander and short-lived Imperial Prime Minister, Yuan Shikai, to take the presidency. Yuan was firmly of the old mould of Chinese personalities and ruled the country like a dictatorship, even declaring himself emperor from December 1915 to March 1916. This did not go down well among the populace who had worked so hard and lost so many to depose the dynastic system. Under pressure of another rebellion, Yuan withdrew the declaration and died soon afterwards, leaving the fledgling republic to infighting among rivals. Coinage bearing Yuan Shikai's head can still be found among the antique markets in China, but are increasingly rare and, therefore, increasingly faked.

Meanwhile, Puyi had been allowed to continue to live in the Forbidden City (until 1924) and the warlord Zhang Xun tried to restore him as emperor following the death of Yuan Shikai. He failed, however, and the Beijing government competed for the next decade with a rival aspiring government, the Guo Min Dang, set up by Dr Sun Yatsen in Nanjing. Russian communist influence infiltrated China during this period and the Chinese Communist Party was set up at a meeting in Shanghai in 1921, at which Mao Zedong was present. Sadly, Sun, the foreign-educated moderate among all the rivalry in China at the beginning of the 19th century, died in 1925. Ironically, both the current communist regime in Beijing and the republican regime now in Taiwan claim Dr Sun and his original movement, helping to topple the Qing dynasty, as the father of their own regime.

The Guo Min Dang was eventually headed by Chiang Kai Shek (Jiang Jieshi in pinyin). But from 1928 to 1937, China was essentially at the whim of warlords and rivalry between the communists and the Guo Min Dang. The Japanese invaded Manchuria, northeast China, in 1931 and set up a puppet government there under Puyi, who was once again declared emperor. He was installed in the new 'Imperial Palace' at Changchun in Jilin province, which has recently been renovated and was opened to the public in 2004. In the meantime, the civil war between Guo Min Dang and the communists was taking its toll on the communists. In 1934, they were forced to flee from their base in the south on the Long March, which took them, led by Mao Zedong, to Yenan in north China's Shaanxi province. Mao's leadership of the communist forces during the Long March made him a legend to many party members and his followers, eventually leading to his appointment as party chairman in 1937.

Realising, however, that a Japanese invasion was far more disastrous to China than internal rivalry, the communists and the Guo Min Dang agreed to a united front against the Japanese in 1937. The Japanese were far better equipped than the Chinese, and soon advanced on Shanghai and the south. On 13 December 1937, the Japanese entered Nanjing, following which was the infamous Rape of Nanjing. The fathers, brothers and sons of between 20,000 and 80,000 girls and women were forced to rape their daughters, sisters and mothers. Japanese soldiers also took part in the raping. Both men and women were massacred, some women escaping certain death only by becoming 'comfort women' for the Japanese army. To this day,

Chinese women, and children born of those rapes, are seeking compensation and an adequate apology from the Japanese government.

The united front lasted until the end of World War II in Asia on 15 August 1945, after which the two rivals started at each other again. The US marines, who entered Tianjin port on 30 September 1945 to help repatriate the surrendering Japanese, stayed until the spring of 1946 initially to mediate peace between the two sides. Soon, however, the US marines essentially became advisors to the Guo Min Dang, until in 1949 when it became obvious that the well-armed and increasingly well-trained Guo Min Dang army could not win against the determined and overwhelming numbers of communist Chinese troops. Chiang Kai Shek retreated, allegedly with much gold and loot and the remainder of the Guo Min Dang army to Taiwan, where the Guo Min Dang party held power on the island until 2000.

CHINA UNDER MAO ZEDONG On 1 October 1949 from above Tian An Gate, Chairman Mao Zedong proclaimed the founding of the People's Republic of China. The Chinese Communist Party under the chairmanship of Mao Zedong since 1937 had attempted to free China from the yoke of foreign colonialism, unequal trade and greedy landowners by giving the land back to the peasantry. Even today Mao is still well remembered for this. But the excesses and utterly disastrous policies of a successful guerrilla leader in times of sovereign peace are too many to describe here. A conservative estimate of civilian murders under Mao runs to almost 38 million, second only to Stalin.

Determined to remain completely independent of the rest of the world while dreaming of overtaking its prosperity within a decade or two, Mao embarked on policies which ran counter to age-old eco-dependencies and established farming practices. In the 1950s, a campaign was started to kill dogs once they were deemed disease carriers. In 1956, sparrows were the target of Mao's campaign to increase food crops, believing that sparrows were eating them. People would bang loud instruments outside to stop sparrows from landing until they became so exhausted that they literally fell out of the sky. Without any sparrows, insects flourished and ruined the harvests. Later, all the grass was pulled up in the cities in order to stop pests from reproducing, and to this day grassy spaces in Chinese cities are few and far between.

Campaigns like the Great Leap Forward of 1958–60 ended in famine and the starvation of over 20 million people, some allegedly resorting to cannibalism. For the most part, officials lied to Mao about the diminishing harvest in order not to anger him and to outdo the already exaggerated numbers of other officials. With Mao's distrust of intellectuals and his hatred of anything 'cultured' and from the past, Mao had millions of academics and writers denounced and killed. This effectively robbed the country of the brain power either to improve the economy or to criticise him personally.

After Mao broke off ties with the Soviet Union in 1960 and expelled all his Soviet advisors, his isolation from the world was complete. But the failure of the Great Leap Forward brought such criticism against Mao that he was forced to import grain in an effort to avert the famines. Needing to crack down on critics, and continuing to believe in the dynamism of perpetual change, Mao unleashed the Cultural Revolution in 1966. Millions of young Red Guards denounced their parents as bourgeois, destroyed thousands of years of Chinese historical relics and drove people to suicide. These Red Guards are now in their forties and fifties, many in managerial positions in state-run businesses and government departments.

2

200000BC	*Homo erectus* lived in northern China – remains have been found in Beijing and Liaoning provinces
5000–1766BC	Neolithic period – silk and pottery from this period found in Banpo, Shaanxi province
4000BC	Rice first grown by Yangshao farmers, then a matriarchal society in today's Henan province
2697BC	The Yellow Emperor Huang Di comes to power
2500BC	Chinese start using acupuncture to treat illnesses
2205–1766BC	Xia dynasty builds dykes and irrigation ditches to control rivers
1766–1122BC	Shang dynasty
1500BC	Chinese characters written on oracle bones used for divination; horses used for pulling ploughs and carriages
1122–771BC	Early Zhou dynasty, who went on to war against the Spring and Autumn periods until 256BC
770–481BC	The Spring and Autumn period
551BC	Confucius born in the Kingdom of Lu near Qingdao; iron smelting introduced to China
481–221BC	The Warring States period
350BC	Chinese invent the crossbow
221–206BC	Qin dynasty; Emperor Qin Shi, first emperor of a unified China
206BC–AD220	Early Han dynasty; Emperor Wu Di also rules over Korea and Vietnam
150BC	Chinese develop the art of lacquerware and silk painting
124BC	Confucianism established as the standard text for official court examinations
50BC	Buddhist influence enters the Middle Kingdom via the trade routes from India
AD150	Korea becomes independent of the Middle Kingdom
221–266	The Three Kingdoms: Wei, Shu and Wu; Wei rule the north
265–316	Western Jin dynasty
317–589	The Tartar invasion from the north partitions China into several smaller kingdoms
589–618	Sui dynasty; China is re-unified
618–907	Tang dynasty considered the golden age of culture
907–960	The Five dynasties and Ten kingdoms; a period of disunity
960–1279	Most of China unified under the Song dynasty; a large part of today's Ningxia region, including the former northern border of

Mao Zedong died in 1976 of Parkinson's disease. He is embalmed in a mausoleum in the centre of Tiananmen Square, where thousands still pay him homage or simply go to gawk at the man who gave independence to China. His excesses during the Cultural Revolution were denounced by the Chinese Communist Party (CCP) a mere five years later. He continues to be revered in the CCP, no longer really because of what he did for China, but because his legacy gives the CCP unchallenged rule over China. It will not be long before he is wheeled into the closets of history, and his mausoleum possibly even moved to the Qing or Ming tomb sites where he will more appropriately fit as the modern-day emperor that he was.

	the Great Wall, is ruled by the western Xia from 990–1227, and the Jin from 1115–1234, who build the Great Wall of Ditches
1275–92	Marco Polo travels through China starting at age 21
1279–1368	Mongols led by Kublai Khan invade from the north to reunite China and form the Yuan dynasty; capital established in present-day Beijing for the first time and Great Wall building is abandoned
1368–1644	Ming dynasty overthrow the Mongols to re-assert a native Chinese dynasty; the Ming quickly becomes inward looking and embarks on the most ambitious of all the Great Walls
1644–1911	The Manchu break through the Great Wall to establish the Qing dynasty
1912	Republic of China set up by Sun Yatsen
1925	Sun Yatsen dies
1927–37	Warlord era plunges China into disunity
1931	Japan invades China, establishing a puppet kingdom, Manchuguo, under the last emperor, Puyi, in the northeast
1937–45	United front anti-Japan resistance
1945, 15 August	Japan surrenders; US marines enter China to expatriate the Japanese
1945–49	Civil war between communists under Mao Zedong and republicans under Chiang Kai Shek (Jiang Jieshi)
1949, 1 October	Mao Zedong's Communist Party wins the civil war and establishes the People's Republic of China on the mainland; Chiang Kai Shek retreats to Taiwan
1966–76	Cultural Revolution; Mao Zedong dies in 1976
1971	The Chinese Communist Party is recognised in the UN as the legitimate government of mainland China
1972	US President Nixon visits China
1979	Deng Xiaoping comes to power, sweeps in wide-ranging economic reforms and establishes the one-child policy
1989, 4 June	Tiananmen Square massacre
1997, 19 February	Deng Xiaoping dies
2008	Beijing Olympics
2010	World Expo Beijing

THE OPEN-DOOR POLICY AND SOCIALISM WITH CHINESE CHARACTERISTICS As could be expected, some chaos ensued after the death of Mao and, coincidentally, the death of his moderate premier, Zhou Enlai, earlier in the same year. It was not long, however, before the economic reformer, Deng Xiaoping, emerged as the de facto leader of China. He never took any of the top jobs in the country, limiting himself to chairman of the military committees of the CCP and the People's Republic of China (PRC), but ensured that his protégés were moved into the positions of PRC president, PRC premier, and chairman of the CCP.

A man with a clear vision of the way forward for China's economy, he introduced the one-child policy in 1979 (see box, page 40) and in 1981 he proclaimed 'socialism with Chinese characteristics' as the guiding policy for China's economy. This firmly put the lid on communist economics. Deng introduced several special economic zones along the coast to attract foreign direct investment, returned farmland ownership to the peasantry and allowed limited (but taxed) profit to small private businesses. This liberalism and open-door policy gradually increased into the economic powerhouse that is the China we see today.

Such economic freedoms are accompanied by the strong hand of Chineseownership of business and the even stronger hand of one-party politics. Socialism with Chinese characteristics is a classic case of sinification of an outside influence. It has happened throughout the millennia of Chinese history and will undoubtedly continue. Whether it is the sinification of settling invaders, such as the Tibetans, the Mongols or the Manchu, or the assimilation of imported views, such as Buddhism, communism or socialism, the Chinese are adept at making an outside influence their own. Taken as part of the very long history of China, communism is just a blip on China's timeline. Capitalism on the other hand was in China long before it entered the East India docks of London.

Deng's strong grip on party politics, belief in the unrivalled supremacy of the CCP and his chairmanship of the military committees of both the party and the government prompted the crackdown against the student protest in Tiananmen Square on 4 June 1989. This was against the wishes of the party general secretary Zhao Ziyang, who was promptly replaced by Jiang Zemin following the end of martial law in the capital.

Deng Xiaoping died on 19 February 1997. The wide-ranging economic reforms he introduced have continued under President Jiang Zemin, and, for so long as this keeps the majority of Chinese shop-happy and better off than they were ten years ago, then the demand for real political change is unlikely to emerge.

21ST-CENTURY CHINA A growing discrepancy in wealth between the rich coastal provinces and the lagging interior is fuelling protests among the rural communities of China, especially as farmers lose land to city development and lines of communication. This is severely testing the central government's ability to hold the country together. Nevertheless, the effective and full transfer of power from President Ziang Zemin to Hu Jintao in 2003 took place smoothly without the usual leadership battles. This was the first time in the Communist Party's history that a transfer of authority has not resulted in a shaky power vacuum for a certain period of time.

The emergence of China in the 21st century as a serious global economic power is no longer disputed. Its trajectory towards a political and military superpower within the course of the 21st century is also a fairly safe bet. This has led to the debate on whether China is a global threat or an opportunity, particularly to America and the world order as we know it. China's enormous investment into Africa, for instance, is turning the West's policy on poverty reduction on its head. President Hu Jintao has been actively promoting China as a country with peaceful intentions and a traditional desire for harmony. The 2008 Olympics will certainly catapult China's entry onto the world stage after decades of marginalisation. Viewing this as a threat will not help the rest of the world cope with a future in which China will increasingly figure as a major player.

The country is divided into 34 administrative areas, consisting of 23 provinces, five autonomous regions, four municipalities and the two special administrative regions of Hong Kong and Macau. Both Tibet and Taiwan are included by the government in the 23 provinces. For the purposes of this book, Northern China along the Ming Great Wall consists of the five provinces of Gansu, Shaanxi, Shanxi, Hebei and Liaoning; the autonomous region of Ningxia; and the two municipalities of Beijing and Tianjin.

GOVERNMENT The governing institutions of China have a similar structure to most countries around the world. The executive branch, headed by a prime minister, is the State Council, which is made up of 50 state councillors, each the head of a government department or agency. Most of the state councillors are senior Chinese Communist Party members, but the State Council is technically separate from the CCP, whose task is to develop policy. The prime minister is Premier Wen Jiabao, who worked under party general secretary Zhao Ziyang in 1989, but who avoided a strong association with Zhao as a sympathiser of the Tiananmen student protests.

CONGRESS The legislative branch is the National People's Congress (NPC), which is housed in the Great Hall of the People on the east side of Tiananmen Square. It consists of 2,985 delegates who meet only once a year in full plenary session. Otherwise, the majority of the NPC's daily work is managed by the NPC standing committee of 150 delegates. The 2,985 delegates are elected every five years from around the country by the municipal, regional and provincial people's congresses. The next NPC election will be held between the end of 2007 and February 2008. The NPC increasingly challenges proposals put forward by the government and will not accept proposals directly from the CCP. It is through this increasingly independent forum that the unrivalled supremacy of the CCP is most likely to be deposed in the next few decades. Aside from debating and passing laws, the NPC also elects the president of the country. Today, the president of the country (and the party secretary general) is the all-powerful Hu Jintao, a chosen protégé of the late Deng Xiaoping. In response to the explosive growth in the economy, the NPC has its work cut out to bring China's outdated and inadequate laws in line with the needs of the private sector and international trade.

JUDICIARY The judiciary is made up of town, municipal, regional and provincial courts, with the Supreme Court of China presiding as the highest court in the country. China's legal system is made up of a mix of customary and civil laws, making it a nightmare to navigate and rife with loopholes. The system is very slow, corrupt and has a habit of using loopholes to throw cases against the provincial government out of the courts. Nevertheless, educated citizens in the provinces are beginning to learn how to use China's vast and complicated legal system against corrupt government and this too is changing China. Ian Johnson, reporter for the *Wall Street Journal*, has done some excellent investigative reporting into this phenomenon in his book *Wild Grass* (see *Appendix 3, Further information*, page 269).

Since dynastic times, China has also offered an alternative to the judiciary. The petition system allows citizens who feel wronged by corrupt judges and courts to come to the China Petition Office in the capital to submit a letter of petition to the government. It is in this way that the government maintains oversight of officials

2

in the provinces. Although this system allows for extraordinary remedies, it is also slow and overburdened. In 2003, the petition office received over ten million petitions, of which only two in a thousand (0.2%) reach a resolution. New regulations brought in at the beginning of 2005 should streamline the system, although there has also been debate about abolishing the system altogether.

POLITICAL PARTIES Contrary to popular belief outside China, there are in fact ten political parties in China. Only one, however – the Chinese Communist Party – is legally granted the right to hold power in the country. The remainder must by law accept national rule by the CCP. One of the ten parties, the China Democracy Party (CDP), refused to accept this regulation when it formed in 1998 as they advocated a nationwide multi-party democracy. As a result, CDP members were arrested in 1998 and sentenced to rehabilitation camps. Most of the other eight legal parties were formed in the 1940s prior to China's proclamation as a people's republic, the oldest two parties being the Revolutionary Committee of the Chinese Guo Min Dang and the China Democratic League. Although these eight legal parties are seen by many as a rubber stamp for 'multi-party consultation' and the Chinese brand of democracy, increasing numbers of members of these non-communist parties are holding positions in government departments and in the courts, where their opinions inform government debate and court decisions. Their opinions are increasingly finding fertile ground also among the younger, more liberal elements of the Chinese Communist Party, who are realising that harnessing some of the trappings of pluralistic democracy, such as the transparency, checks and balances between institutions, elections and appointments is still the best way to curb corruption and foster accountability. The growing voice of these non-communist parties combined with the emboldened parliament will probably eventually usher in true multi-party democracy in China.

The CCP has over 63 million members compared with almost half a million in the remaining eight legal parties.

ECONOMY

Since market economics were introduced in the early 1980s, the Chinese government has dismantled collective farming and let thousands of private companies bloom, from small local enterprises to giant manufacturing concerns. Since the country joined the World Trade Organisation in 2001 – a step that has brought more changes and, above all, access to foreign markets – China has developed into one of the top exporters in the world and is attracting record amounts of foreign investment. The Chinese economy, at US$7,262 trillion gross domestic productivity (GDP) based on purchasing power parity, is currently the world's second-largest economy after the US. This is quadruple what it was in 1978 when the economic reformer Deng Xiaoping effectively came to power. Per capita, however, this works out at only US$5,600 (Purchasing Power Parity). GDP growth is officially estimated at around 9%, one of highest rates in the world, although this has gone into the high teens in previous years threatening overheating of the economy and a possible collapse with significant global repercussions. China had kept its currency pegged to the US dollar for many years, and only in mid 2005 did it introduce a limited floating currency, pegged to an undisclosed basket of currencies. For more on Chinese money, see page 85.

The return of market economics to China has brought almost half of the country out of a subsistence existence. While in 1978 China had some 250 million poor people, this number has been reduced to about 30 million today. But China's

The only thing growing faster than China's economy is its information and communication technology (ICT) sector. The impact of ICT growth is impressive, both in terms of ICT users as well as in terms of the economy. Take the number of mobile phone subscribers, for example, which has been growing over 50% a year since 1999, overtaking the number of fixed telephone lines in 2003. In 2004 alone, the country added another 65 million new mobile phone subscribers (5.4 million new subscribers every month!) – more than the entire population of the UK. While one out of five Chinese today has a mobile phone, there is still much room for growth. The country is home to another one billion potential mobile phone customers.

The internet has also taken off rapidly and more and more Chinese today are online. By the end of 2004, over 7% of the Chinese population was using the internet, compared with 12% worldwide. Internet cafés – although not always easy to find – have spread rapidly, particularly in large towns and villages and are especially popular amongst the young, who gather to watch DVDs, play games and chat. Look for the 网吧 (pronounced **wǎngbā**) sign, which signifies 'net bar/café'. The price and quality of internet access can vary but users will pay ¥2–10 per hour, and high speed/broadband access is often available in larger cities. Chinese-language websites today represent a significant proportion on the world wide web, making the internet an important source of information. Travellers may notice, though, that a number of websites are blocked: the result of government efforts to closely monitor what kind of information internet users can and cannot access.

Nevertheless, the good news for travellers is that they do not need to learn Chinese or adapt to a Chinese keyboard to send emails since keyboards are not 'Chinese' as such. Because the written Chinese language is made up of over 40,000 characters, it is impractical (and for any standard keyboard, impossible) to try to map each character to a single key. For this reason, a number of keyboard input method editors have been designed to allow the Chinese to type using a standard keyboard. One of the most popular is the pinyin method, in which people use the basic Roman alphabet to represent Mandarin sounds and convert these into Chinese characters.

uneven economic growth is causing a growing gap between rich and poor despite the government's efforts to bring the economic boom of the coast to the interior. Over 10% of China lives below the absolute poverty line of less than US$1 per day, while unemployment across the country is believed to be over 20%. Almost 150 million rural Chinese (over 10% of the population) are migrant workers, mostly travelling to the big cities in the hope of finding work (for more on migrant workers, see page 39).

To illustrate the discrepancy in rich and poor it is worth noting that 13% of GDP is made up of agriculture yet almost 50% of China's labour force is employed in this unprofitable business. Over 50% of GDP is made up of industry, which is growing at a rate of 17% per year but employs only some 22% of the labour force. The remainder of GDP and the labour force, each about one-third, works in services and this is likely to see an increase as China becomes more service-oriented.

Energy consumption in China is a concern to world markets as the Chinese demand more and more high-energy products and their economy grows. On average, energy consumption in China is in line with its GDP growth (9%). It is already the world's second-largest consumer of oil after the US. But China is

2

extremely conscious that high demands for fuel are costly and untenable and so is working hard to find alternative fuels and efficient products such as hydrogen fuel-cell vehicles. During the mean time, China had to close one-third of its mines in 2005 because of poor safety and this will affect the availability of coal as a fuel. The majority of these mines are in China's northwest in Shanxi province around Datong. Over 3,000 people died in 2005 due to mine accidents.

3

People and Culture

Out of the 'Hundred Schools' of Chinese philosophy, only two – Confucianism and Taoism – have survived. They have lasted through thousands of years because they have proven the most useful. The Chinese are very practical people – they have no respect for things that sound good but don't work.

Benjamin Hoff, 1992

PEOPLE

China's population of 1.3 billion people is made up of 92% ethnic Han and 8% of other ethnic minorities. The latter group consists of 55 minority groups as recognised by the PRC. At the start of the people's republic, and in true communist spirit, the ethnicities were enshrined in the constitution and given considerable freedoms so long as they accepted the unrivalled rule of the Chinese Communist Party and the government of the PRC. This led to the formation of five autonomous regions, three of which are in the north. Xinjiang is home to the Uighur national minority; Nei Mongol is home to the Mongolian national minority; and Ningxia is home to the Hui Muslim national minority. In the west is the autonomous region of Xizang (Tibet) and in the south is Guangxi, home of many of the southern minorities.

Considering that some say 95% of China's landmass is uninhabitable in its natural format, it is amazing that 70% of China's population lives on 40% of its land. The Chinese have worked hard to cultivate inhospitable ground through terracing and irrigation and the most densely inhabited land is still along the coastal cities and the mighty Yangtze River. Life in the cities is generally good and improving fast, although you don't have to go very far outside Beijing to find people still living without running water, sewage systems and regular electricity. The loess plateau (see page 55), a practically uninhabitable section of the country approximately the size of France is home to a population of 70 million people. In 1995, 40 million of them lived in cave dwellings that backed into the soft loess cliffs and are fronted by a wall with windows. Over half of these have now been rehoused, leaving the fragile loess cliffs susceptible to erosion.

The good life in the towns, where construction is unprecedented and opportunities abound, attracts over 10% (130 million) of China's rural population. Outside of the home county where they are registered, migrant workers have no right to social welfare, housing or medical care. Some are lucky to get jobs as construction labourers, taxi drivers or tourist guides. Some are unlucky enough to get caught by mafia, who run gangs of beggars in the big cities. Often these people are mutilated to gain more sympathy from the rich and so that they can't run away. Ten years ago, beggars were an extremely rare sight on the streets, although they did exist, but were promptly taken away by the police when found. Now, begging

Mao Zedong actively encouraged population growth during his lifetime. So-called 'Revolutionary mothers' with five or more children were given special subsidies and by the end of the 1970s China's population had almost doubled its numbers to 900 million from its population at the start of the people's republic.

Acutely conscious that hungry mouths were a drain on galvanising the economy, Deng Xiaoping put a stop to Mao's policy in 1979 by introducing the one-child policy. Contrary to popular belief outside China, this has only ever applied to urban and ethnic Han majority Chinese. Minorities, single children and those farming the land were allowed to have more children. However, this has not stopped the deaths or abandonment of female babies in an attempt to keep strong sons to farm the land. Even today there are more female than male orphans by far and a shortfall of some 60 million women compared with men. Perversely, female infanticide is leading to the trafficking of an estimated quarter of a million girls and young women into China every year.

Penalties for a prohibited second child vary by province, but most second-child mothers are forcibly sterilised and the family are usually severely taxed to pay for the education and social benefits entitled to everyone. Some couples get around this by saying the second child is adopted from a distant family relative who has just died. Many women in China are automatically sterilised after the first child. The rich are usually allowed to pay for the privilege to have a second child.

With urban Chinese especially in the coastal regions becoming rich, single children with two parents and four grandparents doting over them are becoming spoiled and overweight. This is of concern to policy makers, who fear the rise of individualistic truants that no longer feel the community and filial piety of their elders. In addition, the one-child policy is producing the fastest-ageing population in the world. Nevertheless, Chinese policy makers reiterated the need in 2000 for the one-child policy, which still sees no debate for abolition.

is seen as fair game and can be seen all over large and small towns. Many well-educated, tidy office workers can also be seen begging on the streets after they have lost their job and have nothing else to turn to.

HAN CHINESE The Han Chinese are the predominant ethnicity in all of China and make up the largest ethnic group in the world. In China alone they total over a billion people, almost 92% of the country's population. They took their name from the Han dynasty of 205BC to AD220, although they can be traced back before this period to earlier tribes. The Han Chinese speak a variety of related languages (see *Appendix 1, Language*, page 259), but the predominant language in China today is Mandarin (pǔtōnghuà). All Chinese languages are united by the same script of characters, which was first developed over 3,000 years ago.

MANCHU Almost ten million in number, the Manchu live all over China but higher concentrations of them remain in their northeast homeland of Heilongjiang and Liaoning, as well as in Hebei province. The Manchu are descendants of the Zhushen and Nuzhen nomadic tribes who harassed the northern borders of China in ancient times and finally ruled China as the Manchu Qing dynasty after 1644. They have their own language and writing originating from Mongolian, which was well preserved throughout the Qing dynasty, but has gradually gone into decline.

Most Manchu can now speak only Mandarin, but some communities in Heilongjiang still speak Manchu at home. During the Qing dynasty, the Manchu admired much of Han Chinese culture and assimilated quickly into their customs, religion and even adopted almost wholesale their form of government. The only Manchu custom that was really thrust on the Han Chinese was the practice for men of keeping their hair tied back in a *queue* (pigtail) and shaving the top of their head. In addition, Manchu women were not allowed to bind their feet. Like most dynasties, the Qing were keen to keep the imperial line pure and Manchu wives of the emperor had to be well versed in the Manchu language, customs and culture.

XIBE The Xibe national minority live mostly in Heilongjiang, Jilin and Liaoning, and a few in Xinjiang. They total some 172,000 and speak a Manchu-related Altaic language (the Turkic, Mongolian, Korean and Japanese family of languages) using a script based on Manchu. There is still some debate whether the Xibe are descendants of the ancient Xianbei, who were Turkic, or are Mongolian by descent.

KOREAN There are almost two million Koreans living in China's northeast. They have their own autonomous prefecture in the province of Jilin, but also live in Liaoning (bordering North Korea) and in Heilongjiang and Inner Mongolia. Sizeable communities of Koreans also live in the big cities such as Beijing and Tianjin where their food (especially dog, *kimchi*, and cold mung bean noodle soup) as well as their bathhouses (see page 165) are a speciality. The majority of these Koreans moved to China at the end of the Ming dynasty, midway through the 19th century and after Japan annexed Korea in 1910. They preserve their own language and alphabet, which is taught in Korean schools in Yanbian autonomous prefecture in Jilin.

MONGOL The Mongols, who make up 4.8 million people in China, are also known in Russian as Tartars from the word Tartarus, meaning 'the deepest part of Hell'. It is believed that the word Tartar is also a deliberate modification of the Persian word Tatar, meaning 'Turk'. Although the Mongol Empire did extend through Russia as far as central eastern Europe by the 13th and 14th centuries, they were repelled from there by the Turks, notably the Ottomans, and are ethnically distinct.

In 1207, the Mongol Genghis Khan united a host of nomadic clans and started to expand his rule into China and west into the Arabic and Persian lands. His grandson Kublai Khan expanded his grandfather's conquests to cover all of China and Tibet as the Yuan dynasty, which was eventually forced back into Mongolia by the Ming dynasty in 1368.

Most Mongols today live in the autonomous region of Inner Mongolia, while some live in the bordering northern Chinese provinces. Nomadic by custom, a large number of Mongolians still roam the steppe lands living in yurts and tending herds. They still use their own language and writing.

HUI Today, the Hui ethnic minority total 8.6 million people. They have their own autonomous region of Ningxia, although they are still not the majority there and many Hui live all over China. Nevertheless, the Hui are guaranteed autonomous government in Ningxia and the president of the autonomous government is elected by the Hui national minority.

The Hui are Muslim who started to settle in China along the Silk Road. In the Yuan dynasty (1279–1368), Kublai Khan encouraged the settlement of Arabic, Persian and Turkic people in the Ningxia region. These people assimilated the

Chinese language but kept their Muslim faith and customs. Hui food is wheat based and they do not eat pork, but specialise in lamb dishes and other halal foods. There are over 3,000 mosques in Ningxia alone, and increasing numbers of Hui make the pilgrimage to Mecca every year.

SALAR The Salar ethnic group is about 87,000 strong living mostly in Gansu and Qinghai. They descend from the Samarkand people of central Asia who were first moved here by Kublai Khan during his repopulation of northern China. They have since assimilated with the surrounding Hui, Tibetan, Mongolian and Han people. Although the Salar speak their own language, a Turkic branch of Altaic, they do not have a written alphabet and so use the Chinese script for written communication.

DONGXIANG Descendants of the Mongolians, the Dongxiang national minority live mostly in neighbouring Gansu, Ningxia and also in Xinjiang. They number some 373,000. Their language has no written form and belongs to the Mongolian branch of Altaic.

TU The origin of the Tu, who total 191,000 citizens, is still somewhat disputed, but their language belongs again to the Mongolian branch of Altaic. They live mostly in Qinghai province, with a sizeable community also living in Gansu.

BONAN The Bonan ethnicity number a mere 12,000, who, as the Salar, live predominantly in Gansu and Qinghai. It is not completely clear whether the Bonan emerged from the Mongolian or Hui people, but their language belongs firmly in the Mongolian branch of Altaic. There is no written form of the language.

YUGUR There are also some 12,000 Yugur living in Gansu province. They are an ancient ethnicity whose livelihood in Gansu can be traced back to the 4th century BC. Their language is a very old form of Altaic and has no script.

KAZAK The Kazak, originating from Kazakhstan, live mostly in neighbouring Xinjiang and in Gansu. They total around 1.1 million inhabitants in China. Their language is Turkic Altaic using an Arabic script. They are predominantly Muslim by faith.

TIBETAN Tibetans in China number almost 4.6 million people. Outside Tibet, they also live in neighbouring Qinghai, Sichuan and Yunnan, as well as in Gansu. The Tibetan language belongs to the Sino-Tibetan family and has its own script.

Tibetans in Tibet dispute rule by the People's Republic of China and there is a government in exile in Dharamsala, India, which is headed by the Dalai Lama. Tibet itself has seen three periods of effective rule from Beijing: firstly, by the Mongol Yuan dynasty (1279–1368), when Kublai Khan united the fighting Tibetan kingdoms; secondly, by the Qing dynasty (1724–1911), when they ousted the re-invading Mongols and held Tibet as a vassal state; and thirdly, from 1949 until today, which has seen the most intrusive of rule from Beijing with the lethal suppression of revolt and the mass migration of Han Chinese to rule the province.

Tibetans outside Tibet generally continue to live a strong Buddhist lifestyle tending pasture in highland areas. The Tibetan monastery at Mati (see page 248) is an example of this, although it is now more tourist-oriented than monastic.

LANGUAGE

The predominant language throughout China is Mandarin, known as pǔtōnghuà 普通话 (meaning 'common tongue') or guóyǔ 国语 (meaning 'national tongue') in mainland China. It is also known colloquially as hànyǔ 汉语 (meaning 'language of the Han'). Putonghua belongs to the sinitic branch of the Sino-Tibetan family of languages. There are quite a few dialectic differences spoken throughout the north, and in the south there are six other mutually unintelligible sinitic languages spoken. These are: Cantonese/*Yue*, Shanghainese/*Wu*, Hokkien/*Min*, Hakka, Gan and Xiang. All these languages use the same Chinese character script (for more on script see *Appendix 1, Language*, page 259). The Tibetan branch of Sino-Tibetan languages that are spoken in China are Tibetan, Chin and Yi. The Tibetan languages have a separate script. In the north, the minorities (see above) also speak other Altaic languages (the Turkic, Mongolian, Korean and Japanese family of languages).

The Sino-Tibetan languages are monosyllabic and tonal. Putonghua has over 1,600 syllables, four tones, and over 40,000 characters, each representing one syllable. This means that many characters have the same syllable and tone, so in verbal usage their meaning is often derived from context or combination with other characters/syllables. A minimum of 3,000 characters are needed to be able to read a newspaper.

Appendix 1 gives a quick guide to speaking putonghua as well as useful phrases for getting around and, very importantly, ordering good food.

RELIGION AND BELIEFS

Although communist China has declared itself atheist, there are five registered religions (See *Appendix 2, Glossary* for a definition of key terms used here) in China: Buddhism, Daoism, Islam, Catholicism and Protestantism. These religions are closely monitored and each adherent to one of the five faiths should be registered. In reality, however, many are not. This is partly because different denominations within a faith may not wish to be associated with the dominant registered denomination, and partly because of the recent revival in traditional Chinese faiths (Daoism and Buddhism) and the sheer number of part-time, casual temple-goers has made a mockery of the registration system. In addition, former president Jiang Zemin had sought to build stronger ties with the religious communities, especially the traditional Chinese belief systems. Many temples and monasteries are now being restored, albeit largely for tourism, and many of the monks you will see in the temples are paid to administer the monastery rather than to actually keep the faith. Many more true adherents, however, are flourishing in this more relaxed atmosphere of tolerance of religion. Nevertheless, as is communist China's way, unregistered believers can run foul of the authorities, as is the case with Falun Gong believers. (For a good account of the Falun Gong see Ian Johnson's book *Wild Grass* in *Appendix 3, Further information*, page 269.)

To the main traditional Chinese faiths of Daoism and Buddhism can be added the traditional Chinese philosophy of Confuciansim. All three are more belief systems or teachings in social conduct than religions in the traditional Western sense of these concepts. None believes in a single deity and all are more concerned with conducting life on earth than with one's relation with an omniscient, omnipresent single god. In particular, there are no temples of monks of Confucianism and the closest approximation to 'worshipping' Confucius is the altar or temple of the Three Teachings (Buddhism, Daosim and Confucianism) that can be found in some monasteries. As Chinese beliefs are not based around the supremacy of a single god, they have come to co-exist without resort to the crusades of Christian and Islamic religions. This concept of co-existence is very Chinese in and of itself. Not only do many Chinese believers adhere to all three of the main Chinese beliefs, but they may also have room in their concept of faith to adhere to Christianity or Islam as well (even if this might not be acceptable under strict renditions of these religions). Some Chinese temples or monasteries, such as the Hanging Monastery in Shanxi (see page 201) will even have an altar dedicated to all three beliefs. Some say that a person can, or even should, be Confucian during the day when work has to be done, Daoist in the evening when the duties are done, and Buddhist in helping others and in the afterlife.

CONFUCIANISM Confucianism is a philosophy or set of rules setting out the proper conduct between people in society. It is not defined by the Chinese as a religion. Confucianism maintains that if such proper conduct is adhered to, it will eliminate the need for war. The rules originate from the teachings of Confucius (Kǒng Fū Zǐ 孔夫子 or Kǒng Zǐ) who was born in 551BC. At the time employed as a court official, Confucius preached his beliefs to various rulers, but with little success in converting any of the rulers or of averting war. Amongst his many teachings, Confucius believed that the person most faithful to and enlightened of the rules he espoused would naturally rise as the rightful and benign ruler over an obedient and correct society. Unable to find such a ruler, Confucius left the courts and turned to teaching. He died in 479BC, after which his disciples, especially Mencius, wrote down his teachings in the *Analects* among other writings.

It was not until the Han dynasty (206BC–AD220) that Emperor Wu Di adopted Confucianism as a form of government. The Confucian concepts of hierarchical relationships (subject to ruler, filial piety, younger to older, wife to husband (and his entire family) and friend to friend) suited Emperor Wu Di and subsequent rulers well, which then became the base, often, of an effective dictatorship. For the next 2,000 years, Mandarins of the Chinese imperial courts would have to pass rigorous entrance exams based on the teachings of Confucius and the five Confucian virtues of benevolence, propriety (ancestor worship), moral righteousness, trustworthiness and wisdom. The court rarely, however, epitomised these virtues in practice.

Confucianism has been strongly criticised in the 20th century for its conservatism, which it was believed stifled innovation and shackled China to the past. Mao Zedong himself preferred the legalist leanings of the first unifier of China, Emperor Qin Shi (221–206BC). Modern-day adherents of Confucianism, however, attribute the Confucian values of social order, harmony, hard work and obedience to the successes of China's economy and social progress. Both ancient and new temples to Confucius are seeing a small revival throughout China.

DAOISM Whilst Confucianism gives a set order to the social side of human life, Daoism searches for one's own way (dào 道) with oneself, the Earth and things beyond the tangible. It incorporates, therefore, a spiritual side to its philosophy, and it is defined by the Chinese as a religion. Daoist teachings, exemplified in the Dào Dé Jīng 道德经 (also written as T'ao T'e Ching in the Wade–Giles transliteration, see A Note on Spelling page X), are based on the belief in an all-powerful force making everything relative. Daoists believe that humans are an interference in this force and should seek their minimal impact on the world. Similarly, governments should be minimalist in their impact on society (an early concept of decentralisation).

Daoism originates from the teachings of the hermit Lǎo Zǐ 老子, who is believed to have lived around the same time as Confucius, and also from the teachings of Zhuangzi. The Dao De Jing, however, did not appear until almost 300 years after the death of Lao Zi. Daoism does not have the following of Confucianism or Buddhism, but has been very influential in Chinese science, literature and the arts. Daoist temples can usually be found in most towns, one of the most impressive of which is the active Daoist monastery of Erlangshan in Shenmu (see page 218). Daoist temples differ from

Yinyang symbol with diagram

Buddhist temples in many ways, much of which might not be discernible to the untrained eye. The primary altar in a Daoist temple will be dedicated to Lao Zi himself (a long-bearded fellow with a *yinyang* pendant around his neck). The pendant is usually surrounded by the eight diagrams that make up the divining sticks of the faith.

The same *yinyang* and eight-diagram representation (see above) will also be found on the incense altar in the centre of the temple's primary courtyard. Various altars will exist to the other semi-deities to be found in the Dao De Jing and to various incarnations of Lao Zi including when he appears as a woman. One such deity is the jet-black god of the sea. The last altar at the back of the temple or monastery is almost always dedicated to women in an unusual reverence for women in Chinese society. Daoist temples do not really have priests or monks as such, but teachers called dàoshi 道士. These men are distinguishable by their long beards, black tunics with white leggings and square board hats. Like Buddhist monks, daoshi do not eat meat.

BUDDHISM Unlike Confucianism and Daoism, Buddhism originated outside of China. It entered via the Silk Road from India and took until the end of the Han dynasty in AD220 to really catch on. In the Sui dynasty (AD589–618) the emperor adopted Buddhism as the religion of the nation. However, in a turnaround typical of dynastic change, the ensuing Tang dynasty clamped down on the growing power of the Buddhist monks.

The original Buddha or Enlightened One was the mortal Siddhartha Gautama, a prince born in Nepal in the 6th century BC. Appalled by the cruelty and fellow suffering of humans he abandoned his life in the royal household to seek solace and release. Eventually, through meditation he achieved the enlightenment (*nirvana*) he was seeking and continued the rest of his life on earth teaching what he had learnt as a monk.

This is far too individualistic a path for most socially concerned Chinese, and so most Chinese Buddhists adhere to the later Mahayana school, which believes that ultimate nirvana for the individual cannot be attained before enlightenment for the whole of society. As a result, enlightened individuals in the Mahayana school are known as Boddhisattvas, who go on to aid others on their path to enlightenment. Chinese adherents to the popular form of Buddhism do not believe that enlightenment can be achieved in one's first lifetime, but through reincarnation over several lifetimes. Common folk thus believed that by doing more good than harm in their life they would be reincarnated as a better being, or if they were bad, they would come back as a lesser animal such as a dog or a rat.

In searching out the aid of the Boddhisattvas, the Chinese have built numerous temples to them, such that their position in the hierarchy of relationships has essentially attained that of Confucius-advocated ancestor worship. Popular Boddhisattvas include Guanyin, the Goddess of Mercy, and Amitabha, the God of Eternal Light. The figure of Buddha found in most Chinese temples is a large fat fellow, which illustrates the later life of the Buddhist culture. Indian Buddhas and Buddhas of older schools of Buddhism in China tend to be younger leaner figures, which are usually found in very old temples mostly at the western end of the Silk Road. The Laughing Buddha, a fat sitting figure, which can be found on sale everywhere, is a very popular representation of the Chinese happy-go-lucky attitude to fate.

RELIGION, POLITICS AND SOVEREIGNTY Ever since Buddhist monks became closely embroiled in imperial matters in the 8th century AD, Chinese emperors have kept monks and the clergy well out of government. Religious rituals, rites and divinations often played a part in legitimising the rule of the emperor and many a sacrifice was made in the name of the gods when it suited him. The abundance of religious beliefs and gods meant that the educated Chinaman was usually sceptical of religion, but would often use popular religious beliefs to control the uneducated.

Interestingly, because the Chinese really did believe that the emperor was the Son of Heaven and that China was indeed the Middle Kingdom and centre of the universe (see page 164 for the actual epicentre in Beijing), the Chinese ruling elite did not believe in such things as borders and sovereignty (ie: that lands might belong to another equal monarch and that people of one land should not interfere in the internal political affairs of another land). Instead the Chinese elite believed in spheres or zones of influence. Outside of the Middle Kingdom, modern-day countries like Korea, Japan, Vietnam, Mongolia and Tibet were seen as belonging to the first sphere of influence. The influence of Chinese culture in these countries is evident. In the next sphere of influence belonged the central Asian countries along the Silk Road and the southeast Asian communities of Malaysia and Thailand. Beyond these in Europe were the 'barbarians'. Taiwan belonged firmly in the Middle Kingdom and this ancient belief system is an underlying reason for China's strong calls for reunification between mainland China and Taiwan.

A complex tribute system was adhered to between the lands of the different spheres and the Son of Heaven. Often, however, the emperor poured lavish gifts on those he acknowledged as prince of the land, gifts far in excess of the original tribute offered. In exchange there was usually an understanding that these lands should prevent the barbarians from the outer zone entering the Middle Kingdom, but if the force proved too overwhelming, or neighbouring lands started to quarrel, then the imperial army would step in.

When Queen Victoria sent an envoy in her name to negotiate trading rights with Emperor Xuan Cong in the difficult lead-up to the Opium War of 1840, the envoy refused to kowtow to the emperor as this would signify that Queen Victoria was of a lesser status than the emperor. This was the first real defiance to the Middle Kingdom's belief system. But it took another 70 years to topple. Having learnt the concept of borders and sovereignty the hard way, through wars, concessions and foreign aggression, China is now keen to use such concepts to keep foreigners out. Two centuries too late, this comes at a time when much of the Western world, which had imposed sovereignty on China, is now trying to dismantle it with universal human rights and international trading laws.

Internal disorder invites external calamity The concept of 'internal disorder, external calamity' represented by the four-character phrase nèi luàn wài huàn 内乱外患,

is integral to the Chinese political desire for social order. It is not just the political elite who believe in the concept from a geopolitical standpoint; the concept also applies to family unity. Thus husband and wife, father and son should not quarrel in case it invites trouble for the family as a unit. Many Chinese, even those who took part in the Tiananmen Square protests in 1989, now believe that it was right for the government to have quelled the demonstrations when they did, because the students were no real alternative to the Communist Party. Toppling the government, therefore, would have put the country in chaos and invited the other global powers to carve up China. It is this preference for order that allows the Chinese to endure impingements on their personal freedom which people in the West would find intolerable. With growing corruption at the provincial level, however, it might be only a matter of time before the masses rise up again as in the past to overthrow the communist dynasty.

CULTURE, CUSTOMS AND HABITS

Chinese culture spans over 6,000 years of recorded history, 56 ethnicities, many different religions and numerous influences. China is particularly famous for its silk, tea and porcelain or fine bone china (which is named after the country, not the other way around). For a list of the many inventions that originated in China, see the box below.

Incorporating one-fifth of the world's population, it is not surprising that Chinese culture is so rich. Its writing has influenced Japan, Korea, Mongolia, Tibet and Vietnam. Its cuisine (see page 50) ranges from basic hand-stretched noodles in soup to painstakingly exquisite and refined Qing dynasty imperial dishes. The arts and literature of China are equally beyond listing, including numerous styles of calligraphy; paper cutting; mask, kite and puppet making; Chinese circus, acrobatics and gymnastics; Beijing Opera as well as that of numerous ethnicities; a variety of dress; magic mask shows (see Hua Jia Yiyuan page 154); many indigenous musical instruments such as the èrhú 二胡; wood printing; silk painting; tie-dyeing; modern-day film-making; painting; poetry and literature.

USEFUL CONCEPTS FOR UNDERSTANDING THE CHINESE There are a number of concepts peculiar to the Chinese that are essential to understand if you want to get by in China. If you come from the Anglo-Saxon, Western world then many of these Chinese traits will go against your first instincts, and you may even find them highly irritating before long. Nevertheless, if you can get your head around them, not only will you understand some of the Chinese reactions to some of what you do, but you should also realise that these reactions are not meant to be offensive.

Community and family first Certainly, at least from the time of Confucius (see page 44) if not before, the community and filial piety take precedence over the rights of the individual. This concept ties in with other Chinese reverence for harmony and face (see below). It is a distinctly Asian trait and time and time again, even in Chinese communities in the West, you will see the Chinese sacrifice their own freedoms in order to gain benefits for their family or community. This conversely translates into a lack of regard for what are called by the West 'first generation' human rights: freedom of speech, association, religion and movement. Communism has favoured 'second generation' human rights: right to work, housing, food and health. But these in fact tie in well with Asian concepts of what come first, ie: the greater good of the family and the community. This family- and community-based orientation means that there is enormous respect for the elderly,

The Chinese have a long and illustrious history of inventions, many of which at first were mere toys, and later adopted by the Europeans to reach their full impact. Here is a list of some of the most ingenious creations, most of which we could not today imagine life without.

5000BC	Silk discovered; pottery made in fire kilns
4000BC	Rice cultivated in the south (noodles were already being eaten in the north)
2800BC	Chinese characters first take form
2500BC	Acupuncture used to heal illnesses
2205BC	Dykes built to control flooding; irrigation used to increase arable land
1500BC	Horses used to plough and to pull carriages
1000BC	First Chinese dictionary compiled
513BC	Iron smelting started the use of 'cold' weaponry
350BC	Crossbow invented
150BC	Lacquerware, silk painting and fine pottery
1st century AD	Chang Heng invents the first seismograph to measure earthquakes. Magnetic compasses (pointing south) allow the Chinese to align temples. Cubit rule, calipers, horse breastplates, suspension bridges, the abacus and the ship's rudder are invented. The Chinese divide the calendar year into 365.25 days
AD120	Paper
3rd century	Wheelbarrow (did not come to Europe for another 1,000 years)
AD350	Stirrups
AD593	Printing press
7th century	Gunpowder for fireworks, typeset printing press
AD900	Porcelain
10th century	Rockets
11th century	Playing cards
1498	Toothbrush

and the Chinese will generally see themselves first and foremost as Chinese rather than as an ethnic minority (such as Han, Manchu or Hui) within China. The notable exceptions to this are the Uighur of Xinjiang and the Tibetans.

Population versus privacy The sheer numbers of Chinese in small places, combined with the concept of community and family first, as well as a low income, means that privacy is not something the Chinese are used to, or even see as desirable. This will seem strange and can be irritating to Westerners, especially when the Chinese pick up your books and belongings from the train table to take a look at them, or stare over your shoulder while you are reading, or ask you what seem to be highly personal questions. It is quite common that among the first three topics a Chinese person might ask you about is, how old you are (old age is revered), whether you are married and have children, and how much you earn or how much something you own costs. In the West this might be called 'nosy', but for a lot of Chinese this is normal and in many ways a leftover of communist reinforcement that everything belongs to everybody. As the standard of living in the cities rises, however, affluent Chinese are developing a desire for privacy. This is most visible in the stand-alone fenced houses appearing in the suburbs and in the gated, high-rise communities now appearing in the cities.

Rènao 热闹 There is no exact translation for the word *renao*. It is an adjective essentially describing a situation that is lively, noisy, busy, usually fun (although you might not always agree), and often includes heated debate. Following on again from the priority of community over the individual and population over privacy, the vast majority of Chinese see *renao* almost as a virtue. The more *renao* a situation is, the better. Altogether this gives the Chinese an incredibly high tolerance of both noise and crowds. They might also like elements of tranquillity and solitude, but *renao* is always good. So, be prepared for lively, noisy situations on buses, in trains, in hotels (see page 90) and markets and at any time of day or night. If you want a quiet, relaxing holiday, China might not be the place for you.

Face Owing in large part to the importance of the hierarchy of social relations in Confucianism, there is a strong need among the Chinese not to lose face (diū liǎn 丢脸) in public. This is something like keeping up appearances but not quite as proactive. It relates more to the desire for harmony and the dislike of confrontation (although you will see more of this in China than one might be led to expect). So, for instance, in a market transaction a seller will push up the price for an item if a young couple is buying, knowing that the boyfriend cannot push the price too low in case he loses face in front of his girlfriend for appearing too cheap. In international politics, the social pressure back in China not to lose face means that many political interactions with the Chinese can be satisfactorily resolved behind closed doors, but once an issue becomes public, the Chinese are highly unlikely to back down.

Connections Guānxi 关系 Most business transactions in China are done through connections (*guanxi*) rather than through an open, transparent system with an unknown person. This is not so much because the Chinese do not trust somebody they don't know, but it is because of an age-old system of giving a discount or better service to a known person and the desire to hold or call on favours. The Anglo-Saxon preference not to feel indebted to somebody for a favour does not trump the desire to use one's *guanxi* in China. Guanxi were often the only way to get things done in communist China, and the importance of them should not be underestimated in today's China, even though the increase in affluence in the cities and interaction with foreigners means that more can be done without having *guanxi*.

CULTURAL ETIQUETTE

Very few things can't be done in China's big cities now. **Smoking** (see box page 51) is still ubiquitous, even for women, for whom it used to be very avant-garde. You can discuss anything you like in public including **criticism** of the government, so long as this is on an individual, spontaneous level. Organising a political movement, however, will get you into trouble (such as a visit to the police station and potentially even deportation). The authorities can get very suspicious of journalists and writers and periodically clamp down on them, for which 'rehabilitation' work camps still exist.

On a more positive level, if you **visit** a Chinese family or friend it is polite to bring fruit, especially red fruits such as oranges or peaches. Presents from abroad are always coveted, especially in remote parts of China. In the larger cities, the Chinese can buy so many things that are available abroad (most of them are made in China in the first place nowadays) that even foreign chocolates aren't a big deal any more, although, of course, it's the thought that counts.

If you end up exchanging **business cards**, it is very important to hand your business card to your interlocutor with both hands, to receive theirs with both hands and to leave the received business card on the table face up for the duration of the meeting. Putting the received business card away too hastily shows disrespect.

Generally, if you receive a **wrapped gift**, you are not expected to open it in front of the host, nor should you urge a recipient of your wrapped gift to open it. This avoids the dreadful faux pas of losing face and showing inadvertent disappointment when the present turns out to be exactly that piece of kitsch which friends will mock. (Although it must be said that the Chinese often like memento pieces of kitsch.) When **drinking alcohol**, the Chinese will often take care to ensure that when they clink glasses with each other, their glass is not higher than the host's glass. This often dissolves into a race to be the lowest glass. For food etiquette see *Cuisine*, below.

CUISINE

Northern Chinese cuisine today is a real mix of ethnic, traditional, modern, poor and rich tastes. The staple food of northern China is **wheat**, usually served up as noodles or as **steamed buns** (mántou 馒头). Throughout the north you will come across many different ways of **pulling noodles** (lā miàn 拉面). Mostly, they are served as individual bowls of noodle soup or plates of short strips of noodles with a vegetable and meat mix. **Lamb** (yángrou 羊肉) is the meat of choice in the north, especially among the Muslim communities. It is served in many different ways, but one of the most irresistibly tasty is as skewers of lamb pieces (yáng ròu chuàn'r 羊肉串) grilled with plenty of chilli powder, salt and numb pepper. Very tasty with a beer and a plate of cold boiled peanuts and celery.

Hotpot (huǒguō 火锅), sometimes known as steam boat or shuànyángròu 涮羊肉 , is a delicious Chinese fondue broth in which you cook your own fresh raw ingredients. It is very popular in the north, especially in the winter. Once upon a time, the hotpot pan itself was a copper cauldron over coals in the middle of your table. These days, modern multi-partitioned stainless-steel bowls sit in a hole especially cut out of the table and are heated by gas, which can be more easily controlled. On ordering hotpot, you will normally be presented with a sheet of paper with a list of raw ingredients and their respective prices, which you mark up, letting the waiter know what you want (see the crib sheet on page 264 for a typical hotpot menu). First you order the hotpot soup base. Each establishment usually has its own special recipes, but most importantly you might want to differentiate between spicy hot (là 辣) and not hot (qīng 清). Hotpot broths usually come in meat or fish varieties or a plain starch soup. Many places now offer hotpot bowls with two or three partitions so that you can choose two or three different broths. Occasionally, you will come across places with individual hotpot bowls, but usually it is a set-up best suited for two or more people. After you have chosen all your ingredients, which usually come by the small plate or basketful, then you will also be asked to choose your dipping sauce. Each person chooses their own, which again can be specialities of the house, but the most popular are the peanut or sesame seed sauces. At the end of eating all your dishes, the leftover soup is very tasty by this stage.

A mini personal hotpot served in the mid north is the **sand pot** (shā guō 沙锅). There is a variety of choices, usually consisting of some type of meat or fish, several vegetables and mung bean noodles. At about ¥8 per pot, they are cheap and ideal for the individual traveller.

Any traveller, and particularly those from countries where smoking is increasingly forbidden in public places, will quickly realise that the Chinese smoke a lot, and just about anywhere. Although smoking is banned in some public places in some cities, you would hardly know, and the law is rarely enforced. The World Health Organisation (WHO) estimates that 350 million Chinese – or 36% of the total population and 60% of men – smoke. Cigarettes cost as little as US$0.24 a pack and there are few public efforts to get people to cut the habit, which remains socially accepted. China is not only the world's largest producer of tobacco, it is also home to one in three of the world's smokers. This suggests that the economics of cigarettes are significant, both to the local, and to the international tobacco industry, to whom China is one of the most promising markets. In 2004, the Chinese lit up an estimated 1.8 trillion cigarettes, compared to 388 billion cigarettes in the US, where cigarette consumption has declined by 2–3% a year for the last decade. Stricter laws and government efforts to limit the number of smokers have helped people in developed countries smoke less. This makes countries like China, where the sector is less regulated by state health authorities, even more interesting to the tobacco industry. The results are nefarious: according to one source, 200 million Chinese teenagers are expected to take up smoking and 25% will die between the ages of 35 to 69 due to tobacco-related illnesses. One sign that things might be changing, is the government's recent decision to ratify the WHO's Framework Convention on Tobacco Control, which includes a number of steps to reduce smoking.

There are two types of wheat **dumplings** found in the north. Most common, especially for breakfast, is the steamed bāozi 包子. You will see these steaming away in round bamboo trays on the side of the street. They are usually filled with a minced pork stuffing, but sometimes come with an egg, spinach and vermicelli stuffing, or occasionally other varieties. Be careful not to mix them up with plain steamed buns (mántou 馒头), which can be a bit of a disappointment if you are expecting a tasty filling. Another type of dumpling is the jiǎozi 饺子, which is a northern type of pot-sticker. Usually crescent shaped rather than round, they are either boiled and served as water dumplings (shuǐjiǎo 水饺), or boiled and fried. Both are usually served with black vinegar and soy sauce. Some shops specialise in shuijiao, which can come in dozens of fillings.

For most visitors to northern China, their trip would not be complete without eating **Beijing duck** (Běijīng kǎoyā 北京烤鸭 – previously known as Peking duck). This is roast duck served in slivers and put into a small pancake with spring onions, finely sliced cucumbers and plum sauce. All the ingredients are supplied at your table, where you create the little pancake feasts yourself. Half a duck usually serves two. The waiter will often slice up the duck at your table and then take the leftover carcass to make it into a watery duck soup for you. Modern fusion restaurants often provide an alternative to the traditional plum sauce, or may serve the even tastier southern variety of crispy aromatic duck with your pancakes.

A simple traditional northern Chinese breakfast takes some getting used to. It usually consists of a rice or wheat gruel (thin paltry tasting broth) accompanied by unsalted steamed buns and small plates of very salty pickled vegetables. Tea (unusually for the British) is not normally served at breakfast, so the gruel is your only source of liquid. If you are lucky, boiled eggs rather than hundred-year-old pickled eggs might also be served. Contrary to their name, hundred-year-old eggs are in fact pickled for only 100 days, but they are meant to be able to last 100 years.

People and Culture CUISINE

3

51

People spitting in public is probably the Chinese habit that foreign travellers will find the most difficult to get used to, apart from children urinating in the streets. While there have been several years of government efforts to put an end to spitting, the Chinese (men – women do not usually spit) have not yet dropped this widely prevalent habit. When the SARS (Severe Acute Respiratory Syndrome) epidemic was discovered in China at the end of 2002, the government came under increased pressure to ban spitting and improve overall Chinese health and hygiene. This included the call for more physical exercise to bolster the immune system, washing hands, and serving individual portions instead of sharing food from one plate. With good personal hygiene recommended as one of the most effective ways to prevent the spread of SARS, spitting – which can propel droplets to others and inadvertently spread the disease – was particularly criticised. Various localities, including Beijing, Shanghai and Guangzhou, have imposed fines of up to ¥200 for spitters.

The pickling process turns the egg white a translucent brown, while the yolk becomes a sulphuric blue-green. Definitely an acquired taste for most people. Larger hotels might serve a buffet that includes a variety of steamed vegetables, fried rice, noodles, hot dried milk, coffee, tea and fruit. Western hotels usually serve a full fried and continental breakfast as well. If you can't face a traditional simple Chinese breakfast after your first encounter, then go out early onto the streets and you should find many more palatable alternatives, such as baozi, huntun, hot doufu milk, sweet pots of yoghurt, sweet fried sesame paste, glutinous rice buns and fried dough twists, youtiao. A delicious variation on the youtiao, available early in the morning and often throughout the day, are jiānbing guǒzi 煎饼果子. These are thin pancakes wrapped around a youtiao and depending on your tastes served with an extra egg, spring onions/scallion, and chilli or sesame sauce. The local morning market or street vendors can provide many of these tasty snacks, although there is a move afoot now in many towns to rid the streets of independent vendor stalls (because they aren't usually licensed and don't pay taxes).

Tea is an art form in China. Although you can get black tea (called 'red' tea, hóng chá 红茶) most people drink green teas (lǜchá 绿茶), of which there are many different types and many different prices. In the south, the tea ceremony has made a big comeback and it is beginning also to appear in the north, especially Beijing, Dandong and Yinchuan. It can be a bit expensive, especially if you are only one or two people and you don't really appreciate tea. One of the most popular flowered teas is jasmine tea (mòli huāchá 茉莉花茶). True tea connoisseurs consider jasmine tea to be a bit of a cheap populist alternative to real green tea as it takes the cheaper broken varieties of green tea and adds sweet-smelling jasmine flowers to it. Some of the artwork done with jasmine tea, though, is quite amazing. The leaves can come in a variety of twisted shapes and some are sewn up into 3cm balls which unfurl in the water to become a purple- or red-hearted flower (chūshuǐ fúróng 出水芙蓉). Green teas are renowned for their antioxidant properties and although they are lower in tannin/caffeine than black teas, some people still find them to be stimulants. If you want a completely non-caffeinated tea try chrysanthemum tea (júhuā chá 菊花茶). A big handful of chrysanthemum flowers is usually stuffed in a glass pot and allowed to steep in hot water. It is served with rock sugar, which you can have added to the pot or separately to your teacup.

Another favourite non-caffeinated tea is eight-treasure tea (bābǎo chá 八宝茶). This consists of eight different teas, dried fruits, flowers and rock sugar.

Food etiquette in China can be quite complex. When eating with chopsticks, it is impolite to stick your chopsticks in the bowl of food, but they should be laid on the top of your bowl when not in use or on the chopstick holder at the side of your bowl. It is considered bad luck to cross your chopsticks. Especially after SARS, a fad had started whereby diners would take food from communal plates with one end of the chopsticks and eat from the other end. This practice is not highly observed.

Generally speaking, it is impolite to eat all of the food offered by your host as it shows that they have not ordered enough. At a truly sumptuous banquet, it is even considered a failure on the part of the host if you have to resort to rice, which might not be served until the last course, to satiate your appetite. Soup is usually served with the main course as a kind of drink to go with your meal or it might also be served at the end to wash down the last of your meal. It is never served at the beginning of the meal in a true Chinese restaurant or home.

As the Chinese eat mostly with chopsticks, everything is fairly well chopped up into 'manageable' mouth-size pieces. This does not necessarily mean you can get the whole piece in your mouth, especially as most pieces of poultry and fish will include all the bones. But with dextrous use of chopsticks and biting off chunks of the 'manageable' piece of food, the Chinese can 'hoover' their way through a meal in no time. You might wish to practise at home first with your own chopsticks and a meal of fresh garden peas, a pork chop and a chicken drumstick. To help you with the garden peas, it is useful to know that the Chinese usually bring the bowl up to their mouth and often shovel rice and other food into the mouth using their chopsticks. Bone pieces are usually spat out of the side of one's mouth directly into a pile on the table, which will be cleared up at the end of the meal. It is not considered impolite to slurp your food and the Chinese will often chew on their food with their mouth wide open and talking at the same time. Soup is also often drunk straight out of the bowl.

Like in most societies, it is usually a good idea to see what your hosts are doing first, just to check whether you are sitting with the polite reformist crowd or the slurpy traditional crowd.

4

The Outdoors

Former theories included that loessal deposits were beds of ancient oceans, and even that they were composed of cosmic Saturn-like rings of dust that may have once encircled the globe but somehow rained down in pockets.

Daniel Dillon, 2003

TOPOGRAPHY

The geography of northern China along the Ming Great Wall ranges from mountainous in northeast Liaoning and Hebei provinces, through the grasslands of Ningxia, semi-arid desert of China's loess plateau, and borders the sand dunes of the Tengger Desert of Inner Mongolia. It is the mountainous areas of Hebei and Beijing that most people associate with the Great Wall but, in fact, almost 70% of it lies in the desertified regions of the loess plateau. The Great Wall in these areas is built mostly of rammed earth with little if any use of rock and stone.

SOIL EROSION OF THE LOESS PLATEAU China's loess plateau has the planet's most extensive soil erosion. It extends over most of Gansu, Ningxia, Shaanxi and Shanxi as well as parts of Qinghai, Inner Mongolia and Henan provinces. Containing more nutrients than sand, loess is also much finer. Its silt-like nature is noted as being among the most erosion-prone soils known on the planet. Loess is also extremely sensitive to the forces of wind and water, bearing the dubious honour of being blown or washed away quicker than any other soil type.

Prior to the 19th century, loess was a compelling mystery for geologists seeking to know its origins. Into the last century, however, an apparent agreement was shown between the timing of noticeable waves of loessal sedimentation and the glaciation of the northern hemisphere. China's loess plateau was formed in waves between 2.4 and 1.67 million years ago, helped along by the uplift of the Tibetan plateau, the movements of several huge glaciers across the desert regions and strong winds. It is the world's largest deposit of loess, approximately the size of France. It has a remarkable average thickness of 150m, extending to 330m near Lanzhou.

Some 5,000 years ago, the Tengger and Ordos deserts started to encroach upon the loess plateau. Almost 2,000 years later the Chinese started terracing and irrigating the plateau in an effort to increase water retention and decrease soil loss. These efforts are generally beneficial and help to curb the advance of the desert. From the Han dynasty (221BC–AD206), however, certain policies were started that not only reversed any benefit from terracing but contributed drastically to a trend in widespread soil erosion. For example, woodland areas in the region were stripped of trees in order to provide timber for war fighting and palaces. The remains of denuded forests were then torched in repeated 'scorched-earth' policies to repel the Mongol invasions from the north.

Today, the Lanzhou-based Cold and Arid Regions Environmental and Engineering Institute of the Chinese Academy of Sciences is working hard to counter desertification and soil erosion in the region. A branch office in Shapatou manages the Shapatou Desert Research Centre where you can see samples of the efforts being taken region-wide to reverse soil erosion (see page 234).

Another remarkable effort undertaken by the government to improve soil and air quality on the plateau is the Herculean tree-planting campaign started in 1997. All over the north of China, you will see rows and rows of young trees planted along roadsides. Every spring, the army plants literally millions of saplings, most of which do take root. It will be some decades before the consequences of these efforts will be truly felt and it is not even certain that the policy overall will be positive without other negative side effects. Only in China, however, could such a massive environmental tree-planting campaign take place on a scale likely never seen before in the world. The president said 'Grow trees' and they were grown.

WATERWAYS AND ARSENICOSIS Within the People's Republic of China the Great Wall starts in the east at the Yalu River which forms part of the border between China and North Korea. The Great Wall dips into the Bohai Gulf at Shanhaiguan, which has occasionally been known to freeze. Fresh and inland saline lakes dot north and south of the Great Wall along its entire length.

The wall crosses the Yellow River twice in Shanxi province and Ningxia autonomous region, and even forms part of the defensive system of the northern frontier. The Yellow River is so named because of its yellow-brown colour, derived from the heavy sediments of loess in the water. Allegedly, the Yellow River carries 30 times more sediment than the Nile and almost 100 times more than the Mississippi. Over 90% of this sediment comes from the loess plateau, between 10cm and 10m of which is gradually deposited downstream, and contributing to yearly floods during the summer rainy season, especially where the river is not dredged. Flooding, in turn, contributes to soil erosion of the loess further downstream. Thousands of lives are lost every year due to flooding, earning the river the nickname 'China's Sorrow'.

Much of the Yellow River is irrigated, helping to alleviate the impact of desertification in Ningxia particularly. In addition to irrigation, Ningxia draws water from the extensive aquifer beneath the Helan mountain range between the northwest of the region and Inner Mongolia. There are growing concerns that lowering the water table of the Helan aquifer too fast may cause irreversible environmental damage, as such measures have done in other parts of the world. It is unclear at present, however, just how fast is too fast and what the consequences of too fast would be. As a result, the local authorities seem little concerned with the long-term side effects that another generation will most likely have to deal with rather than themselves, and in the mean time reclaiming desertified land is good for the wine grapes, business connections and their pockets.

The semi-arid nature of the loess plateau means that for the most part, water sources are scarce along the Great Wall. In these regions, water is sought from wells dug deep into the aquifer. This presents quite a problem in the coal-mining areas, especially of Shanxi and Ningxia, where the coal is rich in arsenic (shēn 砷), which can contaminate the water. The United Nations Children's Fund (UNICEF) has been working with the authorities in China to improve water quality and treatment in rural areas where a quarter of the population drinks untreated water. Many years of drinking arsenic-contaminated water can lead to cancer of the skin, lungs and urinary system. Short-term exposure is not known to have lasting effects, but you would still be wise to drink bottled water, unless you can be sure that you are drinking from a safe well. UNICEF has also helped to conduct extensive blanket tests of wells in contaminated regions and be aware that the complex nature of rock formations means that a well a mere 10m from a contaminated well can be safe from arsenic. The authorities encourage people to use contaminated wells for washing and bathing only, but the lack of local understanding about the long-term effects of drinking arsenic-contaminated water means that considerable local education efforts still need to be undertaken.

AIR POLLUTION Air pollution in highly industrialised northern China can be extreme. Smoke from low-quality coal dust bricks used in most of the old and poor homes across China creates a thick, pea-soup smog. In big cities like Beijing, the smog has been so thick that it used to block out the sight of the sun on an otherwise clear day. Modernisation, especially in Beijing, which has committed itself to a Green Olympics in 2008, has helped to clear up visible air pollution, but many poorer regions still suffer badly.

While higher-quality smokeless coal used mostly in industry might not result in visible air pollution, the high aresenic content of China's coal is nonetheless released during burning. In the many cave dwellings in the regions, home stoves without chimneys release coal gases straight into the house. Many families in the poor coal mining areas of Shanxi and Ningxia also use this coal to smoke and preserve food, unaware that their food is now laced with arsenic.

Finally, to add more substance to air pollution, the strong winds across the north carry loess in the air all the way to Beijing and beyond. You will still see Beijingers today wearing headscarves and masks during the early summer windy season in order to avoid inhaling loess. In the loess plateau itself, loess storms can be so thick that you can see only a few metres ahead and feel like you are eating fine sand all day long.

Despite this negative picture of air and water pollution and soil erosion, much of the wall lies in areas mostly untouched or now abandoned by civilisation. Moreover, in the clear autumn, winter and early spring, the skies are clear and crisp, and mountain rivers in Hebei and Beijing thrive with healthy fish and wild edible water plants. For more on these see *Flora and fauna* below.

CLIMATE

Northern China experiences all four seasons. Summer and winter frequently reach extremes of over 40°C and below -20°C respectively. Spring and autumn are usually quite short. Spring in the northeast, around Beijing, Datong and Shanhaiguan, tends to see heavier April showers than in the northwest around Yinchuan and Jiayuguan. Beijing and Datong are also quite windy and dusty in the spring. The dust brought over from the loess plateau (see above) by the westerly winds can be severe enough that Beijing women especially often travel outside with a light veil or a medical mask over nose and mouth, usually when riding a bicycle. Average spring and autumn temperatures range between 5°C and 25°C.

Autumn is the best time to visit the Great Wall, especially if you are going to hike any of it. The changing autumn leaves make for beautiful scenery and fantastic photography. Morning mists give way to warm sunny days and cool evenings. If you are going to hike the wall in the summer then make sure you bring plenty of water, sunscreen or shade from the relentless sun, and insect repellent. Visiting the more remote parts of the Great Wall in the winter is not recommended, not least because most of it won't be visible.

Chinese wildlife is immensely diverse, as can be expected in a topography ranging from desert to mountain to marshes to seaside. The north is home to the extremely rare Siberian tiger, *Panthera tigris altaica*, of which there are believed to be fewer than 100 still living in China. The protected and rare giant panda can also be found in a handful of mountain forests in southern Gansu, where bamboo still forms much of the undergrowth, although its main strongholds are in Sichuan and Shaanxi.

Other wild mammals to be found in the north include rhesus macaque, goral, Manchurian weasel, sable, brown bear, black bear, lynx, northern pika, water shrew, muskrat, and mandarin vole. Deer species include roe deer, Sika deer and the much sought-after spotted deer, which is used in Chinese medicine. Every part of the animal, from the velvet and horns to the blood and the bile are attributed a medicinal purpose. The most sought-after and potent part of the deer is its spotted horn, used to make a tonic. The horns are cut from live deer (which is about as painful as having your tooth sawn off without anaesthetic) allowing new horns to grow the following year. Today, cultivated spotted deer are raised to meet demand, and although wild spotted deer is deemed even more potent, most buyers would not know the difference. The famous Père David's deer is now established by captive breeding in a couple of reserves.

Notable birds of northern China include brown- and blue-eared pheasants, the common pheasant, golden pheasant, black grouse, hawk owl, pine grosbeak, three-toed woodpecker, black woodpecker, mandarin duck and fairy pitta. The fairy pitta is an increasingly rare summer migratory bird, whose forest habitat is decreasing with the encroachment of urban development and logging. The bird itself is also sought after for the caged bird trade. Cranes are rare, but widely revered in China: common, demoiselle, white-napes, hooded and red-crowned cranes all breed in northern China.

There are also many tonic plants, such as the now rare ginseng (*Panax ginseng*), *Astragalus membranaceus, Epehdra sinica* or mahuang, and *Lycium chinense. Lycium chinense*, known more commonly as tea tree or wolfberry, and also as Gou qi zi, Goji, bastard jasmine, box thorn, and matrimony vine, has antiseptic qualities and is also traditionally used to treat anaemia, coughs and vision problems. Recent trials suggest it may also have properties that counter certain cancers. The plant is grown in many monasteries but can also be found in the wild. Another northern Chinese medicinal plant comes from the dogwood family and is known in Chinese as the happy tree (xǐshù 喜树) *Camptotheca acuminata*, which has anti-cancer properties. Siberian dogwood also grows in the north. Many more common flowers such as jasmine and plum blossom are in abundance all over northern China, while edelweiss, rare in Europe, can be found carpeted all over Matisi (see page 248) in Gansu province.

OUTDOOR PURSUITS

Outdoor pursuits in China do not have the tradition of western Europe, but they are growing, especially in affluent centres like Beijing. Hiking and climbing clubs are springing up (see *Chapter 8*, page 168 for contact details of some of the Beijing clubs) as well as biking (page 90) and paragliding (page 167). Kayaking is also attracting participants or try simple sheepskin rafting on the Yellow River (page 232). Good indigenous Chinese outdoor equipment and clothing brands and stores can also now be found so you don't have to bring everything with you if you don't want to or are looking to buy equipment more cheaply in China anyway. For a list of the Chinese outdoor stores of Sanfo see page 84.

WALKING THE GREAT WALL Most outsiders have an image of the Great Wall as a continuous stone structure, wide enough to walk five horses abreast, and just like all the great colour photography of the Great Wall in beautiful magazines like the *National Geographic*. In reality, as discussed in *Chapter 1*, the Great Wall is made mostly of mud, was not designed to be stood on, and is quite discontinuous. As a result, there are a number of important reasons why walking the Great Wall is not as easy as hiking in the Alps, the English Lake District or South America.

Underdeveloped recreational sports Hiking as a recreational sport is not well established in China. Hiking clubs are beginning to start up in Beijing, but outside Beijing most Chinese will think you are either mad for wanting to hike anywhere especially with a big pack on your back, or too poor to afford transport, and anyway, what do you want so see a load of old mud for? The unfamiliarity with hiking as a recreational sport (much of China still can't even afford the time for recreation, and sport is only a forced group activity associated with school, the work unit or the military) means that the etiquette of crossing state or private land is still unknown. Public rights of way such as are available in the UK are unheard of and little of the wall runs through China's many national parks.

Poor mapping Aside from town maps, maps of less than 1:450,000 scale are impossible to get hold of. Military maps of the ground at 1:50,000 or less are still a state secret. This makes hiking without a personal guide really quite difficult, especially when the weather reduces visibility: you come to a junction in the Great Wall (it has a number of offshoots in it) or it just simply disappears. Hiking guides who know the Great Wall are few and far between. In fact there are possibly more foreigners that have extensive experience of hiking the Great Wall than there are Chinese.

Physical safety Unlike most hiking trails, the wall is a fragile manmade structure, made mostly of mud. Foreigners dream of walking on the Great Wall of China, and hear of many tales of armies marching along the wall to defend the Middle Kingdom against the northern Mongol hordes. This was certainly possible on parts of the wall 400 years ago, but today much of the wall lies in ruins. The brick facing of much of the wall that was marched on with horses and armies back then has long since been ransacked by locals for building their own houses or other structures. Lots of the wall, therefore, is literally falling apart and unsafe for hiking on. For many sections it is possible to walk alongside the wall instead of on top of it, but parts of the wall are also along steep and treacherous terrain, making a side walk also difficult. Government-maintained sections, such as the popularly visited Badaling and Mutianyu require an entrance fee. For the rest of the wall, the concept of maintained trails is a long way off.

Damage to the wall For much of the same reasoning expounded above, damage to the wall is another reason not to walk on top of it. As responsible hikers, taking only memories and leaving no trace, it is important to leave the wall intact for others to also experience. In addition, Article 66 of China's Law on Cultural Relics expressly states that (unintentional) damage to a cultural relic (such as the Great Wall) could lead to, at minimum, a warning from the police and escorting from the site, and possibly a hefty fine up to a maximum penalty of ¥500,000 (€50,000). Many organisations are lobbying for stronger laws and enforcement.

Lack of clean drinking sources Another important aspect that makes it difficult to walk for extensive periods along the Great Wall is the lack of safe available drinking water along a lot of the route. As the wall was often built along mountain ridges and/or in inhospitable terrain, there is a lack of water per se along the wall. In other parts of China, such as in Shanxi's coal mining region, the water is frequently polluted with coal, chemicals and arsenic (see page 56). Even with water-purifying tablets, this water could make you at least pretty sick, if not do some permanent damage.

Manmade obstacles Although the wall was never continuous from its eastern to western end, nowadays it is even more cut up by roads, railways, towns, fences and pipelines. Some of these can be walked across, but the growing dominance of the car and the need for alternatives to the already overcrowded trains, has brought ever more motorways to China. These are usually fenced to stop animals and humans wandering onto them mistakenly (or deliberately). Finding convenient crossing points by foot could take you tens of kilometres off your intended hiking route.

Poor infrastructure Poor infrastructure along the wall makes access, accommodation and supplies of food and water sometimes hard to attain. There are many dirt back roads leading close to the wall, but public transport there can be scarce if not simply unavailable. Villages for water and food (and homestays if you are not camping) may be some kilometres from the wall, thus increasing your hiking time considerably. This is bound to change as hiking the Great Wall becomes more popular, and trekking with mules might also start up, but at the time of writing a few supported hikes by foreign tour operators remain the preferred (and expensive way) to hike extensive sections of the wall (see page 66).

No mountain rescue China does not have a mountain or wilderness rescue system, such as those to be found in Europe and North America. So, if you get lost or hurt, you are on your own; or, if you are lucky, at the whim of a local herder. Scaling these walls is not for the unprepared.

Still worth hiking All in all, the Great Wall of China was not designed to be hiked along. Not that that is a reason not to do it. Hiking the wall presents a very serious set of challenges that should not be taken lightly. Realising the great tourist potential of the wall, the government is making more of the wall accessible, which in the long run will benefit hikers and the local economy (see page 19). For the most part, however, until infrastructure is built up along the wall to meet the needs of independent hikers, then supported hikes along the wall are the safest way to hike for more than a day or two between destinations. Nowhere in Chinese law at the time of writing is it expressly forbidden to actually walk on or by the Great Wall if no damage is done, although local restrictions may apply. So, if you are going to hike the Great Wall, just take great care to do no damage, leave no trace, and offend no local (or government official).

ENVIRONMENTAL EFFORTS

Despite Daoist tendencies for harmony with nature, China on the whole is not renowned for its high regard for the environment. Half a century of full-on communism and the illusion of rapid industrialisation has set a course of damage inplace that is difficult for China to reverse. Nevertheless, environmental efforts in China are certainly on the increase. Policy makers know that China cannot

Despite the fact that the Great Wall has been around for two millennia, the hordes of visitors over the last hundred years have been wreaking unprecedented human destruction. In addition, much of the Great Wall lies in remote parts of China in fragile ecosystems and soil types that are easily damaged by both the mark one (bare) and mark two (clad) human foot. The best way not to damage the Great Wall is, of course, not to go near it (or, alternatively, to paraglide – see page 167). But if you do go (and why else did you buy this guidebook?) there are a number of points you should heed to minimise your impact, especially on the wild wall.

1. **Mud wall**. Avoid walking on top of mud wall, no matter how tempting it is, unless there is maintained access to the top.

2. **Semi-arid areas**. In areas suffering from desertification (see page 55) where there is little vegetation, try not to damage the superstrata of the soil and the fragile roots of the limited plant growth. Breaking the topsoil exposes the delicate fine soil beneath which can easily be blown away in the wind or washed away in heavy rainfall. If an established path exists already then stick to that, otherwise you will in fact minimise your impact better as a group by spreading out and not walking the same track along the wall. This is the case at Shuidong (see page 229).

3. **Sand dunes**. Despite how tempting it is to walk the ridge of sand dunes, just like in the movies, it is not good to do so. The desert in China, such as the Tengger Desert, is the result of many years of tree felling and desertification. China is trying to hold back the advance of the desert, so try not to encourage movement of the sand.

4. **Tenting overnight**. For the same reasons as those mentioned above, you can minimise your impact by setting your tent up on hard-standing surfaces if they are available rather than on easily damaged local soil.

5. **Don't litter**. It should go without saying that if you pack it in, then pack it out. The Chinese themselves are particularly bad at litter etiquette, and you may want to consider taking away some of the most offensive trash (such as plastic bottles, ice cream wrappers and cigarette cartons) yourself. This sets a good example and you can go away feeling like you've made up a bit for any damage to the soil.

6. **Donate to local protection**. Although the opportunities to donate to Great Wall charities are very limited, these are likely to mushroom in the near future (see page 99).

continue at current levels of growth with Western standards of waste production without bankrupting resource renewability and causing gridlock on the roads. It is partly for this reason that China has pledged to make the 2008 Beijing Olympics the 'Green Olympics' and a race is currently on between China's major car manufacturers to develop the first home-grown, no-pollution, hydrogen fuel-cell car. The number of environmentally concerned NGOs is increasing and environmental management as a class at universities is well attended. For more on environmental organisations in China see the *Giving something back* section on page 99.

The Outdoors ENVIRONMENTAL EFFORTS

4

5

Practical Information

WHEN TO GO

The best times to visit the Great Wall of China are in late spring and autumn – May to mid June and September to mid November. In winter (late November to early March), much of the wall lies under snow. While this can be picturesque and should certainly not deter visitors to the easily accessible areas of the wall around Beijing, in the more remote areas you will be taking on a bit more of an adventure than the average tourist to China is usually prepared for. In the peak of summer (July and August), aside from the fact that this is the most expensive time to fly to China itself, it is also when the Beijing sections of the wall are inundated with tourists, both Chinese and foreign. The more remote areas mentioned in this book rarely see tourists at any time of the year.

If you are going to hike the wall, the autumn is undoubtedly the prettiest time to do this, especially in the leafy hills and mountains of Hebei and Beijing when the leaves are turning colour. Early spring should be avoided for hiking, especially in the areas west of Hebei. Not only does the earth look particularly barren and dry, the spring dust storms are particularly bad, often bringing visibility down to less than 100m. You can also end up eating dust as you hike for most of your trip.

Those wanting to partake in the Great Wall Marathon (www.great-wall-marathon.com) should check with the marathon organisers in their own country to see exactly when the next race is. It usually takes place in May.

WHERE TO GO/WHAT TO SEE

The Chinese government is taking steps to fully document and preserve the entire Great Wall in all its many iterations. As a result, more areas are being renovated and made more accessible to tourism, while others are being cordoned off precisely so that brash tourists do not destroy pieces of China's most treasured cultural monument. Depending on what you want to experience in your visit to the wall, here is an overview of the most worthwhile sections by province.

Beijing	Simatai to Jinshanling – a 4–5-hour hike along unrestored wall (see page 172). Jiankou to Mutianyu – a 2-day hike for remote access, high ridges and a good trout dinner at the end (see page 176).
Hebei	Laolongtou to Jiumenkou – a 2-day hike from where the wall meets the sea to Nine Gateway via Shanhaiguan, the 'First Pass Under Heaven' (see page 121). Sleep on Panjiakou Reservoir by the sunken Great Wall and take a speedboat to Xifengkou (see page 129).

Gansu	Jiayuguan – the western end of the Ming Great Wall (see page 249).
Shanxi	Boat down the Yellow River from Laoniuwan past Wanjiazhai Reservoir to Baodezhen (see page 193).
	Visit the little-known walled city of Guanwu, the remains of Wild Goose Pass and hike the wall to Bald Head Mountain (see pages 194-195).
	Hike 6–7 hours from Li'erkou hamlet to the Hot Springs Hotel at Luowenzao (or as part of a longer 5-day hike – see page 191).
Ningxia	Hike the Great Wall along the border with Inner Mongolia (see page 231).
	Float down the Yellow River past the Great Wall in sheepskin rafts at Zhongwei (see page 231).
Tianjin	Hike 7–8 hours from Huangyaguan in Tianjin to Jiangjunguan in Hebei (see *Hiking clubs,* page 168).
Shaanxi	Visit the largest stone tower, Zhenbeitai, on the Great Wall, then relax at the nearby Red Stone Gorge health park next to cave dwellings, rock writing and riverside gardens (see page 215).
Liaoning	Peer into North Korea at Hushan, the easternmost end of the Ming Great Wall (see page 119).

MULTI-DAY HIKES AND SUGGESTED ITINERARIES

MULTI-DAY HIKES Multi-day hikes along the Great Wall are only for the well-prepared and the experienced remote-area hiker. It is essential that you read about the difficulties of walking unaided along the Great Wall (see pages 59-61) before you embark on any of the suggestions below:

1. Gubeikou via Jinshanling to Simatai (12 hours or 2 days, page 172)
2. Laolongtou via Shanhaiguan and Jiaoshan to Jiumenkou (2 days, page 121)
3. Li'erkou to Deshengbu (2 days, page 191)
4. Datong (Juqiangbu) to Laoniuwan on the Yellow River (3 days, page 193)
5. Sandaoguan to Zhongwei (3 days, page 231)

More and more tour operators are doing aided multi-day hikes along the Great Wall and, while these are much more expensive, they are safe and enjoyable, especially if you do not speak Chinese. Some of the tour operators have even put together one-month aided hikes along the Great Wall through several provinces. See *Tour operators,* page 66.

GREAT WALL ENTHUSIAST: TWO WEEKS If you wish to use the Great Wall as a theme for your time in the north of China, here are some suggestions of routes to take:

Day 1	Arrive Beijing; book onward ticket to Shanhaiguan.
Day 2	Visit Chongwenmen city wall and another Beijing site of your choice.
Day 3	Train to Shanhaiguan; visit the town and book return ticket to Tangshan.
Day 4	Bus to Laolongtou; start hike towards Jiumenkou, visit Qixian Monastery on the wall, camp overnight by the wall.
Day 5	Continue hike to Jiumenkou; visit Ensi Monastery; taxi back to Shanhaiguan or stay overnight in a farmer's inn (nong jia yuan).
Day 6	Train to Tangshan, bus to Qixian and to Panjiakou. Taxi and boat to Reservoir Lodge.

Day 7	Hike Panjiakou and Xifengkou.
Day 8	Buses to Simatai.
Day 9	Hike Simatai to Jinshanling; camp by the wall.
Day 10	Continue hike early to Gubeikou; buses to Miyun, Huairou and Huanghuacheng.
Day 11	Hike to Xiaoxihu.
Day 12	Return to Beijing.

GREAT WALL INTEREST: TWO WEEKS

| Week 1 | 3-hour train ride to Shanhaiguan; visit Laolongtou, Jiaoshan and Jiumenkou. Weekend trip with a Beijing hiking club. |
| Week 2 | 7-hour train ride to Datong; see Li'erkou wall, hot springs, Yungang Buddhist Caves. |

WIDER CHINA AND THE GREAT WALL
Including Beijing

| Week 1 | Beijing sights. Weekend trip with a Beijing hiking club. |
| Week 2 | Datong, including Li'erkou wall, hot springs, Yungang Buddhist Caves, Hengshan, Hanging Monastery. |

Outside the capital

| Week 1 | Ningxia Hui autonomous region, including Sandaoguan wall, rock art, film city, sauna hotels, desert camel rides to the Great Wall, Yellow River rafting past ancient water wheels. |
| Week 2 | Jiayuguan, last fort of the Great Wall; Lanzhou Yellow River capital. |

NORTHERN CHINA FOR THE NON-HIKER
Itinerary I

Week 1	Beijing sights and shopping; paraglide over the Great Wall. Weekendtrip to Shanhaiguan (2 nights – page 121) to see First Pass UnderHeaven, Walled City and Old Dragon's Head at the Bohai Gulf.
Week 2	Datong sights (2 nights – page 183): Yungang Grottoes, Hanging Monastery, Yixian wooden pagoda (oldest in the world), Wutai sacred mountain and monasteries (2 nights – page 201), Shenmu Daoist temple complex (1 night – page 218).
or	Ningxia province, little-visited home of the Hui Muslim minority: Yinchuan capital (5 nights – page 219), including day trips to Zhenbeipu Film City, Suyukou rock art, Sandaoguan border with Inner Mongolia to see Mongol ponies and the Great Wall. Try Xixia wine, eat hotpot, relax in massage and sauna hotel for the day. Experience tea ceremony and Yinchuan nightlife; find bargains at local antique market; Shapatou desert resort on the Yellow River (1 night – page 234).
or	Gansu special: fly to Lanzhou, train or bus along Silk Road to: Zhangye (1 night – page 244) to see the largest Sleeping Buddha statue in China; bus or train on to Jiayuguan (2 nights – page 249) to visit most western fort of Ming Great Wall and Great Wall Museum; overnight train to Lanzhou (2 nights – page 253) to experience mighty Yellow River; relax in Culture Court over tea, games and Beijing Opera.

There is now a whole army of tour operators who cater for packages to China. All those listed below, in addition to general tourist packages to anywhere in China, also specialise in trips to the more remote parts of the wall and many offer hiking packages, too. China International Travel Service (CITS) was once the only travel operator in China (state run) allowed to serve foreigners. The Chinese themselves travelled through China Travel Service (CTS). CTS would offer lower prices and soon foreigners started to turn there for travel services, too. Now the market has opened up considerably, and there are many excellent private travel and tour operators. As former monopoly services, CTS and CITS have built up an incredible network and have had to become more user-friendly in the face of competition. Some individual CTS and CITS branches are even remodelling themselves with a new name and specialised services.

UK

Audley Travel 6 Willows Gate, Stratton Audley, Oxon OX27 9AU; ☎ 01869 276200; f 01869 276214; e mail@audleytravel.com; www.audleytravel.com

China Direct 109–110 Ferguson Cl, Ferguson's Wharf, London E14 3SJ; ☎ 020 7538 2840; f 020 7536 9088; e info@chinadirect-travel.co.uk; www.chinadirect-travel.co.uk. Offers a good hiking tour of the Great Wall around the Datong area in Shanxi including the great stone Buddhas of Yungang Caves and the Buddhist monasteries of Wutai Shan.

Dragon Cambridge International www.dragoncambridge.com. A new company specialising in liaison with China.

Explore! Nelson House, 55 Victoria Rd, Farnborough, Hants GU14 7PA; ☎ 0870 333 4001; e info@explore.co.uk; www.explore.co.uk. A responsible tourism company, with well-run tours covering the eastern and western ends of the wall.

Imaginative Traveller 1 Betts Av, Martlesham Heath, Suffolk IP5 7RH; ☎ 0800 316 2717; e online@imtrav.com; www.imaginative-traveller.com. Offers a 3wk hiking, rafting and camel-safari tour along the length of the Great Wall.

Intrepid Travel UK 76 Upper St, London N1 0NU; ☎ 020 7354 6169; f 020 7354 6167; e info@intrepidtravel.com; www.intrepidtravel.com

On the go tours 68 North End Rd, London W14 9EP; ☎ 020 7371 1113; e info@onthegotours.com; www.onthegotours.com. China specialist offering group and tailor-made tours.

Regent Holidays 15 John St, Bristol BS1 2HR; ☎ 0117 921 1711; f 0117 925 4866; e regent@regent-holidays.co.uk; www.regent-holidays.co.uk

Silk Steps Deep Meadow, Edington, Bridgwater TA7 9JH; ☎ 01278 722460; e info@silksteps.co.uk; www.silksteps.co.uk. Tailor-made hiking trips to more remote parts of the eastern wall; also offers cycle tours in China including visiting the Great Wall, and runs a number of charity trips.

US

Asian Pacific Adventures 6065 Calvin Av, Tarzana, CA 91356; ☎ 800 8251 680 or 818 881 2745; e info@asianpacificadventures.com; www.asianpacificadventures.com

Backroads 801 Cedar St, Berkeley, CA 94710; ☎ 800 462 2848 or 510 527 1555; f 510 527 1444; www.backroads.com. An environmentally conscious company offering amongst many other trips a 9-day hiking trip from Beijing to Lhasa in Tibet including a day along the Great Wall.

China Travel Service Network PO Box 9515, Newark, DE 19714-9515; ☎ 302 355 0511; f 419 818 3432; www.chinats.com

CITS (California) 975 E Green St, #101, Pasadena, CA 91106; ☎ 626 568 8993; f 626 568 9207; e citslax@aol.com; www.cits.usa.com

CITS (New York) 71–01 Austin St, Suite 204, Forest Hills, NY 11375; ☎ 718 261 7329; f 718 261 7569; e citslax@aol.com; www.cits.usa.com

Intrepid Travel Inc 2511 Ocean Av, Venice, CA 90291; ☎ 310 305 7979 or 866 847 8192; f 866 864 1663; e info@intrepidtravel.com; www.intrepidtravel.com

Helen Cooksley

As a mother of two under-fives I thought that the challenge of walking 45 miles along the Great Wall of China would be out of my reach, but I was wrong. The idea came to me because my son was born prematurely and on his medical equipment was the name MedEquip4Kids. At the time, when he was hooked up to ventilators and fighting for his life, it was just a name that was stamped on his tubes, but a week after he was allowed to come home, I saw an advert in the paper asking for volunteers to raise a minimum of £2,500 for five children's charities (ChildLine, Dreams Come True, MedEquip4Kids, Barnardo's and Kith & Kids); there was that name again.

The fundraising was a challenge in itself and there were times when I truly believed I had failed, especially when my first major fundraising event was unsuccessful. I had organised an auction of promises and advertised in the paper and on radio, but no-one came. I learned from this experience and instead arranged a three-course Chinese meal and auction with the same lots from before, at my local college. With other events such as a cake stall at work and straightforward street collections, the money started to trickle in. I finally banked just under £3,000 with a month to go before the deadline.

The date finally arrived for the long journey to China, taking almost 20 hours in all and the second challenge began the following day. The mornings were early, but that was no different from the kids getting me up. The days were tiring but magical and the views were so amazing, words can't do them justice. Each of the five consecutive days along the Mutianyu, Gubeikou, Jinshanling and Simatai sections of the Great Wall north of Beijing provided a new test of physical and mental endurance. Although our luggage was transported for us to the next hotel, we each carried daysacks, with water and food that were provided for the journey, as well as toilet roll or tissues, and of course a camera. At night we stayed in good hotels, usually two or three to a room, although one memorable occasion had us three to a bed. To round it off, we had two days for sightseeing before returning home.

We were a group of 45 people ranging from 19 to 66, all with their own reasons for taking on this event. Some were very physically fit and others weren't; I had done little training for the event. There was a lovely lady fighting her own battle with MS and another who froze on various sections of the wall due to her fear of heights, but still we all managed to overcome our own limitations and make it over the finish line. The fulfilment and the humbling feeling of helping those less fortunate cascaded over all of us and many tears were shed at the end.

There were two major beneficiaries from this event: the charities with the wonderful work they do, and me. This event has had more of an impact on my life than I thought possible. I look back and still find it hard to believe I achieved such a thing. If you have the opportunity to take on this kind of challenge, embrace it with open arms, don't be afraid of the fundraising and enjoy the experience. While some charities will run a Great Wall trek on their own behalf, smaller organisations may club together to organise such an event. Those groups focusing on the Great Wall will thus change regularly, so the easiest way to find out about a forthcoming trek is to search the internet. Alternatively, you could try contacting one of the tour operators or charities that specialise in organising these trips, such as Silk Steps (see page 66) or Let's Trek for Children (www.actionforcharity.co.uk).

Zephyr Adventures PO Box 16, Red Lodge, MT 59068; 📞 888 758 8687; 📧 info@ZephyrAdventures.com; www.zephyradventures.com. Offers a hiking tour of the Great Wall including a night camping out on the wall itself.

AUSTRALIA
Intrepid Travel 11 Spring St, Fitzroy, Victoria 3065; 📞 1300 360 887 or 03 9473 2626; 📠 03 9419 4426; 📧 info@intrepidtravel.com; www.intrepidtravel.com
Peregrine Adventures 300 Lonsdale St, Melbourne, Victoria 3000; 📞 1300 85 4444; 📠 03 8601 4422; 📧 websales@peregrineadventures.com; www.peregrineadventures.com

CANADA
CITS 5635 Cambie St, Vancouver, BC, V5Z 3A3; 📞 604 267 0033 or 877 267 0033; 📠 604 267 0032; 📧 cits@citscanada.com; www.citscanada.com
GAP Traveller 355 Eglinton Av E, Toronto, Ontario, M4P 1M5; 📞 866 732 5885; 📠 416 260 1888; 📧 info@gaptraveller.com; www.gaptraveller.com
Worldwide Adventures 1170 Sheppard Av West, Suite 45, Toronto, Ontario, M3K 2A3; 📞 416 633 5666 or 800 387 1483; 📠 416 633 8667; 📧 travel@worldwidequest.com; www.worldwidequest.com. Offers an extended 21-day hiking tour of the wall north of Beijing and around Datong in Shanxi.

FRANCE
Ariane Tours Centre Commercial Dunois, Paris 75013; 📞 01 45 86 88 66; 📠 01 45 82 21 54; 📧 bureau@ariane-tours.com; www.ariane-tours.com
CITS 30 rue de Gramont, Paris 75002; 📞 01 42 86 88 66; 📠 01 42 86 88 61; 📧 see website for individual sales representatives' addresses; www.citsfrance.com. Ariane Tours Centre Commercial Dunois, 75013 Paris; 📞 01 45 86 88 66; 📠 01 45 82 21 54; 📧 bureau@ariane-tours.com; www.ariane-tours.com

GERMANY
China Tours Hamburg GmbH Wandsbeker Allee 72, 22041 Hamburg; 📞 040 81 97 380; 📠 040 81 97 38 88; 📧 info@chinatours.de; www.china-tours.de

CHINA
Every town in China has its own travel agencies now; for these see the individual chapters. There are also a few well-established and reliable Chinese travel agents who can arrange tours and tickets for you prior to arrival as well as once in the country. Some of these are:

China International Travel Service Beijing International Hotel, 28 Jianguomenwai St, Beijing; 📞 010 6515 8587/8570; 📠 010 6515 8602; 📧 webmaster@citsbj.com; www.citsbj.com/English
China Travel Service Zidutech Co, #A1, Sanlihe North Rd, Xicheng District, Beijing 100045; 📞 010 6852 4860; 📠 010 6852 4887; 📧 bisc@chinats.com; www.chinats.com

RED TAPE

PASSPORT/VISAS Chinese visas, like visas for most countries, differ according to the purpose of your visit and status in the country. As China opens up to the outside world, some visa requirements have even been lifted for some nationalities for short visits. Always check with your closest Chinese embassy (see page 69) for the latest visa requirements – their websites should cover most of the main requirements, but sometimes websites are not updated.

Most Chinese embassies require that you apply in person for a tourist visa, although often a travel agent can do this for you. Visas usually take four business days to process at an embassy. Expedited service is available for an extra fee, and a mailback system is in place at most embassies. Visas are not tied to specific dates but are valid for use within certain periods: entry into China must be made within three months of the application of the visa, and your passport must be valid for at least six months after your entry. One unused page is needed for the visa itself.

L visa For tourists, visiting relatives, or for other personal matters eg: medical treatment, private research. Duration of stay upon entering China is usually granted for 30 days, but up to 60 days is also possible if you request this in your application. sgl- and dbl-entry visas available.

F visa The business visa for those invited by a Chinese host to conduct short-term business, lecture, intern, read a post-graduate course or partake in a cultural exchange of less than six months. sgl-, dbl- and multi-entry visas available.

X visa For study or intern of more than six months

G visa For transit through China (consult the Chinese embassy of your country of nationality for detailed exceptions to this)

J visa For journalists

D visa For permanent residency in China

Z visa For employment in China

If you want or need to stay in China for longer than the duration of your visa (usually one or two months), you can apply for a **visa extension** at the Foreign Affairs department of the Public Security Bureau (PSB – gōng ān jú 公安局) of the local county. Local PSBs are listed under each town in this book.

The first extension to your L visa is usually granted with minimal difficulty. Further extensions are possible, but your reasons will either need to be more urgent or backed with an invitation or planned travel itinerary, showing that you had thought the extension through from the beginning. Wanting to see more of China, being too ill to travel, or other travel delays are seen as acceptable reasons to extend your visa. Do not mention that you have run out of money, even if you have, nor raise any suspicion that you might be trying to snoop around in closed areas of China or gathering information for publication in any format. An extension usually costs around ¥160, but don't be surprised if the local bureau charges 'surcharges'. Make sure you get a receipt. The **fine for outstaying your visa is** ¥500 per day, so don't even contemplate pushing the envelope by even half an hour.

Chinese embassies abroad Chinese embassies of most use to readers are listed below; for a full list go to www.fmprc.gov.cn/eng.

Australia 5 Coronation Dr, Yarralumla, ACT 2600, Canberra; ℓ +61 2 273 4780; f +61 2 273 4878/5189; ⓔ chinaemb_au@mfa.gov.cn; www.chinaembassy.org.au

Canada 515 St.Patrick St, Ottawa, Ontario, KIN 5H3; ℓ +1 613 789 3434/791 0511; f +1 613 789 1911/1414; ⓔ chinaemb_ca@mfa.gov.cn; www.chinaembassycanada.org

France 11 av George V, 75008 Paris; ℓ +33 1 49 52 19 50; f +33 1 47 20 24 22; ⓔ chinaemb_fr@mfa.gov.cn; www.amb-chine.fr

Germany Markisches Ufer 54, 10179 Berlin; ℓ +49 30 27588 555; f +49 30 27588 221; ⓔ chinaemb_de@mfa.gov.cn; www.china-botschaft.de

Ireland 40 Ailesbury Rd, Dublin 4; ℓ +353 1269 1707; f +353 1283 9938; ⓔ chinaemb_ie@mfa.gov.cn; www.chinaembassy.ie

Netherlands Willem Lodewijklaan 10 2517 JT, The Hague; ℓ +30 70 306 5090/1; f +30 70 306 5085; ⓔ chinaemb_nl@mfa.gov.cn; www.chinaembassy.nl

New Zealand 2–6 Glenmore St, Wellington; ℓ +64 4 472 1382; f +64 4 499 0419; ⓔ info@chinaembassy.org.nz; www.chinaembassy.org.nz

UK 49–51 Portland Pl, London W1B 1JL; ℓ +44 20 7299 4049, +44 797 029 2561 (24 hours); f +44 20 7636 2981/5578; ⓔ chinaemb_uk@mfa.gov.cn; www.chinese-embassy.org.uk

USA 2300 Connecticut Av NW, Washington, DC 20008; ☎ +1 202 328 2500/2551; f +1 202 328 2582;
📧 webmaster@china-embassy.org; www.china-embassy.org

FOREIGN EMBASSIES IN CHINA
Australia 21, Dong Zhi Men Wai Da Jie, San Li Tun, Beijing; ☎ +86 10 6532 2331; f +86 10 6532 4349;
📧 pubaff.beijing@dfat.gov.au; www.austemb.org.cn
Austria 5, Dong Wu Jie, Xiu Shui Nan Jie, Jian Guo Men Wai, Beijing; ☎ +86 10 6532 2061; f +86 10 6532 1505;
📧 peking-ob@bmaa.gv.at; www.bmaa.gv.at/peking
Canada 19, Dong Zhi Men Wai Da Jie, Beijing; ☎ +86 10 6532 3536; f +86 10 6532 4072;
📧 beijing-immigration@international.gc.ca; www.beijing.gc.ca
France 3, Dong San Jie, San Li Tun, Beijing; ☎ +86 10 6532 1331; f +86 10 6532 4841;
📧 consulat@ambafrance-cn.org; www.ambafrance-cn.org
Germany 5, Dong Zhi Men Wai Da Jie, Beijing; ☎ +86 10 6532 2161; f +86 10 6532 5336; www.deutschebotschaft-china.org
Ireland 3, Ri Tan Dong Lu, Beijing; ☎ +86 10 6532 2691; f +86 10 6532 6857; 📧 beijing@dfa.ie; www.ireland-china.com.cn
Netherlands 4, Liang Ma He Nan Lu, Beijing; ☎ +86 10 6532 1131; f +86 10 6532 4689; 📧 pek@minbuza.nl; www.hollandinchina.org
New Zealand 1, Dong Er Jie, Ri Tan Lu, Beijing; ☎ +86 10 6532 2731; f +86 10 6532 4317;
📧 nzemb@eastnet.com.cn; www.nzembassy.com
UK 11, Guang Hua Lu, Beijing; ☎ +86 10 6532 1961; f +86 10 6532 1937; 📧 consularmailbeijing@fco.gov.uk; www.uk.cn
USA 3, Xiu Shui Bei Jie, Jian Guo Men Wai, Beijing; ☎ +86 10 6532 3831/3431; 📧 AmCitBeijing@state.gov; www.usembassy-china.org.cn

CUSTOMS You will be required to fill in a customs form on entering China, declaring certain goods such as perfume, jewellery, electronic items and cash over US$5,000 or equivalent. You may bring in 400 cigarettes and two litres of alcohol duty free. Items brought in over the customs allowance will incur a duty charge. As a tourist you may not bring in items for sale, so when you leave the country, the customs officer may check your copy of your original customs declaration to check if you still have all your declared goods with you. This means that if you lose an item that you declared, or have it stolen, then you will need to make sure that you register this with the police and get a lost/stolen report or you may end up paying duty on it at departure (or buy another camera!).

Certain original cultural items, valuable indigenous jewels and antiques over 100 years old may be prohibited from export. Items that are approved by the State Bureau for Cultural Relics (SBCR) for export will exhibit the red wax seal of the SBCR. It is not easy to check whether an item is a prohibited cultural relic or not, but try asking for the export form at the local Friendship Store (Yŏuyì Shāngdiàn 友谊商店) and allow plenty of time for a reply. In practice, most items bought in local markets for less than ¥1,000 (especially if you were ripped off) and which come from grandma's attic, are common old pieces of nostalgia. Customs officials rarely check for these at departure, but be prepared to have the item confiscated if you do not have the correct paperwork and approval. All the more reason, therefore, to pay no more for your market bargain than you are prepared to lose.

GETTING THERE AND AWAY

✈ **BY AIR** For anyone on a short holiday to China, this is the most convenient way to get there, and thankfully tickets are getting cheaper, despite the rise in oil prices.

International discount ticket agencies There are many online discount air ticket agencies now, most of whom will also offer internal China air tickets. These include:

Dial-a-flight In London; ✆ 020 7464 1018; www.dialaflight.co.uk
Expedia Travel Both in the UK; www.expedia.co.uk, and USA; www.expedia.com
Trailfinders Has many branches throughout the UK; www.trailfinders.com
STA Travel Has many offices worldwide; www.statravel.com

Specialists in China Some agents specialise in cheap flights to China as well as internal China flights. Although internal flight tickets will be much cheaper to buy from an agent or airline in China once you are there, purchasing these in advance will give you the peace of mind that you have the connection you want, and you may save yourself a day or more, as well as hotel bills, if you can plan and purchase a connecting flight. All the tour operators listed on pages 66–68 will also book just flights, if required, usually including internal flights too.

FlyChina Infotek 5300 NW 33 Av, Ste 219, Fort Lauderdale, FL 33309-6356, USA; ✆ +1 954 233 0680 or +1 800 318 1363; f +1 954 233 0670; @ hq@flychina.com; www.flychina.com

Arrival at Beijing International Airport Today's Beijing International Airport, built in 1999, is undergoing further renovation and expansion in preparation for the 2008 Olympics. The airport also serves all domestic flights in and out of Beijing.

A highway links the airport to the third ring road, so getting into town by taxi or shuttle bus (fēijī chǎng bāsì) takes less than an hour. By 2008, there will also be a subway train linking into the expanded underground metro system. A metered taxi into town costs ¥100–150, plus the ¥20 highway toll. Shuttle buses into the city have recently become much more convenient, with tickets costing ¥16 from the airport. Four shuttle-bus lines run every 15 minutes, covering various destinations across the city. If you know your hotel address, but don't know how to get there, ask one of the staff at the shuttle-bus stand who will be able to tell you which is the best bus to get closest to your hotel. You can then take a city bus or taxi from the bus stop. The shuttle bus to Xidan stops at Dongzhimen where you can get bus 107 to the Houhai *hutong* area, location of a number of the hotels listed in this guidebook. Shuttle-bus tickets are sold at the stalls at the front of the buses.

Leaving China A shuttle bus can be picked up every 15 minutes from Xizhimen, Xidan, Qianmen, Dongdan, Beijing International Hotel and Dongzhimen. Buy your ticket at the shuttle-bus counter or the nearest China Post kiosk. The shuttle buses do not stop long at intervening pick-up points such as Dongzhimen, so be ready with your ticket at the bus stop.

Until 2005, you had to pay a ¥90 international airport departure tax. Thankfully China has now joined most of the rest of the world in incorporating its airport tax into your ticket, so you no longer have to worry about having sufficient Chinese money with you on departure. (Internal flights have also incorporated their previous ¥50 domestic airport tax into their ticket prices.) A couple of other unusual regulations that may affect you, however, still appear at Chinese airports. First, Chinese airports, including Beijing International Airport, will take no responsibility for tampered or opened luggage unless it has been plasti-cordoned by the airport packaging counter at the end of every check-in console. Each item cordoned costs ¥10, but note that the cordoning is not a requirement. Second, alcohol that has been bought outside of duty free may not be taken into the cabin, but must be packaged and put in the hold. This is a result of increased security measures since 9/11. If you do not want to put bottles of liquid into your suitcase, then the package counter can package your bottles into a sturdy brown box (big enough for four wine bottles) and plasti-cord it for you, all for ¥10. Any other sealed containers, tins or bottles containing liquids of any sort will be opened by security and given the sniff test to check whether you are taking on dangerous fuels and explosives.

You will need to fill out a departure form before going through security.

BY TRAIN The Trans-Mongolian and the Trans-Manchurian trains (also known as the Trans-Siberian, although this in fact only runs through Russia from Moscow to Vladivostok) from Moscow to Beijing offer an amazing experience. The journey in the summer is more picturesque, and therefore more popular, so you may need to book tickets two or three months in advance. The Trans-Mongolian is more direct, taking only five days to travel the 7,865km from Beijing to Moscow, but requires both a Mongolian and a Russian visa. The Trans-Manchurian takes six days to travel the 9,001km. There is only one train a week for each train in each direction, but with the likelihood of cargo travel increasing along the route, passenger opportunities may also increase in the near future. Both trains pass through seven time zones and must change undercarriages at the Chinese border because of the difference in rail gauge.

Second-class cabins are four berth with communal carriage showers and cost around €200, while first-class cabins are two berth, include a shower and cost around €300. Meals are included on the Chinese portion of the journey but not on the Mongolian or Russian sections. The Russian dining car is an experience in itself. You cannot actually get many of the items on the menu, but paying in US dollars rather than Russian roubles may induce the waiter to find a few more things. You may find it difficult to order at all if you are vegetarian, and for all travellers it is wise to stock up on pot noodles and snacks for the journey. Samovars in each carriage provide constant boiling water for tea, coffee and noodles. At each stop along the way, vendors sell local goods including fresh garden carrots and small newspaper cornets of steaming new potatoes.

Visas Obtaining visas to travel on the Trans-Mongolian or the Trans-Manchurian can be complex and you may prefer to use a travel agent to help you out, even if this is more expensive. There are two types of visa that you can get for both countries: a tourist visa or a transit visa. Both must be obtained in advance (ie: not on the border). The transit visa for both Russia and Mongolia requires an onward ticket and an onward visa, so you must first buy your ticket then buy your visas in reverse order of travel.

Russian visas still require a letter of invitation, which you can get from a reputable organisation if they are inviting you or a Russian travel agent. The transit visa is valid for ten days and as six of these are used travelling on the trains themselves in and out of Moscow, you will have only two full days to stop off in Moscow if you wish to do so. A tourist visa lasting 30 days will give you the run of the country, but your application must then show confirmation of every hotel or host you will stay with and, even in today's modern Russia, you may stay only in hotels that are approved by the Russian Ministry of Foreign Affairs.

Mongolian visas are slightly less hassle to obtain. The transit visa is valid only for two days (just enough to get you through Mongolia). The tourist visa requires a letter of invitation, again from a reputable organisation or a Mongolian travel agent.

Single-entry tourist visas are valid for three months and multiple-entry tourist visas are valid for six months.

Buying tickets In Moscow, Trans-Mongolian or Trans-Manchurian tickets are allegedly available at the railway station, but you may have more luck paying the surcharge to go through a travel agent. Outside of Moscow you will have to purchase your ticket through a travel agent. Many of the travel agents and tour operators listed below can buy tickets for you. In China, tickets can be obtained from the head office of the China International Travel Service (CITS) in the Beijing International Hotel (see www.cits.net/travel/reservation/train.jsp for more up-to-date information on timetables and prices) or from Monkey Shrine (*Room 35, Red House Hotel, 10 Chun Xiu Lu, Dongzhimenwai, Chao Yang District, 100027 Beijing;* ℓ *010 6591 6519;* f *010 6591 6517;* e *MonkeyChina@compuserve.com or monkeychina@hotmail.com; www.monkeyshrine.com*).

BY BOAT Passenger boats to northern China (Dalian, Tanggu or Qingdao) come from South Korea and Japan. Most nationalities can stay in South Korea for 30 days without a visa, and in Japan for 90 days, but check with the nearest embassy before travelling.

✚ HEALTH

with Dr Felicity Nicholson

Make sure you get health insurance that is valid for China before getting into the country, unless you are prepared to pay for any mishaps yourself. Chinese doctors and hospitals expect to be paid in cash on the spot from foreigners seeking treatment; once you have your receipt, appropriately translated, you can usually reclaim the money from your insurer. Outside Beijing, few doctors speak English. Most travel agents abroad will be able to sort you out with the appropriate health insurance, and some give a good deal combining health and travel insurance with insurance against theft.

It is a good idea to get any treatment that you need *before* you go travelling. It is not necessarily any cheaper to get things done in China and standards may not be as high as in your home country. Common illnesses can be treated in China by the pharmacists in any local drugstore, who can also advise you of the nearest family practitioner if you are in need of a doctor. If you need hospitalisation, this is best left till you get home, unless it is an emergency.

Vaccinations are not legally required for entry into China, unless you have come from a yellow-fever-infected area (sub-Saharan Africa and tropical South America), but doctors will advise inoculations against the following to be on the safe side: diphtheria, tetanus, polio, hepatitis A, and typhoid. Hepatitis B vaccinations are recommended for trips of four weeks or more, or if you are working in a medical setting or with children. The course comprises three injections and can be done over as few as 21 days, so make sure that you visit your doctor or travel clinic in plenty of time. Rabies vaccine may also be recommended for longer trips or if you are going to be away from medical help for more than 24 hours. Again the course comprises three injections over 21 days. If you are going to China to study for a year, you will also need to have an HIV test done.

TRAVEL CLINICS AND HEALTH INFORMATION A full list of current travel clinic websites worldwide is available from the International Society of Travel Medicine on

5

www.istm.org. For other journey preparation information, consult www.tripprep.com. Information about various medications may be found on www.emedicine.com.

UK

Berkeley Travel Clinic 32 Berkeley St, London W1J 8EL (near Green Park tube station); ℓ 020 7629 6233

British Airways Travel Clinic and Immunisation Service There are two BA clinics in London, both on ℓ 0845 600 2236; www.ba.com/travelclinics. Appointments only Mon–Fri 09.00–16.30 at 101 Cheapside, London EC2V 6DT; or walk-in service Mon–Fri 09.30–17.30, Sat 10.00–16.00 at 213 Piccadilly, London W1J 9HQ. Apart from providing inoculations and malaria prevention, they sell a variety of health-related goods.

Cambridge Travel Clinic 48a Mill Rd, Cambridge CB1 2AS; ℓ 01223 367362; e enquiries@cambridgetravelclinic.co.uk; www.cambridgetravelclinic.co.uk. Open Tue–Fri 12.00–19.00, Sat 10.00–16.00.

Edinburgh Travel Clinic Regional Infectious Diseases Unit, Ward 41 OPD, Western General Hospital, Crewe Rd South, Edinburgh EH4 2UX; ℓ 0131 537 2822; www.link.med.ed.ac.uk/ridu. Travel helpline (0906 589 0380) open weekdays 09.00–12.00. Provides inoculations and antimalarial prophylaxis and advises on travel-related health risks.

Fleet Street Travel Clinic 29 Fleet St, London EC4Y 1AA; ℓ 020 7353 5678; www.fleetstreetclinic.com. Vaccinations, travel products and latest advice.

Hospital for Tropical Diseases Travel Clinic Mortimer Market Building, Capper St (off Tottenham Ct Rd), London WC1E 6AU; ℓ 020 7388 9600; www.thehtd.org. Offers consultations and advice, and is able to provide all necessary drugs and vaccines for travellers. Runs a healthline (0906 133 7733) for country-specific information and health hazards. Also stocks nets, water purification equipment and personal protection measures.

Interhealth Worldwide Partnership House, 157 Waterloo Rd, London SE1 8US; ℓ 020 7902 9000; www.interhealth.org.uk. Competitively priced, one-stop travel health service. All profits go to their affiliated company, InterHealth, which provides health care for overseas workers on Christian projects.

MASTA (Medical Advisory Service for Travellers Abroad) London School of Hygiene and Tropical Medicine, Keppel St, London WC1 7HT; ℓ 0906 550 1402; www.masta.org. Individually tailored health briefs available for a fee, with up-to-date information on how to stay healthy, inoculations and what to bring. There are currently 30 MASTA pre-travel clinics in Britain. Call 0870 241 6843 or check online for the nearest. Clinics also sell malaria prophylaxis memory cards, treatment kits, bednets, net treatment kits.

NHS travel website www.fitfortravel.scot.nhs.uk. Provides country-by-country advice on immunisation and malaria, plus details of recent developments, and a list of relevant health organisations.

Nomad Travel Store/Clinic 3–4 Wellington Ter, Turnpike La, London N8 0PX; ℓ 020 8889 7014; travel-health line (office hours only): 0906 863 3414; e sales@nomadtravel.co.uk; www.nomadtravel.co.uk. Also at 40 Bernard St, London WC1N 1LJ; ℓ 020 7833 4114; 52 Grosvenor Gardens, London SW1W 0AG; ℓ 020 7823 5823; and 43 Queens Rd, Bristol BS8 1QH; ℓ 0117 922 6567. For health advice, equipment such as mosquito nets and other anti-bug devices, and an excellent range of adventure travel gear.

Trailfinders Travel Clinic 194 Kensington High St, London W8 7RG; ℓ 020 7938 3999; www.trailfinders.com/clinic.htm

Travelpharm The Travelpharm website, www.travelpharm.com, offers up-to-date guidance on travel-related health and has a range of medications available through their online mini-pharmacy.

Irish Republic

Tropical Medical Bureau Grafton Street Medical Centre, Grafton Buildings, 34 Grafton St, Dublin 2; ℓ 1 671 9200; www.tmb.ie. A useful website specific to tropical destinations. Also check website for other bureaux locations throughout Ireland.

USA

Centers for Disease Control 1600 Clifton Rd, Atlanta, GA 30333; ℓ 800 311 3435; travellers' health hotline: 888 232 3299; www.cdc.gov/travel. The central source of travel information in the USA. The invaluable *Health Information for International Travel*, published annually, is available from the Division of Quarantine at this address.

Connaught Laboratories PO Box 187, Swiftwater, PA 18370; ℓ 800 822 2463. They will send a free list of specialist tropical-medicine physicians in your state.

IAMAT (International Association for Medical Assistance to Travelers) 1623 Military Rd, 279, Niagara Falls, NY 14304-1745; ✆ 716 754 4883; ✉ info@iamat.org; www.iamat.org. A non-profit organisation that provides lists of English-speaking doctors abroad.

International Medicine Center 920 Frostwood Dr, Suite 670, Houston, TX 77024; ✆ 713 550 2000; www.traveldoc.com

Canada
IAMAT Suite 1, 1287 St Clair Av W, Toronto, Ontario M6E 1B8; ✆ 416 652 0137; www.iamat.org
TMVC Suite 314, 1030 W Georgia St, Vancouver BC V6E 2Y3; ✆ 1 888 288 8682; www.tmvc.com

Australia, New Zealand, Singapore
TMVC ✆ 1300 65 88 44; www.tmvc.com.au. 31 clinics in Australia, New Zealand and Singapore including:
Auckland Canterbury Arcade, 170 Queen St, Auckland; ✆ 9 373 3531
Brisbane 6th floor, 247 Adelaide St, Brisbane, QLD 4000; ✆ 7 3221 9066
Melbourne 393 Little Bourke St, 2nd floor, Melbourne, VIC 3000; ✆ 3 9602 5788
Sydney Dymocks Bldg, 7th floor, 428 George St, Sydney, NSW 2000; ✆ 2 9221 7133
IAMAT PO Box 5049, Christchurch 5, New Zealand; www.iamat.org

South Africa and Namibia
SAA-Netcare Travel Clinics P Bag X34, Benmore 2010; www.travelclinic.co.za. Clinics throughout South Africa.
TMVC 113 D F Malan Dr, Roosevelt Pk, Johannesburg; ✆ 011 888 7488; www.tmvc.com.au. Consult website for details of 9 other clinics in South Africa and Namibia.

Switzerland
IAMAT 57 Chemin des Voirets, 1212 Grand Lancy, Geneva; www.iamat.org

COMMON PROBLEMS Without stating the absolutely obvious, it is a good idea to be fit and healthy before going on holiday! Many of us though have usually just raced through a work or college deadline before going on holiday, and the time to unwind and relax is just when the common cold or stomach flu takes hold.

Unless you are a seasoned world traveller and have a stomach like cast iron, many people usually get a bout of the trots (lā dùzi 拉肚子) on coming into contact with new foods, and new cooking. In China, this is quite common, especially if you have been eating hot spicy food, and may turn into full-blown diarrhoea (fùjí 腹疾) requiring antibacterial medication to clear it up. If it does, the pharmacy can sort you out; alternatively take some suitable medication with you from home if you are prone to a bit of 'Delhi belly'.

There are many old wives' tales that are alleged to help you deal with this phenomenon. A good remedy for the trots which just keep trotting is to restrict yourself to a diet of well-boiled salted carrots and salted white rice for a day or two. This will bung you up in no time at all, and although somewhat bland, is worth pursuing. Keep off dairy products, eggs and fresh fruit or juice for a few more days and things should return to normal. I have administered this remedy to several travelling partners of mine, for whom it has worked wonders. I must confess to never having had to undergo these rigours myself, because I do have a stomach of cast iron. Always drink plenty of water if you do have diarrhoea, and take in plenty of salt. The locals will recommend tea; others recommend flat Coca-Cola.

As with any travels away from your medicine cabinet at home, it is a good idea to have a small first-aid pack with you in your bag. You can buy these ready made up from any good drugstore at home, such as Boots in the UK, or Walgreens in the US, or you can just make up a small kit yourself from the following items: plasters/Band-aid; painkillers such as aspirin, paracetamol or tylenol; lipsalve; sunscreen;

antiseptic cream and mosquito-bite cream (diluted tea tree oil does well for both); mosquito repellent; spare contact lenses if you wear them. A small sewing kit is useful for when you've eaten too much of the local food and need to re-sew on a button, or your trousers have ripped on a hike in the undergrowth of the Great Wall.

HEALTH AND SAFETY IN THE WILDS
In the wilds, anywhere in the world, health and safety go hand in hand. China's mountains around the Great Wall are not very big, but much of the Great Wall, even in flat terrain, is sufficiently remote, and the wall sufficiently degraded, that without a good hiking map (preferably 1:25,000, 1cm = 0.25km; unfortunately maps of this scale are currently unavailable in China, see page 84) it is very easy to get lost. Make sure you are a proficient hiker before venturing for long hikes along the Great Wall (see page 78 for more advice). Alternatively, go with a guide (see the travel agent or hiking club section in each chapter).

Know the potential dangers of mountaineering and how to deal with them before you set out on a hike, and preferably be first-aid proficient. The list of health and safety considerations below, as well as the advice on page 59, will give you an idea of what you are up against.

Your medical pack for any extended hiking trip (more than two hours) needs to be more than basic, and should contain at least the following: large plasters/ Band-aid and surgical gauze; antiseptic cream and wipes; painkillers; crêpe bandages x 2; surgical tape and zinc-oxide tape; Compeed for blisters; iodine-based water-purification tablets (available from any good mountaineering shop, but hard to find in China); emergency blanket and inflatable splint if you are going on a long trip.

Dehydration In these untamed mountainous regions, the going can get tough, and as in all mountains, water can be hard to find when you need it. Bring plenty of water with you, at least a litre per hour of uphill in the summer, and especially if you don't know where your next water source will be. It is very arid in parts of China and the lack of overhead cover can cause excess sweating. Dehydration will make you tired and prone to injury, and makes some people's vision blur. If you find yourself running short of water, try to conserve what you have left, and take small sips every now and again. Don't over-exert yourself, and breathe through your nose rather than your mouth to stop excess moisture escaping. Keep covered to prevent excess moisture being lost in sweat.

Injury Injuries are usually caused when you are tired and/or are hiking beyond your limits. It is, therefore, important to know what your limit is, and those of your travelling partners, and to recognise when it is time for a rest. Come properly equipped for the task at hand, with good hiking boots and an appropriate overcoat as a minimum. Many Chinese wander around in flimsy, trendy sports shoes, or – even worse – high-heeled shoes. This may suffice for a hike to a popular monument, but will get you in trouble further afield. If you do sustain an injury that would normally require stitching, then bind the wound with a large plaster or surgical tape and then secure it laterally with zinc-oxide tape.

Sunburn Do wear a hat, sunglasses and plenty of sunscreen (available in the pharmacies). The sun in China is stronger than in northern Europe and it is easy to forget this until it is too late. If you do get badly burnt, apply an after-sun cream (not so easily available once in China) or calamine lotion, cover up, and don't go back out in the sun without a total sunblock. A cold, wet, black teabag also works for sunburn if you can't get anything else.

Sunstroke After the onset of dehydration and sunburn, you are heading for heat exhaustion and then sun/heatstroke. While heatstroke can be fatal, if you recognise the early symptoms soon enough you should never get that far. It is usually more difficult to tell in oneself than in others, so watch your hiking partner carefully. The easiest signs to look for are muscle cramps, dim or blurred vision, weakness, irritability, dizziness and confusion. If any of your hiking partners are talking utter drivel (more than normal anyway), are not able to have a logical conversation with you, and particularly if they say they don't need water or to get out of the sun, then sit them down in the shade immediately, loosen any tight clothing, sprinkle water on them and fan them to cool them down. They should take regular sips of water, but not drink a pint down flat (which has recently been found to cause a fatal swelling of the brain). If your hiking partner shows the above signs, and feels sick, and particularly if their skin feels hot and dry (ie: is not sweating), then the body has gone into shutdown mode. They may soon fall unconscious and medical attention is required quickly.

Altitude sickness You are unlikely to suffer from altitude sickness hiking the Great Wall, as it doesn't go much over 1,500m above sea level. If you venture into some of the higher areas (over 2,000m) then you may experience altitude sickness, although this is unlikely as the majority of cases occur over altitudes of 3,500m. No matter how young you are, or how much mountaineering you have done in the past, altitude sickness can hit. The best way to avoid it is to acclimatise over time. If you don't have that option open to you, and you start to feel dizzy, sick and overly short of breath, then the next best thing to do is to stop and rest. If this doesn't help then descend slowly to a lower level (500m is usually adequate), and consider doing something else for the day.

Hypothermia Hypothermia occurs when the body loses heat quicker than it can make it. This is most likely to happen when the body is wet and cold, inactive, hungry and tired. Uncontrollable shivering, drowsiness and confusion are tell-tale first signs. If the person has stopped shivering, is physically stiff, and indifferent to their surroundings, then the body is already in shutdown mode. The person's body temperature must be warmed up immediately with plenty of warm, dry clothing, shelter and warm sweet drinks to increase the blood sugar level. Exercise will not help. At severe levels, skin contact with another warm body, preferably in a sleeping bag, might be required. At this point the medical services should be brought in. Do not heat the person with anything hotter than body temperature, or immerse the person in hot water as this might simply cook outer extremities. Do not rub or massage the person, but warm the core of the body first.

Wild and deadly nasties A number of poisonous snakes and spiders, such as black and brown widow spiders, and some adders and vipers, exist in China. They do not seek out humans, so you are extremely unlikely to come across one. If you do get bitten, then the best thing to do is not to panic, to move as little as possible, and to lower the bitten area below the level of the heart. Do not attempt to suck out the venom, despite what you might have seen at the movies. Get the victim to hospital as fast as possible.

Dr Jane Wilson-Howarth

Long-haul air travel increases the risk of deep vein thrombosis (DVT). Although recent research has suggested that many of us develop clots when immobilised, most resolve without us ever having been aware of them. In certain susceptible individuals, though, large clots form and these can break away and lodge in the lungs. This is dangerous but happens in a tiny minority of passengers.

Studies have shown that flights of over five-and-a-half-hours are significant, and that people who take lots of shorter flights over a short space of time form clots. People at highest risk are:

- Those who have had a clot before – unless they are now taking warfarin
- People over 80 years of age
- Anyone who has recently undergone a major operation or surgery for varicose veins
- Someone who has had a hip or knee replacement in the last three months
- Cancer sufferers
- Those who have ever had a stroke
- People with heart disease
- Those with a close blood relative who has had a clot

Those with a slightly increased risk:
- People over 40
- Women who are pregnant or have had a baby in the last couple of weeks
- People taking female hormones or other oestrogen therapy
- Heavy smokers
- Those who have very severe varicose veins

FITNESS

Clearly, there are different levels of fitness required depending on what you are intending to undertake along the wall. The wall passes through a variety of different terrain, being mostly mountainous in the east and becoming flatter but at higher altitude towards the west. None of the Great Wall lies over 2,000m above sea level, so altitude sickness should not be a problem, although if you suffer from asthma, then the thinner air above 1,000m may affect you. This section does not try to plan out a foolproof fitness programme for preparation for walking the wall, but does try to give a few pointers that you should at least keep in mind. **If you are not familiar with the exercises below, consult your doctor or a fitness instructor before embarking upon them.**

MULTI-DAY HIKES If you have never done a multi-day hike before, then you should certainly ensure you are accompanied by an experienced partner or guide and you should get further (preferably professional) consultation on how to prepare physically. Serious multi-day hikes will require a lot of previous training if you are not already accustomed to them. The best way to prepare for any sport is to buildup strength over time by practising exactly what you will be doing. Few people,

- The very obese
- People who are very tall (over 6ft/1.8m) or short (under 5ft/1.5m)

A DVT is a blood clot that forms in the deep leg veins. This is very different from irritating but harmless superficial phlebitis. DVT causes swelling and redness of one leg, usually with heat and pain in one calf and sometimes the thigh. DVT is only dangerous if a clot breaks away and travels to the lungs (pulmonary embolus). Symptoms of a pulmonary embolus (PE) include chest pain that is worse on breathing in deeply, shortness of breath, and sometimes coughing up small amounts of blood. The symptoms commonly start three to ten days after a long flight. Anyone who thinks that they might have a DVT needs to see a doctor immediately who will arrange a scan. Warfarin tablets (to thin the blood) are then taken for at least six months.

Prevention of DVT
Several conditions make the problem more likely. Immobility is the key, and factors like reduced oxygen in cabin air and dehydration may also contribute. To reduce the risk of thrombosis on a long journey:
- Exercise before and after the flight
- Keep mobile before and during the flight; move around every couple of hours
- During the flight drink plenty of water or juices
- Avoid taking sleeping pills and excessive tea, coffee and alcohol
- Perform exercises that mimic walking and tense the calf muscles
- Consider wearing flight socks or support stockings (see www.legshealth.com)
- Taking a meal of oily fish (mackerel, trout, salmon, sardines, etc) in the 24 hours before departure reduces blood clotability and thus DVT risk
- The jury is still out on whether it is worth taking an aspirin before flying, but this can be discussed with your GP.

If you think you are at increased risk of a clot, ask your doctor if it is safe to travel.

however, have enough holiday to be able to build up to a long multi-day hike. As a result, you will need to find other ways to build up long-term stamina and cardiovascular strength, whilst also increasing the short-term load-bearing strength of the muscles of your legs (and back if you are going to be carrying all your own overnight equipment and supplies).

If you can't do a multi-day hike before you go, then do at least get one or two days in hiking a similar length and terrain to what you will be doing when hiking in China. In addition, build up your stamina by increasing time spent on other steady cardiovascular workouts, such as jogging, swimming or cycling. As a rough guide, you might aim to be able to jog half of your average day's hike, swim a fifth or a quarter of it, and/or cycle twice its distance. This distance should feel 'comfortable' shortly before your multi-day hike.

For more detail on the type of terrain where you will be hiking, see the relevant sections of this guidebook. You should also take note of the tips given in the following day-trip section.

THE DAY TRIP The great majority of visitors to the Great Wall go for just a day. The drop off and pick up point is usually at the same place, so you can easily regulate how little or how much you hike on the wall. Nevertheless, if you really want to earn that

'I hiked the Great Wall' T-shirt, then you'll probably want to hike at least a couple of hours or more, which can be a very serious workout on most of the stone Great Wall.

Most day trips are in the Beijing area, which has some of the wall's best mountainous sections. The Beijing wall at Badaling, Mutianyu, Huanghuacheng, Simatai and Jinshanling follows very steep direct slopes, so you will not be walking along the gentle switchback paths that you might be used to when hiking up a steep mountain. Jiankou wall requires a two- to three-hour steep hike before you even get to the wall itself. The steepness of the slopes along which the wall rises means that the stone steps in the wall are frequently very high, many over 50cm high, and some boasting almost a metre in height.

Finding terrain like this at home to practise on is almost impossible. Nevertheless, two exercises do exist to help you prepare for the forthcoming challenge. Stairmaster (a step machine) is probably the best exercise, although building up to two hours of Stairmaster might not make you popular with other people in the gym. Another good exercise is leg lunges, both forward and backward. In addition, always use the stairs rather than the lift (either up or down) during the months before your Great Wall hike. Try also to walk rather than take the car or public transport for short distances.

As important as building up short-term muscle strength is stretching. Leg stretches, especially for the thighs, *Glutaeus maximus* (bottom!) and calves are the most important. An easy calf-muscle stretch is to stand on the edge of a stair on your toes facing up the stairs and allow your heel to drop below the edge of the stair. A good stretch for the bum is to stand on one leg, bend your other leg up in front of your chest and hold it there with your arms. For the thigh, stand on one leg and clasp your heel with your hand behind you, keeping the knee as close to your standing knee as possible. All stretches should be held for several seconds and repeated equally on both sides several times.

On the day of the hike itself, it is important to stretch, both before and especially after your hike. Some trainers advocate that stretching before exercise should not be done from cold or can be skipped so long as you start off your exercise slowly. Stretching after your hike will need to be done two or three times a day or more, possibly for several days afterwards.

Some may find the use of knee supports, such as the ones available in most good chemists, and a collapsible hiking stick useful for taking the strain off the knees and for helping to prevent injury. It is often the way back down that is most painful after a good climb, and a hiking stick certainly helps to shift weight and strain from the knees to the arms.

SECURITY AND SAFETY

Emergency telephone numbers: police – 110; fire – 119; ambulance – 120.

For the foreigner, China is one of the safest countries in the world to travel in. In tourist areas, it's common enough to come across pickpockets or to have your bag slashed and money stolen, but mugging and rape are almost unheard of. This makes travelling as a woman alone in China (although still unusual in a lot of China) quite a joy. As in any foreign country where you are carrying a lot of cash and valuables, use a money belt or inside pocket to store them away from prying hands. Divide your money so that it is less likely to be stolen all at the same time.

When travelling on trains and buses, especially overnight, secure your luggage to a rail or pole. You wouldn't want to wake up or come back from getting a mug of hot water to find all your bright shiny purchases from Hong Kong having been thrown out of a window to a waiting accomplice at an intervening station.

Gordon Rattray

Raiding and plundering are not the intentions of tourists, but for those with mobility problems the Great Wall is still magnificently inaccessible. Put simply, for full-time wheelchair users there is no easy way to the top, and even people who can walk with difficulty will find it a challenging experience. Zoe Macfarlane has this to say: "I used to be a tour leader for Travel Indochina and I once took a disabled client (who had a severe limp) to the Great Wall at Mutianyu. It was a difficult process and very tiring for him but he was a very determined man. At the top of the wall he took some time out to enjoy his picnic lunch and even walked one section (approx 0.5km). He had about two hours from start to finish and he did not regret any of his time there. My advice for any disabled traveller is to take this into account, decide if you have the commitment to struggle a little (either by being carried, being slow or the walk being arduous), and then go for it!"

The most approachable sections of the wall are at Badaling and Mutianyu. This is not only because there are cable cars at these sites, but also because they are relatively close to Beijing.

At **Badaling** there is a relatively flat surface to reach the cable car. It would need to be stopped briefly to give time to enter and although it is quite small there is room for a wheelchair to be collapsed down and placed inside. The language abilities of the staff here are limited, so a local guide is extremely helpful. At the top of the cable-car journey there are steps up on to the wall, making it only really feasible if you can walk slightly or don't mind being carried. From this point, however, it is still possible to enjoy a picnic lunch amidst spectacular scenery.

At **Mutianyu**, there is a cobbled street with a very steep incline between the car park and the cable car. Once at the cable car (if you are carried there) it is possible to do as at Badaling, but again, at the top there are steps to navigate and then an uneven resting area for photos. It is not possible to get right on to the wall here.

PUBLIC TRANSPORT in China is, in general, not accessible by design, and practically no English is spoken. So, unless you are able to jostle your way (quickly!) up steps and into buses and trains, then taxi or tour operator may be your only options. Private taxis and minivans can be ordered or hired through your hotel reception, and although language could again be a problem, drivers are normally friendly. To avoid confusion later, agree a fixed price for your trip in advance, and don't forget to take into account the extra time necessary for all the manhandling at the wall.

ACCOMMODATION No budget hostels and only a few mid-range and luxury hotels in Beijing have rooms that are accessible. These establishments need to be contacted in advance with details of specific requirements, and even then improvisation may still be necessary.

If you are mugged, robbed or attacked, then report it to the Public Security Bureau (gōng ān jú 公安局 – see individual chapters for local listings). A mugging and especially an attack should also be reported to your embassy, with whom you might want to register if you are going to be staying in China for a month or more.

WHAT TO TAKE

CLOTHING Most of the Great Wall lies at over 1,000m above sea level, so even in the summer, if you are staying near the wall overnight or are likely to get there early in the morning or late in the evening, remember to bring a light overcoat or jacket.

Many Chinese day trippers to the wall will get away with wearing town shoes – heels are not uncommon! Nevertheless, comfortable tennis shoes as a minimum and loose-fitting clothing are recommended – a lot of the Great Wall, even near Beijing, is steep and hard work. For longer treks see the hiking section below.

In towns, casual dress is the norm on the streets, although you'll see a lot of smart dressing these days in Beijing. Many top-notch hotels will not accept shoddy attire in clear need of repair. Businessmen tend to wear short-sleeved shirts in the summer, and you may wish to pack such a shirt or polo shirt if you intend to go to one of the nicer restaurants or bars. Some nightclubs also have a dress code and won't accept jeans and sneakers or anything less than shirt and tie.

Many monasteries may ask you to be decently covered before entering their grounds, so bring a pair of long trousers and shoulder coverings. A light scarf for women may also come in handy for mosques in Ningxia, some of which require women to cover their heads.

In spring and autumn it may be very warm during the day, but in the evening it can also get quite cold, and some hotels may have not yet turned on/or already turned off the central heating, so bring enough warm clothes.

PLUGS, ADAPTORS, CONVERTERS, CHARGERS AND CABLES China's electricity supply is 220 volts and uses a confusing array of two- and three-pinned plugs so a multi-choice adaptor is useful if you are bringing anything electronic. There are several great travel adaptors available now that take a multiple choice of plugs and give multiple options in pins. The sockets most frequently found are the two-pin flat variety similar to that used in North America, or a flat three pin. Adaptors are readily available in most cities, and newer hotels are starting to put multi-sockets straight into the hotel walls, meaning that you can plug your appliance from anywhere around the world straight into the socket. This is one of the brightest hotel ideas to have come out in a long time, but you won't find them in most of the budget lodgings in the more remote parts of northern China.

If you are coming from North America with American electrical appliances, then you can also purchase a power-voltage converter that will convert the 220 volts of Chinese electricity into 110 volts.

In the land of what is fast becoming the leading electronics manufacturer, you can find almost anything for your electrical appliances, and/or get them fixed. The computing and electronics world in Beijing is Hailong DaSha 海龙大厦 (literally 'sea dragon tower') at Zhong Guan Cun in northwest Beijing near the universities. Here you can get anything from the latest iPod and Apple Mac, PCs galore, cameras and videos, accessories and get them all repaired. To get there, take underground public transport to Xizhimen and then bus 106 north to Zhong Guan Cun. Hailong Daxia is on the west side of the road.

TOILETRIES AND MEDICINES You can buy all the basics in China, and in Beijing you can get a lot more besides. For the more remote parts of the wall bring your own contact lenses and solutions. Always bring spare glasses if you wear them. It is a nightmare anywhere in the world if you break your only pair. China's air is very polluted and very dry in winter and spring, so you may wish to bring a good face scrub and plenty of moisturiser if you are prone to dry skin.

Bring a universal wash plug, especially if you will be staying in lower-end accommodation. Otherwise plugs (sāizi 塞子) are easy enough to buy at a local hardware store in larger towns. Small packets of clothes washing powder are also readily available in supermarkets and local shops across China, and some hotels even sell travel packets of them. Most bigger hotels in larger towns will have cheap laundering facilities, although top-notch hotels are also starting to charge Western prices per item. A local launderette can usually wash everything for much cheaper, and some hotels can organise this for you if they do not provide their own laundering service. Budget hotels and dorms do not usually provide towels, so you will need to bring your own.

Small bottles of no-water-required, alcohol-based hand sanitiser like Purells, available in most good chemists or supermarkets at home, are a very good thing to take. Travelling in China, even just around Beijing, is very dirty. Cheaper eating establishments rarely have bathrooms (although they might have a bowl of water for you to wash your hands in), and public toilets rarely have soap (or even water), so hand sanitisers are a good way to prevent the transfer of bacteria.

Chinese hotels usually provide re-usable plastic sandals (cheap to mid-range hotels) or disposable cotton slippers (higher-end hotels) for going to the bathroom, but you might want to bring your own flip-flops if you are prone to picking up foot fungal infections. Medicated foot power is recommended for the same reason.

A basic first-aid pack (see page 75) is also useful, and sunscreen is essential if you are spending any amount of time hiking along the wall.

DOCUMENTS Obviously, a valid passport with visa, tickets and money (see below) are essential. Bring your travel insurance policy document (or a copy of it) with you in case you need it, as there is no point leaving it at home. A copy of the main page of your passport is also useful in the event of loss, and remember to keep it separate from your passport.

GIFTS It is always a good idea to bring family photos and postcards of your home town with you on holiday. They make good talking points and you can give the postcards out as a small gift. Many Chinese have never seen any foreign money, and so you may also want to bring some smaller bills or coins with you from home.

If you are invited into a Chinese home, try to bring fresh fruit for the host. Good supermarkets can usually make you up a nice gift-wrapped basket of fruit. Western sweets and brandy are popular in the more remote areas, and more permanent small souvenirs are also ideal as the Chinese love trinkets.

OUTDOORS AND HIKING Light sports shoes or open-toed hiking sandals like Tevas are fine for walking around or a short hike to a popular monument, but anything more arduous requires suitable hiking boots. Pollution in northern China is so bad and full of black coal dust that you might want to bring extra pairs of dark socks rather than get your feet absolutely filthy after a few hours of hiking. You may also find a long pair of hiking trousers useful as the paths in China are often overgrown and prickly, thorny or full of nettles.

Bring a good daypack and your favourite water container: wide-mouthed Nalgene bottles are far easier to fill than reused plastic water bottles, but my favourite has to be the Camelbak *(www.camelbak.com)*, especially in this arid climate.

If you are planning to hike for several days along the wall or travel from point to point staying in different hotels along the way, then you will undoubtedly be better off travelling with only one bag and preferably a rucksack. Chinese buses and trains can get very, very crowded. It is easier to keep your eye on only one bag or rucksack and your fellow travellers will appreciate it if you are not carting several wheelie bins around. Not that such appreciation would stop them taking their own array of baggage, including live animals.

It does get very hot in the summer, so bring enough clothing so that you can change out of your sweaty T-shirt when you get to the end of your hike. This helps to prevent you from getting a chill, which happens easily when you reach the colder climes of a peak or in the evening.

MAPS Outside China, the most detailed maps currently available are the Nelles maps. For the purposes of this book, the northern and northeastern maps of China cover the Great Wall area and depict the wall in all but Liaoning province. Inside China, more detailed maps of provinces are available, but unfortunately, the maps are mostly in Chinese. Hiking scale maps at 1:50,000 or 1:25,000 or even 1:100,000 are not available.

Town maps are available in most cities, sometimes in English and Chinese, especially for cities that receive many foreigners. It is unusual to find a map of a city anywhere other than in the city in question itself, so you will usually have to wait till you get to the destination city to buy a more detailed map than the one in this book, for instance.

Chinese maps of the world, available in both English and Chinese, are interesting items from a Western perspective as they place the Americas on the right-hand side of the map and Europe on the left, thus putting China and the Pacific Ocean in the centre. Old Chinese maps have north at the bottom of the map, because originally the compass (invented by the Chinese) pointed south.

CAMPING Dedicated basecamp stores are springing up in Beijing but are much more difficult to find outside the capital. So, you may need to stock up on gas-stove canisters and other supplies before leaving the capital, or bring an all-purpose fuel stove and buy petrol from the petrol stations.

Sanfo is the leading outdoor gear store in the country. They sell a variety of Western-branded goods as well as competitive Asian brands and Black Yak goods. Tents, climbing gear, roll mats, MSR and Primus stoves and fuels, Camelbaks, Nalgene, headlamps, compasses, binoculars and a good range of very affordable outdoor clothing can all be found at their stores:

Sanfo Beijing Building 4, Entrance 5, Nancun, Madian; *ℓ* 010 6201 5550; www.sanfo.com.cn. To get to Madian take the underground line 2 to Zhishuitan and then take bus 315, 344 or 345 for 15 minutes to Madian. The shop is located on the south side of Bei Sanhuan, west of the Madian intersection.
Sanfo Beijing Jinzhiqiao Dasha, Guomao, Chaoyang District; *ℓ* 010 6507 9298; www.sanfo.com.cn. Take the west entrance (where Starbucks is) out of the China International Trade Centre and continue west along the north side of the street to the east side of the second block of buildings.
Sanfo Eastern Hebei Province (towards Tianjin) 14–15 Genjiang Dajie, Langfang; *ℓ* 0316 2115 007
Sanfo Gansu Province 1 Youshengnan Lu, Jinshui District, Lanzhou; *ℓ* 0371 3866 757; *f* 0371 3866 760
Sanfo Jilin Province 668 Xikang Hutong, Ziyou Dalu, Changchun; *ℓ* 0431 5643 258
Sanfo Xinjiang Province 8 Mingde Lu, Urumqi; *ℓ* 0991 2817 218
Sanfo Zhejiang Province 1227–1229 Baizheng Dong Lu, Jiangdong District, Ningbo; *ℓ* 0574 8792 3220. Approximately 400m east of the Xin Changdu restaurant.

OTHER USEFUL ITEMS AND LUXURIES A cable lock is advisable if you are doing any long or overnight hard sleeper train or bus trips so that you can secure your luggage to the luggage racks on trains and buses whilst you sleep or wander around. A small LED headlamp is also useful if you want to get some reading done on the sleeper buses, or find yourself in a budget hotel with the dimmest of lighting; this is also useful if you get caught out late at night.

It might seem a bit of a fad, but an iPod or something equivalent is a good way to block out some of the frustrations of travelling in China when you have been on the road a long time. Small, durable and efficient, you can charge them whilst in a modern internet café.

$ MONEY AND BUDGETING

CURRENCY AND CHANGING MONEY Once upon a time, Foreign Exchange Currency (FEC) was the only 'currency' issued to foreigners at banks. 'Funny money' as it was fondly called then was dismantled in January 1994 (along with higher prices for foreigners) and with it went the illegal market for exchanging hard currency for Chinese yuan(¥) 元 (also called kuài 块 colloquially, or officially rénmínbì 人民币 (RMB) meaning 'the people's money').

The yuán 元 is divided into ten jiǎo 角 (or mao in slang) and each jiao into ten fēn 分, although fen are such a small denomination that even the Chinese hardly use them any more. Take care to check your change from vendors as they may try to give you jiao instead of yuan, especially as the colours of the notes look very similar. Coins as well as notes are in circulation for one, two and five jiao, as well as for one yuan. Notes are also available in ¥5, ¥20, ¥50 and ¥100.

The yuan has been pegged to a basket of currencies since July 2005. Exchange rates at the time of going to press (May 2006) were as follows:

US$1 = ¥8.01
£1 = ¥14.60
€1 = ¥10.10

You can get RMB from any bank or ATM, of which there are many all over China. Most ATMs that take Western credit cards (and not all of them do) can also take debit cards. You can still find money changers at some of the big markets in Beijing, but they are hardly worth the stress of thinking that you might get short-changed or receive false notes and coins. You still could not purchase RMB outside of China at the time of writing, but international airports and railway stations in China all have banks, exchange booths and ATMs where you can get hold of what you need. Although you are not meant to take Chinese currency back out of China when you leave, you may change any amount back into your home currency providing you can produce an exchange certificate from the bank where you originally changed it.

Travellers' cheques are the safe way to carry money in China and usually get a better rate than drawing money from an ATM. Even if you prefer to use an ATM, it is still worth carrying spare travellers' cheques for those remote towns (and there are lots of them) where there are no ATMs or the ATM is not working. The head branch of every Bank of China can exchange travellers' cheques and can usually draw money for you against a credit card (but not a debit card).

If you want to bring **cash** to exchange for RMB in China, then you are best bringing popular currencies such as US dollars, British pounds sterling or euro.

BUDGETING Although China is still very cheap, you can quickly spend a surprising amount of money on all the cheap bargains, and in Beijing you can spend a lot of money besides on the high life. Once in China, and if you do not spend too much time in Beijing (where the cheapest bed is ¥80 or US$10 a night), then you could get away with US$100 per week. If you want to take advantage of some of the nicer hotels (not the ¥10 or US$1.20 a night variety) and some really excellent food, then you might want to budget US$250 per week. At the other end of the scale you can pay over US$1,000 a night for a hotel to yourself at the Commune By The Great Wall (see page 149) and over US$100 for a meal for two at The CourtYard (page 154). Hiring a 4x4 with chauffeur would also help to increase your budget considerably.

BARGAINING Some foreigners love bargaining. Others find it difficult, annoying or degrading. For the Chinese, however, bargaining is an integral part of Chinese life, so much so that if you do not haggle with street vendors, they are likely to feel insulted. Foreigners are usually offered grossly exaggerated starting prices, and there is a strong chance that if you are offered a starting price in the hundreds of yuan then you can drop it to one-third and the vendor will still make a killing. Otherwise, you might want to start at half price and set yourself the rule of thumb to pay no more than two-thirds of the asking price. The trick with bargaining is first not to show interest and second to drive a hard bargain by buying several items together. If you try to buy another item from the same vendor where you have just bought something else, there is a very high chance that the vendor will manage to make a lot of money off the next item you buy, even if you got a good price for the first purchase. Walk through the entire market first to get an idea of what is available and ask casually into prices before making a decision to purchase. It is horrible to buy something at the first stall, like the bargain-crazed foreigner that the Chinese think you are, only to find a better item at the next stall at a lower price. In any case, it is usually a conscience saver if you decide how much an item is worth to you and pay no more than that. If you can't be bothered to bargain, then decide your paying price, get your money out and be prepared to walk away if the vendor doesn't like your price. If the vendor lets you walk away then you have probably bid too low. Prices in supermarkets in big cities are usually set now, so there is no bargaining to be had there. Prices in hotels can almost always be discounted (dǎ zhé 打折) unless you book in advance.

TIPPING Leaving a tip for services at restaurants and hotels is not at all common in China, even in the large Western hotels.

GETTING AROUND

Compared with many countries, public transport in China is extensive and cheap although far from exemplary. Nevertheless, as privatisation and ensuing competition takes hold, travel in China will only become more convenient. It can only be hoped that the revolution taking place in some provinces in bus travel will also soon take place in the now quite outdated train and plane travel.

Travelling in China, especially by bus, usually takes place early in the morning. Buses to some destinations do not run after 11.00, making it an extremely early-morning start if you want to get to a place and back in one day. The other reason for travelling early in the morning is that, unless you have reserved a place in a hotel in advance and, therefore, you know where you are sleeping for the night, it is always easier to look for a hotel and bargain down prices during daylight when reception desks are manned. You then have the rest of the day in your new destination to orient yourself and take a look around town.

✈ **FLIGHTS** fēijī 飞机 Internal flights in China are relatively cheap and certainly save an enormous amount of time travelling around the Middle Kingdom's huge interior.

China is just starting to allow for the privatisation of provincial airlines and allowing them to compete with each other. E-ticketing is also coming in (very slowly). These two changes will help to bring prices down and services up, and China's air safety record has improved considerably over the last decade. Gone are the rickety old planes that looked as if they would fall apart if you so much as sneezed. At the moment, however, flights are still far too expensive for the average citizen and so they remain the preserve of party officials and rich east-coast yuppies and businesspeople.

The national carrier, China Air, has CAAC offices in almost every major city and town, even if there isn't an airport there, as well as at most big airports. City and town offices are listed in each chapter. You can also buy plane tickets at your hotel (in mid- to upper-range hotels) through their business or travel centre, usually at no extra cost. A number of web- and phone-based discount travel agents now operate throughout China, and if you speak some Chinese, these can be quite helpful. It should be noted, however, that discounted flights are also available at CAAC offices. Tickets purchased up to two months in advance often get a 50% discount, and 30% discount up to one month in advance, after which the discount depends on how many seats are still to be sold on the plane.

Flights within China usually incur an airport tax of ¥50, which is now included in the ticket price.

TRAINS huǒ chē 火车 Trains are still ridiculously cheap in China. They are convenient for travelling long distances between major destinations, but next to useless for small hops or alighting between destinations. Demand for train travel is so high that tickets are often sold out as soon as they are available, especially for popular tourist routes, which are often bought up by tour operators in advance and sold on at a premium to foreign travellers. It is not unknown in the very busy Golden Week in May or National Week in October for soft sleeper tickets to be sold to foreigners by travel agents for three times their actual price.

At the train's origin or point of departure, train tickets can usually be bought up to five days in advance. If you are worried about getting a certain last train back to the capital in order to make your flight home, then you may want to enlist the help of a local travel agent to help you get your ticket (or take the bus). Seats and sleepers are available on most trains as hard or soft: hard sleeper (yìngwò 硬卧); soft sleeper (ruǎnwò 软卧); hard seat (yìngzuò 硬座); soft seat (ruǎnzuò 软座).

After the point of origin of the train, a small number of tickets might be reserved for purchase in larger towns. Usually these are 'no seat' tickets (wúzuòwèi 无座位) that allow you to get on to the train, but don't give you a seat. If you want a seat (zuòwèi 座位) or sleeper (wòpù 卧铺), then you have to make your way (possibly with all your luggage through several crowded carriages) to the train conductor (usually in the middle of the train), who will let you know if any seats/sleepers are available for purchase.

Once you get a seat, then travel by train is usually very comfortable, and sometimes can be faster than the bus (eg: Yinchuan to Wuwei in five hours by train, or eight hours by bus), because the train does not need to stop for people to eat or go to the toilet. Exactly why China has not increased its train use, especially for shorter commuter stops, gives rise to much speculation. One theory is that the Chinese government is so keen to produce an internationally viable Chinese car that it is deliberately trying to encourage car use and purchase and so is not investing in train travel. Such random conjecture aside, even if the government was to double the price of rail travel, and so increase revenue, this mode of transport would still be great value for money.

BUSES dàbāshi 大巴士 For most journeys in China, buses are by far the most convenient, although they can often be very crowded and very dirty. The significant improvement in road infrastructure has made bus travel almost enjoyable. For travel to a destination within two to three hours, buses often leave every 20–40 minutes from 06.00–18.00. For a four- to five-hour trip, fast direct buses (kuài kè 快客) usually leave every hour or half-hour from 06.00–16.00, and slow buses stopping at a number of stops en route (pǔ kè 普客) usually leave every hour and half-hour from 06.00–18.00. Longer trips may occur only once or twice a day and can get booked up quickly. Such tickets can usually be bought up to three days in advance, however.

In most provinces, minibuses (gōng jiāo chē 公交车) starting in smaller towns normally wait until the bus is full before setting off. This can be frustrating if you are trying to visit a place and come back again in one day, as this system can impinge on your time both in reaching your destination and on your return planning. Once the bus is full, the bus station master may register the number of passengers and check payment by all passengers before the bus is allowed to set off. Once on the road, drivers and their conductors on the slow routes pick up passengers along the way (and usually pocket the money). Even though it is illegal to stuff a bus with more passengers than it is designed to take, it is not unknown for drivers to pack their bus to twice its capacity, demand regular payment, and then ask half the passengers to hide on the floor of the bus when going through a police checkpoint. While this does not conform to European and North American standards of the law-abiding citizen, when stuck in a remote location on the Great Wall late in the afternoon you might just appreciate being picked up by a very full bus which can whisk you back to a decent meal and a good night's sleep.

Sleeper buses (wòpù chē 卧铺车) have become more common in recent years. These incorporate two decks of bunks (barely long enough for a foreigner to lie flat on) with two aisles between three single rows. They are more expensive than day seat buses, but the extra room afforded is worth it if you are on a long journey. The main disadvantage of sleeper buses is that, unless you take the bus to its final destination, you might be dropped off in a town late at night or in the middle of the morning and then need to find a hotel. Although taxis will probably be waiting to take you to your desired destination, it is always difficult to test a number of hotels in the middle of the night in the dark. On the other hand if you are taking the bus to its final destination, then even if it arrives very early in the morning, you are usually allowed to sleep on the bus until dawn or later. Sleeper buses often start around 16.00, allowing them enough time to pick up other passengers along the way if the bus is not full. There is usually a half-hour break in the evening at a very basic roadside restaurant for food and to use the toilet (there is rarely a toilet on the bus).

TAXIS chū zū qì chē 出租汽车 There are two types of taxis in China: official and unofficial. Official taxis are run by firms, usually have meters and drivers are registered, with a photo and ID number of the driver at the front of the car. In main towns these are the only taxis you should take. They should be able to give you a receipt for your journey. Metered taxis should turn on their meter (biǎo 表) very soon after you get in. If they do not then you might want to remind the driver to turn on his meter by saying the word biao and pointing to it. There is a flag fall for metered taxis, which varies by town. In Beijing, flag fall is ¥10. In smaller towns, flag fall can be as little as ¥3. Metered taxis are usually all a similar colour (usually dark red or two-tone green and white or some other combination). Metered journeys must give a certain percentage to the taxi firm, and then the rest is usually kept by the driver, but his petrol, diesel or liquid petroleum gas (LPG) must come out of his profit. This provides the incentive to pick up as many rides as possible and not simply drive around town aimlessly. Car maintenance is usually covered by the taxi firm. Some big cities only allow pick up and drop off at certain designated areas. Main junctions and corners are usually banned in big towns for drop off and pick up.

Unofficial taxis are basically private cars. Whatever money they take, they keep, and without a meter they usually charge many times the price of a metered taxi. A free ride, however, is virtually unheard of, so if you take a private car because there are no metered cars where you are, then make sure you set a price before setting off on your journey. As a rule of thumb private rides are normally charged at ¥1–2 per kilometre.

Many metered taxis will also take private rides, especially to longer or remote destinations, such as the airport, nature reserves or far-flung reaches of the Great Wall, where it is difficult to pick up a return passenger. In such cases, the driver will charge you essentially for the price of a return journey so that he can get back to town. While he will probably pocket this entire sum (minus petrol), you will probably also get slightly less than half the going metered rate, precisely because the driver gets to keep all the money. In an effort to save money, drivers will often try to charge you extra for tolls, or take the back roads, and/or will drive slowly so as to maximise on fuel efficiency.

In general, female taxi drivers are less likely to try to rip you off, are safer and don't usually smoke. Female taxi drivers are relatively easy to find.

UNDERGROUND dì tiě 地铁 The only underground system working in all of northern China is in Beijing (see *Chapter 8* for more information). Tianjin is in the process of constructing an underground system, which should come into effect in 2007.

HITCHHIKING Hitchhiking is not at all common in China, not least because buses are so abundant that you are more likely to have a bus pick you up before a private-car-owning individual will let a stranger into their much-coveted possession. Even if you do get picked up by a private car, there is a high chance that the driver will expect some sort of payment. In fact this is likely to be the only reason they stopped for you in the first place.

DRIVING kāi chē 开车 Foreigners can now drive anywhere in China. The biggest hurdle to driving in China is the requirement for a Chinese driving licence. Getting a driving licence via the normal route requires a resident's permit and costs about US$200 in lessons and tests that are very difficult to pass. An easier (more expensive) option is to buy your Chinese driving licence for US$500 from a broker, many of whom can be found at the back of city magazines such as *That's Beijing, Time Out Beijing,* or *City Weekend.*

Whether you really want to drive on China's crazy roads, however, is another issue altogether. Lane discipline, adhering to speed limits and other general road etiquette is not considered important, if the Chinese have any concept of them at all. Drivers almost never wear seatbelts, even though it is a legal requirement. In addition to the hazards of Chinese driving behaviour, many vehicles in China are, by most western European, North American and even Chinese standards, completely illegal. Vehicle safety inspections and standards are essentially ignored and little enforced. As if a ten-tonne truck sliding into your vehicle is not bad enough, there is every chance that the truck has actually been refitted for 50 tonnes, making its impact on roads, vehicles and humans much greater. Bicycles are another hazard, many of which have practically no brakes to speak of. As a result of all this madness, vehicles in China tend to drive quite slowly and horn honking as a means of indicating presence is common. There is always the odd maniac, however, who drives far too fast for everyone else.

So think hard about driving in China, especially if you are not used to driving in developing countries.

BIKING zì xíng chē 自行车 Biking in China in cities is still very common, but between cities or as a recreational sport is seen by the grand majority of Chinese as a bit odd, to put it mildly. Biking tours are becoming more common in the heavily visited southern regions of China, but in the north, it is still fairly unusual. However, this is changing. Biking clubs are popping up in Beijing and some tour operators also offer biking tours of parts of northern China including the wall (see Silk Steps, page 66).

Cycle China Club ✆ 139 1188 6524; ✉ reserve@cyclechina.com; www.cyclechina.com. Does supported cycle and hiking tours of the Great Wall in Beijing province as well as other cycle rides elsewhere. Costs vary depending on the number of cyclists. Maps of cycle routes are available for those who prefer not to go in a group.

Mountainbikers of Bejing (MOB) ✆ 138 0108 8646; ✉ themob@404.com.au or bjmobsters@yahoo.co.uk

HIKING AND WALKING along the Great Wall is covered in *Chapter 4, The Outdoors*, pages 59-61.

ACCOMMODATION zhùsù 住宿

After years of a communist state-run regimented mentality, followed by a rush for things 'modern', hotels in China tend to be either downright dreadful or at best faceless but functional. Courtyard hotels in the Ming and Qing style are beginning to see a revival, most of which are often quiet and generally fairly well serviced. Family-run hotels, however, with character and charm, a welcoming relaxing atmosphere and a good understanding of customer service are almost impossible to find in China at any price, especially in northern China.

Hotels built in the 20th century are usually shoddy and much the worse for wear by now, unless they have been renovated this century. Even then, it is often too late for the waterworks, which continue to seep the stench of rotting drains. For some bizarre reason, China still does not seem to have cottoned on to the u-bend as a means of blocking smells and improving health and sanitation.

If you can get into a newly built hotel, then it will be in good service. Chinese travellers are very hard on hotels, though, frequently putting out stubs in the carpets, and tracking dirt all over the walls, fittings and furniture. In addition, for a country that still has great cobblers and bicycle menders, hotel maintenance is somehow not high on the list of Chinese virtues. A year or two after opening, shower heads will be bust, toilets don't flush properly (or at all), sinks won't drain, some of the lights and the air conditioning won't work, and the walls, ceiling and floor leave something to be desired.

The Chinese have an incredible tolerance for noise (see page 49), meaning that most hotels are on busy and noisy main streets with paper-thin walls, single-pane windows, and fellow travellers who yell at each other and the floor attendant down the corridor until late at night rather than use the free hotel phone. A TV is a must for information- and technology-starved Chinese, who will almost always have it on in the background, loud, from early in the morning until late at night. If you value peace and quiet on your holiday, then you might want to stick to the popular foreigner hostels, of which there are few along most of the Great Wall, or higher-end hotels.

The Chinese language has a dizzying array of words covering different types of accommodation, and confusingly, the use of the English word 'hotel' does not always imply accommodation, but sometimes only a restaurant. Cheap accommodation abounds all over China if you know what sign to look for, and most places will accept your money even if they are not supposed to. In the bad old days, only approved hotels could accept foreigners, but this practice is dwindling as laws are passed province by province allowing foreigners to stay in any place on offer. That doesn't stop some hotels from refusing foreigners, however.

Budget places are usually found near the train and bus stations. They rarely advertise in English or even pinyin, however, so it is worth getting a grasp of some of the basic characters for accommodation if you want to look for something cheap on your own. No matter whether you stay in a five star or a no star, always remember to ask for a discount (dǎ zhé 打折), which is almost always available, usually up to one-third off the posted rate.

HOTELS Bīn guǎn 宾馆 is the most common word for 'hotel'. These are usually middling to very respectable, offering standard (biāozhǔn 标准) en-suite twins, doubles and triples, and common (pǔtōng 普通) rooms perhaps without bathrooms. The hotel may or may not have a restaurant, and may or may not offer breakfast. Every town usually has a bingguan in the town's name. These were once all state run, shoddy and not usually worth the money. They do provide a certain moulding quality, however, and if you don't know of anywhere else to stay in the town, then 'town name + bingguan' is usually a safe bet. Recently, some of these hotels have been renovated, such as the Beijing Binguan and the Datong Binguan, which now rank among the most expensive establishments in town.

Dàjiǔdiàn 大酒店, meaning literally 'big drink court' is usually a bigger establishment with a restaurant. Again, if it has the town name in front of it then it is usually still state run and the same applies as in bingguan above.

Fàndiàn 饭店, meaning 'food court', is normally only a restaurant, but bigger ones might also offer rooms (but frequently not to foreigners).

Lǚguǎn 旅馆 can be translated as 'travellers inn'. These are generally smaller and cheaper than bingguan, and friendlier and more personal. 'Cheaper' might entail no towels and no toilet paper and you make your own bed (with the bedding provided).

Sìhéyuàn 四合院, literally translated as 'four-sided court', is the typical Ming and Qing dynasty town courtyards. Very few original courtyards are left in big cities like Beijing, and only a handful have been turned into hotels (all listed in this guide). Most have been renovated with en-suite bathrooms, AC, TV and phone, although none has yet got broadband internet access. Rooms are usually small, often decorated with Ming (simple elegant lines) or Qing (more ornate) style furnishings leading to the common descriptor 'bijou'. Ming-/Qing-style enclosed coloured lampshades often adorn lights, leaving rooms a mixture of atmospheric or simply downright dim. The popularity of courtyard hotels is beginning to catch on elsewhere and there is a growing trend in building brand-new courtyard hotels, many with slight adaptations making them larger, lighter and more comfortable.

Shānzhuāng 山庄, meaning 'mountain lodge', has become the craze descriptor for any accommodation or eating establishment out in the countryside, whether it is on a mountain or not. Often fairly secluded by Chinese standards, most have been built in this century and so are relatively modern in conveniences, en suite with on-demand water heaters. Rooms are usually few and fairly basic, and run by a family. Some can be surprisingly large, but rarely have over 50 rooms. A family-run restaurant serving a few good dishes is usually part of the lodge.

HOSTELS zhù sù 住宿 in large characters is usually the sign hung outside cheaper accommodation indicating a place to stay. A Zhusu sign most likely represents one of the following:

Zhāodàisuǒ 招待所, most often translated as guesthouse, provides cheap accommodation, mostly of the putong (common) variety without en-suite bathrooms. Four-, five- and six-bed dormitories are common in Zhaodaisuo. Zhaodaisuo usually have a lot of rooms, and are less likely to accept foreigners than are binguan.
Lǔshè 旅社 or lǔdiàn 旅店, probably best translated as 'travel lodge', also rents a few very cheap rooms, and usually only singles, doubles or twins. Often, communal facilities are extremely basic.

BED AND BREAKFAST This is not really a common notion in China, and the nearest equivalent is the nóng jiā yuàn 农家院, or farmer's inn. In commonly visited areas, especially in Beijing and Hebei provinces, most families have realised that if they convert a room or two they can get a bit of extra income, especially from weekend Beijing yuppies. Some do provide a basic Chinese breakfast as well as other meals if required (at extra cost), but many will also send you off to the local restaurant. In popular tourist sites like Huanghuacheng, nong jia yuan are even being built from scratch with basic en-suite facilities, on-demand water heaters and karaoke sets.

✖ FOOD AND DRINK

Food and drink in China is generally plentiful, cheap, fast and good – the winning combination, if you like Chinese food. For more on cuisine in northern China see *Chapter 3*, page 50. In Beijing, you can get any type of foreign food you want, but outside of the capital this is more difficult. Like anywhere in the world, even Chinese food in China can be cooked badly and take-away food in Styrofoam containers is frequently of low quality. The Chinese have a reputation for eating anything that walks, crawls or flies and much more besides. Offal is a favourite of the Chinese that most foreigners prefer to avoid. Most kinds are cooked in a flavourful sauce, but some, such as mutton tripe soup for breakfast, are best described as revolting. A walk down the night markets in Beijing will reveal stall after stall of deep-fried silk worms, sparrows, locusts, chicken kidneys and hearts. Or you can stick to 'clean' cuts of lamb, chicken, beef and pork.

If you are a **vegetarian** or vegan then eating out in China could pose a problem. Even though there is an abundance of delicious vegetable dishes, most are cooked with a dash of meat or in a wok that may have had a meat dish in previously. Animal drippings or lard are a common cooking ingredient, especially in the countryside. In the big cities, however, some restaurants specialise in tofu cooking and if it is a while since you ate duck or fish or bacon, you can find some remarkable tofu imitations which are very hard to tell apart from the real thing.

Hygiene in a lot of cooking establishments in China leaves much to be desired. If you are particularly prone to food poisoning then you may wish to steer clear of uncooked foods or iced drinks. Most Chinese peel their fruit, including apples, pears and peaches, before eating them.

Even the Chinese do not drink **water** straight from the tap, but boil it first. You might be able to get away with using it to brush your teeth, and some of the upper-class hotels provide filtered water spouts at the wash basin in your room. Take care when you are buying bottled water from remote but popular tourist sites, as occasionally the water bottle is a refill and not the genuine product.

PUBLIC HOLIDAYS AND FESTIVALS

NATIONAL HOLIDAYS

1 January	New Year's Day
January/February	Chinese New Year. Businesses usually shut for the first three days of Chinese New Year and may close for the entire week. The first day falls on the full moon between 22 January and 22 February. Chinese New Year will fall on the following dates in the coming years: 18 February 2007 (year of the pig), 7 February 2008 (year of the rat), 26 January 2009 (year of the ox).
8 March	Women's Day
1 May	International Labour Day. The ten-day-long Golden Week centres around this day and the 4 May Youth Day. Like Chinese New Year and the 1 October National Day, the entire Chinese nation seems to go on holiday. Transport is usually packed and hotels in popular destinations such as Wutaishan and Shapotou often triple or quadruple their prices. Normally quiet parks and streets become a cacophony of blaring loudspeakers and firecrackers. It is best to avoid China during this week or to take a long hike at a remote part of the Great Wall.
4 May	Youth Day
1 June	International Children's Day
1 July	Anniversary of the Chinese Communist Party
1 August	People's Liberation Army Day
10 September	Teachers' Day
1 October	National Day celebrating the foundation of the People's Republic of China in 1949. Government may close for up to one week and once again the whole nation is on the move to favourite destinations.

FESTIVALS The Chinese celebrate a great variety of colourful festivals throughout the year. Below are brief descriptions of the main nationwide festivals.

Spring Festival Spring Festival, also known outside mainland China as Chinese New Year, starts on the first day of the first lunar month of the Chinese calendar. There are 12 or 13 months in the Chinese lunar calendar (*see Appendix 2, Glossary*), which starts between 22 January and 22 February of the Western calendar. In communist times celebrations were relatively sedate, but now the good old Chinese customs are back in force. This generally entails a lot of eating and a lot of noise, usually in the form of strings of loud red firecrackers, and the famous lion dance conducted by several people in costume. In the north, Spring Festival is celebrated by making *jiaozi*, moon-shaped dumplings stuffed with various fillings, boiled and served with black vinegar and soy sauce. The Chinese calendar rotates around 12 animal figures, which occur in the following order: dragon, snake, horse, sheep, monkey, rooster, dog, pig, rat, ox, tiger and rabbit; 2006 is the year of the dog.

Lantern Festival Fifteen days after the start of the Spring Festival is the Lantern Festival. This terminates the festivities of the Chinese New Year with the lighting of lanterns and an almighty fireworks show. The celebratory food of the festival is yuánxiāo 元宵, small sweet glutinous rice dumplings filled with a mixture of sugar, coconut, walnuts, sesame, osmanthus flowers, rose petals, tangerine peel, red-bean paste or mung-bean paste.

Qingming Festival The qīngmíng 清明 or 'clear bright' festival falls in April and is the day for paying respects to the dead. It is generally a private festival, when families meet up to visit ancestral graves and offer food and paper money to departed loved ones.

May Golden Week Less of a festival than simply a week-long holiday, the Labour Day May Golden Week centres around the 1 May International Labour Day and the 4 May Youth Day. China started the Golden Week system in 1999 as a means of ensuring that more people had a holiday and to boost the tourism industry. It certainly seems to have worked and, as with the golden weeks of Spring Festival and the National Holiday, the whole nation seems to be travelling in the May Golden Week to visit family or go sightseeing.

Dragon Boat Festival More of a southern Chinese than a northern Chinese festival, the Dragon Boat Festival falls in the fifth month of the lunar calendar, ie: in June. Dragon boats race each other along rivers in honour of the dragon king while onlookers eat zòngzi 粽子, glutinous rice cooked in pyramid-shaped leaf packets and filled with dates, meat, chestnuts and other delicacies.

Moon Festival The Moon Festival or Mid-Autumn Festival falls on the 15th day of the eighth lunar month, which is generally sometime in September. It is essentially a harvest festival, and also, in ancient days, a time to pay respects to the moon, which was seen as a female (and negative!) character. Moon cakes are eaten, made in the shape of the moon (round not crescent) and filled with delicacies like many of the other treats of Chinese festivals. Of note in many moon cakes is the hard-boiled egg-yolk centre surrounded by sweet lotus, sesame, or red-bean paste. Not quite a Cadbury's chocolate fondant Easter egg, but the Chinese equivalent thereof.

Double Ninth Double Ninth, as its name suggests, falls on the ninth day of the ninth month. The number nine is considered to be the closest that man can come to perfection (ten is for the gods only) and so double ninth (usually falling in October) is particularly auspicious. It is a very old festival, mostly celebrated by older people, and is becoming known in China as the day to pay respects to the elderly. Age is generally revered in Chinese society.

Although **Christmas** is not a traditional Chinese celebration, it is fast becoming a commercial favourite as a means of selling goods and an excuse for a celebration.

1 January has been a holiday in mainland China for some time, and is another excuse for more fireworks and good food.

SHOPPING

Many original and 'genuine copies' of scrolls, branded clothing, jade, lacquerware, tea paraphernalia and some of the best tea in the world, antiques, silk, porcelain, ornaments, kites, coins, mobile phones, fans, swords, papercuts, embroidered linen, masks, woodwork, chopstick sets, pearls, calligraphic items, handmade paper, ethnic tie-dyes, Mao Zedong paraphernalia, melody balls, abaci and a whole host of other things, can be purchased in China for as cheap as your bargaining skills (see page 86) can manage.

Most large cities have a Friendship Store (Yǒuyì Shāngdiàn 友谊商店), where you can purchase many of the items mentioned above, or you can try in the local antique market. See the section on *Customs* (page 70) for what you may take with you out of the country. Beijing is an excellent place for shopping (see page 158 for details on shopping in Beijing) although you might find better bargains in the smaller towns and villages.

PHOTOGRAPHY

China provides an abundance of exciting photographic opportunities. SLR film is available everywhere and is generally cheap to process. Quality of processing in big cities is excellent. Slide film and processing is also available. Digital photography is all the rage, however, especially now with mobile phones. Digital photography processing can be found easily if you want to turn your digitals into printed photographs, and most digital photography stores will also sell memory cards and sticks if you need extras.

Most younger Chinese have no problems with you taking their photo, but for the elderly it is polite to ask first. The few ladies with bound feet who are still living do not usually like to have their photo taken.

For more top tips on photography see the box on pages 96-97.

MEDIA AND COMMUNICATIONS

China is on the same dialogue mobile phone system as most of the rest of the world (ie: not the same as Japan and analogue users in the US). As a result if you have a standard world phone that is enabled to use abroad (some are locked by the manufacturer) then you can buy a **mobile phone** sim card in China for use with your phone.

There are two main mobile phone network providers in China: China Mobile and China Unicom. They cover a variety of regional numbers across China. Depending on what you want out of your sim card, you should check before purchasing whether the sim card allows you to send and receive calls to and from abroad, and can send and receive text messages to and from abroad. At the time of writing there was no Chinese top-up sim card that would allow you all four options.

Local kiosks for magazines and snacks usually have a local **public phone**, which you use first and then get charged according to a meter. Public phone booths taking coins, credit cards and national phonecards are also available in big cities and most towns and villages.

Postal services in China, especially when delivering packages from abroad, are not renowned for their reliability. Sending packages back home out of China is

Ariadne Van Zandbergen

Equipment Although with some thought and an eye for composition you can take reasonable photos with a 'point-and-shoot' camera, you need an SLR camera if you are at all serious about photography. Modern SLRs tend to be very clever, with automatic programmes for almost every possible situation, but remember that these programmes are limited in the sense that the camera cannot think, but only make calculations. Every starting amateur photographer should read a photographic manual for beginners and get to grips with such basics as the relationship between aperture and shutter speed.

Always buy the best lens you can afford. The lens determines the quality of your photo more than the camera body. Fixed fast lenses are ideal, but very costly. Zoom lenses are easier to change composition without changing lenses the whole time. If you carry only one lens, a 28–70mm (digital 17–55mm) or similar zoom should be ideal. For a second lens, a lightweight 80–200mm or 70–300mm (digital 55–200mm) or similar will be excellent for candid shots and varying your composition. Wildlife photography will be very frustrating if you don't have at least a 300mm lens. For a small loss of quality, tele-converters are a cheap and compact way to increase magnification: a 300 lens with a 1.4x converter becomes 420mm, and with a 2x it becomes 600mm. Note, however, that 1.4x and 2x tele-converters reduce the speed of your lens by 1.4 and 2 stops respectively.

For photography from a vehicle, a solid beanbag, which you can make yourself very cheaply, will be necessary to avoid blurred images, and is more useful than a tripod. A clamp with a tripod head screwed on to it can be attached to the vehicle as well. Modern dedicated flash units are easy to use; aside from the obvious need to flash when you photograph at night, you can improve a lot of photos in difficult 'high contrast' or very dull light with some fill-in flash. It pays to have a proper flash unit as opposed to a built-in camera flash.

Digital/film Digital photography is now the preference of most amateur and professional photographers, with the resolution of digital cameras improving the whole time. For ordinary prints a 6 megapixel camera is fine. For better results and the possibility to enlarge images and for professional reproduction, higher resolution is available up to 16 megapixels.

Memory space is important. The number of pictures you can fit on a memory card depends on the quality you choose. Calculate in advance how many pictures you can fit on a card and either take enough cards to last for your trip, or take a storage drive onto which you can download the content. A laptop gives the advantage that you can see your pictures properly at the end of each day and edit

no longer cheap either at ¥100–150 (€10–15) per kilogram for surface mail (píngyóu 平邮) back to Europe. Express Mail Service (EMS tèkuài zhuāndi 特快专 递) is also available at most post offices as well as registered mail services (guà hào xìn 挂号信).

If you need to receive mail in China while on the move then you can use the internationally agreed **poste restante** (cún jú hòu lǐng 存局候领) system. It is not the most reliable of systems and so you may be better off using fax or email unless and delete rejects, but a storage device is lighter and less bulky. These drives come in different capacities up to 80GB.

Bear in mind that digital camera batteries, computers and other storage devices need charging, so make sure you have all the chargers, cables and converters with you. Most hotels have charging points, but do enquire about this in advance. When camping you might have to rely on charging from the car battery; a spare battery is invaluable.

If you are shooting film, 100 to 200 ISO print film and 50 to 100 ISO slide film are ideal. Low ISO film is slow but fine grained and gives the best colour saturation, but will need more light, so support in the form of a tripod or monopod is important. You can also bring a few 'fast' 400 ISO films for low-light situations where a tripod or flash is no option.

Dust and heat Dust and heat are often a problem. Keep your equipment in a sealed bag, stow films in an airtight container (eg: a small cooler bag) and avoid exposing equipment and film to the sun. Digital cameras are prone to collecting dust particles on the sensor which results in spots on the image. The dirt mostly enters the camera when changing lenses, so be careful when doing this. To some extent photos can be 'cleaned' up afterwards in Photoshop, but this is time-consuming. You can have your camera sensor professionally cleaned, or you can do this yourself with special brushes and swabs made for the purpose, but note that touching the sensor might cause damage and should only be done with the greatest care.

Light The most striking outdoor photographs are often taken during the hour or two of 'golden light' after dawn and before sunset. Shooting in low light may enforce the use of very low shutter speeds, in which case a tripod will be required to avoid camera shake.

With careful handling, side lighting and back lighting can produce stunning effects, especially in soft light and at sunrise or sunset. Generally, however, it is best to shoot with the sun behind you. When photographing animals or people in the harsh midday sun, images taken in light but even shade are likely to be more effective than those taken in direct sunlight or patchy shade, since the latter conditions create too much contrast.

Protocol Don't try to sneak photographs without permission, as you might get yourself into trouble. Even the most willing subject will often pose stiffly when a camera is pointed at them; relax them by making a joke, and take a few shots in quick succession to improve the odds of capturing a natural pose.

Ariadne Van Zandbergen (@ ariadne@hixnet.co.za; www.africaimagelibrary. co.za) is a professional travel and wildlife photographer specialising in Africa.

you are receiving a package or an original signed document (in which case get it sent by registered post). To receive post by poste restante, have it addressed backwards as is the custom in China:

Postal code, province, city
(street and number of the specific post office if you know it)
Poste Restante 存局候领
Name

If you do not know the street and number of the specific post office that you want the mail delivered to, then it will go to the main post office of the town. You will need to show your passport and pay a fee of ¥5. If the attendant cannot find your expected mail then ask for a search by your first name as well as your last (the first character of Chinese names is the family name) and write your name down on a piece of paper for the attendant to take on the search.

BUSINESS

Doing business in China is not for the faint-hearted and comes with a severe health warning. The lure of making it rich off a market of 1.3bn people is very strong, but more foreign investors flounder by the wayside than actually make any money. To be successful at business in China takes determination, patience and learning to do things the Chinese way. The topic is far too complex to cover in any great detail here, and fortunately there are many excellent books on the subject available at most good bookstores, including those at larger airports. Some recommendations are made in *Appendix 3, Further information*, page 269.

A few observations are worth making, however, for the general reader and may help to explain some of the encounters you come across in China (or amongst the Chinese at home). As mentioned under *Culture, customs and habits* (page 47), guānxi 关系 (connections) are extremely important for doing business in China, and a serious deal is unlikely to take place without a personal introduction from a native Chinese or a very trusted 'old China hand'. After countless hours of effort and perseverance at courting a potential partner, an agreement might be reached (probably without a contract as this would denigrate the trust built during the courting period), and the all-important banquet dinner with much drinking and merrymaking will signal that the deal is on the right track. Don't be surprised, however, if the partner in whom you have been putting all your hope tells you at the eleventh hour that they have been courting someone else all along and will not be doing business with you – maybe next time.

Although 'sly, underhand and untrustworthy' might be words that spring to mind, this is not true. It is merely that the point of confidence, concepts of partnership and art of transactions are different. The Chinese are past masters of trade, profit and capital, going back millennia. It is in their blood, so to speak, and it is worth keeping this in mind when sitting at the business or dinner table with them. By nature, the Chinese are very hard-working given the slightest incentive, although you might not believe that when you are wading through the red tape presented by an arch-communist local government official of a province in the back of beyond. Fortunately, the pace of change in business in China is phenomenal, even in the interior of western China. Unfortunately, sweeping away corruption and bribery is not happening quite as fast.

It will be important to observe all sorts of etiquette (see *Cultural etiquette* on page 49) and if you can get yourself an auspicious Chinese name for your business card, this will impress your interlocutors and show that you are serious. It used to be almost impossible to get a majority stake in a business in China, but this is beginning to change. As with most developing countries, you might want to take China's human rights record and working conditions into consideration if you are at all concerned about this. You might be also well advised to seek in-country expertise and on-the-ground assistance through the services of an advisory bureau such as the US-China Business Council (*www.uschina.org*).

The only other general thing to add is 'Good luck' – you will need it.

The interaction of the outside world with China is a driving force in many respects. Hopefully, your time in China will be environmentally sustainable and beneficial. If you would like to get involved more personally in issues in China, then consider contacting one of the organisations below, either simply to find out more, or to volunteer or donate.

Global Village of Beijing (GVB) 86, Bei Yuan Lu, Jiaming Yuan, Chaoyang District, Beijing 100101 (100101 北京市，朝阳区，北苑路 86 号，嘉铭园 5 号楼 6 单元 103 室); ☎ 010 8485 9667/9; ☏ 010 8485 9679; 🄴 office@gvbchina.org.cn; www.gvbchina.org. Founded in 1996 as one of the first NGOs in China, this is a non-profit organisation dedicated to environmental education and strengthening civil society. GVB's environmental campaigns focus on the promotion of sustainable development and a green lifestyle. It does this through the production of environmental TV programmes and other publications, the organisation of journalist trainings, the development of green communities, the organisation of public events and forums and several other projects in the field of sustainable development and consumption.

World Wide Fund For Nature (WWF) Room 1609, Wenhua Gong, Beijing Working People's Culture Palace (Laodong Renmin Wenhuagong Dongmen), Beijing 100006 (100006 北京市，劳动人民文化宫东门内文华宫，世界自然基金会北京办事处); ☎ 010 6522 7100; ☏ 010 6522 7300; 🄴 wwfchina@wwfchina.org; www.wwfchina.org. The WWF was the first international conservation organisation invited to work in China in 1980. WWF started work with Chinese scientists on giant panda conservation. Today, WWF China works on many more projects including restoring the Yangtze River wetlands and environmental education.

Part Two

The Wall

6

Liaoning and the border with North Korea 辽宁

It starts from the Yalu River, crossing Yan Mountain, Helan Mountain, and Qilin Mountain, snaking across the deserts and steppes, heading towards Jiayuguan Pass in northwestern China. This imposing Great Wall was built by the Ming dynasty.

Dong Yaohui, 2005

The Ming Great Wall in Liaoning is the most eroded of all the Ming wall. So little of it remains in Liaoning that debate raged for decades about whether this badly damaged mud section of the wall was part of earlier Qin and Han walls, or whether the Ming dynasty had in fact fortified it later on. The existence of a number of Ming dynasty articles found around the wall added to the confusion, but also finally tipped the scales in favour of the pro-Ming proponents. The Chinese Academy of Ancient Architecture finally confirmed in 1992 that the remains of the wall in Liaoning are indeed part of the Ming renovation of the Great Wall. Until that point, people had believed that the 'First Pass Under Heaven' at Shanhaiguan in Hebei province was the easternmost end of the Ming wall in China. The easternmost end of the Ming wall in China, therefore, is in fact near Dandong on the banks of the Yalu River that divides China and North Korea. The earlier Qin and Han walls went further than Dandong into what is now North Korea, but hardly any of these now remain.

Despite taking over 150 years to build the 1,000km of Great Wall in Liaoning province, the Ming paid relatively little attention to this section of their defences. In many ways this attitude ushered in the downfall of the Ming dynasty. The poor construction of the Ming wall in Liaoning, combined with the neglect to its further fortification and defence, made it easy for the Manchu tribes of the northeast to breach the wall, which they had already succeeded in doing by the beginning of the 17th century. When the Ming dynasty finally collapsed under the pressure of internal rebellion in 1644, the Manchus were quick to establish rule over the Middle Kingdom and became the ensuing Qing dynasty. The Qing made minimal attempts to maintain the Great Wall, either in Liaoning or elsewhere in China.

Since its confirmation as genuine Ming wall, the government has completely renovated three sections in Liaoning, at Hushan, Xingcheng and Jiumenkou. Hushan can be explored from Dandong town, while Jiumenkou, a mere 18km from Shanhaiguan, and Xingcheng are best explored from Shanhaiguan (see page 121).

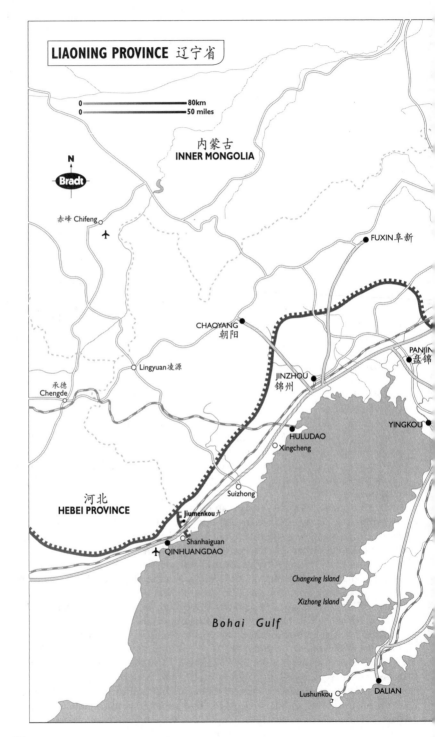

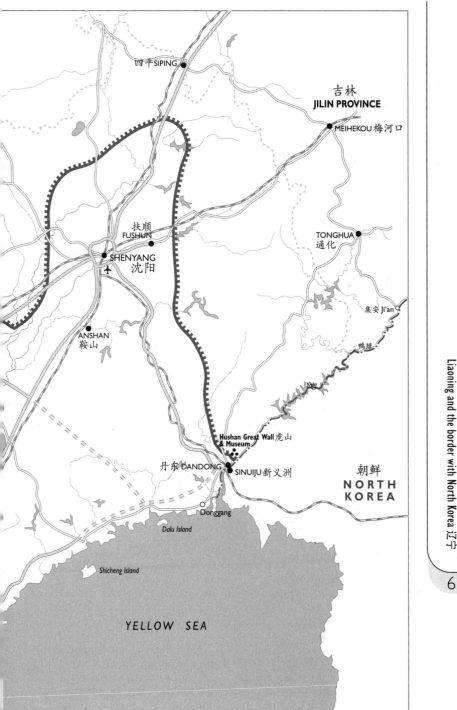

On 16 September 1952, US Air Force Captain Troy 'Gordie' Cope of Norfolk, Arkansas, and his wingman, both flying F-86 Saber Jets from Kimpo Air Base in South Korea, encountered six MiG-15s of the North Korean Air Force. Cope was flying near the Yalu River, separating North Korea from China, on combat air patrol in an area known as 'MiG Alley'. In the ensuing aerial dogfight, Cope lost contact with his wingman and was never seen again.

In 1995, an American businessman saw a metal dogtag belonging to Cope in the military museum in Dandong. He copied the data and reported it to US authorities, yet inquiries to both the Chinese and North Korean governments yielded no further leads.

Then, in 1999, during archival research by analysts of the Defense POW/Missing Personnel Office (DPMO), documents about Cope's shootdown were discovered in Russian archives in Podolsk. These archives held documents that included statements and drawings by the Russian pilots who were flying the MiG-15s for the North Koreans. Also included were detailed reports on the ground search carried out by Russian and Chinese officials in Dandong where the crash site was located.

After DPMO's discussions with the Chinese government in 2003, a team of specialists from the Joint POW/Missing In Action (MIA) Accounting Command excavated the site in May 2004 and found aircraft debris and human remains which were identified in October that year. Dandong citizens and officials assisted the team throughout the excavation. Cope's remains were buried with full military honours in Plano, Texas, on 31 May 31 2005.

Of the 88,000 Americans missing from all conflicts, 8,100 are MIA from the Korean War.

DANDONG 丹东

HISTORY Some form of settlement in the Dandong area goes back to Neolithic times and it has periodically been a frontier town on the northeast edge of China for over 2,000 years. From early times up until 1965, the town here was known as Andong, meaning 'peaceful east'. Reed walls were first built to the north of Andong at the very end of the Ming dynasty in 1618, when the Ming tried to limit local foraging excursions beyond the wall in order to keep peace with their northern neighbours. After the neighbours (the Manchu) overthrew all of the Middle Kingdom and set up the Qing dynasty, they encouraged trading through the wall.

The railway came to Andong in 1909, linking the rest of northern China to Korea. The town started to grow quickly after that, especially from 1931 to 1945 when Andong was under Japanese annexation. Its role as a portal for Chinese troops into North Korea during the Korean war against America from 1950 to 1953 swelled the numbers and significance of the town even further. The Americans bombed the rail crossing across the Yalu River into North Korea in 1950, but this did not stop the Chinese from pouring across the river to the aid of their Korean comrades.

Today, Dandong is a pleasant little city of 2.3 million people, surrounded by hills and the Yalu River. Its climate is less harsh than a lot of places in the heart of China, and so it benefits from richer plantlife and abundant sealife. Most visitors, from South Korea and Japan as well as the rest of China, come to stare at North Korea over the Yalu River. The result is an upbeat atmosphere that is used to tourists.

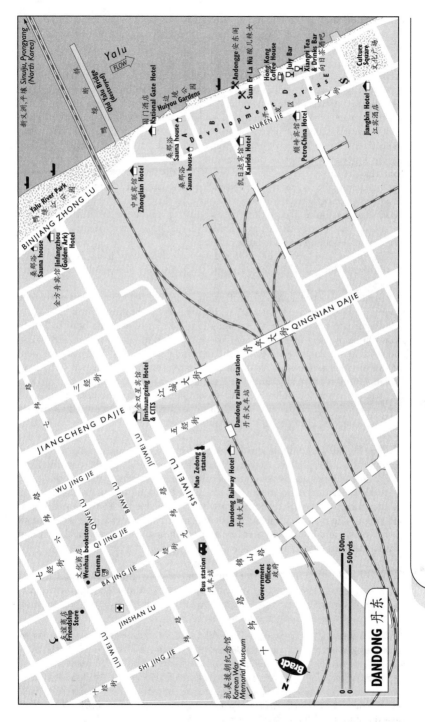

Yalu
FLOW

新义洲,平壤 Sinŭiju, Pyongyang
(North Korea)

鸭绿桥

Old Yalu Bridge
(destroyed)

Andonge 安东阁

Suan Er La Nü 蒜儿辣女

Hong Kong
Coffee House

July Bar

Xiangri Tea
& Drinks Bar 向日茶酒吧

国门酒店
National Gate Hotel

惠园公园
Huiyou Gardens

桑那浴
Sauna house
A

桑那浴
Sauna house
B

D e v e l o p m e n t   a r e a s

NUREN JIE 女人街

Culture
Square
文化广场

Jiangbin Hotel
江滨酒店

凯日达宾馆
Kairida Hotel

顺峰宾馆
PetroChina Hotel

桑那浴
Sauna house

Yalu River Park
鸭绿江公园

BINJIANG ZHONG LU 滨江中路

桑那浴
Sauna house

金方分身馆 Jinfangzhou
(Golden Ark)
Hotel

中联宾馆
Zhongjian Hotel

JIANGCHENG DAJIE

路 三 经 府

路 七 经 府

金叉星宾馆
Jinshuangxing Hotel
& CITS

江城大街

QINGNIAN DAJIE 青年大街

WU JING JIE 五经街

JIUWEI LU 九纬路

路 五 经 府

Mao Zedong
statue

Dandong railway station
丹东火车站

Dandong Railway Hotel
丹铁大厦

QI JING JIE 七经街

路 六 经 府

BA JING JIE 八经街

QIWEI LU 七纬路

BAWEI LU 八纬路

SHIWEI LU 十纬路

路 九 经 府

文化商店
Wenhua bookstore

Cinema

Bus station
汽车站

友谊商店
Friendship
Store

JINSHAN LU

LIU WEI LU 六纬路

SHI JING JIE 十经街

路 山 锦
JINSHAN LU

Government
Offices 政府

十 经 纬 路

抗美援朝纪念馆
Korean War
Memorial Museum

N
Bradt

DANDONG 丹东

500m
500yds

0

Competition amongst hotels and restaurants has brought prices down and quality up, which all in all makes for a nice change if you have spent a bit of time in some of China's less service-minded areas.

GETTING THERE AND AWAY Out of the tourist season the only way to get to Dandong is by train or bus. Soft sleeper berths on **trains** from Beijing (15 hours, ¥383) are often booked up with Korean travellers, so book ahead if you want a sleeper. There is a train twice a day from Beijing to Dandong, leaving Beijing around 03.15 and 17.30 and arriving in Dandong at around 18.15 and 08.30 (the following day) respectively. If you are travelling by train from Shanhaiguan or Xingcheng, then getting a sleeper will not be possible until after you have boarded the train, and your chances of getting one are slim because of the high bookings of berths from Beijing. Taking the day train (07.50 from Shanhaiguan, 09.10 from Xingcheng) can be a pleasant experience if you can get yourself a sleeper once you get on the train (hard sleeper is quite likely), otherwise you will probably be stuck without a seat the whole way. Hard seat carriages are frequently packed with the usual migrant workers travelling up and down the country.

Day **buses** and overnight double-decker sleeper-buses from Beijing (from Dongzhimen long-distance bus station, see page 146) and Qinhuangdao leave every evening.

Flights occur once a week from Beijing, Shanghai and Guangdong during the summer season, but check with CAAC for the latest flight information.

An alternative way to get to Dandong is to take an **overnight boat** to Dalian from Qinhuangdao (10–12 hours, ¥130–400) or Tianjin (13–15 hours, ¥180–720), and from Dalian take a train or bus the remainder of the way. There are frequent buses from Dalian (6 hours, ¥60). An 11-hour overnight train leaves at 19.30 from Dalian. You don't save any time, but it is more comfortable than the bus and you are guaranteed a berth, unlike the train from Qinhuangdao or Shanhaiguan.

Most hotels will help you with onward booking, but the staff at CITS next to the Jinshuangxing Hotel seem to speak more English.

GETTING AROUND Dandong is small enough that you can walk most places in the centre of town. Flag fall for a taxi is ¥6, which will get you anywhere within 3km. The train and bus stations are conveniently right in the centre and less than 1km from the riverfront. As in most Chinese cities, Dandong has an excellent tourist and travel map of the town and region which is available for ¥5 from most hotels and shops. The map even includes a town plan of Pyongyang as well as a country map of North and South Korea. It is mostly in Chinese, but every year the amount of English increases.

WHERE TO STAY In an effort to boost tourism in Dandong, prices have come down a lot, so you usually get very good value for money here compared with other places in China. As tourism develops further, hotel touts will try to tempt you fresh off the train to rooms in cheaper accommodation.

🏠 **Dantie Dasha** 丹铁大厦 (98 rooms) ✆ 0415 2131 031. You can't get any closer to the railway station than this, and considering the wide open square in front of the railway with its larger-than-life statue of Mao, the views are not bad. Trains run between 05.48 and 21.52 only, so sleep is possible. *Standard twin en suite ¥150. Dorm beds ¥30.*

🏠 **Jiangbin Jiudian** 江滨酒店 (100 rooms) Bldg 5 Fangba (*Nu Ren Jie* Ladies Street); ✆ 0415 3153 748; 📠 0415 3142 835. A nice three-star hotel next to Culture Square, with a good restaurant, café, mahjong rooms and business centre. Free internet in most rooms. All rooms en suite. Buffet breakfast included. Top-floor rooms have a partial view of the river. *Standard riverside twin or dbl ¥396. Riverside deluxe ¥566.*

⌂ **Jinfangzhou Binguan** 金方舟宾馆 (142 rooms) 2 Shiwei Lu; ☏ 0415 2162 009. With an excellent location near the Old Yalu Bridge, this hotel is good value for money for the budget traveller. Breakfast included. *Standard riverside twin en suite ¥280. Dorm bed ¥50.*

⌂ **Jinshuangxing Binguan** 金双星宾馆 (56 rooms) 20–2 Shiwei Lu, Zhenxing District; ☏ 0415 2307 888; 🖷 0415 2308 215. Very clean, nicely refurbished hotel, close to the station. All rooms en suite. *Business-standard rooms come with computer and internet ¥398. Standard twins are often without windows ¥296. sgl ¥260.*

⌂ **Kairida Binguan** 凯达宾馆 (31 rooms) Bldg 1 Fangba (*Nu Ren Jie Ladies Street*); ☏ 0415 3459 995; 🖷 0415 3458 999. A small high-quality and more personal hotel than many of the others in town. Top-floor riverside rooms have free internet and a partial view of the river and North Korea over the tops of other buildings. Close to riverside bars and restaurants. All rooms en suite with big showers. Includes breakfast. *Sgl or standard twin ¥298. Riverside twin or dbl ¥398. Rooms by the hour ¥100.*

⌂ **Guomen Jiudian** 国门酒店 (117 rooms) No 1, Huiyou Gardens, Business and Tourism District (*Shangmao Luyou Qu*); ☏ 0415 3157 788; 🖷 0415 3157 228. Chinese standard three star with good rooms directly overlooking the river. Business centre. Restaurants. All rooms en suite. *Standard twins and dbls ¥398. Riverside standard room ¥528.*

⌂ **Shunfeng Binguan** 顺峰宾馆 (41 rooms) East Unit, Bldg 5 Fangba (*Nu Ren Jie Ladies Street*); ☏ 0415 2305 888; 🖷 0415 3143 338. Dbl A standard hotel. Dark rooms which are in need of an overhaul. Often full owing to its good price for a location downtown. Breakfast included. *Dbl en suite ¥240. Trpl ¥100. Sgl bed in a trpl room ¥40.*

⌂ **Zhonglian Dajiudian** 中联大酒店 (161 rooms) No 1, Business and Tourism District (*Shangmao Luyou Qu*); ☏ 0415 3170 666; 🖷 0415 3170 888; www.zlhotel.com.cn. The only four star in town and well worth the money. Right on the riverfront. Views of the Yalu River and North Korea are unrivalled. Ethernet cable to internet in each room. One buffet breakfast included per room per day. Excellent restaurant downstairs, especially for seafood, although a bit pricey. Free sauna, other services and facilities are charged. Room prices given here are for riverside, expect 15% discount for the town side of the hotel. A service charge of 15% is added to all bills. Takes credit cards. *Sgl ¥400, standard twin ¥605.*

✖ **WHERE TO EAT AND DRINK** Cheap and good places to eat here are in abundance, especially if you are a seafood lover. Dog is also on the menu of a lot of the Korean-style places. The riverfront is the place to eat, but cheaper places are many along the Shiwei Lu. There are also a lot of good restaurants along Qi Jing Jie.

✖ **Andongge** 安东阁 The only restaurant directly over the river. Serves a variety of good standard Chinese and Korean dishes. The coffee bar around the corner from the restaurant is also a mellow place to settle back and watch the world go by.

✖ **Suan Er La Nu** 酸儿辣女 (literally Sour Boy Spicy Girl) Yanjiang Kaifa Qu, on the riverfront; ☏ 0415 3127 558. An excellent hotpot place in a new Sino-Korean/Japanese style. Their speciality is hot and sour fish soup (suān tāng yú 酸汤鱼) and river flower dog meat (huājiāng gǒuròu 花江狗肉). Both are very good. No menu in English at the time of writing (see page 264 for restaurant help). If you take the hot and sour fish soup, you'll be asked which fish. Hēiyú 黑鱼 (black fish) is good or just choose one from the tanks at the far end of the room. ¥100 will see you waddling out of the door after a hotpot and a beer or two. Ask for a discount (dǎzhé 打折) when paying the bill and you might just get 10% off.

✖ **July Bar** No 101, Yanjiang Kaifa Qu. Stylish little coffee house and bar, playing a mix of Sino-Korean flavours.

✖ **Hong Kong Coffee House** Yanjiang Kaifa Qu. Opens for breakfast and serves strong coffee and snacks throughout the day.

✖ **Xiangri Cha Jiu Ba** 向日茶酒吧 (Xiangri Tea and Drinks Bar) Yanjiang Kaifa Qu. Modern décor; serving tea and alcohol. Set back slightly from the main street.

WHAT TO SEE AND DO The main attraction for most visitors to Dandong is to stare at **North Korea** (Cháo Xiǎn 朝鲜) over the river. But it is also a pleasant enough town in itself with a long riverside walking area and a bit of nightlife owing to the high number of visitors. The town has a distinctly Korean bias to it because of the high number of South Korean visitors that come to see 'the other side', as the large buffer zone along Parallel 38 between North and South Korea prevents them from doing this for themselves from the south.

6

The **Old Yalu Bridge** just north of the port was built in 1909 as a rail and road connection with (then one-country) Korea. US fighter planes bombed it in 1950 after China came to the defence of North Korea in the Korean War, and now only the Chinese side of the bridge remains after the North Koreans dismantled their half (the stone supports still stand in the water like giant stepping stones). A series of photo display boards along the length of the bridge presents its history and construction. Sadly, however, the captions are only in Chinese. The construction of the bridge was advanced for its time, using a rotating dais in the centre of the bridge to transfer loads. You can still see this today although of course it no longer works. Now, the end of the bridge has been made into a viewing platform where you can pay ¥1 to use a telescope to peer into the obscurity of Sinuiju town on the other side of the river. A small café serves snacks at the land end of the bridge. As at 2005, the new rail and road bridge on the north side of the Old Yalu Bridge can be entered only if you are part of one of the tours to North Korea (see below). Entry to the Old Yalu Bridge is ¥15.

Boat trips along the Yalu take you for a short 20-minute trip into Korean waters and to within metres of North Korean land. If you like boat cruises, it is interesting to see the two different sides of the river, but you won't see much worse on the North Korean side than you can still see in a lot of the poor parts of China. Lots of boats leave from the riverfront so you can pick and choose from standard large boats (¥8 per person, boat leaves when full), to smaller Chinese-looking boats (¥20 per person) and small speedboats (¥25 per person).

The **Yalu River Park** is an excellent alternative to the boat trips if you don't fancy the water version of seeing the area. The park stretches for over a kilometre but the riverside path stretches for several more. Luxury apartments are quickly going up along the riverfront, making the path very pleasant and quite the juxtaposition to the other side of the river. The park itself, like so many parks in China, is a great place to see old people relaxing, playing cards, chess or mahjong or dancing, singing or playing instruments (or all three together). There is a couple of pagodas and the usual decidedly false stone garden. Free entry.

Sauna is *the* big thing for the Koreans, so, strangely enough, there are a lot of sauna houses here. They are generally much more fun if you are a big group – the Koreans usually visit in large business groups – and hetero couples should not expect to see each other much unless they order a tub to themselves. Korean-style sauna houses require you to take your shoes off as soon as you enter the door, don a pair of sandals, slip into a bathrobe, and thereafter you have the run of the place. Restaurants, games rooms, TV and DVD rooms all await the customer. Many also have bedrooms upstairs if you want to stay longer. The restaurant of the sauna house at Block A8 of the business district has a river view. Most of the others are darkened affairs, great for the winter. Other sauna houses are on Binjiang Zhong Lu and Nuren Jie (see map).

The **Korean War Memorial Museum** lies in the southwest of Dandong. It is marginally interesting for its continued depiction of America as the aggressor in the Korean War, but you can probably imagine that without having to go there. There are no captions in English (and there probably won't be in the future considering the subject matter). Although it was North Korea who actually started the war by invading the south, the American retaliation through North Korea to the border with China was hardly going to be taken lying down by the Chinese. The Chinese were keen to ensure that North Korea stayed as a buffer zone between them and the murdering capitalists and so a counter move was in order.

Trips to **North Korea** can be booked through CITS, next to the Jinshuangxing Hotel. Tours start at ¥9,000 for a one-week, extremely chaperoned trip to Pyongyang and other worthy sites. Mixing with the locals is not an option. Your journey will start over the New Yalu Bridge. There are negotiations ongoing to make Sinuiju into a free economic zone that will be open to foreigners without visas. This seems to be some way in the offing, and visiting a free economic zone here is unlikely to have the feel of the real thing.

BEYOND DANDONG

Robert Willoughby

NORTH OF DANDONG Lying 52km northwest of Dandong, just outside Fengcheng, is the stunning Phoenix Mountain (Fènghuángshān 凤凰山) set in its own small reserve *(open May to October 08.00–17.00, admission ¥30)*. Daoist worshippers come here to pray for relief from their illnesses, for the God of Longevity occupies the mountain's west ridge. Every 28 April a 'Medicine King Meeting' is held at one of the temples, but, in company with former T'ang and Yuan emperors who pocked the mountain with their own tributes of temples and pagodas, the mountain's scenery and serenity are worth taking in anyway. Now a premier bolted and railed rock-climbing route, Phoenix Mountain now also boasts a cable car for the weary (¥25 ascent, ¥15 descent). Guides to the area charge ¥100. From Dandong take the slow trains from Dandong (1 hour) or bus (90 minutes) for ¥10.

Within Dandong's boundaries is the Baishilazi Natural Protection Area, a large reserve committed to protecting China's deciduous broadleaf forests; it is both a natural botanic garden and a zoo. Also of note are the Dagu Mountain with groups of ancient temple structures, the Qingshan gully with natural waterfalls, and Dagshan granite outcropping, with beautiful temples in the vicinity.

SOUTH FROM DANDONG For more border-related points, go south of Dandong, following the Yalu to the coast, to Donggo town on the Chinese side. There's not much beyond a container park and a permanent yurt, but here the River Yalu splits around little islands, property of the Democratic People's Republic of Korea (DPRK). A few kilometres further west along the coast is Dalu Island, a 'pearl on the Yellow Sea', and a splendid natural retreat of caves as well as the Camel Peak. It also offers the chance to splash lazily in Moon Bay. It has a bizarre collection of buildings, from T'ang temples to a Danish church and a British lighthouse. There's also the tomb of Deng Shichang, a Chinese captain killed in 1894 as the Japanese fleet sunk the Chinese fleet en route to 'rescuing' Korea from the Tonghak. Ferries run to Dalu (¥86–92).

EAST TO SOUTH KOREA The Republic of Korea (ROK) is also accessible from Dandong on the *Oriental Pearl* ferry from Dandong overnight to Incheon, the major port next to Seoul (☎ 0415 315 2666; f 0415 315 6131). The ferry leaves Dandong at 16.00 on Tuesday, Thursday and Sunday each week and arrives in Incheon the next morning at 09.00. First-class, two-berth cabin: ¥2,590 per person; second-class, four-berth cabin: ¥1,960 per person.

WEST FROM DANDONG West along the northern bank of the Yalu River from Dandong is the town of Changdianhekou, unremarkable except for its own rail terminus, but 3km north of here is the Taipingwan hydro-electric dam. Halfway across the dam is a rusted, padlocked metal gate, another border with the DPRK, and noticeable along the DPRK bank are regular sentry points. It's possible to get a speedboat up and down.

In the regions running northeast from Dandong along the Yalu, the Korean influence becomes more and more marked. In Jilin and Heilongjiang provinces live 1.8 million ethnic Koreans, 800,000 of whom live in the Yanbian Autonomous Prefecture, a triangular enclave forming the last section of China's border with the DPRK.

From the southeast of Liaoning province all the way to Changbaishan are entire Korean villages, visible in the shop signs, bilingual road signs, Korean forms of dress, the density of Korean Protestant churches and the highly conscious bi-lingualism of the locals. Korean communities grow in rural and urban concentration the closer to Korea you are. (Unfortunately, Korea's division manifests itself in the peninsula's diasporas abroad, and in Beijing the distinction between the ROK and DPRK communities is clearly defined.)

History of the border area with Korea
Tides of migration have ebbed and flowed from China into Korea and back for millennia. Some tribes or groups were nomadic, touring the lands before arbitrary borders were defined in search of new lands of plenty when previous habitats were lacking, natural disasters destroyed their crops or ill-treatment posed some kind of threat. They then either resumed their livelihoods elsewhere or formed military forces to resist and possibly oust their homeland rulers. Sometimes, people were given in tribute from one state to another, or were stolen by foreign raiding parties.

The area came under Koguryo control from the late 400s as Koguryo united the Puyo people and ruled all the way up to the Amur River for two-and-a-half centuries. When Koguryo divided into separate states from 668, the northernmost state was that of Palhae. A former Koguryo general formed with the Malgal tribe an army that led a mass migration into Manchuria, settling around today's Jilin. A new state was established, named Palhae in 713, that soon expanded to take over the northern remnants of Koguryo, combining them with the Manchurian gains. The state reached its pinnacle in the first half of the 9th century under King Seon, when Palhae stretched from the Yellow Sea to the Sea of Japan, and from Chongjin in today's Korea up to Yanji, with its capital in today's Chongchun. However, the state was only as stable as its neighbours allowed it to be, and Palhae wasn't exempt from the warring that brought down the Tang dynasty, succumbing to the Khitan in 926. Those of the ruling classes that could escape to their more common kin in the new Koryo state did so. The Koreans joined with the Malgal people and assimilated into Manchurian life, eventually helping found the Jurchen.

Later Koreans were just taken. In 1254, the Mongols returned from Koryo with a booty of 26,000 Koreans. Many returned over the years, and many migrated back, so in 1464, 30,000 Koreans were recorded as living in Liaodong. The 1627 and 1637 Manchu raids on Korea enslaved tens of thousands. Some Korean families somehow earned freemen status and attained minor noble status under the Manchus, but these were the exception.

From 1677, an area one thousand *li* north of Changbaishan was declared off limits by the Qing dynasty that also established a buffer zone just north of the Yalu and Tuman rivers. Any interlopers were thrown back south of the rivers to the Ri, who built a half-dozen garrisons to prevent any concerted northern invasion.

Nonetheless, people continued to migrate across the rivers in fair seasons, dressing down and cutting their topknots to appear more Chinese as they escaped

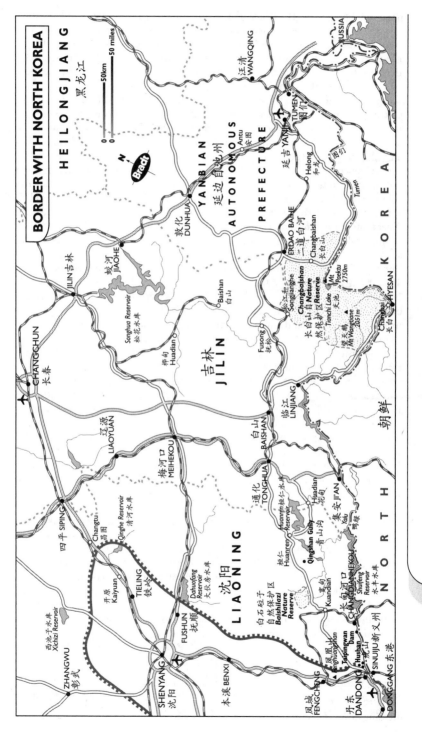

BORDER WITH NORTH KOREA

the harsh life of northern Korea. For two centuries this continued until a string of natural disasters in northern Korea caused a sudden upsurge in migration away from famine. From 1865 the Qing officially allowed Koreans to live and farm in Manchuria and later Dunwha, where Korean farmers pioneered and prospered on the land. Immigration to Manchuria eased as trade with Ri was established, and by 1894 there were 20,000 in Yanbian alone.

It's from those decades of migration that the current Korean population's cultural origins are thought to source. Earlier waves and pockets of Koreans saw their own way of life drowned in the sea of Han Chinese culture. The circumstances of their arrival, often destitute and starving, prevented them reaching any position of wealth and influence to defend their culture. As well as happenstance and convenience, their new rulers demanded the migrants' assimilation, to turn them from obstructive aliens to trusty clanspeople. The Yuan rulers established a governor-general office to rule the Koryo people, as did the Ming. Migrants arriving in early Qing Manchuria were dispersed far and wide. Toleration of Koreans didn't come until the late Qing.

Imperial Japan's attempts to smother Korea's culture were partly what led to a staggering rise in Korean migration in the 20th century. That, and the impoverishment of Korea's peasants, saw migrants into Manchuria surpass 450,000 in number in 1920 to reach 2.1 million by 1945. Many had fled the Japanese but many more were sent there. As Japan's great but subservient brethren, Koreans populating Manchuria secured the territory for their Japanese masters. Only the landscape and sheer numbers allowed for great resistance. Many of the disparate political and military movements that were collectively the Korean National Liberation Movement were based in Manchuria throughout Japan's rule, aiding and abetting Chinese resistance against the Japanese; and thousands of Koreans volunteered for the communist forces in China's civil war of 1946–49, engaging in fighting and liberating cities like Changchun and Jilin.

This assistance to the communist victory was in return for Chinese help in Korea's own struggle against the Japanese and later in the Korean War. Long-term training and support, ideological and material, was also provided by the Soviet Union at this time, where Kim Il Sung refined his leadership skills. The extreme conditions of guerrilla warfare in this part of the world imbued toughness in its veterans that would serve them well.

What to see The roads pass a landscape of forested hills, gulleys and peaks. From Dandong to Tonghua on route 201 is Huanren town, where there's an odd little theme park. From there you can take a powerboat onto the adjacent lake that stretches over the Liaoning–Jilin border to an artist's colony where Chinese artists go and commune with nature, living in a tiny valley in which sit little Gothic-style timber houses. Visitors are welcome to stop off to visit, see their works and hang around for a bizarre but relaxing sojourn.

Further along the way is Huadian, a town on a river where you're almost compelled to stop and try the local fish restaurants.

TONGHUA 41.3° N, 126° E; 40km from DPRK border, Jilin province

This sprawling provincial town hangs onto the lower slopes of the Longgang mountain range, with parts over 1,500m altitude. It doesn't serve any great treats for the visitor and is mainly useful for its proximity to Ji'an.

Where to stay

🏠 **Tonghua Hotel** 同化宾馆 (98 rooms), 22 Cuiquan Rd, Tonghua, Jilin 134001; ✆ 0435 321 2812; 🖷 0435 321 3367. A three-star hotel near the centre of town.

Getting there and away It's an hour's taxi drive from Tonghua to Ji'an. There is an overnight train to Tonghua from Beijing (19 hours, ¥82), then transfer to the Ji'an bus at the long-distance bus station (2 hours, ¥15).

JI'AN *41.10° N, 126.05° E; DPRK border, Jilin province*

This is a small, bilingual city of 100,000, stashed in the mountains flanking the Yalu, but is rich in its ancient history and its tourist industry thrives on ROK tourists coming to what was the capital of the Koguryo Empire. It was established by the Qin 221BC, and noted sights include the Tianxiang Memorial, the Bailuzhou Institute or the Xiyang Palace. Ten thousand ancient tombs and other historical sites including the General's Tomb are around the city, although many are barred to non-Chinese or Koreans. But it doesn't seem that the tourists spend a lot here: the city still has a slightly rundown appearance that fits its remote setting. From Ji'an station a train runs to the DPRK, for which there is fat chance you can get on, but following the tracks to Ji'an Bridge is one viewing point for those coming in and out of the DPRK. Border guards and railway workers may be amenable to fees allowing you to get very close to the dividing line on the bridge that trains steam over daily. The risk's up to you.

Where to stay

🏠 **Ji'an Hotel** 98 Yingbin Lu; ✆ 0435 620 1598. Serviceable rooms for around ¥240.

CHANGBAISHAN NATURE RESERVE *42° N, 128° E; DPRK border, southeast of Jilin province*

This is China's largest nature reserve at over 200,000 ha of virgin forest, a 78 x 53km area across three counties, and has recently become a UNESCO World Biosphere Protection Zone. It is home to the rare Manchurian tiger, sikas, sables, snow leopards and wild ginseng, and as the ground rises up from 500m above sea level to over 2,000m, the forests turn from broadleaf deciduous through pine, spruce, stunted fir and then tundra.

The transformation of the landscape forms the backdrop as you plough skywards, towards the heart of the reserve where sits Changbaishan, meaning 'eternally white mountain', practically the same as the Koreans' Mount Paektu, or 'white-topped mountain'. This crown of volcanic rock surrounds a piercingly clear, round lake in its caldera, the Tian Chi Lake (meaning 'heavenly lake').

The final road to Changbaishan is little more than a dirt track. The tourist buses take around three hours to heave towards Changbaishan through a flat wilderness of clearings between forests of birch, towering Korean pine, Scots pine and Japanese yew, while lorries laden with logs come the other way. When you arrive at the base of Changbaishan itself, evidenced by a car park full of tourists, hawkers, little shops and stalls of T-shirts, medicinal antlers and ginseng, there's a small hotel good for seeing the area in the evening.

From the car park are a few routes up the mountain. For ¥150 a jeep can take you up a series of hairpin bends to the volcano's summit (high above the lake) where the view's terrific if not blocked by fog. To go by foot, the western path is scenic but dangerous enough to entail another charge of 'insurance' and you're given a hard hat to walk up steps sheltered with metal sheet. Fifteen minutes' walk up these stairs is a beautiful waterfall pouring from the lake, cited as the beginning of the Yalu River, and then comes Tian Chi Lake itself. High winds may be blowing between the sharp peaks stabbing the sky round Tian Chi, but the lake itself will be mirror-flat. Many Koreans wade into the scarcely thawed water and sing songs, while the Chinese take pictures. There are also a hundred-odd little towers of piled stones, impromptu pagodas that tourists build.

Although the lake's half Chinese, half DPRK, there's no sign of the border at all in the crater, and it's not obvious outside of it either – no great electric fences or 'LANDMINE' placards about. Once you're free of the crater, it's a landscape (or moonscape) of Scottish moorlands well scored with paths, but be very careful where you stray. One Bristol chap wandered off and came across a hut where he went to ask directions to the nearest Chinese village. The DPRK borderguards inside took him to the nearest DPRK village, where he wasn't badly treated for the two months of haggling the authorities took to get him out.

On Changbaishan's north side is a group of hot springs, identifiable from the hot, steamy air that wafts from them all year. The waters are supposed to be of great medicinal benefit, and some pools can be entered but be careful as they're mostly over 60°C, with an extreme measured at 82°C.

Getting there and away One way to get to Tian Chi is to book a three-day tour through the CITS in Jilin (*1 Chongqing Rd, 132001 Jilin; ✆ 0432 244 3442 or 1304; f 0432 245 6786*), for all transport, accommodation up to and around the lake. There are also ROK specialist firms in Beijing that run tours (they're the organisers of the Korean tour buses you'll see all over the site). Non-Koreans are unusual but most welcome. Contact Beijing Xinhua International Tours Co, Jia 23, Fuxinglu, Beijing China; ✆ 010 6829 6533.

By bus The nearest village to Tian Chi is Erdaobaihe 二道白河. Jilin to Baihe takes seven hours and costs ¥80. Yanji to Baihe takes four hours and costs ¥45. There's also a direct bus from Yanji that takes five hours (¥55). Dunhua to Baihe takes four hours (¥25); there are six buses a day from 0600 to 1200.

Buses from Baihe to Tian Chi leave opposite Baihe railway station from 06.00 until 12.00. The last bus from Tian Chi to Baihe leaves at 16.00.

By train One train leaves Tonghua at 08.45 arriving in Baihe at 17.15; another overnighter leaves Tonghua at 21.05, and arrives at Baihe at 04.36.

By car From Tonghua and Yanji it's possible to hire drivers who will take you to Changbaishan in one-day missions (from ¥400) but from any further places you would have to account for their accommodation.

Where to stay and eat

⌂ Jilin Hotsprings 吉林长白山岳桦温泉 just below the ticket booth; ✆ 0422 574 6069 or 138 044 8956. Entry to the hot springs included in the room price: ¥80.

⌂ Feihu Shanzhuang 飞狐山庄 also near the ticket booth; ✆ 0422 571 8740. Dorm beds ¥50, standard twin or dbl ¥240.

YANBIAN AUTONOMOUS PREFECTURE *Northeast part of the China DPRK border, Jilin province*
Changbaishan sits just on the southernmost corner of Yanbian Autonomous Prefecture (Yonbyon to Koreans). This triangular area on the DPRK's border is home to over half of China's Koreans, who make up half the population, as they have for a century. This population density has meant that Yanbian's Koreans have

been able to defend their ethnicity as a coherent community by being more powerful politically and economically, hence China's communist government recognises the Koreans as a distinct nationality, ethnically separate from the dominant Han Chinese. From 1949, Han Chinese began to repopulate the area, in the cities of Tonghua, Wangqing and Yanji. The Korean nationality is the 12th-largest of China's 56 minorities, although it makes up under 0.2% of the total population. In Yanbian, Chinese and Korean languages are used at varying levels in local government and are taught in schools.

History For centuries before the late 1800s, Yanbian was off limits, kept by the Ming and Qing as an exclusive reserve of primeval forests and virgin land used as royal hunting grounds. The region was only officially to come under cultivation from the 1880s, although many migrants, including Koreans, had surreptitiously begun to till the land before this. It was the Koreans who became most noted for their skills in turning huge tracts of apparently useless land over to wet-field agricultural use. Their reputation for changing this wild frontier into usable paddyfields was something on which the Japanese wished to capitalise when they forcibly populated Manchaca with Koreans, Complicit in Japanese suppression of Korean culture from 1910 onwards were the Chinese warlords who filled the post-Qing power vacuum at the time – although even the Qing hadn't been overtly tolerant of Korean culture.

In that decade Yanbian became a centre of anti-Japanese resistance, and 20 towns recorded disturbances during the 1919 March 1 Movement, formulating the first coherent civilian response to Japan's occupation of Korea. In 1920 major battles were fought between the Japanese and forces of the Korean Provisional government (based in Shanghai). A Korean division wiped out a smaller Japanese force in June, and lost 1,000 troops in heavy fighting around Chung-san-ri (northwest of Changbaishan) in October 1920. Japanese forces retaliated by burning 2,500 homes and schools and killed or imprisoned over 10,000 Koreans in the Yanbian area. Thousands of skirmishes occurred in the 1920s, and small groups later formed into Anti-Japanese Guerrillas or Worker-Peasant Righteous Armies, accruing 12,000 Korean troops in Yanbian by 1932. The Northeast Anti-Japanese United Army (NEAJUA) soon formed, the main resistance force among a myriad of other units that sprung up across Manchuria and the Sino–Soviet border. Many stayed on after 1945 to fight Chiang-Kai Shek's forces, and by 1949 14,000 Koreans had died fighting for the Chinese communists. The People's Republic of China established the Yanbian Autonomous Prefecture in September 1952, which remained a backwater for decades as Koreans and Chinese settled into reconstructing their agrarian lives.

Since the early 1990s, two groups of Koreans have been migrating back to the region. One group is ROK Korean business investors (and lately, tourists) keen to plough hundreds of millions into the area as a centre of Korean industry and commerce in China's industrial northeast and on Russia's border. ROK business has grown since China recognised the ROK in 1992, and the average wage in Yanbian is twice the Chinese national average.

The second group is another migration of refugees from the DPRK following the 1990s agricultural collapse. Hundreds of thousands are estimated to be hiding in China, mostly among the Korean communities that can absorb them and give them shelter and waged work. Whether eking out a living with other Koreans or en route southwards, these illegal immigrants are forcibly repatriated to the DPRK by the Chinese security services, where their fate can be prison or sometimes worse.

A steady rise in refugees storming Beijing's embassies since 2000 raised tensions between the two Koreas and caused great political embarrassment for the Chinese government, particularly as the incidents surged in the run-up to the 2002 World Cup in the ROK. The Chinese are taking the DPRK side (it would be difficult for them not to) and there have been incidents of Chinese troops 'invading' embassies with some violence to retrieve refugees. The barbed wire that now bedecks Beijing's diplomatic quarter is one very visible result of this hard-line policy.

For more information on the plight of refugees and what they are escaping, search for North Korea under the United Nations High Commission for Refugees (*www.unhcr.org*), Amnesty International (*www.amnesty.org*) or the Human Rights Watch (*www.hrw.org*).

YANJI 42.5° N, 129.25° E; Jilin province

The capital of Yanbian is Yanji, a small city of 350,000 people of whom 60% are ethnic Koreans, as seen in the bilingual street signs. The Chinese minority speak less Korean, but Koreans typically speak both languages. Investment from ROK businesses into industry and tourism has been pouring into the city, and it is a prosperous-looking place, with wide roads, lots of glass and steel and shopping malls. There are over 500 Chinese–foreign joint ventures in Yanji. It's easy to get whole-body massages and facials that go on for hours for only ¥60, and Yanji is full of dog restaurants.

In very early September is the Korean folk festival, that exhibits folk arts in painting, dress and food, but also folk customs in song and dance, with competitions such as wrestling, see-sawing and swinging that date back centuries in Korea. But this all takes place at the end of the season when Changbaishan is easily accessible, so time it well. The Tuman River International Art Festival of Yanbian Prefecture is another festival that you should ask CITS about.

Getting there and away No special permits are needed for the Yanbian Prefecture. Yanji is the nearest big Chinese city to Changbaishan. Flights from Beijing to Yanji cost around ¥3,200 return, and from Yanji one-day tours (¥180) to Changbaishan run, the mini-bus leaving at 05.00 to make the five-hour drive and hammering it back by evening. To Yanji daily trains (25 hours, ¥90–620) and flights (2 hours) operate from Beijing.

Tour operators
CITS 4 Yanxi St, Yanji, Jilin 133002; *℡* 0433 271 5018; *f* 0433 271 7906

Where to stay
⌂ **Baishan Hotel Yanbian** 白山宾馆 (389 rooms) 2 Youyi Rd, *℡* 0433 252 666; *f* 0433 251 9493. A four-star hotel, 1km from the railway and 3km from the airport. All rooms are en suite, with TV and AC. Five restaurants serve a variety of food including Sichuanese and Western food. *Standard twin ¥490.*

⌂ **Yanbian Guest House** 3 Yanji Rd, *℡* 0433 512733

⌂ **Postal Hotel** (3*) 68 Juzi Jie, Yanji; *℡* 0433 2910888

⌂ **Xinqiao Hotel** 96 Guangming Lu, Yanji; *℡* 0433 251 7452

⌂ **Xiangyu Hotel** 相遇宾馆 (156 rooms) 62 Gongyuan Rd. A three-star hotel with en suite bath to each room, TV and AC. *Standard twin ¥320.*

Where to eat
There are a lot of dog-meat restaurants – follow the howling (no, really) – or Korean cold noodles are found at Jindalai, 42 Hailan Lu (*℡* 0433 251 3624).

TIGER MOUNTAIN (Hǔshān 虎山) The easternmost section of the Ming Great Wall is at Hushan, Tiger Mountain in English, in the Manchu autonomous county of Kuandian. Hushan Peak is 147m above sea level and commands a view of the Yalu River and border with North Korea in the southeast and the Yuan River in the west. The Chinese, who are quick to see animal shapes in almost anything, have named the mountain Tiger Mountain because of the tiger-like shape that the Great Wall here creates on the mountainside. (There are many Tiger Mountains in China, so make sure you stipulate that this one is in Liaoning province when talking about it.) Almost 1,200m of the wall at Hushan has been completely reconstructed, including three beacon towers and 12 defence platforms.

The Ming built this wall on top of the previous Han and Qin walls, both of which had extended further into what is now North Korea. You can see a photo of this wall as it was prior to reconstruction in 2000 in the Dandong Great Wall Museum at the very end of the Great Wall. It was of a ramped earth construction faced with bricks, like so much of the Ming wall. And as with so much of the Ming wall, the bricks have been mostly 'recycled' by the local farming community to make their own houses.

Today, this reconstructed section looks much older than reborn in 2000, largely because the quality of bricks hardly compares with those used originally. The wall here rises over 100m from entry point to peak. This therefore includes some very steep gradients within the short 1,200m section of the wall. On the western side of the peak, the wall actually stops and only stairs with railings access the higher defence platforms. Steps on the steep gradients are made of stone and are solid with railings on either side. (*Entry ¥30.*)

A small museum on the history of the Great Wall can be found at the far end of the Hushan wall. The most direct way to get to the **museum** is to go over the mountain (30 minutes). However, for those with a little vertigo or weak knees a 1.7km flat road around the bluff of the mountain will take you to the museum in the same amount of time. The small two-floor museum holds a number of Ming dynasty artefacts found around the wall, photographs of the wall and activities surrounding it, as well as pictorial representations of battles, generals and weapons. Unfortunately, there was no English translation at the time of writing. (*Entry ¥10.*)

To get to Hushan, take one of the regular buses leaving from the bus station in Dandong. Buses leave twice an hour between 06.00 and 16.00 for ¥4. Most buses go straight to the car park at Hushan, but some will drop you off at the entrance to the park (Hǔshāntóu 虎山头). It is a ten-minute walk from the entrance to the wall, passing the ticket booth on the way. The bus takes a rather circuitous 40-minute route around the Ai tributary to get to Hushan. A more scenic route in the summer is to take one of the boats from Dandong riverfront for ¥10. Buses back to Dandong out of season can be somewhat erratic, so you might want to consider flagging down a taxi from the entrance to the park. Taxis seem to pass by the entrance with more regularity than the bus, but cost around ¥50 for the one-way metered trip.

NINE GATE ENTRANCE Jiǔménkǒu 九门口 Jiumenkou lies 18km east of 'The First Pass Under Heaven' at Shanhaiguan and the wall from there to Jiumenkou marks the border between Hebei and Liaoning provinces. This section of the Ming Great Wall was built in 1381 on the remains of a wall built here by the northern Qi over 800 years earlier. The pass itself straddles the Jiu River where a nine-gate sluice was built to regulate the water and acted as an obstacle to potential invaders. Each gate originally had heavy wooden double doors, which were opened during the wet summer months to allow the river to flow and stop the towns from flooding. During the dry winter months the doors were closed to help conserve water on the Hebei, inner China, side of the wall and to prevent invaders crossing the shallow riverbed. In its glory days, the pass was known as 'The First Pass East of Beijing' and was the only way to traverse between central and northeastern China.

A replica of the original 110m bridge and some 1,700m of wall was reconstructed at Jiumenkou in 2000, but the double doors were not replaced. A small reservoir has been built north of the pass, replacing the earlier conservation of water south of the pass. Previously, circular walled cities existed on either side of the bridge. The northern city and wall no longer exist, but have been replaced by the park entrance, the new reservoir and a brand-new aviary. The old Ensi Temple, complete with monks, is still there. You can enter for free, pay your respects and be on your way, but photos are not allowed. The remains of the southern walled city can still be seen, though. A small hamlet has grown over the old town and its walls, although one suspects that this too might soon be replaced by a reconstructed model.

For those hiking the 20km from Jiaoshan (see page 127), the trail ends at Jiumenkou as the reconstruction literally 'walls off' the way further up the mountain. Although it is tempting to skirt around the end of the reconstruction through farmers' lands to regain the wall at higher ground, this is not advised at present, and the park wardens and the monks will prevent you from doing so if they catch you. With the present Great Wall fever in Shanhaiguan, there is a high likelihood that the wall beyond Jiumenkou will open up in the next few years and so it is worth asking at the gate pá chángchéng wǎng xī zǒu, kěyǐ ma？爬长城往西走，可以吗？ (Can I/we climb further west on the Great Wall?).

Taxis at Jiumenkou can take you back to Shanhaiguan for ¥50. If none is available and you don't fancy the 20km hike back, then phone your hotel in Shanhaiguan to send around a taxi. In the summer, minibuses may ply the route, but quarrying alongside the road has ripped up the surface and so bus companies are not keen to send less than full vehicles that way.

If you want to cycle to Jiumenkou from Shanhaiguan, the route is through good hilly countryside along a badly surfaced road, so a mountain bike with shock absorbers might be advisable. Take the road out of the north gate of Shanhaiguan for about 800m, then turn right at the first crossroads (ie: don't continue on to Jiaoshan). Follow this road for just over 5km and before really getting into the thick of the mountains turn right at some billboards down a rickety old road and over a small bridge. From here keep following the road for another 12km until you get to Jiumenkou. At the highest point on the road you will be passing the border between Hebei and Liaoning provinces.

There is no accommodation at Jiumenkou at the time of writing, only a few locals selling fruit. The accommodation situation is likely to change in the coming years.

7

Hebei and Tianjin
河北、天津

The stacks of mountains tower beyond the clouds. Cleaved in the middle by an awesome gateway, Created by the will of Heaven.

Anon Chinese Poet

Eastern Hebei, Tianjin (and Beijing) provinces hold the best-preserved sections of the Ming Great Wall. Shanhaiguan and the Old Dragon's Head, where the Ming wall meets the Yellow Sea, was long thought of as the easternmost end of the Ming wall (it is not: see *Chapter 6* for the real easternmost end). It is a rewarding section of the wall to visit and combines well with a trip to Qinhuangdao, the former communist beach playground. Near to spectacular sections of the Ming wall, Hebei province also offers the imperial Qing burial chambers (Qing Eastern Tombs) at Dongling, 30km outside Zunhua, as well as the Qing imperial playground at Chengde, where there remains a collection of scaled-down palaces from all over China. The palaces were nonetheless quite large enough for the Qing princes to live in with a travelling entourage of servants, concubines and other princely necessities. Boat rides on Panjiakou Reservoir sail you across the now sunken parts of the wall.

HISTORY OF THE WALL IN HEBEI AND TIANJIN

The Ji garrison wall dates back to the 6th century. It has seen much reconstruction over the centuries and survived so well through to the 21st century mostly because of the efforts of one man, General Qi Jiguang, commander of the Ji garrison from 1567 to 1583. During his 16 years as garrison commander he renovated over 800km of the Great Wall from Shanhaiguan to Mutianyu (in Beijing province), including almost 30 passes and gateways, and many more watchtowers and beacons. His renovation of the wall used a variety of architectural styles, but for the most part he used a solid base of stone faced with brick. In 1976, the Chinese communist government started patching up the minimal environmental damage from the intervening centuries as well as the damage wielded by both the Allied nations and the Japanese during the first half of the 20th century.

SHANHAIGUAN

Today, Shanhaiguan is a busy little town largely kept alive by tourism to the surrounding Great Wall. Most of the town's walls have preserved their solid brickwork, and for a long time the interior of the walled town was left as it had been for hundreds of years, slowly dilapidating over time while the townspeople moved out to new high rises on the outskirts. Now the old fortified city is going

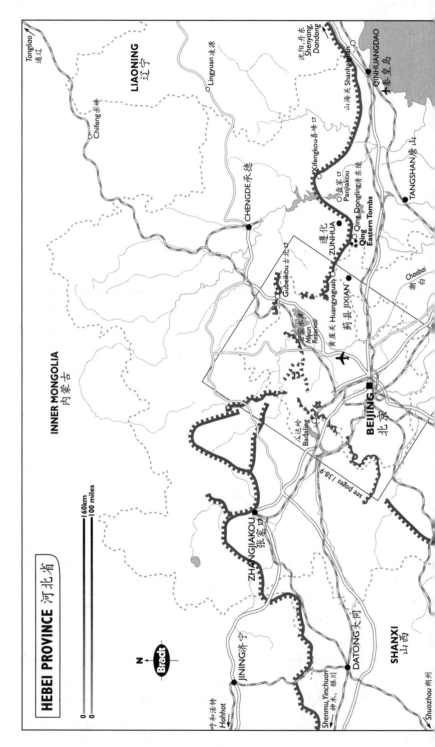

HEBEI PROVINCE 河北省

INNER MONGOLIA
内蒙古

LIAONING
辽宁

Tongliao
通辽

Chifeng 赤峰

Lingyuan 凌源

Shenyang, Dandong
沈阳,丹东

山海关 Shanhaiguan

QINHUANGDAO
秦皇岛

Xifengkou 喜峰口

Panjiakou
潘家口

TANGSHAN 唐山

Qing Dongling 清东陵
Qing
Eastern Tombs

CHENGDE 承德

遵化
ZUNHUA

Huangyaguan
黄崖关

蓟县 JIXIAN

Gubeikou 古北口

Chaobai
潮白

Miyun
Reservoir
密云水库

Badaling
八达岭

BEIJING
北京

see pages 138-9

ZHANGJIAKOU
张家口

JINING 齐宁

DATONG 大同

SHANXI
山西

Hohhot
呼和浩特

Shenmu, Yinchuan
神木,银川

Shuozhou 朔州

N

Bradt

0 ───── 160km
0 ───── 100 miles

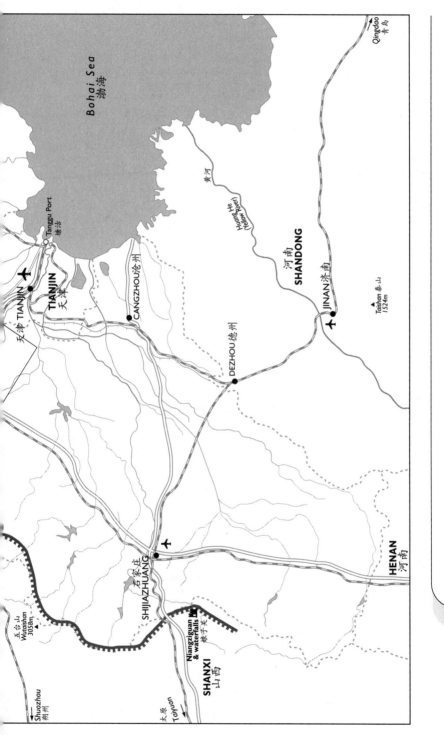

Bohai Sea 渤海

Tanggu Port 塘沽

TIANJIN 天津
天津 TIANJIN

CANGZHOU沧州

黄河

Huang He
(Yellow River)

河南
SHANDONG

JINAN济南

Taishan 泰山
1524m

DEZHOU德州

五台山
Wutaishan
3058m

SHIJIAZHUANG
石家庄

HENAN
河南

Niangziguan
& waterfalls 娘子关

SHANXI 山西

Shuozhou
朔州

太原
Taiyuan

Qingdao
青岛

through a complete overhaul and is being spruced up in time for a projected influx of tourists during the 2008 Beijing Olympics. The plans for it, plastered on the side of a house at the reconstructed drum tower in the centre of the town, look like a sterile and modern imitation of the real thing. It remains to be seen whether the renovations will succeed in keeping the integrity of the old town, or whether it will indeed just become a cheap plastic imitation.

HISTORY Shanhai Pass was thought for some considerable time to be the easternmost section of the Ming Great Wall (now known to be Hushan on the Yalu River border with Korea, see page 119). This misconception was in part created by the alternative name for the pass, First Pass Under Heaven, as inscribed in 1m-high characters above the pass gateway. This pass is also one of the most heavily fortified passes that was built by the Ming dynasty on the whole of the Great Wall. First built in AD583 by the Sui dynasty, the pass was further fortified over the ensuing centuries. By the 13th century, the Ming dynasty had expanded the garrison fort to include an eastern and western outer defensive wall, encompassing the main city fort, and then two satellite defence towns, Weiyuan and Ninghai, on the north and south side of the main city fort respectively. Unfortunately, the western outer defensive wall was dismantled over the course of the last century to make way for the modern-day town that stands there now. In 1933, during the Japanese invasion of China, the town came under significant enemy fire, destroying some of the wall, as well as the Tower for Pacification of Remote Areas (Jingyuanlou). The tower was rebuilt in 1986, and much repair was done to the section where the wall meets the sea at the Old Dragon's Head Lǎolóngtóu 老龙头 Further renovations to Jiaoshan tower were made in 2000, and all 13km of wall between Laolongtou and Jiaoshan will be reconstructed for the 2008 Olympics.

GETTING THERE AND AROUND Direct from Beijing or Tianjin, there are frequent trains to Shanhaiguan, some as quick as a mere three hours for ¥70. From Dandong there are two trains a day, one overnight and one during the day for ¥128. There are more frequent trains from Xingcheng, which take 1½–2 hours. If you are approaching from Panjiakou, you will need to take the bus to Qianxi (see page 129) and then on to Shanhaiguan (one a day early in the morning), or take the frequent bus to Tangshan from where there are many trains to Shanhaiguan. Although this last way is more roundabout, at least the service is frequent.

In theory, there are flights to Shanhaiguan from Beijing and Shanghai, but flight times were proving elusive at the time of writing.

It is easy to walk around all the sites of Shanhaiguan town, and cycling is also an option. Bikes are available for rent, although at the time of writing rental locations in the centre of the walled city were on the move because of the restoration of the town. Ask at your hotel for the most up-to-date information. Taxis also ply the station and tourist sites for customers. They will usually give you an inflated price for a ride, so make sure you always take a metered taxi and that the driver puts on the clock (biǎo 表). Three-wheeler moped rickshaws are also available for slightly less than the taxis. For onward travel to outlying sites see the respective sections below.

The Chinese/English 'Qinhuangdao Traffic and Tourist Map' (Qínhuángdǎo Jiāotōng Lǚyóutú 秦皇岛交通旅游图) is available at the station and other newspaper stalls. It has a small map of Shanhaiguan to Laolongtou, as well as other maps of surrounding towns and areas of interest, and quite a bit of information on public transport in the area. Most of the information applies to the

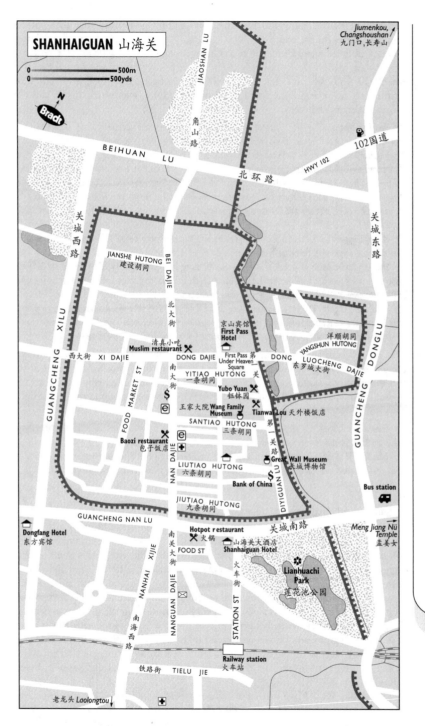

SHANHAIGUAN 山海关

Jiumenkou,
Changshoushan /
九门口, 长寿山

102国道
HWY 102

BEIHUAN LU
北环路

JIAOSHAN LU

角
山
路

N

Bradt

0   500m
0   500yds

关
城
西
路

关
城
东
路

XILU

GUANGCHENG

JIANSHE HUTONG
建设胡同

BEI DAJIE

北
大
街

京山宾馆
First Pass
Hotel

洋顺胡同
YANGSHUN HUTONG

DONGLU

GUANCHENG

清真小吃
Muslim restaurant ✕

西大街 XI DAJIE   DONG DAJIE

南
大
街

DONG

LUOCHENG DAJIE

First Pass 第
Under Heaven 一
Square   关
YITIAO HUTONG   路
一条胡同

东罗城大街

FOOD MARKET ST

$
e

王家大院
Wang Family
Museum

Yubo Yuan ✕
钰体园

Tianwai Lou 天外楼饭店 ✕

SANTIAO HUTONG
三条胡同

DIYIGUAN LU

NAN DAJIE

Baozi restaurant ✕
包子饭店

e
✚

LIUTIAO HUTONG
六条胡同

第
一
关
路

Great Wall Museum
长城博物馆

$
Bank of China

JIUTIAO HUTONG
九条胡同

Bus station 🚐

GUANCHENG NAN LU

关城南路

Meng Jiang Nü
Temple
孟姜女

Dongfang Hotel
东方宾馆

Hotpot restaurant
✕ 火锅
FOOD ST

山海关大酒店
Shanhaiguan Hotel

NANHAI XIJIE

NANGUAN DAJIE

南
关
大
街

Lianhuachi
Park
莲花池公园

南
海
西
路

STATION ST

火
车
街

✉

Railway station
火车站

老龙头 Laolongtou ↓

铁路街 TIELU JIE

✚

Hebei and Tianjin 河北、天津 SHANHAIGUAN

7

125

peak tourist season, so outside this time, you will find for example that many of the proposed buses do not run.

The Public Security Bureau is at 23 Guangcheng Nan Lu (☏ *0335 5073 727*).

🏠 **WHERE TO STAY AND EAT** The entire old town is being revamped at the time of writing, so, aside from the luxurious Jingshan Hotel, everything inside the old town is likely to change.

🏠 **Dongfang Binguan** 东方宾馆 (26 rooms) On the corner of Xinkai Xinlu and Guancheng Xilu; ☏ 0335 5051 376. A bit out of the centre of things but cheap and friendly and safe. *Dorm beds ¥35 each. Standard twin ¥110.*

🏠 **Jingshan Binguan** 京山宾馆 (56 rooms) 1 Dongda Jie; ☏ 0335 5051 130; 🖷 0335 5132 100; 📧 firstpasshotel2188@tom.com. Conveniently located right next to the First Pass Under Heaven and overlooking the new square in front of it, this courtyard-style hotel has retained its Ming/Qing architecture but completely modernised its rooms. Has a good if pricey restaurant and a business centre with email at ¥10 per hour. All rooms en suite with 24hr hot water and includes Western- and Chinese-style buffet breakfast. *Standard twin or dbl ¥580; trpl ¥680; deluxe ¥880; suite ¥1,280.*

🏠 **Muying Lüguan** 牧营旅馆 (8 rooms of 4 beds each) Dong Dantiao Hutong, behind the Shanhaiguan Museum. Extremely basic dormitories. Hot water in the winter only! *¥60 per room.*

🏠 **Shanhaiguan Dajiudian** 山海关大酒店 (67 rooms) 107 Guangcheng Nanlu; ☏ 0335 5054 488 ext 0, or 5064 988. Rather worn dbl. A state-run hotel, but well located 200m from the train station near the south gate of the town. Rooms on the east side of the hotel overlook a small park. Quiet despite being near the train station. *Standard twin ¥195.*

🏠 **Zhongcheng Lüguan** 中成旅馆 (8 rooms) Dong Liutiao Hutong; ☏ 0335 5052 495. A tiny, very basic inn located in the heart of the old town and which may, therefore, be subject soon to the developer's wrecking ball. All rooms have TV, but use communal showers and have no AC. 24hr hot water. Dbl beds available. *¥10 per person.*

The main restaurant streets around the town are along Guancheng Nan Lu and Diyiguan Lu. Dong Dajie has a few places to eat, but they cater for foreign tourists and the quality was dubious at the time of writing. For some really cheap eats try the stalls down at the food market before 13.00, or the stalls behind the bus station. Try also:

🏠 **Tianwai Lou** 天外楼饭店 Diyiguan Lu; ☏ 0335 5052 952. Purportedly sells seafood, but was scarce when this author ate there. Specialises in private dining rooms more than an open restaurant.

🏠 **Yubo Yuan** 钰钵园 46 Diyiguan Lu; ☏ 0335 5051 318. Very close to the First Pass Under Heaven, this restaurant serves delicious sweet and sour pork and steaming bowls of tasty spinach, amongst many other things.

WHAT TO SEE

In and around Shanhaiguan
The fortified city with its largely intact walls and its impressive main east gate is a primary attraction in itself. In addition, nearby is the wall's entry into the sea at Laolongtou – see below. At 25m in height, the main gate still dominates the skyline of the former fortress city. The wall at this point is 12m high and 8m thick. The main gate is topped with a double-tiered 13m-high tower with 68 embrasures for firing arrows on the north, east and south sides of the tower (ie: the sides facing the potential enemy). Shanhaiguan is also known as the First Pass Under Heaven because of this very inscription on the west, inner side of the pass. A square has recently been built on the town side of the gate. At the time of writing the entire square was barricaded off, making it impossible to take decent photos of the gate without paying the entrance fee. Entry to the gate and square is ¥60, including entry to the Great Wall Museum and Wang Family Residence (see below).

The **Great Wall Museum** (*open daily 08.00–18.30; admission included in price of ticket to First Pass Under Heaven*), 200m south of the First Pass Under Heaven, underwent a complete revamp in 2005, which improved what was already a very good permanent exhibition, showing the history, architecture and artefacts of all the Great Wall. Open daily 08.00-18.30. Admission included in the price of the ticket to the First Pass Under Heaven.

The **Wang Family Residence** at Dong Santiao Hutong (*open daily 09.00–17.30; admission included in price of ticket for First Pass Under Heaven*) is the former home of a rich Qing official. The site is well preserved, but you are escorted through the many rooms by a guide, who will elicit payment from you after about five minutes to continue the guiding services. If you know a little about Chinese culture and history at all, then most of the information provided by the guide is self-explanatory and the rest is information overload. Really such a service is designed for the Chinese, who after years of (continued) lack of access to information are hungry for facts and figures and desire a chaperone to take pictures of them in traditional garb. Even if you refuse the continued guiding service, the guide is required to stay with you and harp facts and figures at you so that you feel guilty by the end at not having given them money. A more interesting living cultural note is how Chinese visitors are keen to pose in costume about the place in imitation of Qing landlords and officials, when they grew up learning that such people were immoral. Identity crisis would be too strong a term for this ubiquitous reaction, but there certainly seems to be a bit of confusion in values. Open daily 09.00-17.30. Admission included in the price of the ticket for the First Pass Under Heaven.

South of Shanhaiguan to the Old Dragon's Head
An offshoot of the Ming Wall extends some 25km from Sandaoguan past Shanhaiguan to Laolongtou. Originally, a giant dragon's head carved from stone decorated the end of the wall, making it look like a dragon drinking water from the sea. The head is long since gone, but the name **Old Dragon's Head** (Lǎolóngtóu 老龙头) remains. Two small defensive hamlets, Ninghai and Weihai, were built on the western and eastern side respectively of the Old Dragon's Head. Both settlements were badly damaged by the invasion of the Eight Allied Nations in 1900, but were completely restored in 1986, with the exception of a small portion of the Ninghai wall, which has been preserved behind glass. Just within the main gate of Ninghai is a stone stele inscribed in the hand of General Qi Jiguang, the garrison commander from the 16th century. The stele's inscription says 'A Heaven Built Wall on the Sea'. Weihai is now largely used as administrative offices and was not open to the public at the time of writing.

Today, Laolongtou is a large park, including a stretch of sandy beach, on which you will find a temple, souvenir shops and simple restaurants (avoid the tasteless bowls of noodle soup), a model plane and beach bikes. At the Old Dragon's Head, the tower has been turned into a souvenir shop; there is a model ship, exhibition rooms and a small maze. Arrive early to avoid the loudspeaker-toting tour groups. To get there from Shanhaiguan, take bus 25 from outside the south gate (10 mins, ¥2). From the bus stop, cross the road and proceed south past the museum entrance to the many shops and restaurants around the car park. Large red characters for Laolongtou direct you towards the entrance. Toilets outside the entrance cost ¥0.5, inside the park they are free. (*Entry to the park ¥60.*)

Beyond the park, the wall proceeds for almost 1km along the seafront, then heads north through the southeast of Shanhaiguan's greenhouse district.

North of Shanhaiguan
Until the local government completes restoration of the first 13km of the wall from the sea northwards, the only good place near Shanhaiguan

to start hiking from along the wall is at Jiǎoshān 角山. This well-preserved and steep 3km section of the wall heading north towards Sandaoguan 三到关, is mostly made of stone. Jiaoshan itself is 519m above sea level, rising therefore only a mere 500m from the town of Shanhaiguan. Some of the steps, however, are almost a metre in height, so part of the hike would in fact qualify as a scramble. The ascent to the first watchtower along the way is up a narrow steep-railed ladder, the sight of which is enough to turn back many a faint-hearted hiker. Partway along is the little monastery of Qixian.

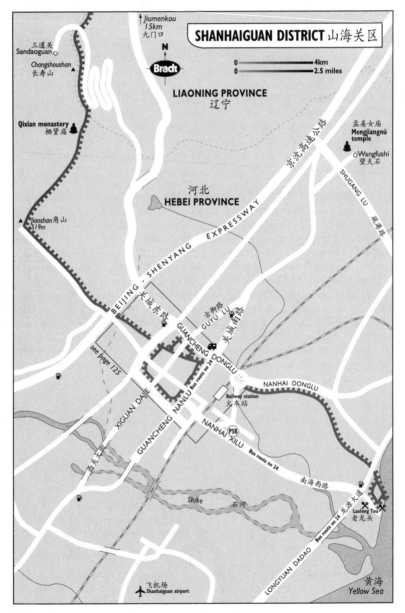

SHANHAIGUAN DISTRICT 山海关区

LIAONING PROVINCE
辽宁

河北
HEBEI PROVINCE

↑ Jiumenkou
15km
九门口

三道关
Sandaoguan ○

Changshoushan
长寿山

Qixian monastery
栖贤庙

▲ Jiaoshan 角山
519m

盂姜女庙
Mengjiangnü
temple
○ Wangfushi
望夫石

京沈高速公路
BEIJING - SHENYANG EXPRESSWAY

SHUGANG LU 蔬菜路

关城东路 GUANCHENG DONGLU

吉街路 GUYU LU

关城南路

see page 125

XIGUAN DAJIE

GUANCHENG NANLU 关城南路

Bus route no 24

NANHAI DONGLU

Railway station
火车站

NANHAI XILU

PSB

Bus route no 24

南海西路

Shihe 石河

Bus route no 24

LONGYUAN DADAO 龙源大道

Laolong Tou
老龙头

飞机场
Shanhaiguan airport

黄海
Yellow Sea

After the monastery, the wall becomes more 'wild' and few people take the wall all the way to Sāndàoguān 三到关 and beyond to Jiumenkou (see page 119) in Liaoning province. Sandaoguan, which lies exactly 5km between Jiumenkou and Jiaoshan, is the junction where the wall branches west towards Panjiakou (see below) and Beijing, and east towards Jiumenkou and Liaoning. It is a 10km hike from Jiaoshan to Jiumenkou. Sandaoguan, meaning 'three-way gate' was indeed constructed of three gates straddling a steep narrow ravine. Two of the gates have now collapsed completely, and little of the last gate remains. It is still easy to imagine, however, the strategic importance of this gateway in the days when paved roads were not so easy to construct. A little further along is Yiyuankou, another important gateway in the wall. It is now in serious need of repair and little visited.

To get to Jiaoshan in peak season, take bus 27 from the south gate. (Entry ¥45.) Outside peak season an unmetered taxi will take you there for ¥10. A chairlift can take you partway up Jiaoshan when the weather is good. Fare ¥25.

East of Shanhaiguan Bianqiangzi, 5km east of Shanhaiguan, is a beacon tower overlooking the Bohai Sea. A further 2km east at Fenghuang Mountain is a small **temple** built for mèngjiāngnǚ 孟姜女 (see box, page 131). In peak season, bus 23 runs to Jiangnü Temple. Out of peak season a taxi will cost you ¥10.

PANJIAKOU RESERVOIR 潘家口水库

Pānjiākǒu shuǐkù 潘家口水库 lies at the gateway of Xīfēngkǒu 喜峰口, or Peak of Happiness. This seemingly auspicious name comes from a bittersweet story that tells of a father and son who had been separated for several years while the father was conscripted to build the Great Wall. Eventually the son sets out to seek his father and finally finds him at Xifengkou. Allegedly, both father and son were so overwhelmed at their long-awaited reunion that they both died there and then of happiness!

Since those giddy days, the Chinese communist government has built a reservoir near Xifengkou. The reservoir has submerged a section of the wall, parts of which become more visible when the water level is low. The wall is very eroded where it enters the water at both the western and eastern sides of the reservoir. The Xifengkou section of the wall on the eastern side of the reservoir is in better condition, and a water platform tout there takes ¥10 for access to the wall from the reservoir. For this fee, you will get to see the faux Ming village built in the shadow of the wall as well as several towers and unlimited walking. The village looks authentic, until you inspect the cement binding between the stones and read the date of the newspapers on the windows: 2004!

Panjiakou town is a long thin town spread out along the lower edge of the reservoir on its western side, by the electricity plant. Many people eke out a livelihood on the reservoir by farming trout, but an increase in tourism is beginning to revitalise the local economy. Boat rides on the reservoir are available through the reservoir manager, Mr Yang (✆ *131 8019 1458*). His boat drivers know how to navigate the many fish farm lines across the water and can take you to Xifengkou for lunch or the water lodge at the western edge of the lake where it meets the wall.

Buses from Qianxi 迁西 leave for Panjiakou twice an hour between 06.00 and 17.00. More buses come to the next village down, Jiuheqiaozhen 旧河桥镇 (the Town of Drunken River Bridge!), where you can either change for the bus to Panjiakou or take a taxi for ¥10. The nearest train stations are Tangshan 唐山 and Fengrun 丰润.

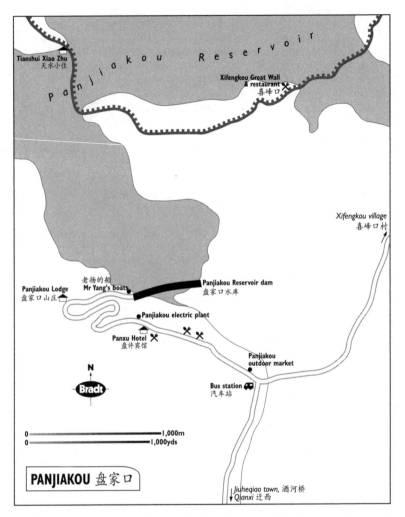

Tianshui Xiao Zhu 天水小住

Xifengkou Great Wall & restaurant 喜峰口

Xifengkou village 喜峰口村

Panjiakou Lodge 盘家口山庄

老扬的船 Mr Yang's boats

Panjiakou Reservoir dam 盘家口水库

Panjiakou electric plant

Panxu Hotel 盘许宾馆

Panjiakou outdoor market

Bus station 汽车站

Panjiakou Reservoir

P a n j i a k o u   R e s e r v o i r

N

Bradt

0 ————— 1,000m
0 ————— 1,000yds

PANJIAKOU 盘家口

Jiuheqiao town, 酒河桥
Qianxi 迁西

Tangshan, which is a major stop on the Tianjin to Harbin line, is well served by trains. Fengrun is on a minor line between Beijing and Qinghuangdao and is served by only four trains a day. Two trains for Beijing leave at 10.00 and 18.00. One train going all the way to Qinhuangdao, Shanhaiguan, Xingcheng and finally Jinzhou leaves at 13.30, and another train going only as far as Qinhuangdao leaves at 15.10

Accommodation at Panjiakou is limited, but good and increasing. Places to eat are scarce so ask at your hotel, and there is a couple of places a few hundred metres down the road when you turn right out of the Panxu Hotel.

Panxu Binguan 潘蓄宾馆 (22 rooms) Main Street (at the north end of the village, opposite the Panjiakou Xuanneng Electricity Plant); ✆ 0315 5895 521/565. This hotel, built in 2000, is a welcome break from some of the 1980s state-run hotels you might have stayed in up until now. Clean and bright with a small terrace for the front-facing rooms. Good value for money. *Standard twin without terrace ¥180, with terrace ¥200. Deluxe ¥400.*

Tianshui Xiao Zhu 天水小住 (4 rooms) On the water at Panjiakou Great Wall; ✆ 138 3287 2505 or 139 3243 2652. This

There are numerous legends surrounding the construction of the Great Wall, many of which relate to the love lost when a conscripted labourer is sent to work on a far region of the wall. The legend of Meng Jiangnü is probably the most famous of all such tales. The story is of a young woman in the 7th century from Shanxi province, who travelled to Shanhaiguan to search for her husband in order to give him clothes for winter. After much searching, and as winter closed in, she eventually learnt that he had died some months earlier from exhaustion. Meng Jiangnü was so heartbroken that she could not stop crying for several days. In fact her grief was so severe that her wailing is alleged to have caused the collapse of some 400km of the Great Wall. Only then did she find the body of her husband, who had been buried in the wall as a lucky talisman. It seems in the end, however, that he had not brought much luck to that section of the wall.

place really does live at, on and from the Great Wall. Chickens scratch about on the spit of land beneath the wall in front of the water platform. Take one of Yang's boats (see above) to get there. Fishing off the platform is also available. Communal shower and toilets. *One dbl, one twin, one three-bed and one six-bed room, all at ¥60 per room.*

QING EASTERN TOMBS — QING DONGLING 清东陵

The Qing dynasty (1644–1911) had two imperial burial sites, one in western Hebei and one in eastern Hebei at Malanyu in Zunhua county. These Qing Eastern Tombs Qīng Dōnglíng 清东陵 are spread out over 2,500km^2 and 15 tombs house the bodies of five emperors, four empresses, one princess and five concubines. Countless other lesser family are also buried around the site. (Entry to all the tombs is with a one-day pass for ¥90.)

Probably the most famous of all these personages is the Empress Dowager Cixi, who effectively ruled imperial China until her death in 1908, shortly before its capitulation to the Republic of Dr Sun Yatsen in 1911. Not only was she renowned for being cruel, she was also incredibly self-centred and politically short-sighted, leading to the fall of the empire. She was the grandmother of Puyi, the last emperor of China (made into cinematographic history through the film of that name, *The Last Emperor*). After a brief period as a puppet king under Japanese rule, Puyi later became a common gardener under the communists and was not given an imperial burial with his ancestors at Dongling when he died in 1967. Like most of the tombs at Dongling, Cixi's was also plundered in 1928 by the warlord Sun Dian and his army, when China fell into warlordism and civil strife. Faithful to his grandmother, Puyi had Cixi's body extracted and then re-interred in the same place later. Her body still lies in the tomb. The grounds of her tomb now show depictions of her life in a less than flattering light, a demonstration of China's distaste of the excesses of the Qing dynasty and her embodiment thereof, as well as a fascination with parading her as one of China's most famous freaks. (Her peculiar habits, including drinking human milk daily, in an attempt to keep young, are well documented.)

A second famous tomb worth visiting is that of the first Qing emperor, Qianlong. The entrance to his tomb, through X-ray screening, is from the top, down a very long set of spiral stairs and through an entrance ornately carved with Chinese, Sanskrit and Tibetan writing. The exit is via a short uphill walk out of the side of the tomb.

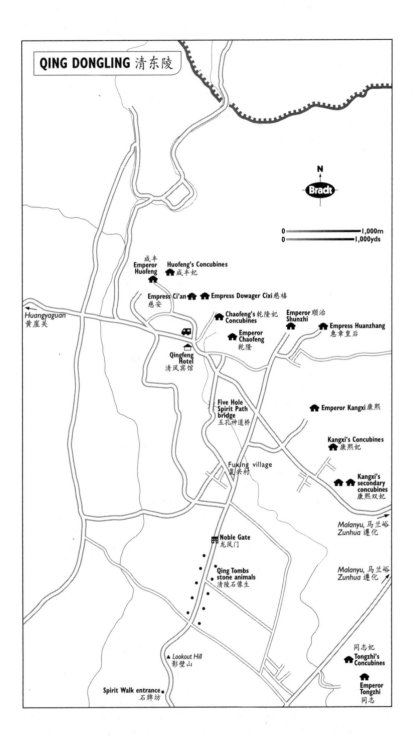

QING DONGLING 清东陵

N

Bradt

0 ————————— 1,000m
0 ————————— 1,000yds

咸丰
Emperor
Huofeng

Huofeng's Concubines
咸丰妃

Empress Ci'an
慈安

Empress Dowager Cixi 慈禧

Chaofeng's 乾隆妃
Concubines

Emperor 顺治
Shunzhi

Emperor
Chaofeng
乾隆

Empress Huanzhang
惠章皇后

Huangyaguan
黄崖关

Qingfeng
Hotel
清风宾馆

Emperor Kangxi 康熙

Five Hole
Spirit Path
bridge
五孔神道桥

Kangxi's Concubines
康熙妃

Kangxi's
secondary
concubines
康熙双妃

Fuxing village
复米村

Malanyu, 马兰峪
Zunhua 遵化

Noble Gate
龙凤门

Malanyu, 马兰峪
Zunhua 遵化

Qing Tombs
stone animals
清陵石像生

同志妃
Tongzhi's
Concubines

Lookout Hill
影壁山

Emperor
Tongzhi
同志

Spirit Walk entrance
石牌坊

Both these tombs and the inner path of carved animals are in easy walking distance (less than 500m) from the centre of Dongling (see below). If you really want to get to the other tombs, minibuses will take you around the entire site for ¥120. A small three-wheeler will take you around the most important sites for ¥30 for two people.

Almost 3km north of Dongling lies the Great Wall just to the north of Yuanbaoshan village. This section of the Great Wall is made of stone face tamped earth and disappears over the hills to the east after a distance of some kilometres. It is in a bad state of repair. Immediately west, the ground is very steep and the wall has all but disappeared.

There are direct buses from Beijing's Dongzhimen bus station to Dongling and zūnhuà 遵化 and several smaller buses ply the route between Zunhua and huángyáguān 黄崖关 via Dongling and mǎlányù 马兰峪, or from Malanyu to Pinggu via Dongling. If you are coming from Huairou, it is quickest to take a morning bus from mìyún 密云 to xīnglóng 兴隆 and then another bus from Xinglong to Huangyaguan (see below). From Huangyaguan, minibuses take over an hour to Dongling for ¥6. You might make it all the way to Dongling in the same day by public transport, but accommodation options are much better at Huangyaguan and the Great Wall there is also more worthwhile.

WHERE TO STAY At the time of writing, Dongling has all of one hotel approved by the tourist board. There are a number of farmer's inns (nóng jiā yuàn 农家院) but, outside of the busiest summer season, you are likely to get ushered into the tourist board hotel instead.

Qingfeng Binguan 清风宾馆 (67 rooms) Yuling Che Yuan Lu Nan, Qing Dongling, Zunhua County; ☎ 0315 6949 216/193. This hotel needed a serious overhaul of its plumbing at the time of writing. Hot water allegedly from 06.00–08.00 and 20.00–23.00, but reserve your room in advance out of season if you want to be sure that the furnace is actually fired up. Considering northern China's water shortage, you will waste more water getting the hot stuff to your tap than you could ever use in one shower. *Deluxe class A rooms (3 rooms) are considerably nicer (but you still have the same water problem) ¥468. Deluxe B with three beds (2 rooms) ¥368. Standard twin class A ¥280. Standard twin class B ¥180.*

THE GREAT WALL IN TIANJIN 天津

HUANGYAGUAN 黄崖关 A small section of the Great Wall passes northeast of the town of Ji in **Tianjin** province. Originally built in AD557 in the Beiqi dynasty, Huangya Pass, which crosses Tianjin province's Ju River, got its name 'Yellow Cliffs' from the surrounding rock formations. The section was well maintained with brick facing during Ming times and the government renovated the site and opened it to the public in 1987. It is worth a visit for its water run-off controls, well-preserved towers, challenging hiking and striking scenery. There is also a larger-than-lifesize statue of General Qi Jiguang at Taipingzhai. It is also much less visited than the sites in Beijing. (*Entry ¥35.*)

One of the main features of the original site at Huangyaguan was **Eight Diagram Street**. It was thus called because of the construction of streets that made up a labyrinthine architectural obstacle at that section of the wall. (Diagrams, made up of combinations of sticks with three whole and three broken lines, were used by the Chinese to divine the future and the luck of future actions.) If invaders tried to avoid the heavily fortified Huangya Pass by skirting south below it, they would end up caught in a maze of streets created to confuse and hinder the enemy. Today an amusement labyrinth has been put in to try to represent the spirit of Eight Diagram Street, but it is a sorry imitation of the original obstacle.

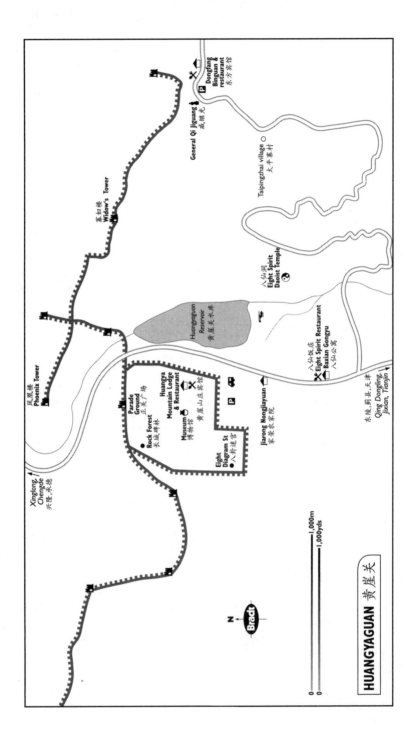

HUANGYAGUAN 黄崖关

Dongfang
Binguan &
restaurant
东方宾馆

General Qi Jiguang
戚继光

Taipingzhai village 太平寨村

Widow's Tower
寡妇楼

八仙洞
Eight Spirit
Daoist Temple

Huangyaguan
Reservoir
黄崖关水库

Phoenix Tower
凤凰楼

八仙饭店
Eight Spirit Restaurant
Baxian Gongyu
八仙公寓

Xinglong,
Chengde
兴隆,承德

Parade
Ground
正关广场

Rock Forest
长城碑林

Huangya
Mountain Lodge
& Restaurant
黄崖山庄宾馆

Museum
博物馆

Jiarong Nongjiayuan
家荣农家院

Eight
Diagram St
八卦迷宫

东陵,蓟县,天津
Qing Dongling,
Jixian, Tianjin

N

Bradt

0   1,000m
0   1,000yds

Aside from the labyrinth, there is also a good museum inside the site, rock character park, gardens, a hotel, restaurants and Eight Diagram fortress. Of the many towers along the length of the Huangyaguan wall, Phoenix Tower, 300m to the north, is a notable renovated roundhouse. It served to shelter the guards on duty as well as their provisions. Outside the site is a small reservoir offering boating and fishing, and nearby is also the temple cave of the Eight Spirits.

East of Huangya Pass is the **Taipingzhai** 太平寨 section of the Ming Great Wall. (*Entry ¥40*). One of the towers on this section of the wall is called Widows' Tower. It got its name from the team of 12 widows who helped build the tower after they had lost their husbands in a war against the invading barbarians from the north.

Getting there and around
Huangyaguan is relatively well served by public transport. Bus 918 from Dongzhimen long-distance bus station in Beijing takes three hours to get to Huangyaguan. There are also minibuses from Xinglong if you are approaching from Huairou area, and there are minibuses also from the Qing Eastern Tombs at Dongling. Regular buses leave from Tianjin and minibuses also serve Huangyaguan from Jixian town (see below). Taxis at Huangyaguan can take you up to Taipingzhai.

Where to stay and eat
There are two mid-budget places to stay at Huangyaguan and another at Taipingzhai. There are also numerous small family hostels and farmer's inns (nong jia yuan). Several farmer's inns on the way up to Taipingzhai are more peaceful and command an excellent view of the valley. Meals are available at the inns and around the car park outside Huangyaguan.

⌂ **Baxian Gongyu** 八仙公寓 (47 rooms) South of the site entrance on the left just after the turning to Taipingzhai; ✆ 022 2271 8897/8110; ☏ 022 2271 8897. Rooms are clean and en suite, although there is no heating outside the state-run system, nor AC in the summer. The restaurant serves generally good food in a courtyard setting or in Mongolian-style huts around the back of the hotel, but avoid the fish stew. *Standard twin ¥160; suite ¥340.*

⌂ **Dongfang Binguan** 东方宾馆 (27 rooms) Taipingzhai; ✆ 022 2271 8658/8655. A wonderful little hotel 8km from Huangyaguan at Taipingzhai Great Wall. All rooms en suite with 24hr hot water, AC and TV. Good restaurant with peaceful outdoor seating. You will need to pay the entrance fee to the wall of ¥40 to get to the hotel, but only for the first day of your stay. *Twin or dbl room ¥120.*

⌂ **Huangya Shanzhuang Binguan** 黄崖山庄宾馆 (64 rooms) Inside Huangyaguan site; ✆ 022 2271 8096/8100. *Standard twin ¥140; deluxe suite ¥390.*

⌂ **Jiarong Nongjiayuan** 家荣农家院 (9 rooms) ✆ 022 2271 8205 or 1300 1388 456. A small nóng jiā yuàn run by a friendly couple. Rooms and facilities are clean and tidy. TV, 24hr hot water for en-suite shower, but communal toilets. Pet pigeons. Washing machine for communal use. *¥10 per person.*

JIXIAN 蓟县 The town of Ji, now in Tianjin province, is over 2,000 years old. If you arrive at the Ming Great Wall in Tianjin via the town of Ji, then it is well worth the extra stop in the town's **Dule Temple**. The temple contains the Tower of the Goddess of Mercy (Avalokitesvara), which is the oldest wooden tower still in existence in China today. The date of its original construction is only known to be some time in the Tang dynasty (AD618–906). The present 23m tower is a reconstruction from 984. Inside the tower, the 16m Goddess of Mercy with her 11 faces is one of the largest in China. She has also withstood almost 30 earthquakes in her 1,000-year lifespan to date.

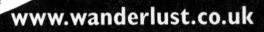

8

Beijing 北京

Though the Fairy's Tower and the Tower for Viewing the Capital are separated only by some 100 metres of the Great Wall, still no-one has ever walked on this part of the wall – it is too thin and is sandwiched between cliffs.

Luo Zhewen, 1995

Even before the Ming moved their capital from Nanjing in the south to Beijing, the walls in Beijing province had been of enormous strategic value. The province has long been a trading crossroads and communications hub between the nomadic tribes to the north and the riches of China's heartland and between the so-called barbarian western regions and the thriving coastland. It was in large part because of this strategic value that the Ming finally moved their capital to Beijing, where it was easier to control the workings of an ever increasing empire and easier to fortify the Great Wall as a defence and trading mechanism.

The Ming Great Wall in Beijing province is the most discontinuous of all the Great Wall provinces. Although it roughly follows the contour of the mountains around the capital in a semicircular configuration to the north, the Great Wall in Beijing – more than any other province – is made up of several layers and locking systems. The Ming interwove the many mountains, cliffs, ravines and valleys with their layers of the wall to produce an intricate defence system of impenetrable obstacles and inevitable, effective killing zones. Today, the Beijing wall has been broken up even further by the high density of roads, railway lines and reservoirs serving the city. It is difficult, therefore, to hike for more than a day or two along the wall in Beijing province without having to break off the hike and start again at another point. Nevertheless, the wall in Beijing is some of the most rewarding of all the Ming wall to walk, in part because of the breathtaking views over acres of mountains, and in part because the sturdy construction of most of the Beijing wall using rock and brick has rendered it least susceptible to erosion.

Erosion, however, has still damaged a lot of the Great Wall, and ransacking it for rocks and bricks has damaged it further. The local government is now renovating more and more of its Great Wall. The most renovated sections at Badaling, the mouth of a four-gated valley, and Mutianyu, both about 70km from Beijing, have become veritable tourist traps, where it is now hard to get a sense of what the wall really was. Huanghuacheng, also in the process of being renovated but not yet at the time of writing administered by the state, and Simatai with its concentration of towers, architectural styles and engineering feats, are much less visited and have preserved more of their original integrity.

All sections of the Beijing Great Wall can be visited from the capital on a day trip, although there are also a few interesting places to stay at the wall if you

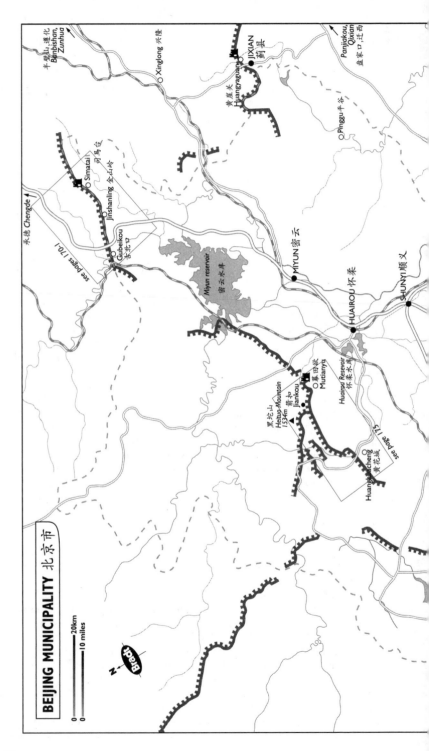

BEIJING MUNICIPALITY 北京市

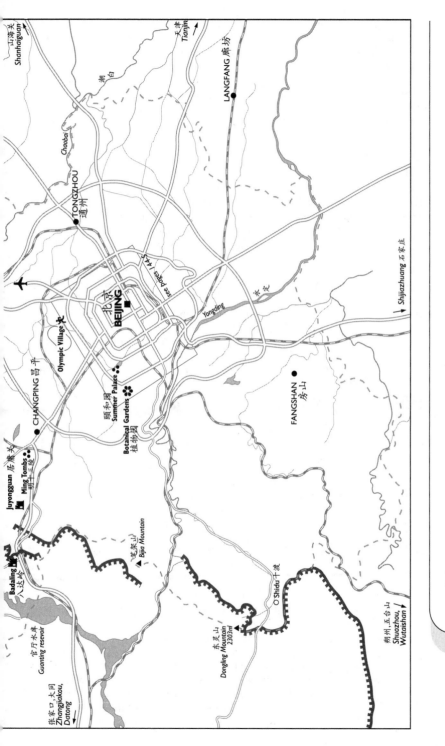

want to enjoy the wall environment out of tourist hours, or intend to do extended hikes on the wall or in the vicinity. Beijing, of course, holds an array of other sites that you might not want to miss, even if your main passion is the Great Wall of China.

Aside from the history section below, everything else in this chapter on Beijing must come with a warning of the enormous likelihood of change in the run-up to the Olympics. The government is overhauling the city big time: no *hutong*, bus route or restaurant is safe from the bulldozer of 'development'.

HISTORY OF BEIJING

CHRONOLOGY

pre 1264	Capital of Jin and Liao kingdoms.
1264	Beijing wrested from Chinese control by Genghis Khan.
1278	Beijing becomes the capital of the Yuan Mongol dynasty of China under Kublai Khan and is known as Khanbalik. The city forms its current layout when Kublai rebuilds the capital and names it Dadu.
1293	Marco Polo visits Khanbalik.
1368	Ming dynasty overthrows the Yuan and moves capital to Nanjing.
1409	Emperor Yongle moves capital back to Beijing and starts to build the city's present layout.
1644	Manchus overrun the city and proclaim themselves the Qing dynasty rulers of the Middle Kingdom.
1860	First Opium War sees the complete destruction of the Imperial Summer Palace by the British.
1900	Boxer Rebellion forces Empress Dowager Cixi to flee the capital for Xian.
1908	Empress Dowager Cixi dies. Boy emperor Puyi ascends to power.
1911	The last emperor Puyi abdicates.
1912	China declared a republic.
1927	Capital of the republic moves to Nanjing and Beijing becomes known as Beiping (meaning Northern Peace).
1949	Capital returns to Beijing after the communist liberation of China.
1972	US President Nixon visits Beijing.
1989	Tiananmen Square massacre on 4 June.
2008	Olympics take place in Beijing for the first time.
2010	World Expo in Beijing.

KHANBALIK – CAPITAL OF THE MONGOL YUAN DYNASTY For some two millennia prior to 1264, Beijing was essentially a backwater trading town between the Chinese, Mongols and Koreans. Then, after Genghis Khan united the Mongol tribes and overthrew the weakening Song dynasty, his grandson, Kublai Khan, moved his Mongol forces into Beijing. By 1278, Kublai was emperor of the new Yuan dynasty of a united China with its capital at Khanbalik (now Beijing).

For another 90 years, the Yuan Mongol dynasty ruled over China from Khanbalik. As noted in the writings of Marco Polo, who lived in Khanbalik for seven years during this period, the Yuan dynasty brought the greatest period of openness and trade between China and the outside world. Kublai started new city walls, within which he also commissioned the building of the Palace of Tranquillities. These were the forerunners of the present Forbidden City. He also ordered the extension of the Grand Canal from Suzhou in southern China to Khanbalik.

BEIJING — MING AND QING RETURN TO ISOLATIONISM The first Ming emperor, Hong Wu, who overthrew the Yuan dynasty in 1368, immediately moved the Middle Kingdom's capital back to Nanjing and clamped down on trade and relations with the outside world. As part of this closed-door policy, he also ordered extensive renovations to the Great Wall along the Middle Kingdom's northern frontier.

The second Ming emperor, and the most forward looking of them all, Yongle, reversed this trend for a while and moved the capital back north, when it acquired its present name, Bei Jing meaning 'Northern Capital'. During Yongle's reign, the Palace of Tranquillities from the previous Yuan dynasty was remodelled and renamed the Imperial Palace. At the same time, this remodelling and enlargement to its present dimensions also set the formation of surrounding streets and suburbs. Emperor Yongle also had the Temple of Heaven, now a World Heritage Site (see page 164), built. Many of the gates and passes of the Great Wall developed small towns and marketplaces around them, where the Chinese people inside the wall would trade with those from outside. Porcelain from the emperor's kilns became known across the trading world and forged the association between fine bone china and the name by which the Middle Kingdom is commonly known by foreigners – 'China'.

Although the capital remained at Beijing after Emperor Yongle passed away in 1424, successive Ming emperors pursued an increasingly isolationist and repressive form of rule. Trade at the outer margins of the Middle Kingdom continued and palace officials grew rich from granting trading rights while screening the emperors at Beijing from this conflict with Confucian values, which held foreigners in contempt.

With control of the outer periphery of the Middle Kingdom waning, Manchu tribes from the northeast were breaking through the Ming Great Wall defences by the 17th century. When internal discontent among the masses ousted the last Ming emperor in 1644, the Manchus quickly took control of the situation and proclaimed themselves the new rulers of the Middle Kingdom under the Qing dynasty.

Concerned little about an invasion from the north, the Qing let the Ming's moneydraining defensive upkeep of the Great Wall fall into decline. The first half of their reign saw an expansion of China's directly controlled lands and with this, trade increased further. The magnificent Imperial Summer Palace (Yuan Ming Yuan) was built during this period. The second half of their reign, however, saw an increasingly inward-looking dynasty concentrate on building decadence and ignoring the encroaching foreigners baying for more trade rights. By the Arrow War (or First Opium War) of 1860, foreign troops had surrounded the city walls and the British looted and burned the beautiful Summer Palace to the ground.

By the turn of the 20th century, internal strife amongst the masses was once again so high that in the summer of 1900 the Empress Dowager Cixi had to flee the capital for Xian. The empress died in 1908, and was buried as the last imperial ruler in her long-prepared mausoleum in the imperial Qing Eastern Tombs at Dongling near Zunhua (see page 131). By 1911, the Qing dynasty was in utter ruin and the last emperor of the Middle Kingdom, Puyi, was forced to abdicate.

REPUBLIC TO COMMUNISM TO SOCIALISM WITH CHINESE CHARACTERISTICS Sun Yatsen, who is seen by both Communist China and the Republic of China (Taiwan) to be the father of their respective movements, returned from exile in 1911 to head up a republican government in Nanjing. But the country fell into civil strife, and various warlords helped by various foreign powers fought for power against each other: the Japanese, foreigners, the republicans and the communists. Mao's Eighth Army eventually encircled Beijing and after marching through the Great Wall's Pass Gully (Guangou, see page 179) they finally liberated Beijing from foreign control in January 1949. Beijing became capital of all China again on 1 October 1949, when Mao Zedong read the declaration of the establishment of the People's Republic of Communist China from Tian An Gate in front of 50,000 happy communists in Tiananmen Square.

Under communism, Beijing, like most Chinese cities has undergone an almost complete facelift. Formerly, under imperial China, houses could not be higher than one storey so that the common people would not be able to look down upon the emperor as he was driven through the streets. The many *hutong* were narrow and irregularly set, so much so that one of the Qing emperors ordered a map to be made of Beijing to facilitate his passage through the city. After liberation, with Soviet help and technology, *hutong* gave way to wide boulevards, ring roads and high-rise faceless concrete-and-tile apartments. Most of the old city wall (except for a stretch at Chongwenmen, see page 142) was dismantled in the 1950s and 1960s to make way for Beijing railway station and open up the city. Air pollution from rapid industrialisation and the continued use of inferior coal-dust blocks for heating and cooking meant that by the 1980s, it was almost impossible to tell whether it was a sunny or a cloudy day in the capital.

After Soviet Russia withdrew its support from China in 1960, and famine set in after several failed harvests, the Great Leap Forward campaign of 1961 saw the same desperate measures in Beijing as elsewhere. Anything made of iron was collected to help push the industrial efforts of the country. But the quality of re-cast iron, made in homemade kilns, was shoddy and had to be thrown out. Silently acknowledging that the Great Leap forward was a failure, Mao's policy of constant revolution led to the Cultural Revolution five years later in 1966. Red Guards rampaged the city, destroying anything that smacked of capitalism, Soviet Russia, bourgeois tendencies, or anything left over from imperial China. Beijing's vast collection of antiques, monuments, palaces and temples, which totalled almost 10,000 after a count in the 1940s, was already badly damaged in the wars and civil strife of the first half of the 20th century. Although the Cultural Revolution finished the rest of them off almost wholesale, some 7,000 have been restored or resurrected now according to the municipal government of Beijing.

After Mao Zedong's death in 1976, Deng Xiaoping ushered in an open-door policy and reinterpreted communism for China into 'socialism with Chinese characteristics'. This brought about a revitalisation first in the south and Shanghai, and then made its way north. Centuries-old rivalry between the north and the south continues as Beijing and Shanghai compete to keep ahead of each other economically, architecturally, culturally and politically. Politically, this has frequently seen a clampdown on outspoken voices in the south and ever more so in the rest of China. After the Tiananmen Square massacre of 1989, in which hundreds of protestors who rallied against corruption and limitations on speech were killed by the army, the government has been much more careful about letting freedom of speech and association flourish. While the economic boom continues to keep most people fed and upwardly mobile, real political freedoms and dissent from Communist Party rule will not be a priority for the average citizen in Beijing.

21ST-CENTURY BEIJING Today Beijing is changing fast. Although the wide boulevards will stay, almost every building from the last century is either being renovated, or torn down for something taller and better, or new storeys are being added. Public toilets (thankfully) are being overhauled (some even have a star-rating system!) and the underground transportation system is being expanded considerably in preparation for the Olympics. Most of the old one-storey *hutong* that were left within the old city walls are being razed to make way for modern hotels, public spaces and pedestrian areas. Some *hutong*, however, are being preserved and are fast becoming the chic 'new China' places to wine and dine.

The city is now home to 15 million people, of whom 60,000 are permanent foreign residents. In addition, Beijing receives tens of millions of visitors every year, only four million of whom are from abroad. As part of China's bid to host the Olympics in 2008, the country promised to overhaul its environmental record and clean up its air, garbage problems and traffic congestion. The government does not want wandering foreign tourists to see the old inferior-quality China of the communist heyday, and you will be lucky (or unlucky, depending on how you look at it) to find it anywhere in Beijing province or a lot of other tourist sites by 2008. This drive to improve the quality of the capital will continue through to the World Expo of 2010. China hopes that the World Expo, which led to the revitalisation of Japan in 1970, will do the same for China.

GETTING AROUND

BY UNDERGROUND Until Beijing finishes its many new underground (dìtiě 地铁) lines (at least five new lines) for the Olympics, navigating Beijing will remain a nightmare for most foreigners. Even then, the new lines will not open up very much of the centre, but will make the outer reaches of Beijing more accessible. For instance there will be a direct line from the airport to Dongzhimen. Until then three lines must suffice: line 1 going east–west following the main boulevard in town, Chang An Jie; line 2 encircling the city core; and line 13 making a loop of the north of the city. (The lines between 2 and 13 are not yet complete.) Some of the central underground stations are being turned into shopping plazas, otherwise most of them are drab affairs. The underground sign is a blue 'D' inside a circle, and dotted around town are signs in English and Chinese directing the way to the underground. Tickets are ¥3 per journey. Make sure you keep your tickets as, very occasionally, the underground ticket staff (they are almost all women) will check your ticket on the way out. The new underground lines will have electric ticket-checking barriers like the ones in London. Each stop is announced on the train in advance in both English and Chinese. See map page 148.

BY BUS Whilst **city buses** (gōnggòngqìchē 公共汽车) are cheap, frequent and cover every main street in Beijing, they can be extremely crowded and, without a grasp of Chinese characters, it is very difficult to know where they are going. If you can get your head around Chinese characters, then Chinese buses are in fact much more user friendly than the old London bus. Almost every bus stop displays a sign showing all the stops of each bus line stopping there, and most also display, in characters big enough for you to see from the bus, the name of the bus stop and which is the next stop so that you know what is coming up. Kiosks around main bus stops, at underground stations and many hawkers on the street sell Beijing travel and tourist maps (Běijīng Jiāotōng Yóulǎntú 北京交通游览图) for ¥4. Although the map is entirely in Chinese, bus numbers and routes are represented for all of Beijing and there are more useful maps of local sites and other information on the back. You'll practically need a magnifying glass to read it however. Most short bus rides are ¥1. Longer rides can cost up to ¥3 on the city

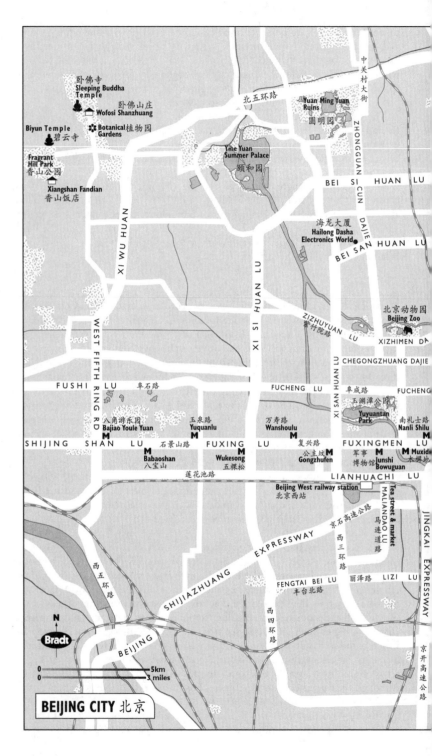

卧佛寺 **Sleeping Buddha Temple**

卧佛山庄 **Wofosi Shanzhuang**

Biyun Temple 碧云寺

Fragrant Hill Park 香山公园

Xiangshan Fandian 香山饭店

植物园 **Botanical Gardens**

北五环路

圆明园 **Yuan Ming Yuan Ruins** 圆明园

中关村大街

颐和园 **Yihe Yuan Summer Palace** 颐和园

海龙大厦 **Hailong Dasha Electronics World**

BEI SI HUAN LU

ZHONGGUAN CUN

BEI SAN HUAN LU

XI WU HUAN

XI SI HUAN LU

北京动物园 **Beijing Zoo**

ZIZHUYUAN LU

普村院路

XIZHIMEN DA

CHEGONGZHUANG DAJIE

FUSHI LU

WEST FIFTH RING RD

阜石路

FUCHENG LU

阜成路

FUCHENG

XI SAN HUAN LU

玉渊潭公园 **Yuyuantan Park**

南礼士路 **Nanli Shilu**

八角游乐园 **Bajiao Youle Yuan** Ⓜ

玉泉路 **Yuquanlu** Ⓜ

万寿路 **Wanshoulu** Ⓜ

SHIJING SHAN LU

石景山路 Ⓜ

FUXING LU

复兴路

公主坟 **Gongzhufen** Ⓜ

军事博物馆 **Junshi Bowuguan**

FUXINGMEN LU

木樨地 Ⓜ **Muxidi**

Babaoshan 八宝山

Wukesong 五棵松

莲花池路

LIANHUACHI LU

Beijing West railway station 北京西站

SHIJIAZHUANG EXPRESSWAY

京石高速公路

西三环路

马连道路 Tea street & market **MALIANDAO LU**

JINGKAI EXPRESSWAY

西五环路

FENGTAI BEI LU 丰台北路

丽泽路 **LIZI LU**

京开高速公路

西四环路

N

Bradt

0 ———————— 5km
0 ———————— 3 miles

BEIJING

BEIJING CITY 北京

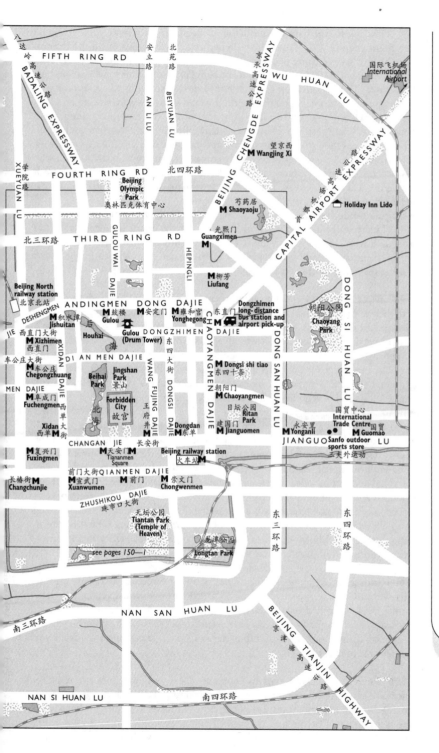

八达岭 FIFTH RING RD 安立路 北苑路

BADALING EXPRESSWAY

学院路 XUEYUAN LU

京承高速公路 BEIJING CHENGDE EXPRESSWAY

WU HUAN LU 五环路

国际飞机场 **International Airport**

AN LI LU 安立路

BEIYUAN LU 北苑路

望京西 **M** Wangjing Xi

机场高速 CAPITAL AIRPORT EXPRESSWAY 首都机场高速

FOURTH RING RD 北四环路

Beijing Olympic Park 奥林匹克体育中心

芍药居 **M** Shaoyaoju

☐ **Holiday Inn Lido**

北三环路 THIRD RING RD

GULOU WAI DAJIE 鼓楼外大街

HEPINGLI 和平里

光熙门 **M** Guangximen

DONG SI HUAN LU 东四环路

朝阳公园 **Chaoyang Park**

柳芳 **M** Liufang

Beijing North railway station 北京北站

DESHENGMEN JIE 德胜门

M Jishuitan 积水潭

ANDINGMEN DONG DAJIE 安定门东大街

M Gulou 鼓楼

安定门 **M**

雍和宫 **M** Yonghegong

东直门 **M** Dongzhimen

Dongzhimen long-distance bus station and airport pick-up

CHAOYANGMEN DAJIE 朝阳门大街

DONG SAN HUAN LU 东三环路

XIDAN JIE 西单

M Xizhimen 西直门

Houhai 后海

Gulou (Drum Tower) 鼓楼

DONGZHIMEN DAJIE

东四大街

M Dongsi shi tiao 东四十条

车公庄大街

M Chegongzhuang 车公庄

DI AN MEN DAJIE 地安门大街

Jingshan Park 景山

WANG FUJING DAJIE 王府井大街

DONGSI DAJIE 东四大街

朝阳门 **M** Chaoyangmen

MEN DAJIE

M Fuchengmen 阜成门

Beihai Park 北海

Forbidden City 故宫

日坛公园 **Ritan Park**

建国门 **M** Jianguomen

国贸中心 **International Trade Centre** 国贸

Xidan 西单大街

Dongdan 东单

M Dongdan 东单

永安里 **M** Yonganli

M Guomao 国贸

CHANGAN JIE 长安街

M 天安门 **M**

Beijing railway station 火车站 **M**

JIANGUO LU 建国路

Sanfo outdoor sports store 三夫外运动

M Fuxingmen 复兴门

M 天安门 **M** **Tiananmen Square**

长椿街 **M** Changchunjie

前门大街 QIANMEN DAJIE

M Xuanwumen 宣武门

M 前门

崇文门 **M** Chongwenmen

ZHUSHIKOU DAJIE 珠市口大街

天坛公园 **Tiantan Park (Temple of Heaven)**

东三环路 DONG SAN HUAN LU

东四环路 DONG SI HUAN LU

see pages 150–1

龙潭公园 **Longtan Park**

NAN SAN HUAN LU 南三环路

京津塘高速公路 BEIJING TIANJIN HIGHWAY

南三环路 NAN SAN HUAN LU

NAN SI HUAN LU 南四环路

buses. Most buses still have a conductor on board, from whom you can buy a ticket. Some require you to have the correct money to drop in a bin at the front of the bus. Many buses require you to get on the front and move to the back to get off. The old white-and-red city buses are at last being phased out for newer green-and-yellow buses. The privatisation of some lines is now also taking place. Yuntong 运通 buses are one example. For a map of their routes go to www.tdzsh.com.cn.

Minibuses (gōng jiāo chē 公交车) ply a lot of the city bus routes along main streets such as Chang An Jie. These are usually a little more expensive (minimum ¥2) but are fast as they stop only at main stops and once they are full they just keep going until the next passenger gets off. This means you are most likely to get a seat. They are not numbered, but might display their final destination in the front windscreen. The conductress (it is usually a woman) shouts the direction of the route as the bus drives at running pace past the stop.

Long-distance buses (cháng tú qì chē 长途汽车) go from main hubs located on the old city walls. These are: Dongzhimen – for the east and northeast such as Huairou, Miyun, Huangyaguan and Chengde. Xizhimen – for buses to the west such as Xiangshan, Shidu and Badaling. Deshengmen – for buses to the north including the Ming tombs and Datong. Qianmen – for places south.

BY TAXI Most foreigners end up taking taxis (chū zū qì chē 出租汽车) to get to where they want to go, and of course if you are two or more people the economics of this makes more sense. The initial fare for flagging down a taxi is ¥10 with a variety of per-kilometre rates thereafter depending on the size of the car. The per-kilometre rate is usually displayed on one of the side windows. Taxi fares are not negotiable, but make sure the driver does indeed run the meter (biǎo 表) in case you do end up getting ripped off. For the time being taking taxis in Beijing is still cheap. However, this is going to change. The rise in the price of oil over 2004 has meant that taxi and bus fares have almost doubled in the past few years. Further rises in the price of oil, coupled with China's increasing demand for oil, will continue to affect the price of fares. In addition, the cheap ¥1.20 taxis are in the process of being phased out before the Olympics because they do not meet the new Beijing environmental standards. The old red ¥1.60 and ¥2.00 taxis will remain. New blue-and-yellow or green-and-yellow ¥2.40 taxis have recently been introduced and the prices may get higher by 2008. By then the economics of taxis may become less tenable for the average traveller. The new underground lines will help to alleviate this, however, and may help to ease congestion, which is dire in Beijing during rush hour (which is most of the day) and especially when it rains – then everybody and his dog is taking a taxi.

BY CAR Hiring a car in Beijing is not really an option as foreigners may only drive in China with a Chinese driving licence and a resident's permit. Even under these circumstances, you had better take an extremely good navigator with you. Negotiating the ring roads, one-way streets and sometimes gridlock traffic will try the patience of any monk. Five- and four-star hotels can arrange hiring a car for you if you are able to take this option.

BY TRAIN There are four train stations (huǒ chē 火车) in Beijing, none of which is connected to another by train or yet by underground. All major lines go out of the main railway station in the southeast of the city. A number of important lines, such as the fast trains to Datong, also go out of Beijing West. Minibuses ply the route between the main station and the west station. They leave from the front of the main railway square when full. Smaller lines to provincial Beijing go out of Beijing South, North and West.

Buying train tickets at Beijing main station can be daunting, as the number of Chinese jostling for tickets at the ten ticket booths outside the right-hand end of the station is constantly too many. You may prefer to get your hotel (at a small cost, usually ¥30 per ticket) to arrange the tickets for you. Or on arrival at Beijing station, before you exit into the square, there is one ticket booth for buying onward tickets. There is also a soft seater/sleeper ticket booth for foreigners inside the soft seater waiting room on the far left-hand side of the main hall.

Taxis from Beijing main station are located at the northwest corner of the station square. Just join the long queue of Chinese waiting for a taxi and avoid the unlicensed unmetered taxi cabbies who will offer to take you to your destination for a cheap price, but, aside from being unlicensed, will mostly charge you twice the going rate or more. You'll notice that Chinese travellers do not use them.

BY BICYCLE Bicycles (zì xíng chē 自行车) are not as abundant in Beijing as they used to be, as wealthy Beijingers turn to the car as their transport of choice (yes, many Beijing mothers now drive their one child to school and back). The bicycle, however, is still by far the quickest way of getting around if you know where you are going and you are not going too far. Most hotels and hostels can organise hiring a bicycle for you if you want to give it a go, and there are plenty of bicycle-hire shops/stalls near popular foreign tourist haunts. Daily rates are usually ¥20, but don't expect a super new and serviced bicycle. Bicycle-repair men are still dotted all over Beijing if you need to get a puncture fixed (or something more serious mended). Bicycle-rental shops usually require a big deposit or your passport as an assurance that you will bring the bike back to them.

ON FOOT Visiting Beijing's sights on foot is exhausting and the city is not really designed for walking and sightseeing. A prudent bit of walking, however, can save you quite some time (and taxi money), especially as traffic frequently gets stuck at junctions or takes a long time to round a major corner. Crossing a road or junction to get a taxi already heading in the direction you want to go can save you both time and money. During the day, walking a little further to an underground station and using the underground for most of your journey inevitably saves more time than taking a taxi for the same distance.

STAYING LONGER

If you think you might want or need to overstay your visa, then you will need to get it extended at the Foreign Affairs Section of the Public Security Bureau:

Beijing Municipal Public Security Bureau No 9, Qianmen Dongdajie, Dongcheng District, 100740 Beijing; e 110@bjgaj.gov.cn

COMMUNICATIONS

There are post offices all over Beijing, including at the airport and in some hotels. Post boxes are recognisable by their dark green colour. Major post offices will also provide their parcel service, EMS. The main post office in Beijing which provides poste restante as well as all the other postal services is at 25 Jianguomen Nei Dajie.

Fedex and DHL services are available at the China World Trade Centre, above Guomao underground station and in some of the big five-star hotels. Calls to a landline number within Beijing are usually free in hotels, although at lower-end

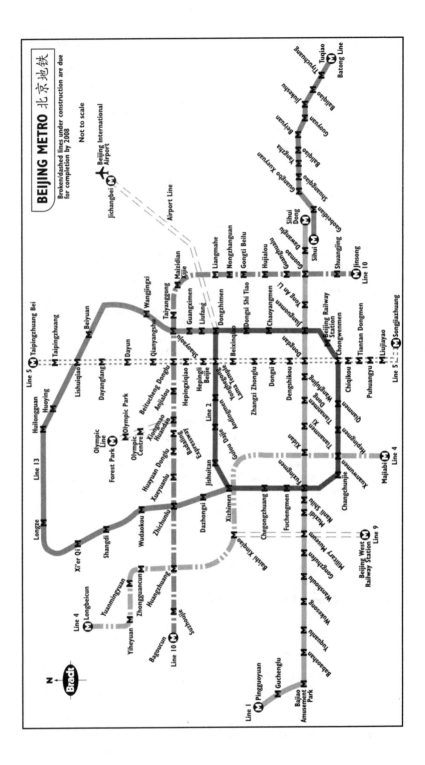

hotels you may need to queue at the front desk for this. Outside hotels, public phones are available for use with coins or cards that can be bought from local kiosks,many of which also have a phone that you can use. Once you have finished your call you will be charged according to their counter.

Mobile phone top-up cards are available all over the place, including in supermarkets and street kiosks. Just make sure you buy the right one (China Mobile or China Unicom) for your phone.

Internet cafés are not as ubiquitous as you might imagine in a country leapfrogging into 21st-century communication. The most common chain of internet cafés is Sparkice. Most hotels now have internet services ranging anywhere from ¥10 per hour to ¥5 for ten minutes, but printing and other business services might not be available or are very expensive. Some of the high-end business hotels now offer wireless internet for free. Beijing University has internet services, and a number of Starbucks are pursuing their global policy of providing wireless connections in their cafés. Starbucks can be found for instance at the west exit of China International Trade Centre Guo Mao, downstairs at Wangfujing's Oriental Plaza and at the Lido Hotel. Passers' By Bar (see page 155) also has free wireless internet access. For a list of expanding wireless hotspots check www.jiwire.com, www.locfinder.com or www.wi-fihotspotlist.com.

WHERE TO STAY

As Beijing tears down more of its hútòng 胡同 in the core of the city, more hotels are becoming available there, obviating some of the frustration associated with navigating city transport to get into central attractions. Most courtyard hotels are located in what is left of the city's central *hutong* area. This guide concentrates on accommodation nearer the centre of town.

OUTRAGEOUSLY EXPENSIVE, BUT IF YOU'VE GOT IT AND YOU'RE HERE...

The Commune By The Great Wall Chángchéng Jiāoxià de Gōngshè 长城脚下的公社 (4 houses) Badaling Great Wall, Shuiguan exit off Badaling highway; ℓ 010 8118 1888; www.commune.com.cn. China's showcase of 21st-century Asian architecture right under the wall. Clubhouse pool included. *Limousine service goes for ¥500 to ¥1,200 for the day. Entire houses go for between ¥7,500 and ¥11,000 per night! Occasionally, they do special offers, so it is worth checking out their website.*

MID-RANGE TO TOP-END WESTERN-STYLE HOTELS

Donghua Fandian 东华饭店 (46 rooms) 32 Deng Shi Kou Xi Jie, Dongcheng District; ℓ 010 6525 7531. Nicely furnished if small rooms. Comes with all the mod cons. *Sgls ¥300; twin or dbl ¥450.*

Dongfang Heping Binguan 东方和平宾馆(101 rooms) 33 Santiaojia, Dongdan, Dongcheng District; ℓ 010 6513 2919; f 010 6524 5047. Opened in 2004, this clean bright hotel is appropriately named 'Oriental Peace' in Chinese as it is surprisingly quiet, despite being a stone's throw from Wangfujing shopping area. Tucked down a very small alley next to Artistic Mansion on Dongdan Santiao. Internet ¥6 per hour. All rooms en suite. Breakfast included. *Sgl and standard twins ¥378; trpl ¥428.*

Huafu Guoji Jiudian 华府国际酒店 (200 rooms) 53 Donganmen Dajie; Dongcheng District; ℓ 010 5120 9588; f 010 5120 9599. Newly opened in 2004, the Chinese-style façade to this hotel opens into a spacious well-lit lobby and spacious clean rooms with all the mod cons including free ethernet connection. One of the three restaurants in the hotel is a mock night food stall street, and you also have the real thing right outside the front door. *Standard twin or dbl ¥600.*

Times Holiday Hotel 时代假日酒店 (120 rooms) 57 Deng Shi Kou Da Jie, Dongcheng District; ℓ 010 6526 9955; f 010 6513 2951. Clean new rooms with free ethernet connection and a gym downstairs. *Twin or dbl ¥640.*

Song He Hotel 松鹤酒店 (300 rooms) 88 Deng Shi Kou Da Jie, Dongcheng District; ℓ 010 6513 8822; f 010 6513 9088; e reservation@songhehotel.com; www.songhehotel.com. Four-star hotel, bright and friendly. Helpful staff. *Standard twin or dbl ¥1,000.*

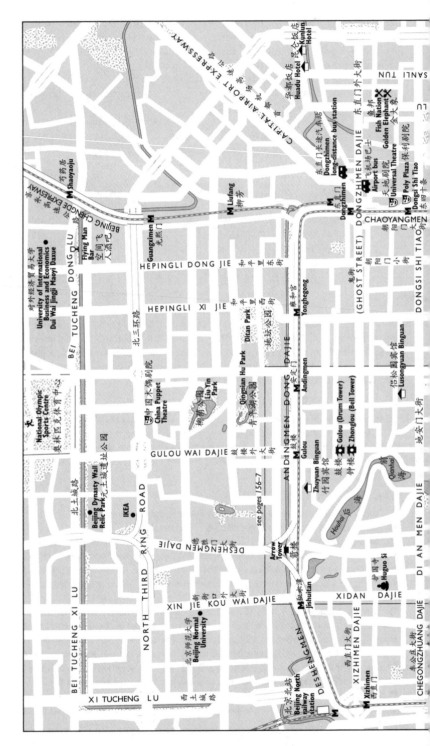

National Olympic Sports Centre
奥林匹克体育中心

University of International
Business and Economics
Dui Wai Jingji Maoyi Daxue
对外经济贸易大学

Flying Man Bar
空间飞人酒吧

BEI TUCHENG DONG LU

Shaoyaoju
芍药居

CAPITAL AIRPORT EXPRESSWAY
首都机场高速

BEIJING CHENGDE EXPRESSWAY
北京承德高速

Huadu Hotel 华都饭店

Kunlun Hotel 昆仑饭店

SANLI TUN

Fish Nation 鱼邦
Golden Elephant 金大象

Dongzhimen long-distance bus station
东直门长途汽车站

DONGZHIMEN DAJIE 东直门外大街

M Dongzhimen 东直门

Airport bus 飞机场巴士
Universal Theatre 天地剧院

Poly Plaza 保利剧院
Dongsi Shi Tiao 东四十条

CHAOYANGMEN

DONGSI SHI TIAO 地四条大街

M Guangximen 光熙门

Linfang 林芳

HEPINGLI DONG JIE 和平里东街

HEPINGLI XI JIE 和平里西街

Yonghegong 雍和宫
M Yonghegong

(GHOST STREET) 鬼街
朝阳门小街

Lusongyuan Binguan 侣松园宾馆

BEI TUCHENG XI LU

NORTH THIRD RING ROAD
北三环路

Ditan Park 地坛公园

Qingnian Hu Park 青年湖公园
Liu Yin Park 柳荫公园
柳荫街

ANDINGMEN DONG DAJIE 安定门东大街

M Andingmen 安定门

Gulou 鼓楼

China Puppet Theatre 中国木偶剧院

GULOU WAI DAJIE 鼓楼外大街

Beijing Dynasty Wall Relic Park
元土城遗址公园

IKEA

北土城路

see pages 156-7

Gulou (Drum Tower) 鼓楼
Zhonglou (Bell Tower) 钟楼

Zhuyuan Binguan 竹园宾馆

DESHENGMEN DAJIE 德胜门大街

Qianhai 前海

Houhai 后海

DI AN MEN DAJIE 地安门大街

Arrow Tower 箭楼
鼓楼

M Jishuitan 积水潭
Jishuitan

XIN JIE KOU WAI DAJIE 新街口外大街

Beijing Normal University 北京师范大学

XIDAN DAJIE 西单大街

Huguo Si 护国寺
护国寺

Beijing North railway station 北京北站

M Xizhimen 西直门
Xizhimen

XIZHIMEN DAJIE 西直门大街

XI TUCHENG LU 西土城路
西土城路

DESHENGMEN 德胜门

CHEGONGZHUANG DAJIE 车公庄大街

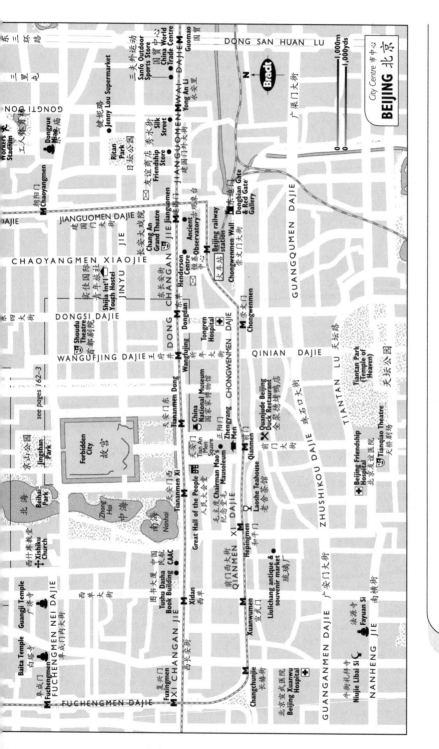

BEIJING 北京

City Centre 市中心

Bradt

N

1,000m
1,000yds

DONG SAN HUAN LU

Workers' Stadium
工人体育场
Dongyue Miao 东岳庙

GONGTIRON

Jenny Lou Supermarket
健妮露

Sanlitun 三里屯

Sanlitu Outdoor Sports Store
三夫户外运动

国贸商城 China World Trade Centre
Guomao 国贸

M Chaoyangmen
朝阳门

Ritan Park
日坛公园

Friendship Store 友谊商店

Xiushui Jie Silk Street
秀水街

Yong An Li 永安里

M Jianguomen 建国门

Chang An Grand Theatre
建国门大戏院

JIANGUOMEN DAJIE

JINYU JIE

CHAOYANGMEN XIAOJIE

Ancient Observatory 古观象台

HANGUOMEN MWAY
建国门外大街

Dongbian Gate & Red Gate Gallery
东便门 红门画廊

DAJIE

Jiajia Int'l Youth Hostel
家佳旅社
Shijia Int'l Youth Hostel
青年旅社

DONGSI DAJIE

Beijing railway station
火车站

Chongwenmen Wall
崇文门大街

GUANGQUMEN DAJIE

Shoudu Theatre
首都剧院

WANGUFJING DAJIE
王府井大街

Henderson Centre 恒基中心

M Dongdan 东单

Tongren Hospital
同仁医院

M Chongwenmen 崇文门

QINIAN DAJIE

TIANTAN LU 天坛路

Tiantan Park (Temple of Heaven)
天坛公园

China National Museum
国家博物馆

Wangfujing 王府井

DONG CHANGAN JIE

M Tiananmen Dong 天安门东

Forbidden City 故宫

Jingshan Park 景山公园

Beihai Park 北海

Xishiku Church 西什库教堂

Zhong Hai 中海

Nanhai 南海

Tiananmen Xi 天安门西

Great Hall of the People
人民大会堂

Tian An Men Square 天安门广场

Chairman Mao's Mausoleum
毛主席纪念堂

Zhengyang Men 正阳门

M Qianmen 前门

Quanjude Beijing Duck Restaurant
全聚德烤鸭店

CHONGWENMEN DAJIE

珠市口大街

Tianqiao Theatre
天桥剧场

Beijing Friendship Hospital
北京友谊医院

ZHUSHIKOU DAJIE

Baita Temple 白塔寺

Guangji Temple 广济寺

FUCHENGMEN NEI DAJIE
阜成门内大街

M Fuchengmen 阜成门

Tushu Dasha Book Building
图书大厦

Xidan 西单

CAAC 民航

XI DAJIE

M Xidan 西单

Hepingmen 和平门

Laoshe Teahouse 老舍茶馆

Liulichang antique & souvenir market
琉璃厂

QIANMEN

M Xuanwumen 宣武门

MXI CHANGAN JIE
西长安街

Fuxingmen 复兴门

GUANGANMEN DAJIE 广安门大街

Changchunjie 长椿街

Beijing Xuanwu Hospital
北京宣武医院

Niujie Libai Si 牛街礼拜寺

NANHENG JIE 南横街

Fayuan Si 法源寺

GUANGANMEN DAJIE

FUCHENGMEN DAJIE 阜成门大街

see pages 162–3

151

🏠 **Novotel Peace Hotel** (344 rooms) 3 Jinyu Hutong (Goldfish Lane), Dongcheng District; 📞 010 6512 8833; www.accorhotels.com/asia. For all the comforts of the Novotel chain, plus an excellent buffet restaurant, The Square. Easy walking distance to the night food market and to Wangfujing. Usually has promotional offers on rooms and business rooms are often cheaper than the listed standard room price. *Twin or dbl ¥1,494.*

🏠 **The Beijing Fandian** 北京饭店 (450 rooms) 33 Dong Chang An Jie, Dongcheng District; 📞 010 6513 7766; www.chinabeijinghotel.com. The closest major hotel on Chang An Boulevard to Tiananmen Square. This was one of the first hotels to open up to foreigners, and is great for its Soviet-style massive halls and lounge areas, although now completely renovated. Even if you don't stay, pop in for high tea and to use the restrooms, toilet attendants in tow. View of the Forbidden City from the top-floor rooms is unrivalled. *There are no standard rooms; all are deluxe and above! Sgl deluxe ¥1,950; Forbidden City suite ¥2,860.*

COURTYARD HOTELS If you are going to travel all the way from China, you may as well stay somewhere that feels authentically and uniquely Chinese. The following are some of the nicest and quietest hútòng sìhéyuàn 胡同四合院 courtyard hotels – all can be booked direct or through www.chinadiscounthotel.com/beijing/index.html. Owing to their popularity, you many need to book well over a month in advance for rooms.

🏠 **Zhuyuan Binguan** 竹园宾馆 (57 rooms) 24 Xiao Shi Qiao Rd, Jiu Gu Lou, Xicheng District; 📞 010 6403 2229. The former home of Qing officials and eunuchs, this hotel, called 'Bamboo Garden' in English, is a veritable garden of peace and close to the restaurants and bars of Houhai, the back lake of the Forbidden Palace. Has its own travel service. *Standard twin ¥540; deluxe ¥620.*

🏠 **Haoyuan Binguan** 好院宾馆 (19 rooms) 53 Shijia Hutong, Dongcheng District; 📞 010 6512 5557; 📠 010 6918 1904; 📧 haoyuanbinguan@sohu.com. This charming *hutong*, right in the centre of town but away from the hustle and bustle is well located near the main Wangfujing shopping area and not too far from the Forbidden City. Standard rooms are bijou and dimly lit. Ming- and Qing-style furnishings in all rooms. The hotel is run by the Haoyuan Women's Association, who are very helpful and who all speak English. Good restaurant. Internet ¥10 per hour. All rooms en suite. Includes breakfast. *Standard twin ¥560; dbl and twin deluxe ¥630.*

🏠 **Jin Ya Zhaodaisuo** 金鸭招待所 (12 rooms) 67–71 Dongsi Liutiao Hutong, Dongcheng District; 📞 010 6401 8823. A small hotel catering mostly to Chinese dinner parties, but therefore all the more authentic. Recently refurbished. *Standard twin ¥550.*

🏠 **Lusongyuan Hotel** 侣松园宾馆 (58 rooms) 22 Banchang Hutong, Kuan Jie, Dongcheng District; 📞 010 6404 0436; 📠 010 6403 0418; 📧 lsyhotel@263.net; www.the-silk-road.com. Clustered around five separate courtyards, this hotel offers huokang-style dbls and Ming- and Qing-style furnishings. Conveniently located between Wangfujing, the Forbidden City and Houhai Lake. Dorm beds downstairs in windowless rooms using a common external bathroom. Runs all the usual tour and travel services for foreign guests. Email ¥5 for ten minutes, restaurant, tea garden and library. Mr Leo's shop two houses down the road offers cheaper internet and tours. *Buffet breakfast ¥30. Dorm bed ¥100. Sgls ¥320; standard twin ¥550; deluxe dbl ¥720; suite ¥950.*

🏠 **Wofosi Shanzhuang** 卧佛山庄 (Sleeping Buddha Hotel 75 rooms) Wofo Si Lu, Haidian District; 📞 010 8259 6066/1459. If you don't want to stay in the constant buzz of the Beijing metropolis, then try this courtyard hotel adjacent to the Sleeping Buddha Temple in the grounds of the Botanical Gardens. The five-courtyard complex often caters for government retreats and comes complete with a bowling alley, 20m swimming pool, sauna and restaurant (all at extra cost). The setting is idyllic, especially in late spring through autumn. The hotel is 90 mins outside the centre of Beijing. By public transport, take the underground to Xizhimen, and then bus 904 to Wofosi Binguan. If you have a lot of luggage you might want to phone the hotel to pick you up from the bus stop. *Standards ¥480–580; dbl ¥680; suite ¥1,180.*

🏠 **You Hao (Best Friends) Mansion** 友好公馆 (52 rooms) 7 Hou Yuan An Si Hutong, Jiao Dao Kou, Dongcheng District; 📞 010 6403 1114; 📠 010 6401 4603. Less a siheyuan than a mix of courtyard, Victorian mansion and Chinese garden all in grey, typical of the republican-era mix of East and West. It was the home of Chiang Kai Shek for a period and then the embassy of Yugoslavia. Japanese restaurant in the grounds of the courtyard. *Sgl, which can also serve as a small dbl ¥450; standard twin ¥560; suite ¥800.*

HOSTELS AND BUDGET

🏠 **Beijing Dongfang Chengguang Youth Hostel** 东方晨光青年旅社 (78 beds) 8–16 Dong Dan San Yiao, Dongcheng District; ✆ 010 6528 4347; 📠 010 6528 4350. You can't get closer to shopping, food markets and an underground station. Five mins walk from Wangfujing underground. When you exit the station at Wangfujing follow the traffic round to the right and it is past the next set of traffic lights on your left. A small train-ticket outlet is located in the entrance of Artistic Mansion (an electronic goods store) between the hostel and Wangfujing. *Dorm bed ¥70; Sgls ¥120; twins ¥150; trpls ¥200.*

🏠 **Downtown Backpackers** 东堂客栈 (67 beds) 85 Nan Luo Gu Xiang, Pingan Dajie, Dongcheng District; ✆ 010 8400 2429; 📧 downtown@backpackingchina.com; www.backpackingchina.com. A newly opened backpackers' haunt run by seasoned Chinese backpackers, and conveniently located in the preserved hútòng area near popular Houhai Lake. Laundry, book exchange, internet. Bars and hangouts in the immediate vicinity. All rooms are en suite and include free breakfast. Free pick up from the airport if you book for more than three days. Offers reasonably priced travel and tour options. *Dorms from ¥50; dbl or twin ¥160.*

🏠 **Beijing Saga (Shijia) International Youth Hostel** 北京实佳国际青年旅社 (86 beds) 9 Shijia Hutong, Dongcheng District; ✆ 010 6527 2773; 📠 010 6524 9098; 📧 sagayangguang@yahoo.com.cn. Friendly, clean youth hostel in a quiet hutong setting, 20 mins from Wangfujing pedestrian shopping street and the night food market. Restaurant and self-catering available. Internet café, washing machine and clothes-drying line, beer garden and lots more. Happy to help with onward travel and accommodation booking. *Dorm bed ¥80; Sgl ¥100; twin ¥180.*

🏠 **Poachers' Inn Friendship Youth Hostel** Yǒuyì Qīngnián Lǚshè 友谊青年旅社 (58 beds) 43 Bei Sanlitun Lu, Chaoyang District; ✆ 010 6417 2632/2597; 📠 010 6415 6866; 📧 poacher43_cn@sina.com; www.poachers.com.cn. Sandwiched between the popular Poachers' Inn and The Tree, in the street west and parallel to the Sanlitun Bar and café street. *Dorm bed ¥70; twin ¥180.*

🏠 **Tailong Binguan** 泰龙宾馆 (60 rooms) 51 Dong An Men Da Jie, Dongcheng District; ✆ 010 6525 7908. This hotel is right at the Donghuamen night market and close to Wangfujing. Clean and bright rooms with duvets and good showers. Friendly staff. No breakfast, no lift, no internet. *Standard twin ¥220; trpls ¥360.*

✗ WHERE TO EAT

There is an abundance of places to eat in Beijing and most are good and cheap. Some of the old favourite haunts are still going strong despite the massive redevelopment of the city in the run-up to the Olympics. In addition to traditional dishes, such as General Bao's chicken, stir-fried aubergines and Beijing roast duck, Beijing is also seeing a turn towards more modern, experimental and fusion cooking. The turnover in eateries as Beijing redevelops itself makes it difficult to keep track of what is still around or what is new. As with the *Entertainment* section below, the best way to find the latest, hippest and recommended places to eat is to pick up a free copy of *That's Beijing, Time Out Beijing* or *Beijing Talk* from any big hotel lobby, youth hostel or the Red Gate Gallery (see page 165). Until you get that far, a few restaurants and eating districts follow below.

✗ **Dongzhimen Nei Dajie** 东直门内, also known as Ghost Street (Guǐ Jiē 簋街), has a number of places where you can get bowls of handmade lā miàn 拉面 – (literally 'pull noodles' after the way in which the dough is pulled to form long strands of noodles) as well as lamb skewers and one of the most popular courtyard restaurants in the city, Hua Jia Yiyuan. Ghost Street is easily recognisable by its many red lanterns, hung out to keep the ghosts at bay.

✗ **Sanlitun, Houhai** and the west side of **Chaoyang Park** (see *Entertainment* below for more details) also offer some excellent Chinese restaurants as well as many world alternatives in case you are hankering for food from back home after a month or more of rice and noodles.

✗ **Wangfujing Snack Street** wángfǔjīng xiǎochī jiē 王府井小吃街 holds an array of tiny restaurants offering snacks and dishes from all over China. Iron plates (tiěbǎn 铁板) of sizzling meat and veg, hotpots (huǒguō 火锅) and steaming bowls of noodles accompany more lurid plucked sparrows and larvae grilled on skewers. A nightly performance of Beijing Opera takes place at the south end of the main alley and the north end is a plethora of stalls selling knick-knacks and souvenirs for those wanting mementoes of their trip to the Middle Kingdom. There is plenty of outdoor seating. The alley is tucked away behind a set of shops on the west side of the southern end of Wangfujing, straddling the trafficked and pedestrian parts of the street. Look for a narrow opening between the dense shops.

✕ **The Donganmen Night Market** Dōng'ānmén Shìchǎng 东安门市场 also offers a range of tempting dishes for you to eat along the street. Turn left at the north end of the pedestrian section of Wangfujing to see the long row of red- and white-lanterned stalls between 18.00 and 22.30.

Other great places to eat include:

✕ **The CourtYard** Sì Hé 四合 95 Dong Hua Men Da Jie, Dongcheng District; ☏ 010 6526 8883; ✉ restaurant@courtyard.net.cn; www.courtyardbeijing.com. Very classy fusion cuisine with a Chinese twist in a former courtyard overlooking the Forbidden City moat. For the location and the quality menu, the price is not so bad. You will definitely want to dress up for this restaurant. Discreet entrance shaded by bamboo on the north side of the Forbidden City car park. Truly excellent food, using the familiar knife-and-fork concept. Book ahead to be sure of a table. All staff speak English. Art gallery downstairs. Cigar divan upstairs. *Main courses start at ¥165. Open evenings only 18.00–22.00.*

✕ **Hua Jia Yiyuan** 花家怡园 235 Dongzhimen Nei Dajie (Gui Jie), Dongcheng District; ☏ 010 6405 1908. This beautiful courtyard restaurant serves a variety of Beijing, Sichuan and Guangdong dishes. Try their Beijing roast duck with traditional plum sauce and fusion sweet chilli sauce, and their tofu balls with vegetables. Nightly performances of the mask dance and other magical feats usually take place around 20.00. The restaurant is often packed by 19.00, so book ahead or be prepared to wait for a table – it's worth it. *Open daily almost around the clock 10.30–06.30.*

✕ **Fish Nation** Yúbāng 鱼邦 2 Sanlitun Bei Lu, Chaoyang District (around the corner from Poachers' Inn); ☏ 010 6415 0119. In case you are hankering for something from home, here you can find battered cod and chips with malt vinegar and ketchup.

✕ **Golden Elephant** Jīn Dàxiàng 金大象 7 Sanlitun Bei Lu, Chaoyang District; ☏ 010 6417 1650. Indian and Thai food at a very reasonable price. Lhasi, lamb and good seafood dishes. *Open daily 11.30–midnight.*

✕ **Green Angel Vegetarian Restaurant** Lùsè Tiānshí Cāntīng 绿色天食餐厅 57–5 Dengshi Xikou, Dongcheng District; ☏ 010 6524 2476. This restaurant is a fine example of the amazing imitations of meat that can be done with tofu and other meat substitutes. Try their fish in red sauce, meat skewers or smoked duck. They even do vegetarian Beijing roast duck with the wheat wraps and plum sauce. You'll find the restaurant on the north side of the street above a semi-precious stone shop. There is usually a couple of waiting staff standing outside ready to usher you upstairs. The shop downstairs also has a small stand of packaged vegetarian imitation meats for you to buy and take home.

✕ **The Source** Dōu Jiāngyuán 都江源 14 Banchang Hutong, Nan Luoguxiang, Kuanjie, Dongcheng District; ☏ 010 6400 3736. In the courtyard next to the Lusongyuan Hotel, this Sichuan fusion restaurant combines hip and traditional. Beautifully restored building. Especially recommended, all the more so if you are a single or pair of travellers as the set menu allows you to try eight or more dishes, which in most restaurants would only be available to a big group. *¥80 per person for their set menu, which can be Sichuan spicy hot or* wēilà *(non-spicy). Open daily 12.00–23.00.*

✕ **Xiao Shan Cheng** 小山城 (Little Mountain Town) 251 Dongzhimen Nei Dajie (Ghost Street), Dongcheng District; ☏ 010 8402 9856. Traditional busy hotpot (huǒguō) place serving plates of raw meat, fish and vegetables for you to cook in delicious soups bubbling at your table (see huǒguō menu helper, page 264). *Open daily around the clock.*

ENTERTAINMENT

See *Time Out Beijing, That's Beijing* or *Beijing Talk* in your hotel lobby for a full current listing of opera, acrobatic shows, music, cinema, drama, galleries, museums, bars, clubs and other shows and exhibitions. Below are a few to get you started:

CHINESE PERFORMANCE ARTS

Chaoyang Theatre Cháoyáng Jùchǎng 朝阳剧场 36 Donghuansan Bei Lu, Chaoyang District; ☏ 010 6507 2421. Magic show, including the mask dance, every evening 18.00–19.00. Chinese acrobatics (that does stuff with bodies and limbs enough to make your eyes water) every evening 19.15–20.20. Beijing Opera (unless you've had some sort of introduction to this, then it is more likely to hurt your ears than be enjoyable) every evening 19.20–20.20. Beijing Opera and magic special every evening 20.40–21.40.

You can also enjoy street performances of Beijing Opera for free at the Wangfujing food market (see page 153) and magic shows at Huajia Yiyuan (see page 154) while you eat.

BARS AND CLUBS Beijing has a thriving and wide-ranging bar and club scene. Sanlitun, despite the building site that is being created around it, still holds the highest concentration of bars, cafés and clubs in the city, albeit they are now mostly south of Worker Stadium Street. Other hang-out scenes are the south gate of Worker Stadium, the west side of Chaoyang Park and Bar Street Jiǔ Bā Lù 酒吧路 running south of the south gate of Chaoyang Park, and around Houhai. Here are a select few:

Boulder Bar 1 Shenggu Jiayuan, Anzhenqiao, Chaoyang District; ✆ 010 6444 1965. Where you can literally practise a bit of bouldering and go for a drink. Has the first and largest climbing wall in China. Harnesses and climbing shoes available for rent. *Open daily 08.30–midnight.*

Poachers Inn 43 Bei Sanlitun Lu, Chaoyang District; ✆ 010 6417 2632. At the bottom of the Poachers' Inn Friendship Youth Hostel (see page 153), this is still one of the most popular party atmospheres in Beijing. Drinks are cheap and cheerful, disco tunes rock the night away. The slightly quieter and more relaxed **Tree** is round the back, opposite the youth hostel entrance. *Open daily from 20.00 till the last person is thrown out.*

Public Space 24 Sanlitun, Chaoyang District. The first café-bar to open up on Sanlitun and still going strong. *Open daily 10.00–02.00.*

Red Yard 14 Yangwei Hutong, Meishuguan Houjie, Dongcheng District; ✆ 010 6403 1584. Hutong atmosphere, relaxed and inexpensive. *Open daily 11.00–midnight.*

Passers By Bar 108 Nan Luo Gu Xiang, Dongcheng District; ✆ 010 8403 8004; ✉ bar@gk01.com; www.gk01.com. Courtyard bar, restaurant and café with mellow music, a good menu and free wireless internet. Bring three books in exchange for one of theirs from their extensive library.

Touch 8 Qianhai Beiyan, Xicheng District; ✆ 010 6618 0809. Great in the summer to relax around the courtyard fish pond. *Open daily 18.00–03.00.*

Watch Bar 22 Dongshuncheng Jie, Dongcheng District; ✆ 010 6407 0115. Hosts fantastic photography exhibitions on the walls while you sip a drink or two. *Open daily 14.00–02.00.*

Zone 12 Houhai Xiyan, Xicheng District; ✆ 010 8403 1419. A good place to zone out in big lounge chairs in front of the lake when you've had enough of Beijing's madness.

TEAHOUSES Tea shops, where you usually buy the stuff but can also sample a pot or two, are springing up all over the place, including Wangfujing. Maliandao (map page 144) is the street most famous for purchasing tea. However, if you want to experience an original teahouse, where people would while away the afternoon eating cold snacks and sipping tea, or want to taste something more discerningly in the new Beijing style, then visit some of the suggestions below. Many of the big hotels, such as the Beijing Hotel on Chang An Jie, also offer English afternoon tea.

Fu Family Teahouse Chájiāfù 茶家傳 8 Jiao Ting, Shiqiao Dong, Deshengmen Nei Da Jie, Xicheng District; ✆ 010 6616 0725. Offers teas in an enclosed Ming pagoda-style setting overlooking Houhai Lake. Makes for a nice tranquil getaway after the bar fervour of Houhai. Same owners as the Noble Restaurant next door. *Both open daily 11.00–midnight.*

Lao She Teahouse 老舍茶馆 Building 3, Qianmen Xi Dajie, Xuanwu District; ✆ 010 6303 6830. Renowned for where the famous early communist writer Lao She wrote many of his novels, such as *Teahouse and Rickshaw Boy*, which criticised the decaying society that the Qing dynasty had become. The teahouse itself though is a stark reminder of the 1920s vaudeville-type decadence that juxtaposed itself against outdated Chinese traditions. Like the Sherlock Holmes pub in London, this teahouse is heavily touristed.

Qing Feng Guan Teahouse 清风官 32 Dayanyue Hutong, Nanchang Jie, Xicheng District; ✆ 010 6603 5979. Just west off Tiananmen Square, this teahouse is dedicated to Chinese traditional arts, such as calligraphy, painting, and playing the gǔqín 古琴 (a type of zither). *Teas start at ¥100 per pot. Open daily noon to midnight.*

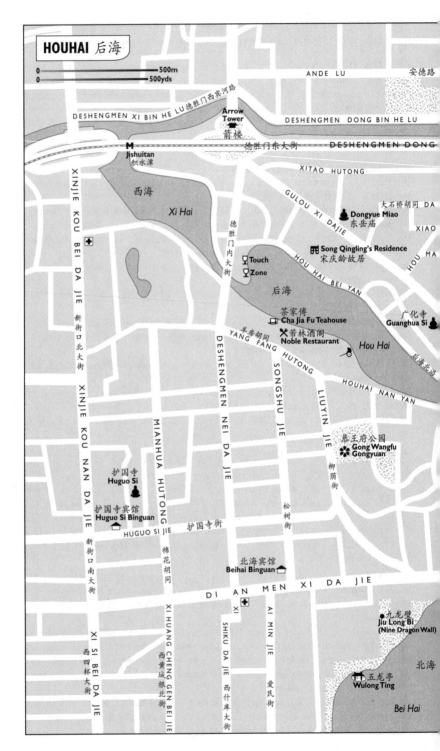

HOUHAI 后海

0 ——————— 500m
0 ——————— 500yds

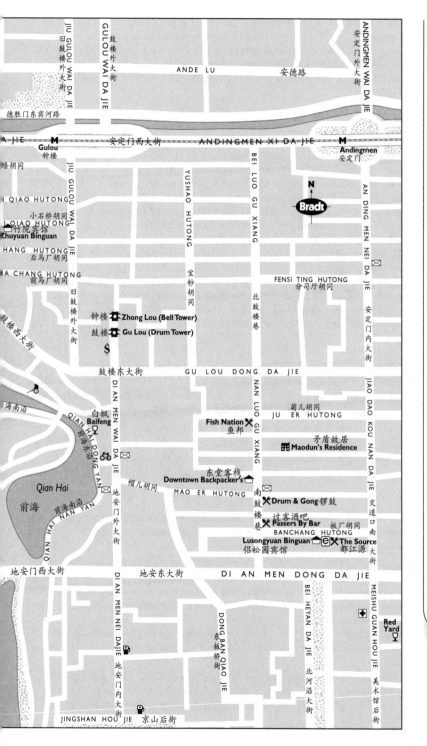

Rose Garden Henderson Centre, (the entrance is street side) Beijing Zhan Jie, Dongcheng District; ✆ 010 6518 1812. Plush attempt at an *olde Englishe tea shoppe*, although it is in fact very new and windowless. Still, it is the best place to get that cup of decent English black tea, served strong enough to stand a spoon in it if you like it that way. High tea, complete with white sliced bread cucumber sandwiches with the crusts cut off, scones, rich fruit cake, biscuits and tea comes at ¥80 per person. You might want to dress up a bit to sup there. 10% service charge added to all bills. *Open daily 09.00–20.00.*

SHOPPING

Beijing (and most of the east coast) is fast becoming one massive shopping mall, not unlike many modern cities. Bargaining at street stalls (for tips on how to bargain see page 86) is slowly giving way to fixed prices in posh boutiques. Many subway stations are being turned into shopping precincts such as the Oriental Plaza between Wangfujing and Dongdan stations. Wangfujing's pedestrian section is still the most popular with both Chinese and foreigners for a leisurely mix of a bit of everything. Xidan is another popular area for shopping but stretched over a major intersection. The Friendship Store, now an institution in itself, offers quality goods tailored specifically for foreigners. Once upon a time it was the only place where foreigners were officially allowed to buy, and it was the only place to accept Foreign Exchange Certificates (see *Money and budgeting*, page 85). While it is more expensive than bargaining on the street or in Silk Street, it is a convenient one-stop shop if you don't have much time. All the staff speak English and the store accepts credit cards. An ATM is located on the ground floor.

ANTIQUES AND SOUVENIRS liúlíchǎng 琉璃厂 is the pedestrian street renowned for its antiques, Chinese traditional crafts and all sorts of other 'genuine' souvenirs. This is where you can bargain away till your heart is content for Chinese fans, wall paintings, swords (tàijí 太极), old coins, jade turtles, calligraphy brushes, papers and ink, watercolours and many, many other things. To get there take the underground line 2 to Hepingmen and from the southwest exit either walk ten minutes down Nan Xin Hua Jie or take bus 7 or 14 one stop to Liulichang.

Smaller souvenirs can also be bought at the Wangfujing food street (see page 153).

BOOKS AND MAPS There is a number of bookstores in Beijing where you can buy foreign-language books and a variety of maps. Backpacker hostels and hotels with a lot of foreigners also run book exchanges.

Beijing Book Building Běijīng Túshū Dàshà 北京图书大厦 17 Xi Changan Jie, Xidan. This is the mother of all bookstores in China. Over ten floors of books and book-related items. If you can't find a book here then you are unlikely to find it anywhere in China. Chinese-authored guidebooks in English and Chinese on Chinese provinces and towns are on the ground floor immediately in front of the main entrance. Take the northeast exit out of Xidan underground and the store is right behind you.

The Friendship Store Yǒuyì Shāngdiàn 友谊商店 Jianguomen Wai Dajie. Has a small useful section of books on China, learning Chinese, foreign magazines and newspapers, and travel guidebooks for a lot of the rest of the world.

Xinhua Shudian 新化书店 218 Wangfujing Dajie, Dongcheng District; ✆ 010 6513 2842. A mere seven floors of books. Maps of Chinese provinces, Chinese auto atlases, and maps of other countries are on the left after you enter the main door. Take the Wangfujing exit (northeast) from the underground station and the shop is less than two mins north up the street.

CLOTHING AND SILK The much-revered **Silk Street** Xiùshuǐ Shìchǎng 秀水市场, which for 20 years was down a narrow alley to the northeast of Yonganli underground station, has now become a six-storey grandiose affair with its own entrance from the subway. Prices have not gone up too much in this time. Bargains can still be had and bargaining is still the rule. Clothing and fabric items are available in all sorts of material, not just silk, and includes Gore-tex, linen, cashmere and plenty of fake stuff. The top floor also offers bolts of silk, which you can buy by the metre, as well as tailoring services. On the silk side you will get everything from Union Jack silk underwear to tablecloths and cushion covers. There is an ATM at the entrance to the underground at the bottom of Silk Street.

Silk Street can make for quite a high-pressure buying experience, with vendors harking at your every move. A much less overwhelming experience can be found in the passageway connecting Silk Street to the other side of the Changan Jie main road. Much the same stuff is on offer and the starting price is usually much lower.

Other areas for silk include the Silk and Cotton Store on Wangfujing, and the Friendship Store. Both also offer tailoring services.

Xidan's **Times Square** also offers a lot of boutique shopping, and the International Trade Centre (Guó Mào 国贸) touts upmarket brands, both national and international.

ELECTRONICS If you are after anything electronic, whether the real thing, fake, or home-grown alternatives, then **Hailong Dasha (Sea Dragon Tower** 海龙大厦) at 1 Zhong Guan Cun Dajie is the place in Beijing to get it. In fact the whole of Zhong Guan Cun Dajie is a big electronics shopping arcade. To get there take the underground to Xizhimen and then take bus 106 or 808 for about half an hour to Zhong Guan Cun. The store is on the west side of the street just south of the pedestrian overpass.

For cheap mobile phones, international and Chinese models, go to the **mobile phone market** (shǒujī shìchǎng 手机市场) at Xidan Dajie. The street is lined with mobile phone shops, including branches of China Unicom, China Mobile, Nokia, Sony Ericsson and others. A lot of hawkers also ply the street, and a lot of the rest of the Xidan area, claiming to get you discounted phones.

FOOD FROM HOME If you are travelling in China for a month or more, and especially if you have been in the back of beyond eating from roadside stalls, there will probably come a point when you will hanker after some foodstuffs from home to sustain you through to the end of your trip. Several Carrefour hypermarkets have come to the outskirts of town, but far more accessible than these is the chain of **Jenny Lou** 珍妮璐 supermarkets, who will deliver free of charge to anywhere within 25km of their stores. These sell everything from your familiar black and herbal teas, Pringles crisps, Marmite, cheese, German breads and pretzels to imported wines and local vegetables. Whatever you yearn for, if you can't get it here, then you probably can't get it anywhere in northern China. You'll find a friendly Jenny Lou's at:

West Gate of Chaoyang Park; ✆ 010 6501 62496
Sanlitun Bei Xiao Jie; ✆ 010 6461 6928
4 Ritan Bei Lu; ✆ 010 8563 0626

And, of course, McDonald's is now almost everywhere.

OUTDOOR GEAR With Bejing's yuppies now clearing increasingly greater amounts of disposable income after having been stuck in the office all week, outdoor pursuits are becoming a more popular weekend activity. As a result a flurry of outdoor sports shops have emerged around **Madian** on the third ring road north of Deshengmen. Chinese outdoor sports brands are also beginning to appear, whose goods are certainly competitive with Western brands and are actually much cheaper. One such company is Black Yak (*www.blackyak.com.cn*) which is working with the International Friends of the Great Wall (see page 20) to promote a countryside code. By far the best store for outdoor gear is **Sanfo** 三夫, whose flagship store, complete with climbing wall, is at Madian. Sanfo has a second outlet near the China World Trade Centre, and five other stores around the country (see page 84). They sell a variety of Western-branded goods as well as competitive Asian brands and Black Yak goods. Tents, climbing gear, roll mats, MSR and Primus stoves and fuels, Camelbaks, Nalgene, and a good range of very affordable outdoor clothing can all be found at their stores.

Sanfo Bldg 4, Entrance 5, Nancun, Madian; ☎ 010 6201 5550; www.sanfo.com.cn. To get to Madian take the underground line 2 to Zhishuitan and then take bus 315, 344 or 345 for 15 mins to Madian. The shop is located on the south side of Bei Sanhuan, west of the Madian intersection.
Sanfo Jinzhiqiao Dasha, Guomao, Chaoyang District; ☎ 010 6507 9298; www.sanfo.com.cn. Take the west entrance (where Starbucks is) out of the China World Trade Centre and continue west along the north side of the street to the east side of the second block of buildings along.

TEN THINGS TO SEE AND DO IN BEIJING PROVINCE

There is so much to see in Beijing, especially if it is your first time here, or even if it is a repeat visit. As this guidebook, however, is primarily about the Great Wall, a shortlist of only ten things ranging from the most popular to the more outlandish, or specific to the wall, has been drawn up here. Shopping (see above) could swamp any remaining spare time you might have in the city.

THE FORBIDDEN CITY 故宫 (See map pages 162-163) The Forbidden City, as it is still popularly known in English, is officially now the **Palace Museum**, and called Old Palace (Gugong) in Chinese. From its foundation by the Ming dynasty in 1420, until the fall of the ensuing Qing dynasty in 1911, it was the epicentre of the world as the Chinese knew it. In fact it was the heart of what the Great Wall was renovated and extended for by the Ming and Qing dynasties, as it housed the emperor himself, who was none other than the one mandated by Heaven to rule the world. The complex of courtyards, receiving halls, gardens and pavilions make up almost 0.75km², protected by some 4km of wall and moat. Common people were not allowed into the palace, or if they did enter, it was rare to come out alive. Now it is a main attraction for millions of Chinese and the first courtyard will usually be filled with Chinese from around the country who come to marvel at the outer walls and only imagine the interior, as few from the countryside can afford the ¥60 entry fee. Once inside the main palace the ratio of Chinese to foreigners changes dramatically. The central passage to any of the halls is often closed, now merely to preserve the aura of what in the past was the preserve of only the emperor himself. Notably, the central bridge to Tian An Gate leading up to an enormous portrait of Mao Zedong that hangs over the central passage through the gate, is blocked off to common folk and guarded by a soldier of the People's Army.

Much of the palace was being renovated in 2005, requiring tedious and intricate work – a roller brush was not the tool of choice for any of the ornate and gold-leaf ceilings. By the end of 2006, however, all the side chambers and courtyards should be open again. It is an awe-inspiring stroll through the palace, although many of the reception halls sometimes come as an anti-climax after you've seen the fifth enormous throne in the middle of an ornately but badly lit and largely empty, cavernous room. By the time you are halfway through the palace, a Starbucks café copy, tucked away in a side hall, beckons you for much-needed sustenance, along with a number of run-of-the-mill Chinese eateries, drinks stands and ice cream stalls. A small garden at the back of the palace makes a pleasant break from the austere courtyards hitherto.

Most people enter via the main gate, Tian An (see below), to the south. In the summer, queues for tickets can be long and crowded. For a more calm approach to the palace, enter via the back gate. The walk from the pleasant garden through increasingly grand courtyards to view Tiananmen Square at the end of your journey certainly helps to build up rather than deflate the climax. Bus 814, which halts at Gùgōng 故宫 bus stop on Jing Shan Qian Jie right outside the back gate, takes you back to Haoyuan Hotel. Bus 5 on the northwest side of the Imperial Palace takes you back towards Downtown Backpackers and Lusongyuan Hotel. The entry fee for the palace is ¥60. A good map of the palace with short descriptions of the main halls in English, Japanese and Chinese costs ¥3.

TIANANMEN SQUARE 天安门广场 The southern and main entrance to the Forbidden City, **Tian An Gate**, meaning 'Gate of Heavenly Peace', provides one of two good viewing points from which to survey Tiananmen Square below you. There you can stand above the enormous portrait of Chairman Mao and imagine impressive Army Day parades or the speech given by Mao upon the foundation of the People's Republic of Communist China on 1 October 1949. The security survey done on the gate considers it a prime target for terrorism, especially considering the number of banquets, receptions and ceremonies that take place up there. As a result no bags are allowed onto Tian An Gate, and they must be deposited for ¥2 at the designated bag counter. (*Entry onto the gate is ¥15.*)

A slightly better and less-frequented place from which to view the square is Zhengyang Gate at the south end of the square. A permanent exhibition of what the area looked like before the city walls were torn down is also well worth the visit. (*Open daily 08.30–16.00. Entry ¥10.*)

The square was redesigned and enlarged to its present size in 1959, so that it can now hold up to 500,000 soldiers on parade, ten times its original capacity. To the west is the **Great Hall of the People** 人民大会堂 – more affectionately known in English as G-hop. This is the nearest equivalent of a parliament or assembly for China. Communist Party cadres debate laws and matters of state here when it is in session. And when it is not, it is open to the public daily 08.00–16.00. (*Entry ¥35.*) You will be paraded around a selection of the 29 reception rooms, which are not really very much to write home about except to say that you have been there.

On the east side of the square is the **Chinese Revolution and History Museum** 中国革命历史博物馆. Unless you are a real history buff, both of these are not really worth the time of day. If you are already familiar with China's history, then they are somewhat curious for their rendition of history for the purposes of educating the masses. (*Entry ¥10.*)

Mao's mausoleum 毛主席纪念堂 is a scary affair in the southern half of Tiananmen Square, on the central axis of the city. Thousands of Chinese pay homage to him every day. You are not allowed to take any bags, but must instead

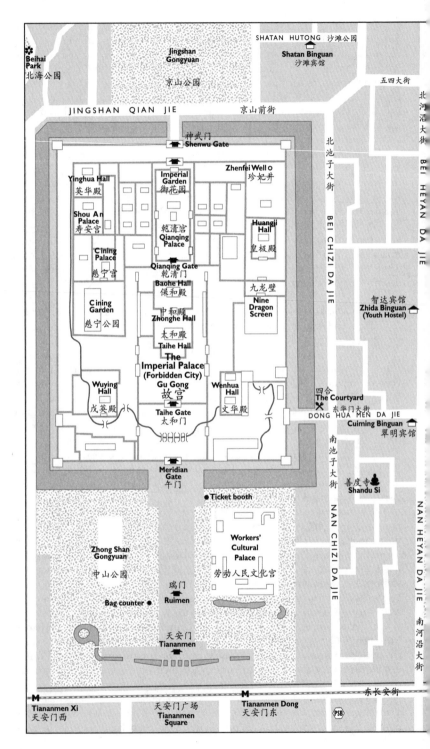

SHATAN HUTONG 沙滩公园

Beihai Park
北海公园

Jingshan Gongyuan
京山公园

Shatan Binguan
沙滩宾馆

五四大街

JINGSHAN QIAN JIE   京山前街

北河沿大街

BEI HEYAN DA JIE

Shenwu Gate
神武门

北池子大街

Zhenfei Well ○
珍妃井

Yinghua Hall
英华殿

Imperial Garden
御花园

BEI CHIZI DA JIE

Shou An Palace
寿安宫

Huangji Hall
皇极殿

Qianqing Palace
乾清宫

Cining Palace
慈宁宫

Qianqing Gate
乾清门

九龙壁

Baohe Hall
保和殿

Nine Dragon Screen

Zhida Binguan
(Youth Hostel)
智达宾馆

Cining Garden
慈宁公园

Zhonghe Hall
中和殿

Taihe Hall
太和殿

The Imperial Palace
(Forbidden City)

Wuying Hall
武英殿

Gu Gong
故宫

Wenhua Hall
文华殿

四合
The Courtyard
东华门大街

DONG HUA MEN DA JIE

Taihe Gate
太和门

Cuiming Binguan
翠明宾馆

Meridian Gate
午门

NAN CHIZI DA JIE

善度寺
Shandu Si

● Ticket booth

Zhong Shan Gongyuan
中山公园

Workers' Cultural Palace
劳动人民文化宫

NAN HEYAN DA JIE

南河沿大街

瑞门
Ruimen

Bag counter ●

天安门
Tiananmen

M

东长安街

M

Tiananmen Xi
天安门西

天安门广场
Tiananmen Square

Tiananmen Dong
天安门东

PSB

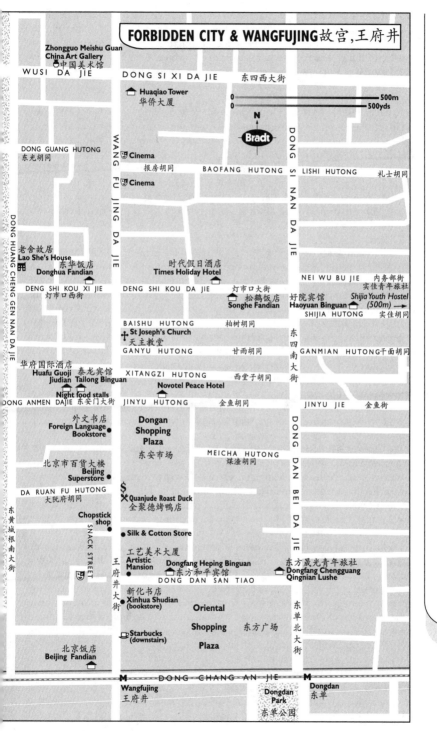

FORBIDDEN CITY & WANGFUJING 故宫,王府井

Zhongguo Meishu Guan
China Art Gallery
中国美术馆

WUSI DA JIE 五四大街

DONG SI XI DA JIE 东四西大街

Huaqiao Tower
华侨大厦

0 ———— 500m
0 ———— 500yds

N

Bradt

DONG GUANG HUTONG
东光胡同

WANG FU JING DA JIE 王府井大街

Cinema
报房胡同

BAOFANG HUTONG

LISHI HUTONG 礼士胡同

DONG SI NAN DA JIE 东四南大街

Cinema

Lao She's House
老舍故居

Donghua Fandian
东华饭店

Times Holiday Hotel
时代假日酒店

NEI WU BU JIE 内务部街

DONG HUANG CHENG GEN NAN DA JIE 东黄城根南大街

DENG SHI KOU XI JIE
灯市口西街

DENG SHI KOU DA JIE 灯市口大街

灯市口大街

Songhe Fandian
松鹤饭店

Haoyuan Binguan
好院宾馆

Shijia Youth Hostel
实佳青年旅社
(500m) →

BAISHU HUTONG 柏树胡同

SHIJIA HUTONG 实佳胡同

St Joseph's Church
天主教堂

GANYU HUTONG 甘雨胡同

东四南大街

GANMIAN HUTONG 干面胡同

Huafu Guoji
Jiudian
华府国际酒店

Tailong Binguan
泰龙宾馆

XITANGZI HUTONG 西堂子胡同

Night food stalls

Novotel Peace Hotel

DONG ANMEN DAJIE 东安门大街

JINYU HUTONG 金鱼胡同

JINYU JIE 金鱼街

Foreign Language
Bookstore
外文书店

Dongan
Shopping
Plaza
东安市场

DONG DAN BEI DA JIE 东单北大街

Beijing
Superstore
北京市百货大楼

MEICHA HUTONG 煤渣胡同

DA RUAN FU HUTONG
大阮府胡同

Chopstick
shop

Quanjude Roast Duck
全聚德烤鸭店

SNACK STREET

Silk & Cotton Store

Artistic
Mansion
工艺美术大厦

Dongfang Heping Binguan
东方和平宾馆

Dongfang Chengguang
Qingnian Lushe
东方晟光青年旅社

DONG DAN SAN TIAO

Xinhua Shudian
(bookstore)
新化书店

Oriental

Shopping

Plaza

东方广场

东单北大街

Starbucks
(downstairs)

Beijing Fandian
北京饭店

M DONG CHANG AN JIE M 东长安街

Wangfujing
王府井

Dongdan Park
东单公园

Dongdan
东单

王府井大街

check them into the luggage counter for ¥10 per piece. Once in the mausoleum you will file past his preserved body without being allowed to stop or take photos. Most Chinese buy flowers to lay at the designated flower collection points. Mao himself had wanted to be cremated and one wonders for how long he will stay on show before being moved to a less prominent location. (*May–Sep open daily 07.00–11.30, Oct–Apr open Tue and Thu 08.00–11.30. Entry free.*)

TEMPLE OF HEAVEN PARK Tiān Tán Gōngyuán 天坛公园 The Temple of Heaven consists of a number of buildings and two altars inside 273ha of grounds. Originally commissioned by the second Ming emperor, Yongle, it was considered by both the Ming and the Qing to be the Middle Kingdom's most sacred temple. For this reason amongst others it was designated a UNESCO World Heritage Site (see page 21) in 1998. The main attractions of the temple are the Hall of Prayer for Good Harvests (including the Altar for Bumper Crops) and the Round Altar. Both are connected by the 360m-long marble Red Step Bridge, which is intersected by the Echo Wall and the Imperial Vault of Heaven.

The circular **Hall of Prayer for Good Harvests** at the north end of the **Red Step Bridge** is the building most people associate with the Temple of Heaven. It is certainly large and impressive, but you are not allowed into the hall itself. Rebuilt several times since its original rectangular construction in 1420, it came to represent the four seasons, the 12 months of the year and the 12 divisions of night and day. In 1971, when the UN recognised the government of the People's Republic of China as the rightful sovereign of China (instead of Taiwan), Premier Zhou Enlai presented a 15m-long silk carpet of the Hall of Prayer for Good Harvests to the UN secretary general. The carpet, which now stands in the Palais des Nations regional headquarters of the UN in Geneva, is a masterpiece of perspective. No matter where you stand in relation to the carpet, it always looks as if you are facing the doorway to the hall. This perspective is not in fact present from the grounds of the hall itself, which are enclosed by a relatively tight wall.

The **Round Altar**, built in 1530, consists of a large round dais made up of nine concentric circles, which sits on a square base. It was seen to be the ultimate union of Heaven and Earth. The Ming and Qing believed that Heaven was round and that the Earth was square (and flat, even up until 1911). The very centre of the altar was seen as the very centre of the world and when the emperor sat on his throne here, his mandate as Son of Heaven would allow him to converse between Heaven and Earth.

The **Imperial Vault of Heaven** (also known as the Celestial Warehouse), originally built in 1530, was rebuilt to its present shape in 1752 during the Qing dynasty. The Imperial Vault is enclosed by the circular **Echo Wall**. Allegedly, if one person stands at the eastern side of the wall and another at the western side of the wall both facing north, they can speak to each other without having to shout, owing to the resonance of their voices around the wall. Arrive first thing in the morning if you want to have any hope of actually achieving this before the place fills up with visitors shouting at each other around the wall.

The surrounding grounds of the temple, dense with half-century-old cypress trees, lawns and flowers, are worth visiting in themselves and provide plenty of opportunity to get away to a quiet corner, bench or pathway, where you will come across a few elderly citizens going for a walk or practising some traditional Chinese arts. (*The park opens daily 08.30–20.00. Entry ¥15.*) The Hall, Imperial Vault and

Round Altar cost an extra ¥20 for entry to all three. Ticket booths for the buildings close at 17.00, with the buildings closing at 17.30.

CHONGWENMEN WALL 崇文门 If you really don't have the time to spend a day visiting the Great Wall, but want to get a sense of what the Ming defensive systems entailed, then go down to Chongwenmen Dajie. The last length of Beijing's city wall, almost 2.5km in length, still stands alongside this street. The rest of the city wall, bar a few gates that now stand in the middle of roundabouts, was dismantled during the 1950s and 1960s, despite strong opposition from local people. Now the government is trying to renovate or reconstruct what little is left of it.

Chongwenmen Wall has thus been set in a pretty little park which you can walk through alongside the wall, and future plans by the government also intend to open up the top of the wall to walkers. Chongwen Gate (now destroyed) used to be the tax office for the Ming and Qing dynasties. As you walk through the park you will also see remnants of some of the first railway in Beijing as well as an old signal station. At the eastern end of the park is **Dongbian Gate**, perfectly preserved and well worth the ¥12 entry fee. (Right behind Beijing's main train station, it is also a great place for trainspotters.)

Since 1991, Dongbian Gatehouse has housed the **Red Gate Gallery** (✆ *010 6525 1005;* ✆ *010 6582 4861;* 📧 *redgategallery@aer.net.cn; www.redgategallery.com*), one of the oldest contemporary art galleries in Beijing. The architecture and massive beams of the building are worth the visit in themselves, but the ground and top floors also display interesting exhibitions of contemporary art, and the second floor holds a permanent exhibition of life at Dongbian Gate from the time it was built. If you are lucky, the gallery director, Brian Wallace, might even give you a cup of Chinese tea on a cold day. *That's Beijing, Time Out Beijing* and other free city magazines are also available at the gallery. (*Open daily 10.00–17.00.*)

There are two ways to get to Chongwenmen Wall. The most direct is to go to Chongwenmen underground station, come out of the southeast exit and head down Chongwenmen Dajie. Alternatively, and to get to the Red Gate Gallery directly, take the subway to Jianguomen, come out of the southwest exit and head south for two blocks.

ANCIENT OBSERVATORY Gǔ Guānxiàngtái 古观象台 The site of this observatory, at 2 Dongbiaobei Hutong, opened in 1442, and makes for a welcome respite from the hustle and bustle of Beijing. It holds an exhibition of early meteor findings, star charts and sightings of Halley's comet. In addition, the rooftop and courtyard garden display armilliary, sundials and navigational aids from the 15th century. A small shop inside sells some information on the museum and the usual paraphernalia. The museum is directly behind the southeast entrance of Jianguomen underground station. (*Open daily 09.00–17.00. Entry ¥10.*)

HAN JIANG KOREAN BATH HOUSE Hàn Jiāng Sāngná Yù 汉江桑拿浴 After a day or several of hiking the Great Wall, this Korean bath house at 9 Xiao Yun Lu, San Yuan Dong Qiao, Chaoyang District (✆ *010 6460 5086*) might be just the thing your sore limbs need. Your initial entry fee will get you into the wet area: standing and sitting showering options with complimentary toiletries, hot tub, steam rooms and sauna. Thereafter, massage, medicinal cupping and scraping, exfoliating scrubs and a shoe shine (!) will cost you extra. A small buffet is served free of charge from 18.30–22.00 and a variety of great dishes can be ordered throughout the day and night. Whilst the wet area is divided into men and women, there is a mixed dry room offering board games and tea. Next door in the resting room, large lounge chairs and pyjamas could find you whiling away some time watching DVDs. From Dongzhimen underground station, take bus 18 or 614 to San Yuan Dong Qiao, then walk east for five minutes along Xiao Yun Lu. (*Open 24/7. Entry is ¥30 for women and ¥48 for men.*)

BOTANICAL GARDENS AT XIANGSHAN Zhíwù Yuán 植物园 The Beijing Botanical Gardens are not necessarily the most impressive in the world, but they do house the greatest collection of the plants of northern China. May through October is the best time to view many of the plants you might see along the length of the Great Wall, and the gardens are a good escape from Beijing's high-rise buildings and overloaded traffic. The park's greenhouse also displays many plants from around the world, as well as an impressive orchid display and a desert room for cacti.

Sleeping Buddha Temple (Wòfó Sìmiào 卧佛寺庙) is located inside the gardens as well as the Sleeping Buddha Hotel (see page 152). The temple is known as the Sleeping Buddha Temple because of its large copper cast statue of Sakyamuni passing into nirvana. To get there (to the temple, that is; nirvana takes a bit more work), take bus 904 from Xizhimen underground station. Take the northwest exit from the underground and continue walking west along the side of the intersection overpass for 500m to the bus stop. Get off at Wofosi, which is one stop after Wofo Shanzhuang and one stop before the last stop at **Fragrant Hills Park Xiangshan**香 山 . (*Entry to the gardens is ¥50; entry to the Sleeping Buddha Temple is ¥35.*)

MING TOMBS Míng Shísān Líng 明十三陵 If you take one of the tourist buses to Badaling (see page 179) then you will spend half the day at two of the Ming Tombs and a jade factory. Unless you are a real tomb fan, there's not really a lot to see here, despite their importance as the graveyard of the Ming emperors. All the jewels and treasures were raided during the warlord period of the 1920s. The main hall in the grounds of the Chang Tomb is constructed with some impressive Nanmu hardwood tree trunks from southern China. The tourist buses give you 45 minutes here. (*Entry ¥45.*) The Ding Tomb is more impressive with its underground vault, but Qianlong's Tomb at Dongling (see page 131) is better. The tourist buses drop you off first at the jade factory and in total you have 90 minutes to get through the jade factory and visit the underground tomb and museum. (*Entry ¥60.*) Bus 314 (07.00–18.00) shuttles between Chanping and both tombs for ¥3. For a high-rise overview of the Ming Tombs take a tandem paraglide trip over them for ¥500 (see box opposite).

CYCLING THE HUTONG AND BEIJING UNDERGROUND DEFENCE SYSTEM A trip to China would not be complete for many without a bicycle ride. A rewarding route is around Houhai Lake and through the *hutong* of the northern half of the centre of the city. Many hotels can arrange bicycle hire for you at around ¥20 for the day, or you can go over to Houhai and rent a bike from there. Tandems and tricycles are also up for rent. If you don't fancy doing the work yourself, two-seater pedicabs are available all over the city and especially at Houhai.

Soon after the founding of the People's Republic of China, realising that the Great Wall was useless against atomic bombs and anyway the enemy wasn't coming from the north anymore, Mao set about building an extensive underground bunker system. When it was finished it was meant to be able to hold all of Beijing's residents for up to six days with food and water. (What they would have done after that doesn't bear thinking about.) Much of this underground defence system has now been turned into shopping malls and the subway system, but much of it still exists. If you would like to join a guided cycle tour through some of the system, contact the Cycle China Club (☎ *139 1188 6524; www.cyclechina.com*).

THE GREAT WALL IN BEIJING

The Ming Great Wall in Beijing province has a variety of offshoots, which, along with the main arterial wall, totals almost 630km of wall. Not even 150km of it is in decent condition and therefore open to tourists. In the run up to the Olympics, however, Beijing Municipality alone has budgeted ¥600m (US$72m) on heritage preservation, including renovation of Huanghuacheng, Jiankou, Chadaocheng and Gubeikou Great Wall sections.

Very little of Beijing's wall is longer than 10km without a break of some nature (see map pages 138-139) which makes multi-day hikes in Beijing more difficult. Special permission (not to everyday hikers) is required to see the closed sections, such as the Tower for Viewing the Capital and Fairy Tower at Simatai, and even then, great care should be taken not to damage what little is left of the Beijing Ming all. (For more on China's laws governing the protection of the wall and whether you will be violating them or not, see page 59.) Fortunately, the highest concentration of fortifications is in the better-preserved sections. Of the 827 fortifications along the Beijing Ming wall, almost half are in the sections that are open. The rest of this chapter gives an insight into the more accessible parts of the wall, some of which

PARAGLIDING AT SIMATAI GREAT WALL AND THE MING TOMBS

This must be the ultimate way to visit the wall without having to do all that hard-work-uphill stuff. There are two paragliding schools in Beijing offering beginner courses and tandem flights for those wanting to learn and/or take this view of the Great Wall.

Superwing ✉ zoomrace@sina.com; *www.superwing.com.cn* A Chinese-run club. Beginner courses take place at Mangshan, 40 minutes outside Beijing, where you can learn to fly while viewing the Ming Tombs. Beginner courses take between five and ten days depending on how quickly you learn and how good the weather is. A beginner course starts at ¥2,500. If you are already a paraglider, but don't want to lug all your equipment to China, then you can hire sails and harnesses from Superwing at ¥350 for the day.

The Flying Man School (☎ *010 6495 6790 or 138 8158 8584;* ✉ *hoefu@hotmail.com; www.flying-man.com*) Honoured to have Alex Hofer, the 2003 paragliding world champion, among their paragliding instructors. Fluent in German, French, Spanish and English, Hofer and his two Chinese staff offer beginner and advanced pilot courses as well as tandem flights. *Beginner courses ¥2,985; advanced courses start at ¥5,000 for ten flights. Tandem flights ¥500.* The Flying Man School also has a cool little bar on Beitucheng (see map page 150) where you can start and end the day.

A good paragliding day depends on the weather, so be prepared for cancellations. The schools will try to wait for six sign ups before going ahead with a flight day. There might be a lot of waiting around before you get your half hour of tandem glory in the air. You can usually spend most of that time, however, wandering around the Great Wall. All in all it is well worth the wait and might be the closest you will get to feeling like an angel.

are only just becoming known to foreign visitors. To hike some of the more inaccessible parts of the wall in Beijing province contact one of the hiking clubs at the end of this chapter.

RECOMMENDATIONS AND TIMINGS Badaling is very overcrowded and tacky so, if you can, go for any of the other sections of the Great Wall in Beijing. If you don't have much time (ie: if you have only one day for the Great Wall and do not want to stay overnight) then, at present, you are limited to signing up to a tour provided by one of the hotels, or taking one of the tourist buses to Badaling. Taking public transport, you can reckon on the following timings for visiting the Great Wall in Beijing:

Badaling	½ day	See page 179
Badaling and Juyongguan	1 day	See page 179
Mutianyu	1 day	See page 174
Huanghuacheng	2 days	See page 177
Jiankou	2 days	See page 176
Gubeikou, Simatai and Jinshanling	2–3 days	See below

CAMPING AND HIKING TRIPS GOING TO THE GREAT WALL There are a number of clubs based in Beijing who frequently camp or hike along the lesser-known and more inaccessible areas of the Great Wall in Beijing province, such as Dongshan and Jiangjunguan near Huangyaguan. Like most clubs, they usually have a regular programme and welcome newcomers even if it is for only one trip. For more up-to-date information contact one of the following clubs:

Beijing Hikers ☏ 139 1002 5516; ✉ info@beijinghhikers.com; www.beijinghikers.com or www.bjhikers.com (in English and Chinese). The club does several family-oriented and more challenging trips each year to lesser-known areas of the Great Wall as well as other places in Beijing province. Their trips usually cost between ¥200 and ¥500 and include snacks and drinks and an English-speaking guide. Trips are always at the weekend and some are overnight.

China Volksports Association 17D Bldg 1, Century Mansion, 45 Xiao Guan Beili, Chaoyang District; ☏ 010 8489 6319–21; ✉ bytsy@mrqh.com or iw@mrqh.com; www.chinawalking.net.cn. This long-standing club became a member of the International Federation of Popular Sports in 2004. They offer weekend hikes twice a month to lesser-known parts of the Great Wall in Beijing province, and over the course of ten years they intend to hike the entire length of what is left of the Great Wall, so guided trips to places beyond Beijing are also possible. They also do longer hikes to other parts of China. Their website is in English, Chinese, Japanese and German.

High Club ☏ 010 8589 3796; www.highclub.cn. A smaller club than the two above, also doing hikes to the Great Wall in Beijing as well as to other places.

Many hotels and hostels offer one night of camping with or without an outdoor barbecue on the wall. These usually take place at Badaling and cost anywhere upward of ¥200 per person; tent, sleeping bag and food supplied.

THE GREAT WALL MARATHON As if hiking the wall is not difficult enough, if you want a real challenge try running a 5km or 10km marathon along it. The marathon takes place once a year, normally in May, and changes location from year to year. This event has been running since 2001 and if you want to participate you must sign up in advance. *(For the latest information see www.great-wall-marathon.com.)*

GUBEIKOU, SIMATAI AND JINSHANLING 古北口、司马台、金山领 (See map pages 168-9) In any rough rendition of a continuous wall, the Gubeikou section of the Great Wall, some 120km northeast of the capital, is seen as the start of the Great Wall in Beijing province. The section extends from Heiguan (Black Gate) past the Simatai Reservoir and Jinshanling to Gubei Gateway. Along its 10km length are 67 towers, some spaced as close as a mere 50m apart. The most interesting of these are **Storehouse Tower, Fairy's Tower** and the **Tower for Viewing the Capital**. Fairy's Tower and the Tower for Viewing the Capital are closed to the public due to the unsafe, almost vertical access.

Gubeikou Gǔběikǒu 古北口
A rundown little place, Gubeikou is a mixture of bits of old China, an unhealthy lashing of centralised planning and some attempts at modernity. The pass itself was dismantled by the Japanese on their way to Beijing in 1937, starting the Sino-Japanese War of Resistance. The locals have long since ransacked the adjoining wall for its stones. The wall now limps along the hills, a mere shadow of what can be found in the 'protected' areas of Jinshanling and Simatai further east. Two tunnels for traffic are the only elements reminiscent of the once mighty pass. The authorised way to get to see the wall at Gubeikou is to go into the Panlongshan Scenic Park south of the tunnels. Walking back through the traffic tunnel from Gubeikou to get there is not advised as you will seriously risk your life in the unlit passage. Either take a taxi or hike back along the river and cross the road from where you can see the approaching cars. *(Entry to the park is ¥20.)*

Simatai 司马台
The Simatai section of the Ming Great Wall is reputed to be some of the most inaccessible and precipitous of the whole wall. The wall here follows a prominent ridge line that stands out like the horned back of a dinosaur. The most precipitous section was built in such difficult terrain that parts of it are only a single wall some 40cm wide at the top. This section of the wall is not designed to be walked along and it is now shut off to the public. Sky Bridge and Sky Ladder are also in this area closed to the public (see box on page 173).

Getting there The turn-off for Simatai lies 10km to the south of Gubeikou and from the turn-off it is another 10km to Simatai Park. This park is less visited than Badaling and Mutianyu and so the hawkers are fewer and their stands are not yet permanent. Once you are inside the park area, there is much more space to enjoy the view of the wall without feeling hassled by someone selling you a T-shirt and other knick-knacks. Inside the park, there are two reservoir lakes with boating and fishing, a cable car, funicular, cable slide, hostels and restaurants. The lakes are renowned for their hot and cold springs on the far side of the Great Wall. These keep the mean temperature of the lake at 38°C throughout the year. Unfortunately, swimming is not allowed as the water is considered to be too deep. *(Entry to the park ¥35; cable car one way ¥35, return ticket ¥60 (does not run in the slightest inclement weather); funicular ¥20 each way.)*

As yet, there is no regular public transport to Simatai. At the weekends, tourist bus 12 leaves outside Xuanwumen underground station in Beijing between 06.30 and 08.00; ¥60 for the round trip including Chinese guide in the bus. You must return on the same bus or stay the night. Otherwise try taking the Chengde-bound bus from Miyun (¥12) or from Dongzhimen long-distance bus station in Beijing (¥20), and ask the driver to let you off at the turn-off to Simatai. If you are staying overnight then you can ask your hotel to pick you up. For day trippers, hiking and hitching is the only way to finish off the last 10km. A taxi from Beijing costs ¥400, from Huairou ¥200, and from Miyun ¥150.

Park facilities Within the park, there is a courtyard youth hostel and a more upmarket hotel, both of which have restaurants. In the road up to the park there are

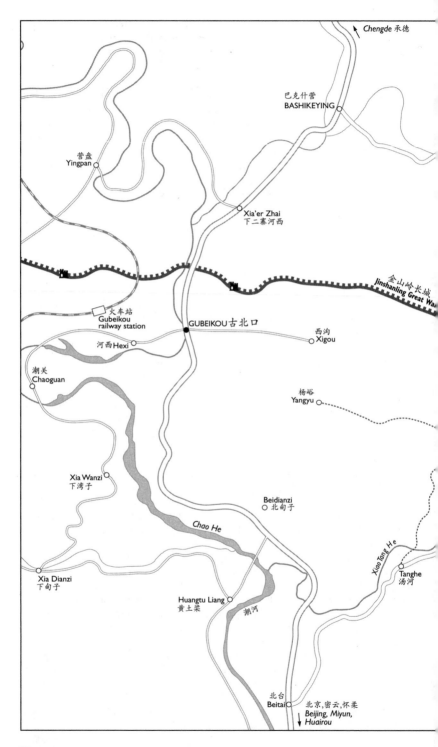

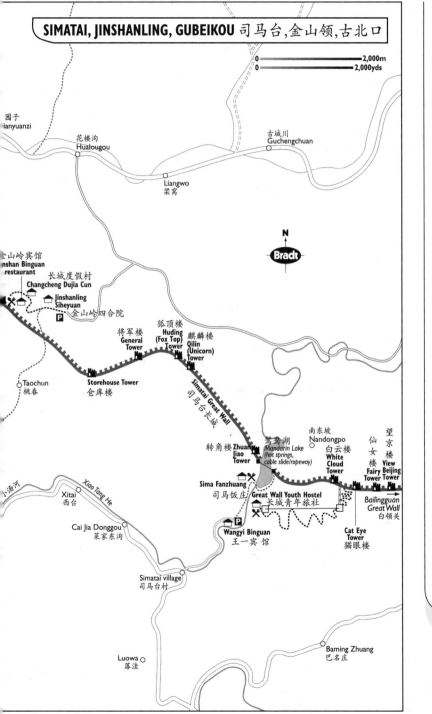

SIMATAI, JINSHANLING, GUBEIKOU 司马台,金山领,古北口

0   2,000m
0   2,000yds

园子
Tianyuanzi

花楼沟
Hualougou

古城川
Guchengchuan

Liangwo
梁窝

N

Bradt

金山岭宾馆
Jinshan Binguan
restaurant

长城度假村
Changcheng Dujia Cun

**Jinshanling
Siheyuan**
金山岭四合院

将军楼
**General
Tower**

狐顶楼
**Huding
(Fox Top)
Tower**

麒麟楼
**Qilin
(Unicorn)
Tower**

○ Taochun
桃春

Storehouse Tower
仓库楼

Simatai Great Wall
司马台长城

望京楼
**View
Beijing
Tower**

仙女楼
**Fairy
Tower**

白云楼
**White
Cloud
Tower**

南东坡
Nandongpo

鸳鸯湖
*Mandarin Lake
(hot springs,
cable slide/ropeway)*

转角楼 **Zhuan
Jiao
Tower**

Sima Fanzhuang
司马饭庄

Great Wall Youth Hostel
长城青年旅社

*Bailingguan
Great Wall*
白领关

**Cat Eye
Tower**
猫眼楼

小渤河
Xiao Tang He

Xitai
西台

Cai Jia Donggou
莱家东沟

Wangyi Binguan
王一宾馆

Simatai village
司马台村

Luowa ○
落洼

Baming Zhuang
巴名庄

several good places to eat offering farmed trout. Many of these are farmer's inns (nóng jiā yuàn 农家院) where a bed costs a mere ¥20.

🏠 **Great Wall Youth Hostel** Chángchéng Qingnián Lüshè 长城青年旅社 (27 rooms) Inside the park at the bottom of the hill; ☎ 010 6903 5159; 📠 010 6903 5922. Courtyard hostel. *All rooms have three beds and a bathroom; ¥180.*

🏠 **Sima Fanzhuang** 司马饭庄 (25 rooms) Inside the park and part of the restaurant on the left before you go down the hill to the lake and the wall; ☎ 010 6903 5311; 📠 010 9603 5655. Plain, tidy rooms. Nice restaurant and a great coffee terrace. *Hot water 07.00–09.00 and 19.00–21.00. Dbl or twin ¥260. Bunk ¥70.*

🏠 **Shan Shui Cheng Dujia Shanzhuang** 山水城度假山庄 (11 rooms) Around 500m in front of the Simatai ticket booth on the south side of the road; ☎ 010 6903 5122 or 133 8116 9609. The proprietress, Zhang Fenzhen, runs a tidy little place with a small restaurant specialising in home-farmed trout. Fishing in their ponds is also possible. *All rooms en suite. Trpl ¥50 per person; dbl ¥80.*

🏠 **Wangyi Binguan** 王一宾馆 (27 rooms) 20m west of the Simatai car park; ☎ 010 6903 3108. This two-storey white building near the ticket booth was in need of some renovation at the time of writing. *All rooms are dbls or twins with a bathroom and 24hr hot water; ¥180.*

For paragliding off Simatai, see the box on page 167.

Jinshanling 金山领

Jinshanling 金山领 Jinshanling lies halfway between Gubeikou and Simatai. It is the least visited of the three Great Wall sections along Beijing province's northern border, as it is a little further to drive to, and correspondingly the park is not as well kept as at Simatai. East of Shalingkou entrance onto Jinshanling Great Wall is the **Storehouse Tower** and **Dajinshan Watchtower**. Storehouse Tower was exactly as its name describes, a storehouse. This was unusual for a tower partway along a section of wall and not next to a castle. The tower was used for a short period, however, as a garrison headquarters and this in part accounts for its large size. Thestorehouse itself is located on the inside of the Great Wall (ie: on the south side of the tower) and the whole tower is further protected by extra walls and barriers. West of Shalingkou entrance is the way to Gubeikou.

Getting there Access to Jinshanling is through Gubeikou into Hebei province. It is, therefore, the furthest away from Beijing by bus or car. From the turn-off on the main road it is another 4km to the park gate.

Park facilities There are three places to stay at present at Jinshanling, all within the grounds of the park run by the Beijing office for Jinshanling (☎ 010 8402 4628).

🏠 **Jinshan Binguan** 金山宾馆 (36 rooms) All en suite with TV and AC. *Trpls ¥360; dbls or twins ¥240.*

🏠 **Jinshanling Siheyuan** 金山领四合院 (15 rooms) At Chinese three-star standard – less than satisfactory waterworks, but a cute traditional Chinese courtyard setting. *Trpls ¥255; twins ¥220.*

🏠 **Changcheng Dujia Cun** 长城度假村 (8 bungalows) Each bungalow accommodates up to eight people with its own cooking facilities. *Bungalow ¥450.*

Hiking from Simatai via Jinshanling to Gubeikou

As it's one continuous section it is possible to walk from Simatai via Jinshanling to Gubeikou or vice versa in about 12 hours, or you might prefer to space it over two days and stay at the Jinshanling Binguan or camp overnight. You will have to pay both entrance fees for access to Jinshanling and Simatai. As with all hiking on the wall, take sufficient water as there are no springs or streams up there, and of course take back all your rubbish with you.

Starting from Simatai, you can save yourself an hour of uphill hiking by taking the cable car and *via ferrata* (¥55). This isn't always open, however, and particularly not early in the morning if you are attempting to do the whole section in a day.

The section of the wall from Fairy Tower via Sky Bridge and Sky Ladder to the Tower for Viewing the Capital is closed to the public for safety reasons. Below is a description of what you would miss:

Climbing Fairy Tower and the Tower for Viewing the Capital were never for the faint-hearted. If you are at all scared of heights then you would be reduced to a dithering wreck here. A grade-three scramble in parts, what can take a mere 20 minutes to traverse if you are nimble and fearless can take over two hours for others even with the help of a guide and a confidence rope. Between the Tower for Viewing the Capital and Fairy Tower is a 100m built-up section of the wall, which traverses the peaks of Kulong (Cavity) Mountain. The top of this section of the wall, known as Sky Bridge, is barely 40cm wide in some places and sheer cliffs drop away to either side. This bridge leads on one side to the bottom of 'Heavenly Stairs' (also known as Sky Ladder), a narrow steep trail with some thirty 'stairs' leading to the top of Fairy Tower. The 'stairs' are actually built-up walls giving the impression of stairs from a distance, but in fact being too high to scale in a single step.

Fairy Tower, allegedly the home of a fairy, is a mere 100m from the Tower for Viewing the Capital. Although Sky Bridge connects them, climbers generally used to descend here to ascend another 1,000m to the Tower for Viewing the Capital. On a clear day it was said to be possible to see the outskirts of Beijing from here with the naked eye, but these days, even if you bring binoculars, Beijing centre will be hard to see well because of the pollution emanating from the capital's surrounding heavy industry. As China progresses towards its promised Green Olympics in 2008, the most environmentally friendly ever, there is hope that one day, soon, the capital will be seen again clearly from this tower.

Once you have covered the Simatai section (two to three hours), you might want to stop in the park restaurants for something to eat, or if you have come well prepared on the food front then cross the bridge over Mandarin Lake Reservoir to continue on to Jinshanling. At the west side of the bridge you will need to pay ¥30 to pass through the Jinshanling entrance.

Between Simatai and Jinshanling the wall is the lesser trodden of these two sections and so you can expect to walk on the wall between vegetation growing up from between the rocks during spring and summer. From Simatai Bridge to Jinshanling entrance takes four to five hours.

You might want to call it a day at this point and stay at the Jinshan Binguan (see above). Continuing from Jinshanling to Gubeikou, the undulations become easier, but the wall also becomes more ramshackle. By the time you drop down into Gubeikou some four hours later, evidence of stone looting is obvious. Take care not to damage the wall further when walking on this section.

Accommodation at Gubeikou was non-existent for foreigners at the time of writing, so you need to either flag down one of the many Chengde coaches going back to Beijing (¥12), take a slow night train back or get a taxi to take you round to Simatai or Jinshanling back to the hotels. Trains from Gubeikou station leave around 03.00, 04.50, 09.50 and 16.00.

Alternatively, do the route in reverse starting at Jinshanling and ending up at Simatai Hotel. Transport back to Beijing from Simatai is more frequent than from Jinshanling. Trains to Gubeikou leave Beijing North Station at around 08.00, 16.30, 19.15 and 21.15.

Beijing 北京 THE GREAT WALL IN BEIJING

8

MUTIANYU TO HUANGHUACHENG 幕田峪、黄花城 The Mutianyu to Huanghuacheng

section of the Ming Great Wall covers some of the most precipitous ground in Beijing province. As a result, it seems to provide the ultimate Great Wall challenge to many Beijingers, who go on work trips to conquer the wall here. Tourist buses from Beijing go only to Mutianyu and public transport to other sections is variable. This may change as the government plans to put more of this section of the wall under the management of the Department of Tourism. Mutianyu has been under the management of the Department of Tourism since 1987. Huanghuacheng looks to follow suit by 2006 and Jiankou may not be long after that.

Huairou 怀柔 is the nearest big town to this section of the wall and generally serves as a hub to access each place by public transport as there is no direct bus along the back roads linking access points to the wall. Sprawled around one of the main reservoirs serving Beijing, Huairou is a growing town catering for Beijing yuppies who can afford to live outside the city. The town itself is not much to write home about, but the northeast side of the reservoir, which you might see on the way to Mutianyu, is picturesque. None of the hotels along the wall yet takes credit cards, so you might want to top up with cash at the ATMs at the Bank of China, and the Industrial and Commercial Bank of China in Huairou. Bus 916 leaves from the Dongzhimen long-distance bus station to Huairou between 08.50 and 16.15 every day. Get off at huìyì zhōngxīn 会议中心 (conference centre – although it doesn't look at all as if you might be outside a conference centre). Buses leave frequently, take one and a half hours and cost ¥6. If you are keen to take the bus option to your final destination, then make sure you stay on the 916 until Huairou huiyi zhongxin, and don't get dragged off one stop early by taxi drivers who will claim there is no public bus to where you are going. From Huairou huiyi zhongxin a number of minibuses (gōng jiāo chē 公交车) serve Huanghuacheng direct, Mutianyu and Jiankou almost, and Miyun (where you can catch onward buses to Gubeikou and to Xingfeng for Huangyaguan and Zunhua in Hebei).

Huairou is also the nearest place to this section of the wall where you can reliably get a taxi. If you are stuck in Huairou or in a mountain village and need to get a taxi, try Lei Haili's taxis (☏ *136 0122 3606)*. Léi Hǎilì 雷海立 himself is from the area, is very knowledgeable about access points to the wall, and has a keen sense of the mountains' natural beauty and the need to conserve it. He can take you for a tour of all the places below in four hours for ¥150 or eight hours for ¥300.

Mutianyu 幕田峪 Mutianyu is only 70km north of the capital, but its winding approach makes for a slower journey than the one to Badaling and this also makes it all the more scenic. Its main fortification, **Zhengguantai**, is easily recognisable by its unusual three-tower formation and can be seen above you as you approach the main tourist entrance. It was built in 1404 by General Xu Da.

Getting there There are fewer options for getting to Mutianyu than are available for Badaling. A taxi from Beijing centre costs around ¥400. Tourist bus 6 leaves between 06.30 and 08.00 from outside Xuanwumen underground station at weekends and holidays only between April and October. After a two-hour journey with a Chinese guide, you will have only a couple of hours to enjoy the Mutianyu site before going on to the Ming Tombs and jade factory. Your bus will return to Xuanwumen by 18.00 and you aren't supposed to swap buses. This does not

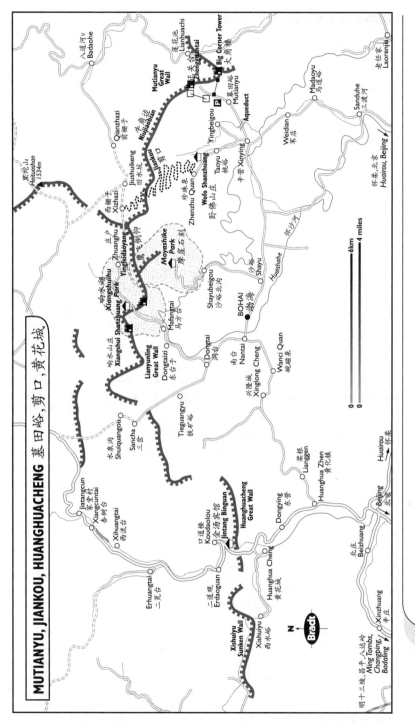

MUTIANYU, JIANKOU, HUANGHUACHENG 慕田峪, 剪口, 黄花城

Badaohe 八道河v

Heituoshan 黑坨山 1534m

Qianzhazi 前栅子

Jiushuikeng 旧水坑

Xizhazi 西栅子

Zhuanghu 庄户

Yingfeidaoyang 鹰飞倒仰

Niujiaobian 牛角边

Jiankou 剪口

Jiankou 旧水坑

Zhenzhu Quan 珍珠泉

Lianhuachi 莲花池

Zhengguantai 正关台

Big Corner Tower 大角楼

Mutianyu Great Wall

Mutianyu 慕田峪

Madaoyu 马道峪

Sanduhe 三渡河

Laorenjia 老任家

Yingbeigou 鹰背沟

Taoyu 桃峪

Xinying 辛营

Weidian 苇店

Aqueduct

Wofo Shanzhuang 卧佛山庄

Xiangshuihu 响水湖

Xiangshui Shanzhuang Park

Moyashike Park 摩崖石刻

Shayubeigou 沙峪北沟

Shayu 沙峪

Huaishahe 怀沙河

BOHAI 渤海

Lianyunling Great Wall

Dongtaizi 东台子

Mafangtai 马方台

Dongtai 洞台

Nantai 南台 Nailong Cheng

Wanci Quan 碗磁泉

Xinglong Cheng 兴隆城

Tieguangyu 铁矿峪

Shuiquangou 水泉沟

Sancha 三岔

Liangen 梁根

Huanghua Zhen 黄花镇

Dongying 东营

Jiatangcun 家堂村 Xiangcuntai 香树台

Xihuangtai 西浒台

Jintang Binguan 金汤宾馆

Koudaolou 口道楼

Huanghuacheng Great Wall

Huairou 怀柔

Beizhuang 北庄

Erhuangtai 二浒台

Erdaoguan 二道观

Huanghua Cheng 黄花城

Xishuiyu Sunken Wall

Xishuiyu 西水峪

Ming Tombs, 明十三陵·昌平·八达岭 Changping, Badaling

Xinzhuang 辛庄

N

Bradt

6km
4 miles
0
0

Beijing 北京 THE GREAT WALL IN BEIJING

8

Huairou, Beijing 怀柔·北京

Beijing 北京

175

provide you with any more time there anyway. The entire trip costs ¥50, excluding entry and cable car fees.

Otherwise you should take bus 916 to Huairou huiyi zhongxin (see above) and then take a taxi to Mutianyu for ¥50–60. For ¥4 there are the blue painted gong jiao che minibuses that leave three times an hour to **Dongtaizi** 东台子 , passing through Xinying village on the way.

Park facilities Mutianyu was the second area of the wall (after Badaling) to come under government management. Although it is slightly less touristed than Badaling, owing to its slower approach, there are still more hawkers' stalls than you could possibly buy T-shirts from and plenty of restaurants besides. The layout of Mutianyu, however, has a more old-world feel to it. The car parks are less visible than at Badaling, and the narrow cobbled approach gives a better sense of the bartering and trading that might have gone on here in days of old.

Much more modern in approach, however, are the two cable cars and toboggan slide built to transport you up and slide you back down with the minimum of effort and maximum of exhilaration. The ten-minute ride will save you a whole 50 minutes or more of Stairmaster. (Entry to the wall is ¥35.) The cable car is an additional ¥35, and the cable car/toboggan combined costs ¥55. There is an additional ¥1 insurance fee which is compulsory but has not been incorporated into the cable car prices. For those who want to rent out the top floor of the top cable car station contact the Mutianyu Great Wall Cable Car Services (✆ 010 6162 6894; ℻ 010 6162 6824; www.cablecar.com.cn). Alternatively, try the Mutianyu Great Wall Tourist Service (✆ 010 6162 6505; www.mutianyugreatwall.com).

Xinying 辛营 The minibus claims to go to Mutianyu, but actually stops 4km short in Xinying. (Xinying, incidentally, means 'labour trading post', harking back to the days when this village would have been the processing point for forced and recruited labour to build the Mutianyu wall.) If there aren't many people on the bus by then, and the other passengers don't mind, you might be able to persuade the driver to take you to Mutianyu Great Wall. If not, the chances of finding a taxi to take you the remaining 4km are very slim. The hike however is beautiful and you will pass under two crossings of the aqueduct built in the early 1950s to serve Mutianyu village. On the way you will also pass a number of nong jia yuan where you can stay the night for as little as ¥10.

Jiankou 箭扣 A few kilometres west of Mutianyu, Jiankou rises over 1,000m from its lowest point to its highest, and is no simple walk in the park for those wanting to stroll its sturdy but as yet unreconstructed walls. From the fish farm at the bottom of the mountain base, it is a two- to three-hour hike to the wall. Follow the path keeping to the left of the gully up to the saddle of the ridge. Once on the wall, you will need to walk around quite some vegetation growing on the wall itself. The highest peak is called Ox-horn Wall (Niú Jiǎo Biān 牛角边) owing to the sketch it creates of an ox horn on the hillside. Another animal-like formation is the Upside Down Flying Eagle (Yīngfēi Dàoyǎng 鹰飞倒仰), which leads down to the village of **Xizhazi** 西栅子 on the north side of the ridge.

Compared with the cable car options and even compared with the ease of access onto Huanghuacheng, this really is the place to test Mao's saying 'You are not a (wo)man until you have climbed the Great Wall'. At the time of writing you can't even buy a Great Wall T-shirt at the bottom, although this would be the hike that would certainly qualify you for wearing such an item. People rarely risk any other way down than the same route they came up. A much shorter hike of less than an hour is possible from the north side of the ridge from the village of Xizhazi, but that is almost a four-hour drive from Huairou. In addition, a return to the fish farm at the bottom of the mountain heralds mouthwatering dishes of trout at the terrace restaurant whilst you enjoy the setting sun.

Getting there and facilities Again, the gong jiao che towards Dongtaizi 东台子 will drop you off at Xinying 辛营, leaving you a 5km hike in to Jiankou. A taxi from Huairou costs ¥50–60. If you want to stay the night nearby, there are plenty of nong jia yuan for ¥10 a person on the road leading up to the fish farm.

⌂ **Sleeping Buddha Mountain Lodge** Wòfó Shānzhuāng 卧佛山庄 (32 rooms) ✆ 010 6162 6090. Offers more classy rooms just before the fish farm. *Standard twin ¥220.*

For a more remote mountain feel, there is a couple of *nóng jiā yuàn* above the fish farm right at the trailhead.

Lianyunling 连云领

Further west of Mutianyu and Jiankou is Lianyunling. This part of the wall can be accessed via a little-visited stone park called Móyá Shí Kè 摩崖石刻 (literally 'cliff cutters'). The park itself is known for its Ming dynasty rock engraving and for its scenery. (Entry to the park is ¥12.) A small side branch of the wall dips into the park. It is easily seen from within the park, but hard to access. A small cliff slopes off one side of the wall and a narrow precipitous path leads up the other side until reaching some makeshift steps to scramble onto the wall. There is also a small mountain lodge in the park.

⌂ **Móyá Shí Kè Shānzhuāng** 摩崖石刻山庄 (15 rooms) ✆ 010 6163 2507/1692. Communal bathrooms. *Five-person huokang (communal bed) ¥150; standard twin ¥100; dbl ¥120.*

Xiang Shui Hu 向水湖

East of Huanghuacheng is Towards Water Lake Xiang Shui Hu. The lake for the most part has dried up, although a stream running through the park still provides for false waterfalls and fishing ponds and other water features. A branch of the Great Wall runs through the park, as well as a fully renovated beacon tower. (Entry to the park is ¥20.) A large hotel complex (120 rooms) caters mostly for groups and will also take independent travellers (✆ 010 8960 2185/2888; *www.xiangshuihu.com – Chinese only as part of the large Huairou.net site; standard twin ¥280.*)

Huanghuacheng 黄花城

Huanghuacheng is reputed to be one of the most well built sections of the Ming Great Wall. The general who built it, Cai Kai, was beheaded for painstakingly taking too long over building it and using too many men. When this section of the wall, however, was the only section to successfully repel invading Mongols years later, Cai Kai's name was resurrected and he was reburied with honours near Huanghuacheng.

In the 1970s, a reservoir was built north of the wall, mostly using the large hewn rock blocks from the wall itself. While the reservoir now looks strong and sturdy, the wall has suffered from erosion and the weaker interior of mud and stone gapes open for all to see like a sore wound. Hidden behind the roadside vendors is the original pass through the wall. Now the road just runs roughshod through the torn-down section of the wall immediately west of the original pass.

In recent years, Huanghuacheng was known as the 'wild wall' as it had been left unreconstructed by the government and was essentially free to access. Those days are numbered. In 2004, the government started ¥12m (US$1.5m) of renovation work to Huanghuacheng, allegedly with original materials and traditional techniques. After a formal opening in 2007, the area is likely to require an entry fee. Until then, as with many parts of the 'wild wall', local farmers charge between ¥2 and ¥4 to walk through their private property. While many visitors think this is an affront, the argument by local farmers that the fee is compensation for the increasingly severe erosion to their land, and the extra maintenance work needed as a result, is an extremely valid one. (For more on the need for sustainable tourism around the Great Wall see pages 18-20; 61).

In anticipation of the build-up in tourism at Huanghuacheng, following the lead of government control of Badaling, Jinshanling and Mutianyu, the locals are fast building new restaurants and mountain lodges (shānzhuāng 山庄). The name 'mountain lodge' is somewhat misleading, as none of them to date is in the style one might have come across in the Rockies or the English Lake District, with roaring fireplaces, wooden floorboards and a quiet atmosphere. Many of Huanghuacheng's mountain lodges have been built with karaoke-crazed weekend groups in mind, so just how quiet they might be on a Friday and Saturday night is debatable. Firecrackers also seem to be a popular pastime with Chinese day trippers. Nevertheless, Huanghuacheng is surrounded by beautiful scenery especially in late spring and in autumn, and makes for excellent hiking, even if you choose not to climb the wall itself. For more information on Huanghuacheng see www.huanghuacheng.com (Chinese only).

Getting there Options for getting to Huanghuacheng are changing rapidly. Even though it is only some 70km north of Beijing, it can take up to three hours to get there by public transport. A taxi from the centre of Beijing is much quicker but can cost over ¥400. By public transport, take bus 916 to Huairou huiyi zhongxin (see above). At Huairou huiyi zhongxin, blue minibuses (gong jiao che) leave three times an hour towards Huanghuacheng and Xingshutai. The journey to Huanghuacheng can take up to another hour and a half and costs ¥4.5. Minibuses will drop you off at any of the guesthouses or lodges along the road. Alternatively, a taxi from Huairou will whisk you there in less than an hour for around ¥60. By the time the wall is 'opened' to the public under the management of the State Administration for Cultural Heritage (SACH), more public options may have opened up, including the old 916 public bus route from Huairou to Huanghuacheng (not to be confused with the current 916 from Beijing to Huairou). Taxis back to Huairou or Beijing may be more difficult to find, especially out of season and during the week, so you may want to keep the number of the taxi who dropped you off. The last gong jiao che leaves Huanghuacheng for Huairou at 18.00.

Where to stay and eat Accommodation at Huanghuacheng varies from the reservoir-side Jintang Shanzhuang catering for large groups, to smaller family-run newly built 'lodges', farmer's inns or 'ranches' and a number of very low-end budget places offering platform beds (huokang). Beijingers as well as foreigners have idealised the concept of staying with a local farmer, even though none of the farmer's inns here will be anywhere near what it is like for real. Places to eat abound at the intersection of the wall with the main road, and most lodges have their own restaurant.

⌂ **Cang Po Fu Restaurant and Guesthouse** 仓坡扶餐厅旅店 (12 rooms) Huanghuacheng Shuiku, Huairou District; ✆ 010 6165 2377 or 0136 6121 8838. On the right-hand side of the road, 100m before the reservoir, where a variety of restaurants and guesthouses are being built. Ask the bus driver to drop you off at Cang Po Fu. Friendly, helpful staff and good cooking. Try their zhá xiǎo yú 炸小鱼 (fried little fish, deep fried with heads and tails) for something truly local. Communal bathrooms with round-the-clock hot water; the water might be cold in the morning after the thermo-solar heaters have got cold overnight. Clean rooms with overhead fans. *Four-person bedrooms and five-person huokàng all at ¥60 per room.*

🏠 **Shanlihong Nongjia Dayuan** 山里红农家大院 (12 rooms) 1 Huanghuachengjia, Jiuduhe, Huairou District; ☏ 010 6165 2090. Take the gong jiao che heading for Xishuiyu to get to this pleasantly named 'Hawthorn Ranch'. The view from the terrace restaurant onto the Great Wall is spectacular at sunset. Snooker room, karaoke and constant hot water. *In the main building, four suites comprising two twin rooms and a bathroom cost ¥150 per suite. One dbl suite ¥200. In the back yard, there are six huokang sleeping four, with bathroom, cost ¥60 per room.*

🏠 **Jintang Shanzhuang** 金堂山庄 (64 rooms, dbls, trpls and suites) 1 Huanghuacheng Shuiku (reservoir), Huairou District; ☏ 010 6165 1134/1188. This large, almost conference-like facility is right on the Huanghuacheng Reservoir. Offers karaoke, a bowling alley, swimming pool and much more besides, but no outside line from your room despite the promising-looking phone. Hot water only between 20.00 and 22.00, but very hot and plenty of it. Cash only, pay upfront, including ¥104 room key deposit. *Standard twin rooms ¥298; trpls ¥328; suite ¥488; deluxe suite ¥888.*

🏠 **Laoli Kezhan** 老李客栈 (3 rooms) Huanghuacheng Shuiku, Huairou District; ☏ 010 6165 1211 or 0136 9351 4508. Quaint, very budget place down on the river below the reservoir. Steps lead from the road down over a wooden 'suspension' bridge. Unless you sleep at the guesthouse, Old Li charges ¥4 to cross his bridge and land to access the Great Wall. Very basic communal shower and toilet, although Old Li claims that renovations are in the offing. Karaoke TV and microphone are available. His little shop after the bridge sells batteries, juice, firecrackers and other bits and pieces. *One seven-person huokàng and a four-person huokang at ¥10 per person, and a dbl room at ¥40 for the room.*

🏠 **Longfu Shanzhuang** 龙福山庄 (12 rooms) Erdaoguan, Huairou District; ☏ 010 6597 6609. This red lodge with white iron railings is easy to spot on the far side of the temple-like entrance of the road to Baiyunchuan village. The restaurant terrace has a sunset view on the Great Wall and the rooftop has a view of the Great Wall and supporting watchtowers in almost all directions. Separate karaoke room. *Seven standard twins en suite ¥80. Four* huòkàng *for four people each en suite ¥48. One dbl suite ¥220.*

🏠 **Qifengle Cottage** 旗风乐 (2 rooms) Around 500m south of the bridge before Huanghuacheng Cun; tel 010 6165 2030 or 0135 2216 5800. Good food, and offers guiding services. *Basic rooms at ¥20 per person.*

Camping at Xiao Xi Hu 小西湖 Little West Lake Xiao Xi Hu is another small natural park just outside the village of Xishuiyu, west of Huanghuacheng. A section of the wall there is now submerged under a manmade lake. Beijingers often come here to camp out for the weekend by the lake and enjoy an evening around a small campfire (fires in the rest of the camp are forbidden because of the risk of fires going out of control in the dry foliage). Take a taxi or gong jiao che from Huairou.

GUANGOU – BADALING AND JUYONG PASS 关沟－八达岭、居庸关 Northwest of Beijing is the valley of Guangou (Pass Gully). In ancient times it was one of the easiest ways across the surrounding mountains of Beijing, but at almost 20km in length it was also a convenient geographical killing zone. As a result the Ming dynasty built, renovated and enlarged a total of four fortified passes through the valley: Nankou (Southern Gate), Juyongguan (Pass of Conscripts), Shangguan (Upper Pass) and Badaling (Eight Way Valley). Once trapped between the southern and northernmost gates (Badaling), the enemy was easily slaughtered. Few emerged from the Southern Gate alive.

Badaling 八达岭 Despite the convenient trap of Guangou, Badaling was designed to not even allow the enemy into the valley in the first place. Restored to its former glory, a visit to Badaling today shows the impressive engineering feat that is Badaling. Here the wall is almost 8m high and 6m across. With a 4.5m inside width, the walkway atop the wall was designed to allow ten men or five mounted horsemen abreast to march along the wall from fortification to fortification as reinforcements were required. Fortified towers at the Badaling section of the Great Wall are never more than 500m apart, which makes it today one of the most impressive sections of the wall to view for as far as the eye can see. It is also,

however, heavily touristed with all the trappings that that entails and is, therefore, in the eyes of this book, the least-recommended section of the Great Wall to visit.

Badaling is a veritable amusement park all of its own, without even having to get on the wall itself. In fact some of those who never make it onto the wall merely get a photo of themselves superimposed onto a background of the Great Wall. A more 'upmarket' version of this gimmick is to have a VCD (Video Compact Disk) made of yourself on a flying carpet gracefully bobbing over a backdrop of gorgeous Great Wall.

For those who would rather walk down than up, there is a cable car which will take you up to a high point (where you must still pay the ¥60 entry fee, as well as ¥45 for the cable car). Unless you come by private taxi, then by the time you walk to the cable car from the lower bus park, you may as well just hike up the wall. On the way to the cable car you will pass numerous hawker stalls, restaurants, the Badaling Hotel (which does not have any rooms), the museum and the 360-Degree Cinema. Despite the kitsch around it, the free entry into the cinema for the 15-minute film of the wall is actually well worth it, even if you are going to see more of the wall in China.

Getting there There are a number of ways to get to Badaling. Most hotels will provide **tours**, often with English-speaking guides. Depending on the number of people on the tour, hotel tours can range from ¥100 to ¥200 per person, excluding entry fees. Chinese **tourist buses** 1–4 are much cheaper at ¥50 per person (excluding entry fees) and include a visit to Juyongguan and to the Ming Tombs. All buses, usually 16 seaters, depart when they are full: bus 1 departs from Qianmen 06.00–10.00; bus 2 leaves Dongdan 06.30–09.30; bus 3 from Xidan 06.30–09.30 and bus 4 from Xizhimen 06.30–09.00. These include a Chinese-speaking guide who will provide a stream of information while you are on the bus, but leave you to yourself at the sites visited. All buses are back at their departure station by 18.00 and you must stay with your bus. Depending on how early you leave, the tour itself gives you about 90 minutes at Juyonguan, two hours at Badaling, 45 minutes at the Chang Ming Tomb, and two hours at the Ding Underground Tomb and the jade factory (yes, all tours have their sales tie). If all you want is a quick look at the wall, then this type of tour is sufficient. If you want to control your own time, then take the even cheaper alternative of local bus 919 from Deshengmen for ¥8. The local and tourist buses will deposit you at the lower car park and so you must walk up the hill to the wall and the throng of hawker stalls that await you.

Two slow trains a day, leaving Beijing North Station at around 09.00 and 15.20, take two-and-a-half hours to Badaling Station to the east of the main pass for ¥6. Return **trains** leave Badaling around 15.15 and 19.30. A taxi to Badaling for the day costs around ¥500.

Where to stay Accommodation at Badaling is limited by the highway, the lack of a real community in the area, and the fact that Beijing is close enough and well enough connected by public transport that visitors tend to go back to the capital in the evening. The misnamed Badaling Hotel is in fact only a restaurant and very large souvenir store. The one place of note to stay near Badaling is **The Commune**, a showcase of 21st-century Asian architectural design. Even if you can't afford the prices per house for the night (see page 149), it's still worth viewing the houses and stopping at the restaurant for a bite to eat. Cantilever House offers great views of the Great Wall. Bamboo Wall House is minimalist and serene in nature, whilst Furniture House or Suitcase House offer a more post modern wild feel. The Commune and its surroundings sum up modern China very well – 2,000 years of

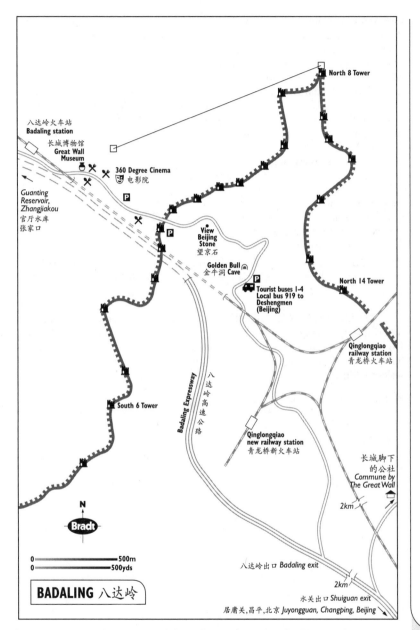

八达岭火车站
Badaling station

长城博物馆
Great Wall Museum

360 Degree Cinema
电影院

Guanting Reservoir, Zhangjiakou
官厅水库
张家口

North 8 Tower

View Beijing Stone
望京石

Golden Bull Cave
金牛洞

Tourist buses 1-4 Local bus 919 to Deshengmen (Beijing)

North 14 Tower

Qinglongqiao railway station
青龙桥火车站

Badaling Expressway

八达岭高速公路

South 6 Tower

Qinglongqiao new railway station
青龙桥新火车站

长城脚下的公社
Commune by The Great Wall

2km

N

Bradt

| 0 | | 500m |
| 0 | | 500yds |

BADALING 八达岭

八达岭出口 *Badaling exit*

2km

水关出口 *Shuiguan exit*

居庸关,昌平,北京 *Juyongguan, Changping, Beijing*

history juxtaposed against leapfrog designs, partly shoddy, partly exquisite craftsmanship, which leaves you unsure of whether you feel overwhelmed or confused.

The next gate down from Badaling along Guangou Gully, **Upper Gate** has not been well preserved. It is much eroded and hard to access.

Juyong Pass 居庸关

Juyong Pass on the other hand has worn well over the years and in 1993 it was fully restored. This pass, meaning 'Pass of Conscripts', existed as early as the first Qin Great Wall, built 770–476BC. Its present name is reminiscentof the scale of forced labour used by the Qin dynasty to build the first Great Wall. It has been rebuilt many times over the millennia and has been known under as many different names. It now stands almost as it did after its last enlargement during the Ming dynasty. The major modification is the enlarged passages through the pass for the railway and the highway. A reservoir has also been added outside the walls.

The Ming pass at Juyong forms part of a 4.5km wall enclosing the small garrison town and the original Qin pass, made of marble and richly engraved with Buddhist carvings and long inscriptions in a variety of Asian scripts. The reconstructed garrison town is sadly devoid of residents and so appears the mere mock-up that it is. Nevertheless, there are a few Chinese craft shops, including a man hand-painting T-shirts for ¥60, and some places to buy snacks. Sometimes outdoor concerts and exhibitions are held along the wall and the entire enclosure can be walked in two to three hours. Hardly anyone does this, so you'll have most of the wall to yourself once you get past the crowds. *(Entry ¥40.)*

If you want to stay at Juyongguan, there is a hotel outside the enclosure on the far side of the reservoir.

🏠 **Changcheng Gukezhan** 长城古客栈 (12 rooms) Juyongguannei, Chuanping District; ☎ 010 6977 8888. The hotel had seen better days at the time of writing but offers basic clean rooms en suite with 24-hour hot water. No breakfast. *dbls, twins and trpls for ¥180.*

REST OF THE GREAT WALL IN BEIJING The Southern Gate at Nankou town unfortunately no longer exists, although it was still very much present when Frank Dorn drew his map of Beijing in 1936 (copies of which can be bought in Xinhua bookstore on Wangfujing and Xidan in Beijing). Further west of Badaling, the wall scales the Bijia Mountains and disappears into southwestern Hebei.

9

Shanxi 山西

If we take advantage of the respite to complete construction of border walls at Xuanfu, Datong and Huamachi; construct many large fortified villages inside; call upon the people to cultivate completely so that grain becomes cheap; would it not be possible to guarantee security?

Ming official, 15th century

Shanxi province effectively served as the third ring of defence around the capital, after Beijing province itself and then Hebei. This province contains most of China's inner wall, which extends some 400km from where it crosses the Tang River in the east to where it joins the outer wall at Beibao/Kouzishang. The outer wall bordering Inner Mongolia extends another 400km from Yongjia Castle in the east to Laoniuwan on the Yellow River. A southern offshoot of the wall also runs from Wutai Mountain along the border with Hebei.

The walls in Shanxi province are mostly constructed of rammed earth and are sometimes referred to as the Purple Great Wall owing to the colour they acquired from mixing the local yellow earth with the more sturdy red earth imported for building. Rammed earth erodes quickly if not constantly maintained and so much of the wall is already completely destroyed. Take care not to add to the destruction of the wall by climbing on top of it if you are walking along any of these sections. Some of the highlights of the wall in the province are the hike from Li'erkou to Yanggao hot springs resort; where the Great Wall meets the Yellow River; and the fortified towns of Guanwu and Wild Goose Pass.

These parts of the wall are not much visited, although supported hikes along them are beginning to emerge. The province also offers a number of other famous sites that are well frequented. These include the Hanging Monastery, Yungang Carved Buddha Grottoes, the ancient Ming dynasty town of Pingyao, and the 3,058m-high sacred Wutai Shan and a number of famous monasteries associated with the sacred mountain. Datong city, accessible by train but not plane, makes a good base to explore the province's 1,000km of Great Wall and its prolific number of fortified villages.

DATONG 大同

HISTORY Datong's history goes back over two millennia. By AD383, it became the capital of the northern Wei dynasty, which ended in AD534. While it languished in obscurity for almost 1,000 years after that, in the Ming dynasty Datong became the headquarters of the Shanxi garrison zone, thus increasing its importance for trade and defence. Datong's legendary claim to fame relates the love story of the mythical dragon and phoenix that now symbolise love and harmony between man (the dragon) and woman (the phoenix). The story dates back to the time of Emperor

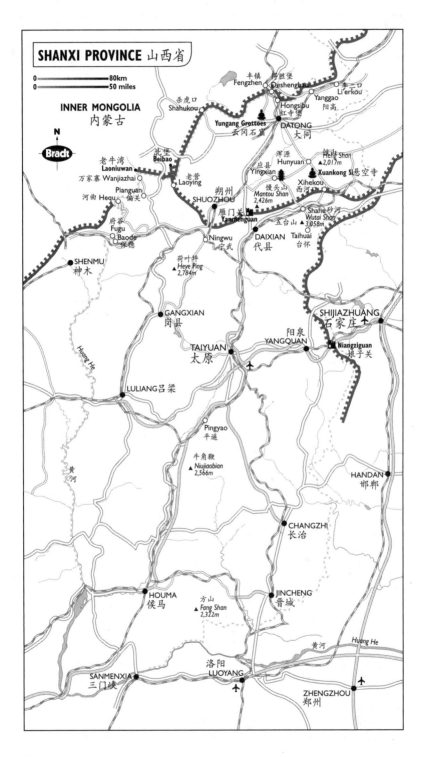

SHANXI PROVINCE 山西省

0 ————— 80km
0 ————— 50 miles

INNER MONGOLIA
内蒙古

N

Bradt

丰镇 得胜堡
Fengzhen Deshengbao
李二口
Li'erkou
杀虎口 Yanggao
Shahukou 红寺堡 阳高
Hongsibu
Yungang Grottoes DATONG 大同
云冈石窟
北堡 浑源 恒山
Beibao Hunyuan Heng Shan
应县 ▲2,017m
Yingxian Xuankong Si悬空寺
老牛湾 西河口
Laoniuwan 老营 Xihekou
万家寨 Wanjiazhai Laoying SHUOZHOU 馒头山
Pianguan 朔州 Mantou Shan
河曲 Hequ 偏关 2,426m 沙河
雁门关 Shahe 砂河
Yanmenguan 五台山 Wutai Shan
府谷 Ningwu DAIXIAN ▲3,058m
Fugu 宁武 代县 台怀
Baode Taihuai
保德
SHENMU
神木 荷叶坪
Heye Ping
2,784m

GANGXIAN
岗县 SHIJIAZHUANG
石家庄
阳泉
YANGQUAN Niangziguan
TAIYUAN 娘子关
太原
LULIANG吕梁

黄
河 Pingyao
平遥

牛角鞭
Niujiaobian HANDAN
2,566m 邯郸

CHANGZHI
长治

HOUMA 方山 JINCHENG
侯马 Fang Shan 晋城
2,322m

黄河 Huang He
SANMENXIA 洛阳
三门峡 LUOYANG
ZHENGZHOU
郑州

Huang He

Zhengde of the Ming dynasty, who fell in love with a local Datong girl, Li Fengjie, while in Datong on inspection of the garrison. The dragon and the phoenix, which go back much further than the Ming dynasty, have become personified in this love story.

Over the centuries, Shanxi and the wider region have suffered from massive deforestation (see page 55). As a result, this area is blighted by frequent dust storms in the spring and flooding throughout the Yellow River delta during the summer rains. In 1997, a reforestation programme was started in Shanxi. The army plants trees every spring, and year by year the province grows greener, but whether reforestation will succeed in reversing environmental degradation has yet to be seen.

Aside from the environmental effects of deforestation, Shanxi also suffers from widespread air pollution as a result of extensive coal mining. Datong is the capital of China's coal industry. Although this industry does keep the province financially liquid, the conditions for those working in the coal pits remains appalling. The safety record of the mines has been a cause for concern in recent years with pit explosions in the Datong area killing hundreds.

GETTING THERE AND AROUND There is no airport at Datong. The nearest airport is at Taiyuan (see page 205). CAAC's representative office in Datong is at 14 Yingbin Dong Lu; *✆* 0352 5101 777/747.

Datong is well served by buses and trains. Several trains (seven hours) leave from Beijing main station, including one overnight train. Soft sleepers are booked up fast by tour groups, so book ahead early. Hard sleepers cost ¥93. Faster trains (five hours) leave during the day from Beijing West. Direct buses (4½ hours) leave from Xizhimen long-distance bus station, four per day, for ¥91.

Once in Datong, the city is spread out enough that you'll want to take a taxi (minimum fare ¥6) or buses between the train station and main sights. Bus 4 leaves from the train station through the centre of the old fortified town past the Drum Tower and on to Xinkaili, where bus 3 goes to the Yungang Grottoes. Bus 15 goes from the train station past Hongqi Square and towards the hotels on Yingbin Lu. Bus 8 goes to Hongci Castle.

There are four long-distance bus stations in Datong:

Old Long-Distance Bus Station Jiù Chángtú Qìchē Zhàn 旧长途汽车站 Xinjian Bei Lu, near the corner with Xinhua Jie; *✆* 0352 2818 411; a 15-minute walk from the train station. Hohhot two per day (4–5hrs, ¥45). Minibuses to Wutaishan every hour 06.00–14.00 (4hrs, ¥40); Fengzheng via Desheng Castle (1hr, ¥15); Tianzhen (¥30).

New Long-Distance Bus Station Xīn Chángtú Qìchē Zhàn 新长途汽车站 Yantong Xi Lu; *✆* 0352 6036 784 or 6020 870. Lingqiu via Hengshan and the Hanging Monastery Xuankong Si (¥30); Hunyuan every hour (2hrs, ¥20); and to Shahe/Wutaishan station (¥30).

New South Bus Station Xīnnán Qìchē Zhàn 新南汽车站 Xinjian Nan Lu; *✆* 0352 5025 222. Beijing several per day (4hrs, ¥100); Taiyuan every 40 minutes 07.00–18.30 (3½hrs, ¥70); Yingxian every hour (1½hrs, ¥20). Bus 30 from the train station goes to New South Bus Station.

Bus Station at the Train Station Opposite the Hongqi Hotel. Has smaller buses and minibuses going to more local destinations.

A couple of very good **tour operators** can help you with hotel bookings, onward travel, and tours to various sights around Datong and Shanxi.

CITS Inside the main train hall; tel/f 0352 7124 882 or 510 1326; mob: 130 0808 8454; e railwaystation-info @datongcits.com; www.datongcits.com. The very helpful English-speaking Gao Jinwu can arrange all your travel needs, including budget hotels. CITS tours for ¥100 each (minimum five people, excluding entrance tickets) go to two of: Yungang Grottoes, Hanging Monastery, Hengshan Mountain, Yingxian Wooden Pagoda, and the Ancient Great Wall

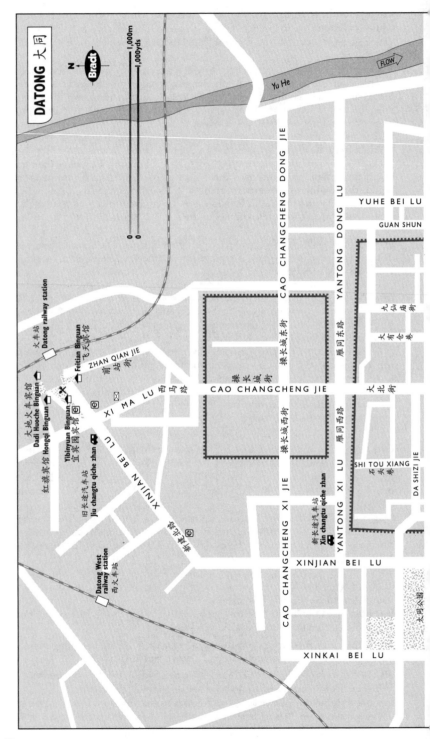

DATONG 大同

FLOW

Yu He

Bradt

N

0 1,000m
0 1,000yds

YUHE BEI LU

GUAN SHUN

CAO CHANGCHENG DONG JIE

YANTONG DONG LU

九仙庙街

大有仓巷

CAO CHANGCHENG JIE

大北街

DA SHIZI JIE

SHI TOU XIANG
石头巷

YANTONG XI LU

雁同西路

雁同东路

操长城东街

操长城西街

CAO CHANGCHENG XI JIE

XINJIAN BEI LU

新长途汽车站
Xin changtu qiche zhan

XINKAI BEI LU

太阳公园

新建北路

XINJIAN BEI LU

Datong West
railway station
西火车站

旧长途汽车站
Jiu changtu qiche zhan

红旗宾馆 Hongqi Binguan

大地火车宾馆
Dadi Huoche Binguan

宜宾园宾馆
Yibinyuan Binguan

XI MA LU 西马路

ZHAN QIAN JIE
前站街

Feitian Binguan
飞天候馆

火车站
Datong railway station

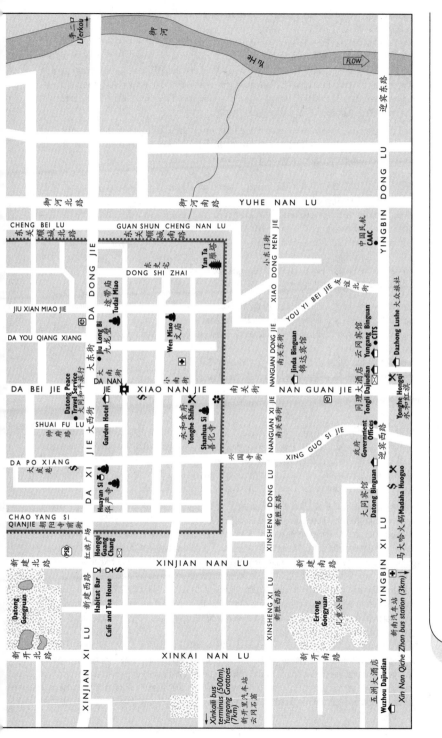

(Hongcibu and Deshengbu). For other tours see their website. They also run a ten-day Great Wall and Shanxi sights tour. Open daily 06.30–20.30.

Datong Peace International Travel Service Dàtóng Hépíng Guójì Lǚxíng 大同和平国际旅行 36 Shuaifu Lu; ☏ 0352 2025 816 or 139 0352 1876; f 0352 2018 158; @ gsjzlx@yahoo.com.cn; www.skyler.cn. Mr Skyler Gao, who speaks excellent English, can provide you with slightly more tailored trips than CITS, as well as all the usual travel booking services, and can get you up to 40% discounts on more expensive hotels (minimum ¥200) in Shanxi. One of their drivers available for tailored trips, Zhang Hong, has detailed experience of the Great Wall in Shanxi, and he also doesn't smoke! Peace International has another office in Taiyuan.

Once in Datong, there are some excellent maps in Chinese of the province, the Datong city area and of Datong town itself. The kiosks around the train and bus stations and the magazine stores all sell them.

MONEY AND COMMUNICATION The main branch of Bank of China on Yingbin Xi Lu, opposite the Datong Hotel, cashes travellers' cheques, gives credit-card advances and exchanges foreign currency. Open every day including weekends 08.00–18.00. At the time of writing, the only bank with an ATM accepting foreign credit and debit cards was the Bank of China on Xiao Nan Jie. Some branches of the other banks, including Industrial and Commercial Bank of China, and China Construction Bank also exchange foreign currency.

Internet cafés are many:

Liansuo Wangba 连锁网吧 Xinjian Bei Lu, near the train station, opened in 2005 and has modern computers and software in a light and airy atmosphere. Open 24hrs at ¥2 per hour.

Qiankun Wangba 乾坤网吧 99 Da Dong Jie. Nice setting, friendly staff. Open 08.00—midnight with Windows 2000 at ¥2 per hour.

Nongchao'er Wangba 弄潮儿网吧 Xinjian Bei Lu. Windows 98 at ¥2 per hour.

Xunyu Wangba 训雨网吧 78 Nan Guan Jie. Only Windows 98 at ¥2 per hour.

Wangyuan Wangba 网缘网吧 Xinjian Bei Lu. Dark, dingy atmosphere with Windows 98. Charges foreigners ¥5per hr.

WHERE TO STAY Most of the accommodation in Datong has centred in the past around the train station or outside the south city walls. With the reconstruction of much of the centre of the city, new hotels are popping up inside the old city walls. Although these might be on the more expensive side, they are very good value for money and are right at the heart of the sights, shops and cafés.

🏠 **Dazhong Lüshe** 大众旅馆 (20 rooms) 36 Yingbin Dong Lu; ☏ 0352 5102 149. Located 70m down a small alleyway opposite the Tongli Hotel. Sunny, serviced rooms run by friendly staff. Make your own bed, bring your own toilet paper, hot water can sometimes be scalding. Useful town and regional maps on the lobby walls. Bus 15 runs from the train station to the City Government Shì Zhèngfǔ 市政府 bus stop. From there proceed 200m east, across the crossroads to the alleyway. En suites have 24hr hot water. *Standard twin en suite ¥80; twin or dbl with AC en suite ¥100; two-, three- and four-bed dorms using communal showers with limited hot water ¥60 per room.*

🏠 **Feitian Binguan** 飞天宾馆 (110 rooms) 1 Zhan Qian Jie; ☏ 0352 2814 348; f 0352 2813 483. A Chinese two star getting past its sell-by date, but conveniently close to the train station if you don't mind the sound of regular train whistles. Restaurant and sauna. *Standard twin ¥160; common dbl ¥140; trpl ¥210; bed in a four-person dorm ¥35.*

🏠 **Garden Hotel** Huāyuán Dàfàndiàn 花园大饭店 (108 rooms) 59 Da Nan Jie; ☏ 0352 5865 888; f 0352 2061 435; @ gardenhotel@sina.com. By far the nicest hotel in town and centrally located not far from the Drum Tower. Two restaurants, one serving Brazilian buffet (¥128 per person), and an airy coffee hall on the second floor. All rooms with free ethernet connection, deluxe dbls have a window through from the bedroom to the bathroom, suites have a jacuzzi bath in addition. Breakfast included. Takes credit cards. *Standard dbl or twin ¥620; sgl ¥580; deluxe suite ¥1,280.*

🏠 **Jinda Binguan** 锦达宾馆 (17 rooms) 64 Nan Guan Jie; ☎ 0352 2450 292. Guaranteed 24hr hot water at this bathhouse hotel with big communal showers and scrub beds. *En suite only in the deluxe, ¥380. Standard twin ¥68; with AC ¥88. Room for 2hrs ¥38.*

🏠 **Dadi Huoche Binguan** 大地火车宾馆 (78 rooms) Immediately to your left on exiting the railway station; ☎ 0352 7121 263. The friendly railway staff, who run this basic but serviced hotel, will tell you that it is the safest place in town to stay at, as it is within the railway square which is monitored by the police. There is a small restaurant downstairs, and a shop on each floor. *Plenty of dorm beds at ¥10 per person. Standard twin en suite ¥120.*

🏠 **Hongqi Dafandian** 红旗大饭店 (120 rooms) 11 Zhan Qian Jie; ☎ 0352 5366 111; 🖷 0352 5366 222. Very good value for money and a stone's throw from the train station — walk 50m west of the station (two o'clock direction from the station exit). A three star with sauna, two excellent restaurants, business centre with internet at ¥10 per hour, and direct dial to your room. Their restaurant is over water (glass floored including red goldfish) and offers a lot of Chinese specialities. Try their lamb back, or hotpot in the hotpot restaurant. English-, German- and Japanese-speaking staff. Chinese buffet breakfast included. *Standard twin ¥338; suite ¥568. Room by the hour ¥80.*

🏠 **Tongli Dajiudian** 同理大酒店 (50 rooms) 18 Yingbin Dong Lu; ☎ 0352 5024 114; 🖷 0352 5024 888. A nice bright, clean, three-star hotel, recently refurbished, with two floors of popular restaurant. Breakfast included. No internet. *Common twin ¥218; standard twin or dbl ¥250; suite ¥260.*

🏠 **Yibinyuan Binguan** 谊宾园宾馆 (30 rooms) Xinjian Bei Lu; ☎ 0352 2811 317–9. Friendly staff, cheap rooms, near the station. *Standard dbl ¥78; common dbl ¥50; sgl ¥40; trpl ¥15 per bed.*

🏠 **Yungang Binguan** 云岗宾馆 (158 rooms) 21 Yingbin Lu; ☎ 0352 5021 601; 🖷 0352 5024 927. A Chinese three star and already rather worn despite its refurbishment and upgrade to duvets several years ago. There is a restaurant, bank, post office and gift shop, but no internet and no breakfast. *sgl ¥380; standard twin ¥400; suite ¥680.*

✖ **WHERE TO EAT AND DRINK** Datong restaurants are many and good. The grand majority of them are on the main north–south street through town along Cao Changcheng Jie, Da Bei Jie and Xiao Nan Jie. Early in the morning you can often see the entire restaurant staff paraded for inspection outside their restaurants. Some even do team sports like tug-of-war before breakfast. Unfortunately, breakfast street stalls, familiar in many other cities, appear to have been banned from Datong's streets, so you will need to find a restaurant for breakfast in the mornings if it is not included in your hotel.

✖ **Café and Tea House** On Xinjian Nan Lu, corner with Da Xi Jie at the popular Hongqi Square. A relaxing atmosphere playing country music and other mellow tunes. Japanese-style seating area available downstairs. Open 10.30–midnight.

✖ **California Beef Noodle King** Xinjian Bei Lu, close to the train station and start station for the city buses. This chain of restaurants with their familiar red sign (the logo is reminiscent of Kentucky Fried Chicken's Colonel Sanders) offers a variety of cheap noodle dishes and snacks. Beef or chicken noodles ¥7. Sweet coffee ¥3, but no tea. Open 06.00–22.00.

✖ **Habitat Bar** On Xinjian Nan Lu, corner with Da Xi Jie, next door but one to the Café and Tea House; ☎ 0352 2034 789. A very cool, if pricey, pub complete with red British telephone box and interesting postcards on the toilet walls. Open 11.00 till late. Live music in the evenings.

✖ **Hongqi Huoguo** 红旗火锅 11 Zhan Qian Jie; ☎ 0352 5366 888. Much reputed in the city, the huoguo restaurant of the Hongqi Dafandian does indeed serve very good hotpot with a great variety of ingredients to select from.

✖ **Latino's Buffet** Garden Hotel, Xiao Nan Lu; ☎ 0352 5865 888. Once you've had enough of Chinese food and crave something a little more Western, Latino's buffet is the place to come. At ¥128 per person it is a little pricey, but you get endless amounts of Brazilian roast meats and seafood, including crab, caviar and some less than popular sushi. Comes with live Brazilian music.

✖ **Madaha Huoguocheng** 马大哈火锅城 Yingbin Xi Lu, opposite the Datong Hotel and very near the Bank of China main branch; ☎ 0352 5033 107. A popular hotpot restaurant serving all the usual favourites.

✖ **Tongli Dajiudian** 同理大酒店 18 Yingbin Dong Lu; ☎ 0352 5024 114. On the second and third floors of the hotel, this restaurant is great for looking out onto the street and serves excellent food including Chinese specialities from around the country. Try their Mongolian roast lamb (měnggǔ kǎo yángròu 蒙古烤羊肉) served on a sizzling hotplate, and their hand vegetables (shǒucài 手菜 – a type of stringy spinach).

✖ **Yonghe Hongqi Meishicheng** 永和红旗美食城 8 Yingbin Dong Lu; ☎ 0352 5101 333. Sister restaurant to the one below but more upmarket. Avoid the pineapple sweet and sour pork.

✖ **Yonghe Shifu** 永和食府 Corner of Xiao Nan Jie and Shanhua Si Lu; ☎ 0352 2059 199. A big busy restaurant serving lots of good Chinese dishes as well as hotpot.

WHAT TO SEE The heart of Datong's sights and shopping lies around and to the west of the **Drum Tower**. If you are staying near the station, then hop on bus 4 for ten minutes till you see the obvious red painted drum tower in the centre of the city and save yourself the 3km dull hike into town from the station. The bus turns west just before the Drum Tower. Have ¥1 per person ready to get on the bus, as you'll need to put it in the money box at the front on entering; the driver does not give change. The Drum Tower itself is not open to the public. The old city walls of Datong are mostly destroyed already, even though they still readily appear on town maps. There's not much of them to visit, but you will see them periodically as you ride the buses around town and the surrounding areas.

Jiu Long Bi 九龙壁 (Nine Dragon Screen) is the front screen to the former residence of a very rich official in old Datong. If you have seen a jiulongbi before, perhaps in the Forbidden City in Beijing, then this one on its own is hardly worth the ¥10 entry fee.

Of the three **monasteries** in Datong, only (the upper) Shàng Huáyán Sì 上华严寺 Monastery is really worth the visit. Xià Huáyán Sì 下华严寺 and Shànhuà Sì 善化寺 are essentially now exhibition sites, with a few local artefacts on display with no English description. Shang Shanhua is still a working monastery. The way to Shang Huayan is along a small pedestrian street selling souvenirs and incense sticks. *(Entry ¥60.)*

Yungang Grottoes Yúngāng Shíkū 云冈石窟 usually make it on to many package tours of China. They are the largest statues of Buddha to be carved into rock that are still in existence after those now destroyed in Afghanistan. Carved into the sandstone cliffs in the 5th century, they remain a popular tourist attraction for both foreign and Chinese tourists. The majority of the statues have deteriorated since their heyday and the front of Cave 20 has long since fallen away, exposing the statue of Buddha directly to the elements. The semi-decayed state of the statues shows quite clearly how the figures were 'carved'. After a rough rendition of the statue in the cave, holes were made into the figures for sticks. Onto these sticks a layer of material and plaster was laid giving each figure a smooth and more easily defined finish. After hardening, the plaster cast was then painted to give the figures their near lifelike appearance. *(Entry ¥60.)*

To get there by public transport is quite easy. Take bus 4 (leaves from the train station) to its final stop (zhōngdiǎn 终点) at Xīnkāilǐ 新开里. From that bus stop walk back 30m to the starting stop for bus 3, diagonally opposite the final stop for bus 4. From here bus 3 will take you the half-hour journey to the grottoes. It's one of only two places that foreigners usually go on that bus (Guānyīn Táng 观音堂 'Hall of the Goddess of Mercy' being the other) so you'll probably get plenty of helpful people telling you when you have got there. The grottoes rise up on your left after all the coal mines along the way, so you will see them a couple of minutes in advance of your stop. Guanyin Tang is a 15-minute ride on bus 3. There are several buses you can take back from Yungang Grottoes which will let you off at the bus 3 final stop. The last bus 3 back to Datong leaves at 19.30.

THE OUTER WALL

Before Inner Mongolia became an integral part of China, the outer Great Wall in Shanxi province served alternately as a defensive structure and as a control point for trade and customs. The Mongol hordes to the north, when not fighting the various Chinese dynasties, were busy trading with Datong city, and so the Desheng and Hongci castles used to be well maintained for both purposes. During the Ming dynasty, the defence of the outer wall was charged to Datong garrison, which had under its responsibility 827 beacon towers, 72 castles and one-twelfth of the empire's army.

Today the outer wall can roughly be divided into three sections. The easternmost section from the wall's entry into the province until the motorway heading north out of Datong is the cleanest and flattest section. A two-day hike alongside this section of the wall from Li'erkou to Changcheng village is pleasant and easy going. A third and fourth day hiking to the village of Hongcibu is more challenging, rising over the hills. From there to Deshengbu village is flat again.

A five-day hike along a second section from the western side of the motorway to where the wall meets the Yellow River at Laoniuwan takes you north of the heart of Shanxi's mining industry. Pretty in the autumn, this section should be avoided in the spring when the wind whips up not only loess sand but also fine coal dust. Until China moves on to cleaner fuels, this section will always leave your skin black at the end of the day.

From Laoniuwan a third section of the outer wall follows the eastern side of the Yellow River. Pleasant enough to hike, boats are also available to take you up or downstream to Debaozhen, where the wall enters Shaanxi province.

China Direct and CITS (see page 185) do multi-day supported hikes of the Great Wall including parts of all three sections below.

LI'ERKOU TO DESHENGBU HIKE

The Great Wall enters Shanxi province a couple of kilometres north of Mashikou (Horse Market Gate). It follows the mountain ridge south until Toutaizi, when it heads east and down into Shanxi to the little village of Lǐ'èrkǒu 李二口. Villagers live right at the Great Wall, tending fields of cherry and plum trees, vegetables and their flocks of sheep. It is an idyllic setting in the spring when the fruit trees blossom or in the autumn when the trees turn golden. If you are going to camp here at the beginning or end of a hike along the Shanxi wall, be sure to check with the villagers that they are happy for you to camp there, and pay them a little (¥5–10) for using their land and water from the village well.

To get to Li'erkou, there are buses and trains from Datong, Zhangjiakou or Beijing to nearby Tianzhen, from where you can either take a taxi the remaining 6km (¥10) or wait for a bus heading for Xinghezhen. Taking the bus, get out at Waguankou after crossing the railroad and the aqueduct and head west down the unpaved tree-lined track to Li'erkou (3km). Taxis from Datong will take you there in three hours for ¥200, or you can arrange drop-off, pick-up and an overnight stay at the Yunmenshan Hot Springs Resort through Peace International Travel Service for ¥500 (see page 188). On the way to Tianzhen at kilometre marker 87 is the abandoned walled town of Shilipucun, which stands as a good example of cave dwellings which quickly deteriorate after people are moved out to live in the new high-rise buildings of the towns.

From Li'erkou a narrow path follows the wall through the cherry and plum orchards of the village, soon leading to open fields. Take care during this section not to damage the water channels and crops of local farmers. The wall from here to Datong hugs the foot of the mountain range that separates Inner Mongolia and Shanxi. It does not, therefore, follow the actual 'frontier' between the two provinces and you cannot see into Inner Mongolia. The wall is made of adobe mud bricks and is very eroded. In parts, it disappears altogether. Keep following the foothills and you will pick it up again.

After some 25km (a good eight hours' walking), you will pass to the north of the larger settlement of Luowenzao, from which a dirt track road heads north through the wall into Inner Mongolia. A few kilometres after this, the wall passes within 2km north of two hot spring hotels. This is a good place to camp for the night and use the sauna facilities and restaurants, or stay at the hotels themselves. The first, Jinshuai Hot Springs Hotel, is older and already in need of some upkeep. The second, **Yunmenshan Hot Springs Resort** Yúnménshān Wēnquán Dùjiàcūn 云门山温泉度假村 (38 rooms) *(Zhuashanmiao Village, Luowenzao, Yanggao County ℂ 0352 6776 000)* opened late in 2004 and has good clean rooms and facilities, including a restaurant. All facilities are indoors. Male and female bath and sauna areas are separate. The water is a comfortable 34°C and is piped to the communal showers at the baths as well as into the bedroom suites, which have a shower and wooden soak tub; ¥288. Standard twins also come with 24-hour hot water but no tub; ¥158. Rooms can also be rented by the hour for ¥68.

A second day's hike of a further 25km from the hot springs to the village of Changcheng is also easy going, flat and follows the contour of foothills. The wall passes 2.5km north of the small, rundown town of **Yanggao**. The mud walls of the old town are in the usual state of disrepair, the roads are mostly unpaved and bloated dead piglets can be seen littering the streets along with all the rest of the usual rubbish. Keep walking along the wall north of the village of Sikebu to avoid Yanggao unless you are in need of provisions. Thereafter, the wall takes again to the hills, making for a more strenuous hike still heading west. It is 17km from the hot springs to the village of Zhenchuankou, which is a good place to camp for the night before the next 10km push on to Hongcibu village.

Approaching the village of **Hongcibu**, the wall descends the hills towards the Yu River. An old watchtower can be seen at the top of the next ridge to the north. At the river the wall heads north-northwest along the east side of the river towards Deshengbu. An offshoot also branches southwest and joins up again with the outer wall at Black Earth Gate Heitukou. Hongcibu village itself is on the west side of the river (no bridge, just a shallow ford with stepping stones). The rammed earth old village wall can still be seen, unrenovated and dilapidated. Nowadays, there is also an electricity-generating plant to the north of the old walled town. A small shop in the village sells basic supplies of drinks, food and toiletries. Hongcibu is a 30km drive from Datong on bus 8 from the train station (07.00–17.00; ¥3), taking about 50 minutes. The last bus 8 back to Datong from Hongcibu is at 18.00.

From Hongcibu, following the wall on the east side of the Yu River, it is another 10km along the wall to Déshèngbǔ 德胜堡. The railway also follows the river along the valley floor and the road lies further to the east. Deshengbu boasts the last surviving original wooden gate to a city embedded in the actual northern frontier wall. (A number of fortified towns within China still have their original wooden gates.) At Deshengbu town you can pick up a taxi (¥50) or minibus (¥10) to Datong. (Bus 8 ends at Baoziwan, halfway between Hongcibu and Deshengbu.)

JUQIANGBU TO LAONIUWAN Between Deshengbu and Jùqiángbǔ 拒墙堡, there is a railway, several roads and the soon-to-be-completed new highway to Hohhot. At Weilu, the wall then skirts around the foothills of Mount Pinding (elevation 2,060m). The wall runs within 15km of the heart of Shanxi's mining towns. At **Shahukou**, the local government is renovating the wall and old gateway, and will undoubtedly start charging soon for access to the wall. Near Shahukou is another old walled village, Youweizhen. This is also probably soon to be renovated by the local government for tourism consumption. During the mean time it remains a poor rundown town that could certainly benefit from a boost to the local economy. To get there by public transport from Datong, take a minibus from the old bus station to Youyixian and change for a bus heading for Helinge'er.

Further west, the wall at Qidun has two well-kept watchtowers, **Jinpai and Xusi towers**. The wall then proceeds past **Beibao** where the inner wall branches off, and the outer wall proceeds on to Old Bull's Bend Lǎoniúwān 老牛湾 on the Yellow River.

Both CITS and China Direct can run supported hikes of this arduous section (see pages 185 and 66 respectively).

ALONG THE YELLOW RIVER The stretch of Great Wall along the Yellow River is not as easy as might be imagined. Shanxi's honeycombed soil structure is widely prevalent here and the wall rises and falls according to the ancient erosion gullies in the land. Laoniuwan, where the Great Wall meets the Yellow River is slowly becoming more frequented and is indeed quite spectacular. If you don't fancy the hike, speed or slow boats can take you from Laoniuwan to Wanjiazhai Dam in ten or 30 minutes respectively. Both options cost ¥200. The speedboat takes up to eight people, while the slow boat takes up to 30 passengers. The 35m suspension bridge at Wanjiazhai Dam costs ¥6 to cross.

A good option for overnighting at Wanjiazhai is the **Wanjiazhai Binguan** Wànjiāzhài Bīnguǎn 万家寨宾馆 (61 rooms) (✆ *0350 7641 089)*. Located 2km uphill from the dam in a complex for the dam company staff, this hotel offers clean serviced twins for ¥160, single occupation ¥150. Following the road around to the back of the company complex (or through the back gate from the company compound) is the one-street town of Wanjiazhai. There are a few small restaurants to eat at here, including hotpot and dumpling places. One good clean restaurant is Chuányuán Jiǎozi Guǎn 船员饺子馆 (✆ *0345 7641 088)*, offering deep-fried baby Yellow River shrimp for ¥15, Shanxi Kronen beer for ¥5 a bottle and plates of delicious vegetables. The landlord, Zhangyou, is an added bonus. His restaurant also offers a few cheap rooms at ¥50 each.

Boats downstream from Wanjiazhai are also possible at the bottom of the dam. The ride to Baodezhen takes two hours on the slow boat for ¥500.

Piānguān 偏关 served the outer Great Wall along the Yellow River as a garrison fort. It lies close to the mighty Yellow River where it could command most of the 50km of river that makes up part of the Great Wall defensive structure here. To help guard this easy crossing point in the river, a further four walls were built in the area, three to the north of Pianguan and one to the south. Two hundred beacons and watchtowers reinforced this strategic gateway, but little remains to be seen of them now. Pianguan remains a bustling town, although much of its town wall has been destroyed. The main gate to the city has been reconstructed and now looks somewhat odd straddled by two modern concrete and tiled shopping complexes on either side. There are several buses a day to Pianguan and Wanjiazhai from Ningwu. The bus station is next to the reconstructed gate of the town. The nearest main railway station is Baode on the east side of the Yellow River.

THE INNER WALL

The inner wall of Shanxi stretches from Beibao in the west where it branches off from the outer wall south and then east, past Ningwuguan, the Wild Goose Pass at

Yanmenguan, Pingxingguan and then over the southern offshoot of the wall into Hebei province. One of the first towns that the inner wall passes on its way south from North Castle is the fortified town of **Laoying**. Little more than a village today, the mud walls are still intact, but the area inside them is now used mostly for cultivation. The village suffers from lying on Shanxi's main coal belt, and is none too pretty to visit, but interesting nonetheless. Buses to Pianguan or Wanjiazhai from Datong stop at the village.

PASSES The inner Great Wall of Shanxi rides the tops of the Wutai and Heng mountain ranges. Defensive walls have been built along these ranges as far back as the Warring States in 343BC. There are three important passes in Shanxi's inner wall, which are known as the 'outer passes' (in relation to the 'inner passes' in the Hebei inner wall). All three passes served strategic defensive points in the wall and so were well built but have since fallen into significant disrepair.

Nìngwǔguān 宁武关 lies between Pianguan and Yanmenguan at the town of **Ningwu**. It served as a garrison for reinforcements of soldiers to the passes on either side and by 2005 there was not much left there to visit save the original gateway to the town. It is easy to get to, however, by train direct from Datong and so can serve as a useful start or finish to hiking the wall.

Yànménguān 雁门关 was once known among the Chinese as one of the nine strategic forts of the world. Yanmen means **gate of the wild geese**, which is believed to be a reference to the remoteness of this pass. Many famous Chinese battles were fought here and, before the two great dynasties of Liao and Song were conquered and united by the Nuzhen at the beginning of the 12th century, the wall along the Heng mountain range was the border between the two dynasties. Defensive positions straddled either side of the border: Yingxian to the north for the Song dynasty and Daixian to the south (see below). The wall at Yanmenguan is one of the few parts of the wall in Shanxi to be built of brick and stone, signifying the importance of the fortification. The first fort there was built in 1374. It was enlarged several times until it spanned almost 1km in circumference. Unfortunately, little remains of the original fort, but the leftover scars of battles from the much earlier Han period (206–25BC) can still be found outside the pass. Large mounds of earth indicate the burial places of generals and commanders who fell in battle. The larger the mound the more senior the officer. To the west of Yanmenguan is the fort of **Baicaolingkou** where General Yang Ye beat the invading Qidans in 980.

The site at Yanmen is now under local government control, and several features are in the process of reconstruction. Most of the site, however, is largely untouched. Just inside the entrance to the site is the small settlement of Yanmen. It is particularly dilapidated, and the few very poor people who live there at present will probably be moved out to make way for an alley of restaurants and hawkers in due course. *(Entry ¥25.)*

Less than 6km from Yanmen is the old walled city of Guǎngwǔ 广武. It is one of the few remaining walled cities that has mostly retained its brick facing and has not had a larger town built up around it. As a result, you can view it as you approach it almost as one might have done hundreds of years ago. The few inhabitants who still live inside will be moved out to a new settlement that is being built for them. It is unclear at the time of writing exactly what plans the local government has for the original buildings that were inside the walled city of Guangwu.

From Guangwu it is easy to access the wall, which you can see atop the hills behind the mud walls. Crossing the underpass into the very small town of

Guangwu proper, small footpaths lead up to the wall from the roadside. The southwest ridge can be followed for several kilometres firstly alongside, and then bisected by, the new motorway. A southward hike of several kilometres is then required to where the motorway disappears into a 5.6km tunnel. At this point you can then ascend over the tunnel to the other side of the motorway and hike all the way back up the west side of the motorway to regain the wall. The wall then proceeds west, mostly intact, for 50km to the town of **Yanfangkou**, where local roads and rail have replaced much of the wall.

Taking the wall northeast from Guangwu, it heads up towards **Bald Head Mountain** (Mántou Shān 馒头山) (2,426m above sea level). The wall further east is particularly eroded, but remnants of it are ever present in the names of the villages along the Heng mountain ridge: Justice City Gully, Great Wall Village, Six Man Camp, Big Stone Castle, Glad Justice Camp, Spirit Gully.

The wall picks up again through Four River Gate, Sihekou. Part of this wall east of the village still contains stonework and a number of towers top the hills. West of the village the wall has been ravaged of stones and only mud remains. The village itself of only some 200 houses is relatively easily accessible by bus in the mornings, but there is no hotel or restaurant. At the unmarked bus stop on the side of the road is an unmarked shop selling a very few items. Ask in the village to have it opened up if you want some peanuts or buns. The village is served by the buses running between Shahe (Wutaishan train station, one hour, ¥15) and Datong (two hours, ¥20) via Hunyuan (Hengshan, 30 minutes, ¥10). After Four River Gate, the wall proceeds intermittently towards the town of King's Village, Castle Wang Zhuangbu. South of this is the pass of Pingxing (meaning fairness). There is very little left of the pass walls, but the site remains staunchly in the minds of the Chinese on account of a 1937 battle in which the Japanese Itagaki Division tried to take the pass from the Eighth Route Army. They didn't succeed. A large memorial to those fallen in that battle now stands on the hill outside Pingxingguan.

Where to stay

Soup Head Hot Springs Hotel Tāngtóu Wēnquán Bīnguǎn 汤头温泉宾馆 (40 rooms) At Tangtou Village at kilometre marker 102.5 on the road between Hengshan and Lingqiu; ℓ 0352 8466 084. If you are around this area and in need of a good place to stay, this hotel has clean, warm, quiet rooms all en suite with water piped from the hot springs. Sauna, baths and scrub (open 08.30–22.00) come free of charge with a scrub mitten and toiletries for those staying at the hotel. The restaurant offers good food, including the delicious local 'meat fried mountain mushrooms' (ròuchǎo shān mógu 肉炒山磨菇) at ¥20. All food is half price for those staying at the hotel or using the baths. The hotel is one of the few places in northern China where you can hear frogs croak at night. *Standard twin ¥200; common twin ¥120.*

SHUOZHOU 朔州 A useful base for visiting Yanmen Pass, Guangwu old city and Ningwu Pass is the town of Shuozhuo. It was also originally a walled city and the inner mud of the old city walls still existed in 2005. By then the city government was in the process of fixing torn-down sections using metal girders and rods. Part of the northern wall has already been renovated, and many of the old houses inside the wall are being torn down for new concrete-and-tile affairs. Still, the hustle and bustle inside the walled town is real and reminiscent of old times. You'll find people selling all sorts of goods, including pitiful pets, on every street.

The **Chongfu Temple** on Dong Jie was built in AD556 and contains some early stone carvings of various Buddhas as well as cast iron and copper Buddhas. The second hall has 1,000 paintings of Buddha, each with a different expression. The temple has a surreal feel to it as you wander around listening to recordings of

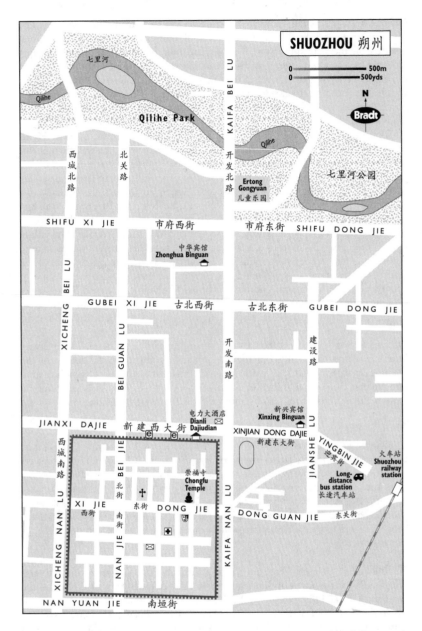

SHUOZHOU 朔州

0   500m
0   500yds

N
Bradt

七里河
Qilihe

Qilihe Park

开发北路
KAIFA BEI LU

七里河公园

西城北路
北关路

Ertong
Gongyuan
儿童乐园

SHIFU XI JIE   市府西街   市府东街   SHIFU DONG JIE

中华宾馆
Zhonghua Binguan

XICHENG BEI LU

GUBEI XI JIE   古北西街   古北东街   GUBEI DONG JIE

BEI GUAN LU

开发南路

建设路

JIANXI DAJIE   新建西大街   电力大酒店   新兴宾馆   Xinxing Binguan   新建东大街

XINJIAN DONG DAJIE

Dianli
Dajiudian

西城南路

BEI JIE
北街

崇福寺
Chongfu
Temple

DONG JIE
东街

XI JIE
西街

NAN JIE
南街

XICHENG NAN LU

JIANSHE LU

YINGBIN JIE
迎宾街

Long-
distance
bus station
长途汽车站

火车站
Shuozhou
railway
station

DONG GUAN JIE   东关街

NAN YUAN JIE   南垣街

Buddhist chants coming from the incense shop on the east side of the temple mixed in with whatever is playing in the local cinema to the south. Unsurprisingly, it is no longer a working temple with monks, although plenty of people come here to worship and light incense.

The new development around the northern and eastern sides of the temple had failed to attract shop owners and investors at the time of writing. Instead some of the buildings were the sleeping quarters of squatters and migrant builders. Human excrement littered the square on the eastern side and the stench was overwhelming.

There are a number of places with decent accommodation in Shuozhou, and lots of cheap accommodation by the train and bus station.

🏠 **Zhonghua Binguan** 中华宾馆 (67 rooms) 45 Kaifa Nan Lu; ✆ 0349 2032 111/195; 🖷 0349 2030 602. A good quiet hotel north of the old walled city and train and bus stations, with big rooms. Not as clean as it could be. All rooms en suite with TV. *Standard twin ¥198.* Chinese buffet breakfast included in the room price.

🏠 **Dianli Dajiudian** 电力大酒店 (90 rooms) Xinjian Xi Dajie; ✆ 0349 2023 534. A good, serviced and friendly hotel right in the centre of town. Small shop and restaurant. Free breakfast and sauna. All rooms en suite. *Free computer terminal and internet in the deluxe rooms, ¥198. Standard twin ¥128; common twin ¥100.*

🏠 **Xinxing Binguan** 新兴宾馆 (200 beds) At the northeast end of Xinjian Dong Dajie; ✆ 0349 202 3668/4035. Cheap and basic. Less than welcoming staff. *Standard twin A class ¥35 per bed. Standard twin B class ¥25 per bed. Three-person room ¥15 per bed. Four-person room A class ¥10 per bed. Four-person room class B ¥8 per bed.*

DEFENSIVE TOWNS
Nestled between the Heng and Guancen mountain ranges, Yìngxiàn 应县 town is tucked away south of Datong and off the main road. It served as the defensive town of the Liao dynasty against the Song dynasty during the late 10th and 11th centuries. In 1056, a nine-storey wooden pagoda was built which still stands today. At 67m in height it is the **highest wooden pagoda** in the world, even after almost one millennium. Archival records from the pagoda note that the structure was also used by the Liao army as an observation post to espy movements from the Heng mountain range to the south.

Today, Yingxian is a busy little town, mostly living off its main tourist attraction of the wooden pagoda. Most buses and taxis will drop you off at the entrance to the short pedestrianised shopping street in front of it. After 1,000 years, the pagoda is starting to lean noticeably to the north. Entry to the pagoda at ¥60 also allows you up to the first floor past a poor gentleman who is meant to ensure that you don't get lost or trip up the stairs in the dark. A couple of LED lights might help to achieve the same result or at least give him some reading light. If you have seen a number of other pagodas made without nails before, then this one will not stand out particularly. It's worth a stopover if it is on your way to another destination, but you may not find it worth a detour. Buses to Yingxian from Datong take 90 minutes. leaving from the New South bus station every hour 06.00–17.00 for ¥20.

Dàixiàn 代县, south of the Heng mountain range, served as a defensive town from as early as the Han dynasty (2nd century BC) The town has a bell tower dating from the 12th century and a drum tower from the 14th century. Both were used as part of an alarm system along the length of the wall to warn inhabitants and neighbouring towns of invasion. The original drum tower built in 1374 was burnt down in 1471, but was quickly rebuilt, and refurbished again in the Qing dynasty. At almost 40m in height it also served as an observation post and is taller than Tiananmen in Beijing. The two signboards on the tower read 'First Tower of Yanmen' and 'Audible in All Directions'. The bell of the 20m-high bell tower is the original from its construction in the 12th century. Buses to Daixian leave from Datong and Shuozhuo. It is 40km by road between Yanmenguan (see page 194) and Daixian.

THE SOUTHERN OFFSHOOT OF THE WALL – WOMEN'S PASS
Niángzǐguān 娘子关 The southern offshoot of the wall along the Hebei–Shanxi border extends some 300km almost as far as Qinquan Mountain. Along this section of the wall, the most well-known fortification is Niangziguan (Women's Pass). A pass was first built here in the 7th century and allegedly called Weize (Reed Pond) Pass after the many reed

9

ponds by the river running along the bottom of the ravine here. Although these no longer exist, the river, natural warm waters and 34m waterfall remain.

Soon after Weizeguan was built, legend says that Emperor Li Yuan, the first emperor of the Tang dynasty (AD618-907), ordered his daughter, Princess Pingyuan, to take command of the pass with a garrison of female warriors. This was either very forward thinking of the emperor or he was desperate to ward off the enemy. Unfortunately, Princess Pingyuan does not appear elsewhere in Chinese folklore and so it can only be presumed that she did not have to fight any great battles. Anyway, the pass has been known as Niangziguan ever since.

The pass has been renovated several times as it is a key passageway between Hebei and Shanxi provinces. Even today, the Shitai Expressway linking the Hebei capital of Shijiazhuang and the Shanxi capital of Taiyuan is not far away, and the railway between the two towns runs just behind the pass. The present pass dates from 1542 in the Ming dynasty. In 2001, the local government started to develop the area, including the waterfall and local lake just east of the pass. The wall itself, of which little was left is being reconstructed. The pass and the small hamlet inside it remain largely intact. Despite the heavy coal dust from the transport of coal on the road below to the local electricity plant, the pass, its bow-eaved housing and gateway tower (now a small temple) are worth the ¥20 entry fee.

Getting there The most comfortable way to get to Niangziguan is by train from Shijiazhuang (three hours, ¥15) or Taiyuan (four hours, ¥20). Otherwise you can take a bus there direct from Shijiazhuang (three hours, ¥20), or from Taiyuan. The bus trip from Taiyuan requires two buses. The first leaves from Taiyuan Jiannan bus station every 15 minutes 06.00–20.00 for the 120km journey to Yangquan (two hours, ¥25). In Yanguan, ask to get let off at the long-distance bus station Chuantu Qiche Zhan by the river, for a little minibus for the 40km journey through mountain scenery to Pingyanghu (1½ hours, ¥6), which is the lake park next to Niangziguan. Minibuses leave every 40 minutes 08.00–17.00. If you get dropped off at Niangziguan, then you can walk the 20 minutes through the charming main street (enter through the new Chinese eaved archway and don't walk along the main coal road) or take a taxi (bargain down to ¥5 for the five-minute ride). If you get dropped off at Pingyang Lake then it is a ten-minute walk back west along the main coal road to the entrance to Niangziguan and the town. Buses back to Yangquan leave every 40 minutes. The last bus back leaves at 18.00. Buses from Yangquan back to Taiyuan leave every 15 minutes. The last bus leaves at 20.00.

What to see and do It is worth staying overnight in Niangziguan to explore the waterpark, waterfall and small lake a little more as well as the surrounding countryside and other parts of the wall. Dinghies can be hired for ¥10 to sail the 1km stretch from the river waterwheels outside Niangzi Pass entrance to the end of the reservoir. The waterpark Shui Liang Dong Pubu containing the waterfall and lake cost ¥15 to enter, and an additional ¥15 for a ride on the larger motorised boat on the 1km lake. As you walk along the path inside the park to the lake, you will see a number of twigs set into the rocks. People who put a small twig in the rock like this believe it will bring them health and ward off illness. Some of this rock is in fact petrified tree branches and roots, which form a weave of laced rock where river erosion has cut into the rock over the millennia. At least one source of water in the park is from a deep hot spring. At 18°C, this water never freezes in the winter, and it is clean and pure enough to drink.

There are two places to eat inside the park: a small stall by the pumphouse serving pancakes and noodles, and Shuishang Leyuan, a small restaurant above the

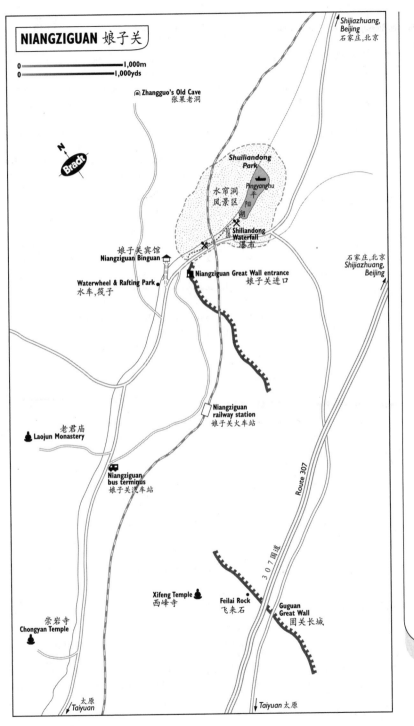

NIANGZIGUAN 娘子关

0 ————————————— 1,000m
0 ————————————— 1,000yds

Shijiazhuang, Beijing
石家庄,北京

Zhangguo's Old Cave
张果老洞

Shuiliandong Park

Pingyanghu
平阳湖

水帘洞
风景区

Shiliandong Waterfall
瀑布

娘子关宾馆
Niangziguan Binguan

石家庄,北京
Shijiazhuang, Beijing

Waterwheel & Rafting Park
水车,筏子

Niangziguan Great Wall entrance
娘子关进口

Niangziguan railway station
娘子关火车站

老君庙
Laojun Monastery

Niangziguan bus terminus
娘子关汽车站

Route 307

307国道

Xifeng Temple
西峰寺

Feilai Rock
飞来石

Guguan Great Wall
固关长城

崇岩寺
Chongyan Temple

太原
Taiyuan

↓ Taiyuan 太原

Shanxi 山西 THE INNER WALL

9

199

children's park overlooking the river. Shuishang Leyuan serves all the usual Chinese dishes as well as the local speciality of battered Kui tree flowers.

Where to stay and eat There is plenty of cheap accommodation around the train station if you wish to stay (or miss the last bus back), and there is also the new three-star **Niangziguan Binguan** 娘子关宾馆 (98 rooms) (☎ *0353 6031 454)*. The hotel has a swimming pool, gym, children's indoor play area, underground car park, restaurants and small garden. *(Standard twin ¥160)*.

In addition to the pass, the local government has also sectioned off another area of the wall, called Old Pass Gu Guan, south of Niangziguan. To get there take a taxi from Niangziguan for ¥20, or follow the ridge from Niangziguan wall south for 10km. *(Entry ¥20.)* Other sites in the vicinity include **Zhangguo Old Cave** and park *(Entry ¥15)*, Five Dragon Spring *Wu* Long Quan *(Entry ¥3)*, a riverside family house *(¥6)*, and **Laojun** and **Chongwen** temples.

WALKING TOURS OF THE GREAT WALL IN SHANXI China Direct, based in London (see *Tour operators*, page 66), do a two-and-a-half-week package tour, including seven days of hiking in Shanxi for just under £2,000 for two people. Trekking sections are no more than 25km per day and are not all linked; occasionally there is a car drive from one destination to the next, which also carries all your luggage to each night's destination. Once in China, the seven-day hiking tour of Shanxi, leaving from and returning to Datong, costs £670 per person (minimum two people).

CITS in Datong (☎ *0352 7124 882/510 1326; www.citsdatong.com)* does a supported ten-day hiking and camping tour, including most of the best sights of Shanxi province. *(Minimum 15 people per tour at US$120 per person per day.)*

OTHER PLACES OF INTEREST IN SHANXI

MOUNT HENG TEMPLE COMPLEX Enduring Mountain (Héngshān 恒山), lies 70km southeast of Datong. It is only one of a circle of mountains known as the Northern Heights, Beiyue. At 2,017m above sea level, Mount Heng is average by Shanxi standards, but boasts a prolific number of temples and monasteries. Entry to the foot of the mountain is ¥25 plus ¥1 for insurance (the insurance also covers the Hanging Monastery). Taxis or buses going up to the car park midway up the mountain must also pay for the driver, otherwise it's a 3km hike from the bottom of the mountain to the car park. At the car park there are numerous places to eat and also an intermittent cable car, which can take you up the next leg of the mountain and save you a 20-minute hike when it is working. Cost for the cable car is ¥25 up, ¥20 down, or ¥35 return. Once you have made it up to the next level, it is another ¥35 to get into the monastery complex. From here it is another hour or more to the peak of Mount Heng.

To get to Mount Heng (and the Hanging Monastery, see below) take one of the minibuses (¥30) from the new long-distance bus station. In the summer these will go all the way to the Hanging Monastery and Mount Heng. In the off-season, some buses will go only as far as Hunyuan at the bottom of the mountain range. From there, take a taxi or a motorbike ride up the mountain for ten minutes to Mount Heng or the Hanging Monastery. Alternatively, take the bus to Lingqiu and ask to be dropped off at Xuankong Si. About an hour into the journey, the bus passes the picturesque if decrepit old mud village of Donggetuopu, standing proud like an island in the middle of the riverbed.

HANGING MONASTERY The Hanging Monastery (Xuánkōng Sì 悬空寺) lies at the foot of Beiyue on the north side of the valley. As a result it gets sunlight only early in the morning, so you will need to arrive before 11.00 to get sunlit photos. Of all the many temples in China, this one is certainly unique in its construction, and unlike many mountain temples the ascent to this one is not strenuous. Early forms of the monastery go back over 1,500 years. One room of interest among the 40 or so in the monastery is the Hall of Three Teachings, housing Buddhist, Daoist and Confucianist figures, and is seen as a symbol of the peaceful co-existence of Chinese teachings. *(Entry ¥60.)*

MOUNT WUTAI (3,058M) AND BUDDHIST MONASTERIES Five Peak Mountain (wǔtáishān 五台山) is one of the four sacred mountain ranges of China, along with Emei Shan in Sichuan province, Putuo Shan in Zhejiang province, and Jiuhua Shan in Jiangsu province. There are five terraces to the range: North Terrace Beitai Ding at 3,058m; East Terrace Dongtai Ding at 2,976m; South Terrace Nantai Ding at 2,474m; West Terrace Xitai Ding at 2,773m; and Middle Terrace Zhongtai Ding at 2,890m. These ridge peaks surround the village of **Taihuai**, which lies at about 1,700m. The mountains are dotted with 108 temples and monasteries, a concentration of which are in and around Taihuai.

If you want to visit a working temple or monastery in China, then it is worth saving yourself for Taihuai. Although visitors here can be many, especially during peak times like Labour Week in May and National Week in October, there are sufficient temples and space that you can find some relative tranquillity. If you enjoy hiking and fresh air, it is worth spending a few days or more here. Locals sometimes feel that it is dangerous to access the peaks, especially when there is the possibility of snow (still possible in May and as early as October). However if you are well prepared, then hiking and camping in the mountains is rewarding.

Getting there and around During the peak season, Taihuai/Wutai Shan is well served by buses and there are two trains a day from Beijing and Taiyuan to the nearest train station, Shahe. Shahe, also called Wutaishan Zhan, is 48km from Taihuai, where buses regularly shuttle the 90-minute journey between the station and the mountain town for ¥20. This is by far the most scenic route to the mountain temple village of Taihuai and the journey takes you up to the saddle (2,900m) between East Terrace and North Terrace. The major stops for the trains through Shahe/Wutaishan train station are as follows:

Taiyuan 07.34, Daixian 11.50 and 18.40, Shahe 13.00 and 19.50 respectively, Beijing South 21.30.
Beijing South 06.30, Shahe 15.15 and 08.20, Daixian 16.20 and 09.20 respectively, Taiyuan 21.15.

There are four buses a day to and from Beijing (433kms, six hours) in each direction. The last bus to Beijing from Taihuai leaves at midday. There are six buses a day to and from Taiyuan. Buses leave Taiyuan Dongke Qiche Zhan at 08.00, 09.30, 11.00, 11.30, 12.30 and 13.30. During the peak holiday week in May and October, extra buses might be added depending on demand. Buses from Taiyuan cost ¥50 and take between four and five hours, depending on whether they use the motorway or not. If the driver takes the motorway, the toll fee is not included in the ticket and so the conductor will solicit ¥2 from each passenger for the toll.

On entering the mountain range, your bus will stop at a mountain checkpoint, where each visitor must pay a ¥90 entry fee. Insurance at ¥5 is also available butnot compulsory. At this point, maps of Taihuai and the surrounding temples and mountains are also available in English and Chinese. These are usually cheaper

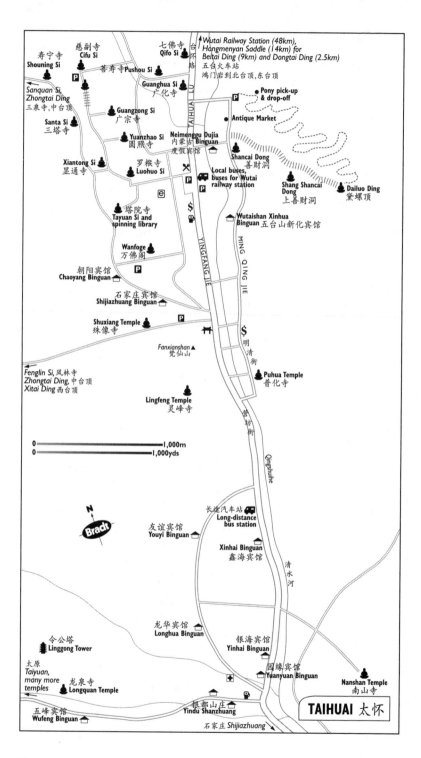

Shouning Si 寿宁寺
Cifu Si 慈副寺
Pushou Si 菩寿寺
Qifo Si 七佛寺 台怀路
Wutai Railway Station (48km),
Hongmenyan Saddle (14km) for
Beitai Ding (9km) and Dongtai Ding (2.5km)
五台火车站
鸿门岩到北台顶,东台顶
Sanquan Si,
Zhongtai Ding
三泉寺,中台顶
Guanghua Si 广化寺
Pony pick-up
& drop-off
Guangzong Si 广宗寺
Antique Market
Santa Si 三塔寺
Yuanzhao Si 圆照寺
Neimenggu Dujia
Binguan
内蒙古
度假宾馆
Shancai Dong
善财洞
Xiantong Si 显通寺
Luohuo Si 罗㬋寺
Local buses,
buses for Wutai
railway station
Shang Shancai
Dong
上善财洞
Dailuo Ding
黛螺顶
Tayuan Si and
spinning library
塔院寺
Wutaishan Xinhua
Binguan 五台山新化宾馆
Wanfoge
万佛阁
Chaoyang Binguan
朝阳宾馆
Shijiazhuang Binguan
石家庄宾馆
MING QING JIE
YINGFANG JIE
TAIHUA LU
Shuxiang Temple
殊像寺
Fanxianshan
梵仙山
明
清
街
Puhua Temple
普化寺
Fenglin Si, 风林寺
Zhongtai Ding, 中台顶
Xitai Ding 西台顶
Lingfeng Temple
灵峰寺
营坊街
0   1,000m
0   1,000yds
Qingshuihe
N
Bradt
Long-distance
bus station
长途汽车站
Youyi Binguan
友谊宾馆
Xinhai Binguan
鑫海宾馆
清
水
河
Longhua Binguan
龙华宾馆
Yinhai Binguan
银海宾馆
Linggong Tower
令公塔
Yuanyuan Binguan
国缘宾馆
Taiyuan,
many more
temples
太原
Longquan Temple
龙泉寺
Nanshan Temple
南山寺
Wufeng Binguan
五峰宾馆
Yindu Shanzhuang
银都山庄
Shijiazhuang 石家庄
TAIHUAI 太怀

in Taihuai itself: ¥5 for a plastic-coated A2-size map; ¥3 for a colour-paper A2-size map; and ¥2 for the old map of Taihuai on a handkerchief (Chinese characters only).

Taihuai town is fairly compact, but outlying temples can be some distance away. There are minibuses (gōng jiāo chē 公交车) which travel frequently up and down the main road, and will pick up and drop you off anywhere on their route. Fare ¥2. Taxis are also available, but they have no meter and so you will need to negotiate the price. The starting price is usually a rip-off at ¥20 for 4km; try not to pay more than ¥5. The long-distance bus station is 1km south of the Taihuai Zhen bus station, which has buses to Shahe/Wutaishan station and outlying temples.

Money and communication There are a number of branches of the Bank of China, the Industrial and Commercial Bank of China as well as other banks in Taihuai. The main branch of Bank of China is just south of Taihuai town bus station (not the long-distance bus station). It changes currency, but not travellers' cheques.

Most of the bigger hotels have internet access; otherwise the Flying Space Internet Café fēiyǔ wǎngba 飞宇网吧 is available in the centre of town. Ask in the centre for its location in this complicated maze of mostly unnamed streets.

Where to stay and eat Taihuai is inundated with places to stay, and more are being built. During the peak period, many hotels will be fully booked, or can be booked only through a travel agency such as Peace International Travel Service (see page 188). However, even at Taihuai's busiest times you can still turn up and find rooms in all ranges from as little as ¥20 per bed to ¥580 per standard twin room. Accommodation in Taihuai town itself is more expensive than in outlying hotels or along the quiet Ming Qing Jie (a street imitating architecture from the Ming and Qing eras, but lacking the busy lifestyle).

Chaoyang Binguan 朝阳宾馆 (38 rooms) Near Ten Thousand Buddha Pavilion *Wanfoge*; ☎ 0350 6545 318 or 139 3414 9142; ☏ 0350 6545 583. This new courtyard imitation hotel is on the edge of Taihuai, slightly away from the crowds but conveniently close to the centre. All rooms en suite with 24hr hot water. Restaurant at the hotel. *Standard twin ¥380; common twin ¥288; trpl ¥396. Extra bed ¥80. Room by the hour ¥50.*

Neimenggu Dujia Binguan 内蒙古度假宾馆 (40 rooms) On the road to the southern bridge towards Dailuo Ding; ☎ 0350 6545 993 or 135 0970 5353. Along with a string of small hotels on this small road, it is conveniently located near the main sites and the centre of town, but with rather inflated prices. Bargain down out of season. No breakfast, but there is a restaurant. All rooms en suite. *¥100 per bed.*

Shijiazhuang Zhaodaisuo 石家庄招待所 (15 rooms) Near Zhuxiang Temple; ☎ 138 3508 2414. Clean, bright, small twins with dark but serviced en-suite rooms and 24hr hot water. *¥20 per bed.*

Wufeng Binguan 五峰宾馆 (270 rooms) Near Dragon Spring Temple *Longquan Si*; ☎ 0350 6548 988 or 139 3400 8412; ☏ 0353 6548 998. One of the better hotels in the Taihuai area, this Chinese three-star has a restaurant serving buffet or à la carte in the evenings and a free buffet breakfast in the morning accompanied by auctioneers selling scroll art. The entrance to the hotel is graced by an enormous fake tree. The hotel also has a sauna, 24hr hot water, laundry service, internet centre and gift shop. *Standard twin ¥580; trpl ¥680.*

Wutaishan Xinhua Binguan 五台山新化宾馆 (27 rooms) 11 Ming Qing Jie; ☎ 0350 6542 339; ☏ 0350 6542 536. Clean serviced rooms in the quiet street of Ming Qing Jie on the east side of the river. *Standard twins and four-bed rooms ¥108.*

Places to eat in Taihuai are also abundant and good, but a bit pricey. Most foods have to be trucked in from outlying towns, and local specialities such as táimó shāoròu 台蘑烧肉 (local wild mushrooms and slivers of fried pork) or juécài 蕨菜 (fiddle heads – the rolled tips of wild ferns) are only seasonal and laborious to collect. At ¥80 a dish, the taimo shaorou are very tasty, however, and allegedly anti-carcinogenic. Very bright green juecai are a little more affordable at ¥15 per dish. The interestingly named bùbù gāo shān 步步高山 , meaning 'step by step ascend the mountain' is a fried dough dish dusted with sugar. Meat dishes are not so easy to find in this monastic retreat town, and are also expensive.

What to see and do There are so many temples and monasteries in Taihuai town and in the mountains that it is difficult to know where to start. Most people get up at the crack of dawn to have an early breakfast and start their first monastery at 07.00. The more popular among them are Green Snail Peak Dailuo Ding Monastery, Pusa Ding Monastery, and Tayuan Si. Other rewarding temples in the outskirts of town are Dragon Spring Temple Longquan Si and Puhua Si with its Sleeping Buddha. Entry to the temples generally costs about ¥4–5. In peak season the monasteries are a veritable tourist trap complete with lots of plastic souvenirs and the unique possibility of having your photo taken and superimposed above your temple of choice as if you are levitating.

Green Snail Peak Dailuo Ding Monastery is perhaps so named because of the snail's pace at which people generally end up ascending the 1,080 steps to the monastery entrance (1,080 being a multiple of the 108 beads on a monk's rosary). The monastery itself is not especially spectacular, but the view from the top of the whole valley, and especially the snow-clad North Terrace, is spectacular. For those wishing a less strenuous ride up the mountain, a chairlift occasionally works for ¥35, or horses can be hired from ¥25 up to the monastery via the back path and ¥20 back down again. At the bottom of the monastery path is a big market selling souvenirs. To get there, cross the bridge at the north end of the town to the eastern side of the river.

Pusa Ding Monastery is also up a set of appropriately numbered steps, but this time only 108. There are a number of steles in this monastery in the writing of Ming and Qing emperors. To get there, keep walking upwards from the town bus stop and square.

Tayuan Si contains the largest stupa in the valley. In addition, it boasts many prayer wheels, a revolving sutra case in the two-storey building at the back of the temple, a gaudy memorial to Mao and his brilliant footsteps, and the many monks prostrating themselves to Buddha. Take the second left after the town square to get there.

Puhua Si lies at the southern end of Ming Qing Jie. At the time of writing it was being renovated in order to accommodate overnight stays. At the back of the monastery is the Lying Buddha Temple Wofosi, with a large copper-cast figure of Sakyamuni gaining nirvana. The temple was damaged by a mudslide during heavy rains several years ago and is currently undergoing reconstruction.

Dragon Spring Temple Longquan Si is an extensive site with an intricate marble carved entrance and Ming dynasty flagpoles. Set away from the main town, it is quieter and more contemplative than most of the temples at Taihuai, yet still easy to reach. The local bus can drop you off there.

To hike to **Dongtai Ding** (East Terrace 2,976m) and **Beitai Ding** (North Terrace 3,058m), take the early bus to Shahe/Wutaishan train station and ask to get off at the saddle between the two mountains (Hongmenshi). The 30-minute journey costs ¥10 and will take you up to 2,900m. From the marble-arched saddle, it is an hour's walk up the trail to the monastery at Dongtai Ding, which you can see from the saddle. Until the road to Beitai Ding is finished (2006?) it is a hike of several hours and a 1,000m climb to Beitai Ding, only to be yattempted by experienced hikers with the right gear for staying out overnight.

Taiyuan is the capital of Shanxi province. There may not be much that you would normally visit Taiyuan for, but it has the only regular airport in the province and so you may find yourself arriving or leaving via this city. It is also usually from here that people go on to Pingyao (see above) or Wutaishan (see page 201). As the capital, it is big, modern, and full of ATMs. Although it still lies firmly in China's coal mining belt, its parks and extensive riverside areas make it feel somewhat cleaner than smoggy Datong and a lot of the rest of Shanxi. Being much further south, Taiyuan warms up earlier in the year than Datong.

GETTING THERE AND AROUND As the capital of the province, Taiyuan is well served by transport.

The **airport** is 15km southeast of the centre of town. Minibuses to the airport for ¥10 leave in time to meet flights from the main CAAC office *(158 Yingze Dajie;* ℓ *0351 4042 903)*, which is located on the south side of the street, west of May 1 Square. Return buses from the airport run only from 11.00 (first arrival) to the last flight arrival at midnight. So if you get caught sending someone off to the airport early in the morning your only way back will be by taking a return taxi, which will charge around ¥25 metered. Taxis to the airport cost ¥50 unmetered, and will make you pay the highway toll or will take the back roads which will add an extra ten minutes to an otherwise 30-minute journey. Taxis won't take you there metered as they cannot be guaranteed to pick up a return passenger. Taiyuan to Beijing single airfare is about ¥700.

The **train** station is at the east end of Yingze Dajie.

There are four **bus** stations in Taiyuan:

Long-Distance Bus Station Chángtú Qìchē Zhàn 长途汽车站 Yingze Dajie. For major routes to Beijing, Datong, Shuozhou, etc.

Jiannán Qiche Zhan 建南汽车站 for buses to Yangquan (to change for buses to Niangziguan).

Dong Kezhan for buses to Wutaishan (4–5hrs, ¥50).

Xi Kezhan 西客站 for buses to Pingyao and Daixian.

Taiyuan is sufficiently large that walking to sights and amenities is time consuming and tiring. Taxi flag fall is ¥7, which will take you most places in town. Bus 1 ploughs up and down Yingze Dajie from the train station and past the river.

The head office of the **Public Security Bureau** for extending visas and reporting theft is at 9 Houjia Xiang *(ℓ 0351 2023 011)* at the northeast corner of Wuyi Guangchang.

MONEY AND COMMUNICATION Many banks in Taiyuan have ATMs that take foreign credit and debit cards. The main Bank of China is at 288 Yingze Dajie *((ℓ 0351 8266 286)*, just west of Yingze Park.

Internet cafés are sporadic but increasing:

Shiji Wangba 世纪网吧 at the New Century Shopping Plaza on Lu Xiang Lu. ¥5 per hour.
Honghu Wangba 红狐网吧 in the Hot City Club, 11 Yingze Dajie. Open around the clock. ¥4 per hour.

WHERE TO STAY AND EAT If you find yourself having to stay here overnight, there are lots of big fancy hotels on Yingze Dajie and cheaper ones around the train and bus station. Also, try one of the following:

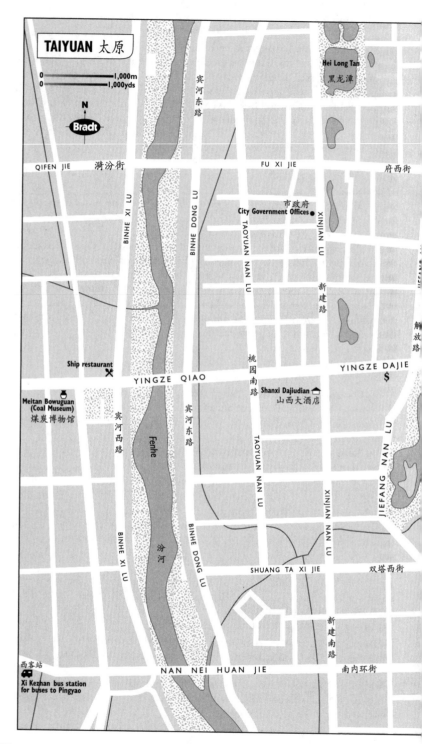

TAIYUAN 太原

0 ———————— 1,000m
0 ———————— 1,000yds

N

Bradt

Hei Long Tan
黑龙潭

宾河东路

QIFEN JIE 漪汾街

FU XI JIE

府西街

BINHE XI LU

BINHE DONG LU

市政府
City Government Offices ●

XINJIAN LU

新建路

TAOYUAN NAN LU

解放路

Ship restaurant ✕

YINGZE QIAO

桃园南路

Shanxi Dajiudian ⌂
山西大酒店

YINGZE DAJIE

$

**Meitan Bowuguan
(Coal Museum)**
煤炭博物馆

宾河西路

Fenhe

宾河东路

TAOYUAN NAN LU

JIEFANG NAN LU

汾河

XINJIAN NAN LU

BINHE XI LU

BINHE DONG LU

SHUANG TA XI JIE
双塔西街

新建南路

西客站
**Xi Kezhan bus station
for buses to Pingyao**

NAN NEI HUAN JIE

南内环街

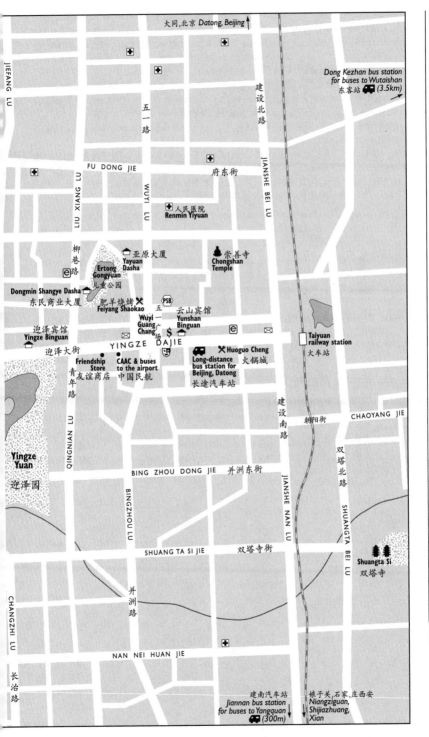

大同,北京 *Datong, Beijing* ↑

Dong Kezhan bus station
for buses to Wutaishan
东客站 🚐 *(3.5km)* →

五
一
路

建
设
北
路

JIEFANG LU

FU DONG JIE

WUYI LU

LIU XIANG LU

柳巷路

府东街

JIANSHE BEI LU

人民医院
Renmin Yiyuan

亚原大厦
Yayuan Dasha

崇善寺
Chongshan Temple

Ertong Gongyuan
儿童公园

Dongmin Shangye Dasha
东民商业大厦

肥羊烧烤
Feiyang Shaokao

PSB

五一广场
Wuyi Guang Chang

云山宾馆
Yunshan Binguan

迎泽宾馆
Yingze Binguan

YINGZE DAJIE
迎泽大街

Friendship Store
友谊商店

青年路

CAAC & buses to the airport
中国民航

Huoguo Cheng
火锅城

Long-distance bus station for Beijing, Datong
长途汽车站

Taiyuan railway station
火车站

QINGNIAN LU

BINGZHOU LU

建
设
南
路

朝阳街

CHAOYANG JIE

Yingze Yuan
迎泽园

BING ZHOU DONG JIE 并洲东街

JIANSHE NAN LU

双
塔
北
路

SHUANGTA BEI LU

SHUANG TA SI JIE 双塔寺街

并洲路

Shuangta Si
双塔寺

CHANGZHI LU

长治路

NAN NEI HUAN JIE

建南汽车站
Jiannan bus station for buses to Yangquan (300m) 🚐

娘子关,石家庄,西安
Niangziguan, Shijiazhuang, Xian ↓

🏠 **Dongmin Shangye Dasha** 东民商业大厦 (200 rooms) 86 Liu Xiang Lu; ☎ 0351 4185 588. A little worn, but serviced. Situated in the noisy shopping street of Liu Xiang Lu, so ask for rooms at the back (houmian de fangjian) if you want something quieter. Although back rooms face the nearby pleasant Children's Park Ertong Gongyuan, the view is blocked by the neighbouring building. Ethernet connection available in all rooms. Restaurant serves good food, but avoid the hot fruit soup. Room price includes Chinese buffet breakfast. *Standard sgl or twin ¥288.*

🏠 **Shanxi Dajiudian** 山西大酒店 (560 rooms) 5 Xinjian Nan Lu; ☎ 0351 4043 901; 📠 0351 4043 525. For a long time, this was the most comfortable establishment in town, but is fast being outdone by renovations along Yingze Dajie. Comes with all the mod cons including a good buffet breakfast. *Standard twin ¥950.*

🏠 **Yayuan Daxia** 亚原大厦 (30 rooms) Haizibian Rd; ☎ 0351 4044 678/668. A quiet hotel round the back of the Children's Park with odd bits of furniture but clean rooms. *Standard twin ¥138; sgl ¥118.*

🏠 **Yingze Binguan** 迎泽宾馆 (280 rooms) 189 Yingze Dajie; ☎ 0351 4043 211; 📠 0351 4043 784. A classy four star, better value and more convenient than the Shanxi Dajiudian, but not as quiet. *Standard ¥780.*

🏠 **Yun Shan Fandian** 云山饭店 (50 rooms) 99 Yingze Dajie; ☎ 0351 4964 862. Small basic rooms, all en suite, and with TV and AC. Prices include breakfast. *Standard twin ¥200; sgls ¥138; trpls ¥240.*

There is an abundance of restaurants on Yingze Dajie and along the busy shopping street of Yinxiang Nan Lu. Snacks are available in the early morning and late evening around Wuyi Guangchang, Tonger Gongyuan and Yingze Yuan.

✕ **Feiyang Shaokao** 肥羊烧烤 (Fat Lamb Grill) Wuyu Lu on the northwest corner of Wuyi Guangchang. Serves cheap skewers of almost anything imaginable. Very good lamb skewers (Yáng ròu chuàn' r 羊肉串儿).

✕ **Huoguo Cheng** 火锅城 16 Yingze Dajie. Your standard steamy hotpot establishment.

WHAT TO SEE AND DO
Taiyuan is largely a big shopping town. **May 1 Square** Wuyi Guangchang is a popular place for people to hang out in the evenings, as are **Yingze Park**, the **Children's Park** (Ertong Gongyuan) and the **riverfront**, which has a long paved area and park on the east side. To get to the riverfront take bus 1 to Yingze Bridge East Yingze Qiao Dong. At Yingze Bridge West is the China National Coal Museum. Here you will find anything you might want to know about coal (in Chinese only) except the answer to the valuable question: 'When is it going to run out?' Outside the southwest gate of the Children's Park is a bird market on Sundays.

There are several temples and museums, none of which is spectacular. The Double Pagoda Shuang Ta southeast of the train station is a nice place to get away from the shopping frenzy of Liu Xiang Lu and Shangma Jie.

10

Shaanxi 陕西

The denuded hills and earth coloured villages of the Loess Plateau rolled by. Once, this had been fertile forests and steppes, one of the birthplaces of Chinese civilization. Nearby was the grave of the Yellow Emperor, mythic founder of the Chinese people. He and other rulers had protected this cultural heartland by building fortifications not far from here that later became known as the Great Wall.

Ian Johnson

After meeting the Yellow River at Laoniuwan and Wanjiazhai Dam in Shanxi province, the Great Wall follows the Yellow River until Hequ, where it continues southwest towards Shenmu town, Yulin and Jingbian, before heading west to Dingbian and northwest into Ningxia autonomous region. Over 880km in length, the Ming wall in Shaanxi was built on top of the ruins of the Qin wall of some 15 centuries earlier. The Ming wall in Shaanxi has not survived much better and most of it has eroded away or become covered in sand from the Mus Us Desert to the north in Inner Mongolia. Despite the poor preservation of the wall itself, however, its path can be traced by linking the 210 original Qin towers and beacons that are still visible. For those wishing to hike the path that was the wall in Shaanxi, the going is tough desert conditions, best done with a guide who knows the area (contact Explore! page 66).

Otherwise northern Shaanxi offers a few highlights, little visited by foreigners, allowing for the full-on China experience. Shaanxi is most well known for the terracotta army of its capital, Xian. Many tourists are disappointed with the site, which only reveals a small portion of the 8,000 terracotta soldiers. Xian's town architecture can be more enthralling, but it is difficult to get away from the tourist trappings and stalls that overwhelm the town. Towns in northern Shaanxi, however, such as Yulin and Shenmu, have no souvenir stalls – just plenty of authenticity, and people who have seen only a handful of foreigners, if any. Both are up and coming towns, oases in the desert, with lively parks and squares, growing rich on local oil and coal deposits. Whilst this is healthy in some ways, it belies the suppression and poverty of the masses out in the countryside which you will see if you go hiking in the province (see Johnson's *Wild Grass* for more on this, page 269). Yulin's old town and extensively renovated town wall are attractions in themselves, while Shenmu's Daoist Erlang Shan temple complex is the best ¥10 ever spent on fully working temples.

YULIN 榆林

HISTORY Yulin was an important garrison town in the time of the Ming dynasty, a testament to which is the size of Zhenbei Tower to the north of the town. Today, Yulin is a town growing rich from oil found nearby in the late 1990s. Its extensive

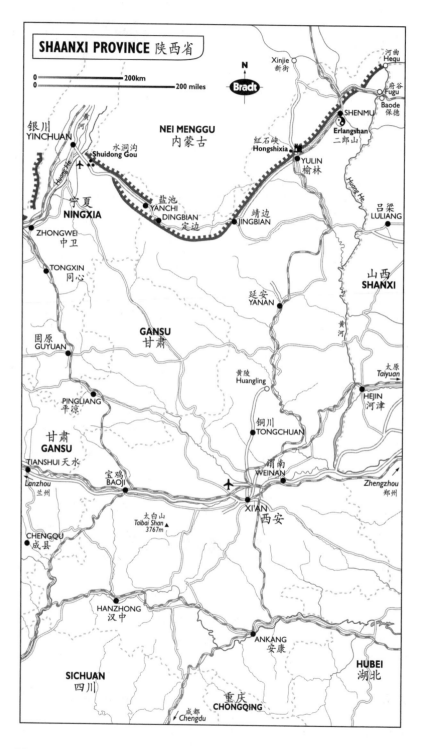

town walls are slowly being renovated as are its drum and bell towers and temples. The old town is already essentially pedestrianised, and offers some of the cheapest (and most basic) accommodation in the town. Hints of Islamic influence grace the town, which is mostly modern and clean.

GETTING THERE AND AROUND Yulin has a small airport 10km to the east of the town (✆ *0912 3884 777*). There are no direct **flights** to and from Beijing, but daily flights to and from Xian are operating (¥600). With the changing face of tourism in China, it is always worth checking with CAAC, especially during the summer months, whether there are other flights or changes to flight plans. A taxi to the airport is ¥10.

Yulin's **train** station is slightly outside town in the southwest. It lies on the Xian–Hohhot line, so there are no direct trains from Beijing, Datong or Yulin. There are two trains a day between Shenmu and Yulin.

Buses in and out of Yulin are more frequent and more convenient. The bus station is also conveniently located near the centre of town and within walking distance of a number of hotels. Buses to and from Shenmu take three hours for ¥20. The Yinchuan day bus leaves at 08.00 and arrives at 16.00 for ¥59. The sleeper bus leaves at 15.30 with an hour's stopover in Jingbian for dinner and arrives in Yinchuan at 06.00 for ¥90. This bus travels within a few kilometres of the Great Wall for most of its journey, but you will not see very much of it until you get into Ningxia. The Shaanxi side of the route is dusty and dull. Night bus tickets can be bought up to three days in advance. Buses to Xian at 07.30 and 18.00 take 12 hours for ¥121. Buses for Yanan take four-and-a-half hours for ¥45, leaving every 20 minutes 06.30–11.00. Buses for Qingyun leave when the bus is full (usually every 40 minutes) for ¥6. Outside the bus station are the usual stalls selling fruit and snacks for bus journeys, as well as a number of Uighur men selling chunks of Xinjiang Bābāgāo (粑粑糕), which consists of a lot of dried fruit and nuts, a bit like a Snickers bar without the chocolate – very tasty and also makes good trail food.

The centre of Yulin is small enough to walk around on foot. The two main streets are known colloquially as First Street Dì yī Jiē 第一街 and Second Street Dì èr Jiē 第二街. Di Yi Jie is the central, north–south street running through the old town, signposted as Bei Da Jie and Nan Da Jie. Di Er Jie is the busy shopping street running north–south on the west side of the old town, signposted as Xinjian Nan Lu. **City buses** 1 and 7 run up and down Shanglang Lu and Xinjian Lu. Buses 5 and 6 ply Changcheng Lu. Bus 3 runs from Guangji Dasha at the corner of Renmin Lu and Changcheng Bei Lu to Zhenbeitai Great Wall tower. All bus rides are ¥1.

Flag fall for Yulin's tiny **taxis** is ¥4.80, but most taxis will take you unmetered within town for ¥5 so that they can keep the money rather than give it to the taxi firm. A taxi to Zhenbeitai, or Hongshixia is ¥10.

A town **map** printed in 2003 of the city and surrounding towns (in Chinese) can be bought for ¥5 at a number of bookstores as well as the drinks and ice cream stall outside Hongshixia. This was the best map available at the time of writing. A 2002 map of the town and its administrative prefecture (in Chinese) can be bought for ¥10 at the kiosk to your right as you enter the bus station, but it is not as good as the 2003 map. Annoyingly, there are no street numbers on the busy shopping street of Xinjian Nan Lu, and shop owners don't know their street address numbers either, so you just have to ask if you are looking for something specific.

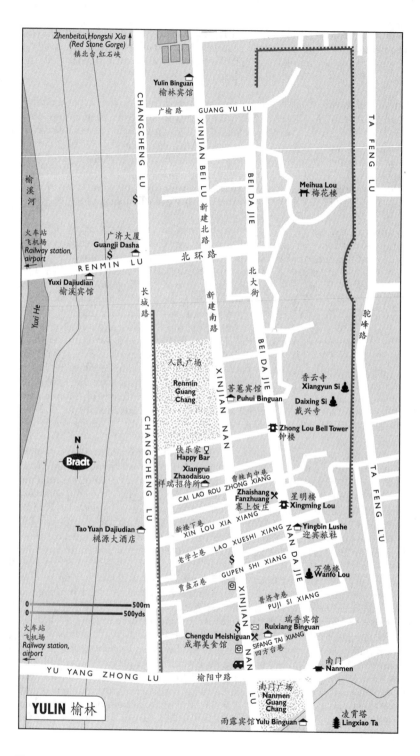

Zhenbeitai, Hongshi Xia
(Red Stone Gorge)
镇北台,红石峡

Yulin Binguan
榆林宾馆

广榆路　GUANG YU LU

CHANGCHENG LU

XINJIAN BEI LU
新建北路

BEI DA JIE

TA FENG LU

榆溪河

火车站
飞机场
Railway station,
airport

广济大厦
Guangji Dasha

RENMIN LU

北环路

Meihua Lou
梅花楼

Yuxi Dajiudian
榆溪宾馆

Yuxi He

长城路

新建南路

北大街

人民广场
Renmin
Guang
Chang

XINJIAN NAN

BEI DA JIE

香云寺
Xiangyun Si

菩蕙宾馆
Puhui Binguan

Daixing Si
戴兴寺

驼峰路

N

Bradt

Zhong Lou Bell Tower
钟楼

快乐家
Happy Bar

Xiangrui
Zhaodaisuo
祥瑞招待所

曹辣肉中巷
CAI LAO ROU ZHONG XIANG

Zhaishang
Fanzhuang
赛上饭庄

星明楼
Xingming Lou

ZAN DA JIE

TA FENG LU

Tao Yuan Dajiudian
桃源大酒店

新楼下巷
XIN LOU XIA XIANG

老学士巷
LAO XUESHI XIANG

Yingbin Lushe
迎宾旅社

0   500m
0   500yds

贾盘石巷
GUPEN SHI XIANG

普济寺巷
PUJI SI XIANG

万佛楼
Wanfo Lou

XINJIAN

火车站
飞机场
Railway station,
airport

Chengdu Meishiguan
成都美食馆

瑞香宾馆
Ruixiang Binguan

四方台巷
SIFANG TAI XIANG

南门
Nanmen

YU YANG ZHONG LU
榆阳中路

南门广场
Nanmen
Guang
Chang

LU

雨露宾馆 Yulu Binguan

凌霄塔
Lingxiao Ta

YULIN 榆林

212

Latrines in Yulin are dire. Aside from hotels, most establishments will point you in the direction of public toilets. One of the cleaner ones is the serviced public toilets on the southwest corner of Renmin Lu. Usage fee ¥0.5.

MONEY AND COMMUNICATION The main branch of the Bank of China on Renmin Lu (✆ *0912 3258 365*) changes currency and travellers' cheques. Open daily 08.00–18.00. A number of ATMs along Xinjian Nan Lu also accept foreign credit and debit cards.

The main post office with EMS is on Xinjian Nan Lu (✆ *0912 3235 196)*. Open daily 08.00–19.00.

There are lots of internet bars along Xinjian Nan Lu, usually hidden underground with a small entrance on to the street. Try:

Heimayi Wangba 黑蚂蚁网吧 Xinjian Nan Lu; ✆ 0912 3829 681. Underground with lots of terminals, a few of which have Windows XP. Drinks available, toilets should be avoided. ¥3 per hour.

Shiji Long Wangba 世纪龙网吧 Xinjian Nan Lu, opposite the Ruixiang Hotel. ¥3 per hour.

Changtong Wangba 畅通网吧 Xinjian Nan Lu, south of the post office. ¥3 per hour.

WHERE TO STAY AND EAT Yulin has the usual variety of accommodation, but nothing very high end. This will undoubtedly change, and at the time of writing two big new hotels were being built on Xinjian Nan Lu and South Gate Square. Lots of budget accommodation was available in the old town, but this is also likely to change as the old town is renovated further. Look for the familiar signs zhāodàisuǒ 招待所 or lǚshè 旅社. Most will take foreigners, although some still use the excuse that they are not approved for foreigners if they don't want you in their hotel. The quietest accommodation is out of town altogether.

Guangji Dasha 广济大厦 (98 rooms) Changcheng Lu corner with Renmin Lu; ✆ 0912 3895 158. Conveniently located at the northwest corner of the old town and at the bus stop of bus 3 to Zhenbeitai Great Wall tower and Hongshixia, but is noisy and characterless. *Standard doubles en suite with breakfast ¥170.*

Xiangrui Zhaodaisuo 祥瑞招待所 (11 rooms including 3 doubles) Cao La Rou Zhong Xiang; ✆ 131 5401 4651. Opened in 2005, this tiny hostel, smack in the centre of the old town, is convenient, quiet and friendly. *Only two standard twins en suite ¥70; remaining common twins and doubles use communal bathrooms, ¥40.*

Puhui Binguan 普惠泉宾馆 (66 rooms) Xinjian Bei Lu; ✆ 0912 3260 605. Friendly staff at this average hotel opposite the lively People's Square Rénmín Guǎngchǎng 人民广场 make up for the otherwise noisy rooms. Ask for quieter ones at the back. One of the two hotel restaurants can provide breakfast (not included). *Standard twins with bathroom ¥138; common twins without bathroom ¥100; by the hour ¥30.*

Hongshixia Shengtai Gongyuan 红石峡生态公园 (15 rooms) 8km north of Yulin; ✆ 139 9221 0088. This recently opened resort (see page 215) has a small courtyard hotel with 11 rooms and four small bungalows, all furnished in a Ming-style setting with northern Shaanxi stone and en suite, but no shower and no hot water (kettle provided). Nevertheless, the tranquillity offered by the resort is exquisite compared with the mid-range hotels on the noisy streets in Yulin or after a period of hardcore travelling in China. All rooms have modern TVs and fantastic black-and-white photos of the surrounding countryside and farming life. Courtyard restaurant, teahouse, Chinese gardens and views of the mud remains of Great Wall towers in the distance. Take bus 3 from Guangji Dasha to the Gorge (¥1) or a taxi for ¥10. *Courtyard twins and one double ¥100; bungalows ¥120.*

Ruixiang Binguan 瑞香宾馆 (34 rooms) Sifang Tai Xiang, 10m off Xinjian Nan Lu; ✆ 0912 3254 366. A clean, serviced hotel, slightly less noisy than some of the others right on busy streets. Has a small restaurant, breakfast included. All rooms en suite. *Standard twin ¥168; trpl ¥198; by the hour ¥50.*

Yingbin Lüshe 迎宾旅社 (11 rooms) 123 Diyi Lu; ✆ 0912 3282 635. This is the real thing: courtyard accommodation, centre of the old town, only one communal toilet available, no shower, no breakfast, very friendly. *Unbeatable prices: twin or double ¥20.*

🏠 **Yulu Binguan** 雨露宾馆 (45 rooms) Shanglang Bei Lu, right on Nanmen Square. Some rooms have a good view of the square and are a little quieter. All rooms en suite, breakfast included. *Standard twin ¥138; common twin ¥138; by the hour ¥30.*

Yulin is not yet big on fancy, expensive restaurants, but those are surely to come. There are lots of small places to eat on Diyi Jie and Di'er Jie, as well as street stalls down the alleys off Di'er Jie. The most charismatic and memorable places to eat, however, are north of the town near Hongshixia.

✕ **Chengdu Meishiguan** 成都美食园 Xinjian Nan Lu; ✆ 0912 3237 139. This might not be the gourmet park its name suggests, but it has good dishes for one person, and serves all the usual favourites as well as huntun and baozi at good cheap prices.

✕ **Nongfu Shanzhuang** 农夫山庄 (meaning Farmer's Lodge) is at the turning to Hongshixia through an archway which misleadingly reads Zhèjiǔyuàn 蔗酒院 (meaning The Rum Yard); ✆ 0912 3828 585. This big courtyard restaurant surrounded by cave dwellings serves local as well as more standard Chinese fare. Each 'dwelling' comes complete with a huokang platform for resting or eating, a dining table, TV and karaoke machine. Try their baby Chinese cabbage in cream of chicken broth (jīyóu wáwacài 鸡油娃娃菜) amongst other delicious local dishes.

✕ **Fengyuan Mengu Bao** 丰源蒙古包 500m south of the turning to Hongshixia, on the east side of the road. Serves Mongolian fare in yurts.

✕ **Red Stone Gorge Restaurant** At the health resort Hóngshíxiá Shēngtài Gōngyuán Fàndiàn 红石峡生态公园饭店; ✆ 139 9221 0088. This courtyard restaurant specialises in local farm-style cooking such as black potato dumplings (Hēilènglèng 黑愣愣) and a variety of local fish.

✕ **Zhaishang Fandian** On First Street just south of the Drum Tower. A popular place to eat in the old town, with big plates of shuijiao dumplings and all the usual dishes. Try their qīngtāng yángròu 清汤羊肉, clear soup with lamb, for a refreshing flavourful, gingery soup.

There are several discos, dance halls and karaoke clubs on Second Street. A nice café-bar to hang out in for an evening on Renmin Guangchang is **Happy Home** Kuàilè Jiā 快乐家. It has a half-decent variety of drinks and coffee, with mellow music, plastic trailing plants and dimmed lighting.

WHAT TO SEE IN AND AROUND YULIN
Yulin's **old town** has been well preserved. Aside from a few modern buildings along Di Yi Jie (such as the town police station and a couple of schools), all the old hutong and courtyards remain intact. Di Yi Jie, so called because it was literally Yulin's first street, is officially called Bei Da Jie and Nan Da Jie. At the time of writing, the street was being repaved and all the old towers along the street were being reconstructed. Only the **Drum Tower** dividing Bei Da Jie and Nan Da Jie is truly original and shows interesting influences of Islam in its architecture, making it stand apart from the other Ming-style reconstructed towers in the town. **Fragrant Cloud Temple** Xiāngyún Sì 香云寺 and **Bring Gladness Temple** Dàixìng Sì 戴兴寺, hidden away in the *hutong* against the back wall of the town, are good little finds if you can get to them.

The town wall has remained largely intact, including most of its original brickwork. The defaced sections are slowly being renovated and soon the South Gate, facing South Gate Square, will be on full display. The main square in town is **People's Square** Rénmín Guǎngchǎng 人民广场, halfway up Xinjian Lu and inside the old town area. There is an exhibition hall at the north end of the square and the spacious grounds are often the location of practising Chinese dance troupes. Even the bus station is within the old town walls and buses enter through an old town gate in the wall.

Some 7km north of Yulin old town is Zhènběitái 镇北台 'Suppress the north platform', one of the **largest towers on the Ming Great Wall**. Its name comes from its function of keeping the Mongols at bay, although its original purpose was to defend the marketplace of Hongshan, which was authorised in 1564 when the emperor designated it as one of 11 trading places along the wall. Here, the outlying Mongols would trade with the Han people from inside the wall. The market itself was enclosed in a four-storey building, 30m high and 130m in circumference. Later, in 1587, Zhenbei Tower was built to help protect the market.

By the 20th century, little of the tower and the protective wall for the market remained. In 2002, local government set about rebuilding the tower, but the protective wall and marketplace were still in ruins at the time of writing. The tower rises up in four layers like an Escher painting in the middle of the desert. A man on the tower steps can rent you a pair of binoculars for ¥2, with which you can view the desert beyond the oasis of Yulin. Besides that, the site offers little else. There is no wall to see snaking off into the distance, just a few stumps of a mud tower or two nearby. *(Entry ¥20. Open 09.00–20.00 in the summer; until dusk in the winter.)* A taxi from Yulin costs ¥10 to the site, and there is usually a couple of taxis at the ticket gate waiting for return rides. Alternatively, take bus 3 from Guangji Dasha (07.00–19.00) for ¥1.

A more time-consuming and interesting site nearby is **Red Stone Gorge** Hóngshíxiá 红石峡, which houses 44 cave dwellings in its 12m-high cliffs. If you have got this far, then Hongshixia is well worth a visit for its lush garden-like atmosphere, pagodas and the massive inscriptions on the cliffsides. The inscriptions were the dedications of visiting poets and writers to the greatness of the Great Wall and to the cultural exchange that the trading outlet provided.

Hongshixia is one stop before Zhenbeitai on bus 3. To walk there from Zhenbeitai (20 minutes), head back south on the main road towards Yulin for a few minutes and take a right (west) at the sign in big Chinese red letters saying '红石峡 1000 米' (Hongshixia 1,000m). At the end of the road is the entrance to Hongshixia. *(Entry ¥20.)*

Around 100m before the Gorge is the small 'health resort' of Hóngshíxiá Shēngtài Gōngyuán 红石峡生态公园. Opened in 2003, this resort has converted a small stretch of the river into a tiny cove beach, complete with a Ming-/Qing-style courtyard hotel (see page 213), teahouse, waterwheel, outdoor swimming pool and Chinese garden features. Popular during weekends in the summer, it is deserted most of the rest of the year, making it very peaceful and relaxing. It also has a good restaurant serving local food. *(Day entrance to the resort, open 09.00–17.00, is ¥10.)*

SHENMU 神木

Growing rich off coal and oil in the province, Shenmu is an expanding town with some reasonably good town planning, a few tourist sites worth visiting and a lively, happy-go-lucky atmosphere. Although the Ming Great Wall was once a major feature of the town, it has since been decimated. The stumps of a few beacons and towers can be seen in the distance, and two towers in the town have been renovated, but are not worth the time of day (one has basically been turned into an open latrine). What is of note here is one of the best and most easily accessible working Daoist temple complexes in China for a mere ¥10 entrance fee, namely Erlang Shan, and the relaxed atmosphere of a town growing rich.

GETTING THERE AND AROUND From the east along the wall if you have not hiked in, the most comfortable way to get to Shenmu is by **train**. The daily 07.20 train to Shenmu from Datong passes along some of the Great Wall. Although the train goes all the way to Shenmu North Station Shénmù Běi 神木北, you can buy tickets only

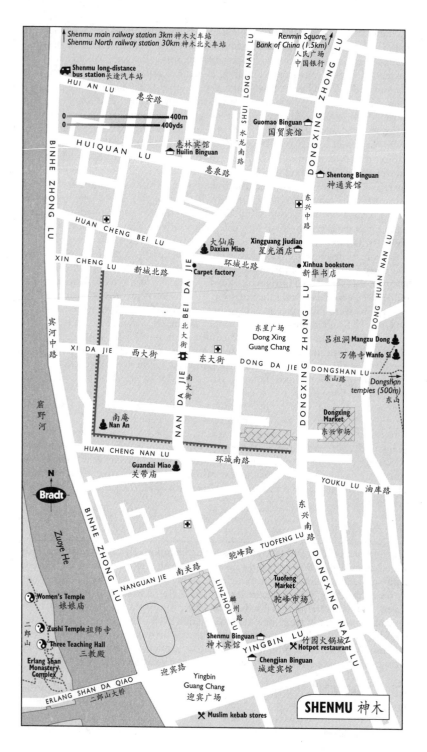

Shenmu main railway station 3km 神木火车站
Shenmu North railway station 30km 神木北火车站

Renmin Square,
Bank of China (1.5km)
人民广场
中国银行

Shenmu long-distance
bus station 长途汽车站

HUI AN LU 惠安路

SHUI LONG NAN LU 水龙南路

ZHONGXING LU

DONGXING LU

0 ——————— 400m
0 ——————— 400yds

HUIQUAN LU 惠泉路

惠林宾馆
Huilin Binguan

Guomao Binguan
国贸宾馆

Shentong Binguan
神通宾馆

BINHE ZHONG LU 宾河中路

HUAN CHENG BEI LU

东兴中路

XIN CHENG LU 新城北路

大仙庙
Daxian Miao

Xingguang Jiudian
星光酒店

Xinhua bookstore
新华书店

DONG HUAN NAN LU

BEI DA JIE 北大街

环城北路
Carpet factory

XI DA JIE 西大街

北大街

东大街

东星广场
Dong Xing
Guang Chang

吕祖洞 Mangzu Dong

万佛寺 Wanfo Si

NAN DA JIE 南大街

DONG DA JIE

DONGXING LU

DONGSHAN LU
东山路

Dongshan
temples (500m)
东山

南庵
Nan An

Dongxing
Market
东兴市场

HUAN CHENG NAN LU 环城南路

Guandai Miao
关带庙

YOUKU LU 油库路

N

Bradt

Zuoye He 窟野河

东兴南路

TUOFENG LU 驼峰路

Tuofeng
Market
驼峰市场

DONGXING NAN LU

NANGUAN JIE 南关路

LINZHOU LU 麟州路

BINHE ZHONG LU 宾河中路

Women's Temple
娘娘庙

二郎山

Zushi Temple 祖师寺

Three Teaching Hall
三教殿

Erlang Shan
Monastery
Complex

Shenmu Binguan
神木宾馆

竹园火锅城
Hotpot restaurant

YINGBIN LU

Chengjian Binguan
城建宾馆

ERLANG SHAN DA QIAO
二郎山大桥

Yingbin
Guang Chang
迎宾广场

Muslim kebab stores

SHENMU 神木

216

at Datong as far as Shuozhou. Once on the train, the ticket conductors will sell you the onward ticket for the very same seat to Shenmu Bei. This bizarre set-up is because of the division of management of the line between Shanxi and neighbouring Shaanxi provinces. A hard seat ticket to Shuozhou ¥9, onward to Shenmu is ¥19. A soft seat to Shuozhou is ¥16, onward to Shenmu ¥33. Shortly after Shuozhou, the train passes through a picturesque section of the inner wall at Jiugeta. Once in Shaanxi, after crossing the Yellow River (about 12.30), the much-deteriorated stumps of old beacon towers along the old Ming wall can be seen from the train all the way to Shenmu. The train arrives in Shenmu North Station at 13.30.

Shenmu North train station (℡ 0912 8252 252/072) is not connected by rail to Shenmu main line station. Numerous unmetered taxi and minibus drivers await the arrival of the 13.30 train to take passengers the 30km on to Shenmu (¥10 per person) or the three hours on to Yinchuan (¥30).

The main line train station in Shenmu is in the northwest of the town on the west side of the river. Two trains a day leave for Yulin, Yanan and Xian at 13.30 and 15.30 (¥12 hard seat). The 15.30 is meant to wait for passengers from the 13.30 before moving off, but this rarely happens, and so if the 13.30 is late then there is a high chance that you will miss this next train.

The long-distance **bus** station in Shenmu is on Binhe Road at the junction with Huian Lu. Buses for Yulin leave every 20 minutes (¥20). Buses are also available to the usual major destinations: Beijing, Hohhot, Baotou, Yanan, Xian, Taiyuan, Daliuta, Jingbian, Dingbian, Yinchuan.

Shenmu town is elongated north–south along the Chuye River. It is easy enough to walk around on foot, and its three bus routes also all plough up and down the main street, Dongxing Lu, and can take you from Erlang Shan temple complex in the south all the way to the north of the town in ten minutes.

The **PSB** (Public Security Bureau) is on Dongxing Zhong Lu (℡ 0912 8332 711.)

The main branch of the **Bank** of China is on Dongxing Bei Lu (℡ 0912 8333 674. Open Mon–Fri 08.00–11.30 and 14.00–17.00.) They change travellers' cheques and currency, but there is no ATM.

WHERE TO STAY AND EAT Shenmu has a few decent hotels and lots of cheap places as usual. The **Shenmu Binguan** (℡ 0912 8312 003) was under renovation at the time of writing and is likely to offer top-notch accommodation by 2006.

⌂ **Chengjian Binguan** 城建宾馆 (40 rooms) Yingbin Lu on the northeast corner of Yingbin Guangchang; ℡ 0912 8311 192. Conveniently located with a great view of Erlang Shan temple complex. Opened in 2005, the rooms are clean but only time will tell how well serviced they will be. Friendly staff. *All two- and three-bed rooms are en suite, but no breakfast. ¥40 per bed.*

⌂ **Guomao Binguan** 国贸宾馆 (66 rooms) Dongxing Zhong Lu; ℡ 0912 8326 657. Basic with TV, phone and en suite, and set back from the main street a little. *Standard twin ¥138.*

⌂ **Huilin Binguan** 惠林宾馆 (45 rooms) Huiquan Lu; ℡ 0912 8328 887 or 135 7127 5988. Clean and comfortable with good discounts, but still a bit noisy. *Standard twin ¥128; common twin ¥60.*

⌂ **Shentong Binguan** 神通宾馆 (60 rooms) Dongxing Zhong Lu; ℡ 0912 8326 773. This hotel is the worse for wear and noisy on the main street. Friendly staff. *Standard twin en suite ¥50; common twin en suite ¥40.*

There are lots of little places to eat in Shenmu, but high class is hard to find. Try the **hotpot** place Zhúyúan Huǒguōchéng 竹园火锅城 on Yingbin Lu, or the many little **Muslim kebab shops** on the south side of Yingbin Guangchang. Yingbin Guangchang itself is a popular place for going out in the evening and you'll see lots of people there gathered around stalls, the bumper cars for the kids or ballroom dancing to a portable stereo.

WHAT TO SEE AND DO The main attraction in Shenmu is the **Erlang Shan temple complex** at the south end of town on the west side of the river. This complex, perched along the steep high ridge of a hill overlooking the town, is well worth the steep climb to the top. The trail past the dozen or so temples also leads further to the back of the hill, where you can wander for some time past graveyards and take in the tranquillity of the surrounding hills. The temples are maintained by a few monks, who are very happy to engage in a conversation (in Chinese) regarding your home country. The last temple on the site is dedicated to women. *(Entry ¥10.)*

In **Dongshan** (meaning Eastern Mountain) overlooking the town is another temple complex, and the possibility of quiet hiking. Although two strands of the Great Wall once joined up in Shenmu forming four branches of wall from the old walled city outwards, none of it is really left in the town now. Two towers have been reconstructed, one within a compound which cannot be accessed, and the other at the north end of the town has basically been turned into an unofficial and unmaintained human latrine. Neither site is worth visiting. Stumps of old beacon towers can be seen in the distance around the town.

Within the old town, the Drum Tower remains intact in the centre and a bell tower can be found to the west of the Drum Tower near a small carpet factory. The road between the two is essentially 'funeral street' where you can see a number of shops making coffins and funeral wreaths.

11

Ningxia 宁夏

The Da Xia had been utterly devastated by Kublai Khan's grandfather, Ghenghis, and what had been the Tangut capital Chongxing was renamed Ningxia, 'pacification of the Xia'.

Arthur Waldron

Ningxia autonomous region is a small pocket of land, whose government is run by the predominant minority of Hui Muslims (see page 41). Their freedom to practise Islam is preserved in their autonomous status, and despite China's somewhat repressive control of religion, over 2,000 practising mosques exist in Ningxia region. Sandwiched between the Mus Us Desert to the east and the Tengger Desert to the west, the Ningxia pocket is a fertile sliver of land covering the Qingshui River connection with the mighty Yellow River. The region has remained powerful since irrigation from the Yellow River and its abundance of tributaries started in this area some 2,000 years ago. Waterwheels, following age-old construction techniques, dot the landscape. The northern horn of the province is further shielded by the Helan mountain range, which separates the Inner Mongolian city of Bayan Hot from access to the fertile Yellow River plain. Made of tamped earth (see page 13), the Ningxia Great Wall marks the northern border of the region and has been relatively well maintained over the centuries by the local people themselves, because of its pivotal role in keeping out invaders from the north. Military strategic thinking up to the Ming dynasty maintained that a pincer movement on the capital city of Yinchuan would cause a major breach on the Middle Kingdom's northern defences and lay open a direct path to inner China, the Silk Road, as well as access to the wheat bowl of the north. The area was considered so valuable that four walls were built to surround the Yinchuan plain.

Today, Yinchuan is a pleasant city and, coupled with Ningxia's exemplary public transport, makes a good base for exploring a lot of the Ningxia sections of the Ming Great Wall, as well as its many other attractions. At almost 1,000m above sea level, summers are warm during the day, and thankfully cooler during the evening. The province's 2,000 years of irrigation have long turned the former desert around the Yellow River into a veritable oasis, lush with paddy fields and vineyards.

YINCHUAN 银川

HISTORY Palaeolithic remains, artefacts and rock carvings in Ningxia province go back 10,000 years, and up until 5,000 years ago the region is believed to have been rich steppe land and forests. What caused the region thereafter to become desert is still unclear. As early as the first years AD, however, settled tribes started to irrigate the mighty Yellow River and tame the creeping desert. Nomadic tribes frequented the region all the way through to 1032 when the Dangxiang tribe settled and dominated a large swathe of land including today's Ningxia province.

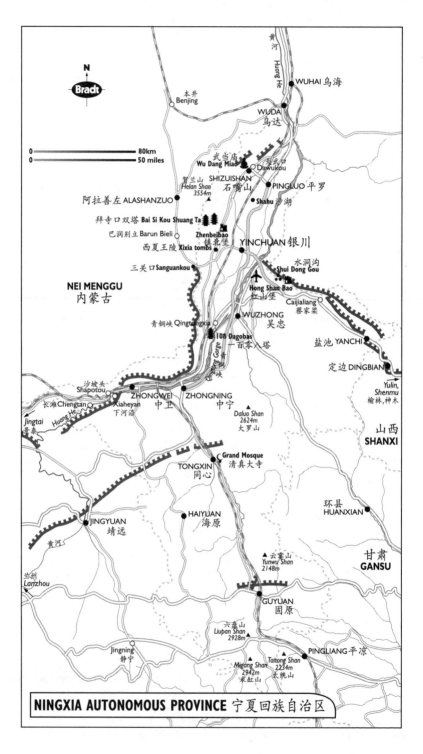

N

Bradt

0 ———————— 80km
0 ———————— 50 miles

黄河
Huang He

WUHAI 乌海

本井
Benjing

WUDA
乌达

武当庙
Wu Dang Miao

大武口
Dawukou

贺兰山
Helan Shan
3554m

SHIZUISHAN
石嘴山

PINGLUO 平罗

阿拉善左 ALASHANZUO

Shahu 沙湖

拜寺口双塔 Bai Si Kou Shuang Ta

巴润别立 Barun Bieli

Zhenbeibao
镇北堡

西夏王陵 Xixia tombs

YINCHUAN 银川

三关口 Sanguankou

水洞沟
Shui Dong Gou

NEI MENGGU
内蒙古

Hong Shan Bao
红山堡

Caijialiang
蔡家梁

青铜峡 Qingtongxia

WUZHONG
吴忠

108 Dagobas
一百零八塔

盐池 YANCHI

定边 DINGBIAN

Yulin,
Shenmu
榆林,神木

沙坡头
Shapotou

长滩 Chengtan

Xiaheyan
下河沿

ZHONGWEI
中卫

ZHONGNING
中宁

Jingtai
景泰

Huang He

Daluo Shan
2624m
大罗山

山西
SHANXI

Grand Mosque
清真大寺

TONGXIN
同心

HAIYUAN
海原

环县
HUANXIAN

JINGYUAN
靖远

黄河

甘肃
GANSU

兰州
Lanzhou

云雾山
Yunwu Shan
2148m

GUYUAN
固原

六盘山
Liupan Shan
2928m

PINGLIANG 平凉

Jingning
静宁

Migang Shan
2942m
米缸山

Taitong Shan
2234m
太统山

NINGXIA AUTONOMOUS PROVINCE 宁夏回族自治区

Xingqing, today's Yinchuan city, became the capital of the Dangxiang, or western Xia dynasty, which ruled until 1227.

The year 1227 marked the overthrow of the western Xia by the unifier of the Mongol hordes, Genghis Khan. Thereafter the province became known as Ningxia, meaning 'pacification of the Xia'.

In 1958, the province was made an autonomous region for China's Hui Muslim minority. The Hui minority are scattered all over China, but are concentrated in Ningxia province where they make up almost one-third of the population.

GETTING THERE AND AWAY Yinchuan Airport is 25km southeast of the old town on a direct highway just outside the South Gate Nanmen. There are four **flights** most days to and from Beijing for ¥1,070, as well as flights to Shanghai, Guangzhou, Chengdu, Taiyuan, Xian, Lanzhou, Urumqi and other cities. The **CAAC** office is at Minhang Dasha, 540 Changcheng Dong Jie (corner with Shengli Jie) (*f 0951 6912 222, or 0951 6913 456 (24hrs))*. Minibuses from outside Minhang Dasha transport departing passengers to the airport for ¥15 on the hour or half-hour prior to departing flights. It is best to enquire in advance as to what time the scheduled bus is for your flight. Minibuses also meet arriving passengers and transport them back to town for ¥15. A taxi to the airport is ¥60 and takes 30 minutes.

The **train** station (*f 0951 5046 271*) is inconveniently in the new town on Xingzhou Lu, 10km west of the old town. Trains to Beijing take 20 hours and run twice a day for ¥270 for a hard sleeper. Four trains a day run to Qingtongxia (one hour, ¥5) and Zhongwei (2½ hours, ¥12). The 06.50 goes on to Wuwei (arrives 14.00, ¥22), Zhangye (arrives 17.30, ¥34) and Jiayuguan (arrives 20.30, ¥76), but book at least four days in advance as the few tickets reserved for Yinchuan sell out fast.

The **South Gate Long Distance – Bus Station** Nán Mén Chángtú Qìchē Zhàn 南门长途汽车站 (*f 0951 6032 157*) is usefully in the southeast of the old town and within walking distance of a number of cheap hotels. Most major-destination buses arrive and leave from this bus station. Overnight buses serve the city from Beijing, Xian, Yulin and Lanzhou. The bus from Yulin can arrive as early as 02.00, but you can sleep on the bus until the morning. (Alternatively, if you can't sleep and don't want to pay for a night in a hotel, take a taxi to the Mingxiuguo 24-hour teahouse (page 226) and hang out on the private room sofas.) Buses to Zhongwei take three hours and leave every 30 minutes for ¥15. Buses to Bayun (Inner Mongolia via Sanguankou) leave every 20 minutes, costing ¥10 to Sanguankou and ¥25 to Bayun.

North Gate Travel Bus Station Běi Mén Lǚyóu Qìchē Zhàn 北门旅游汽车站 (*f 0951 6738 245*) is at 580 Qinghe Bei Lu. Buses for Dawukou, Shizuishan and Desert Lake Shahu leave from here. There is a very helpful Travel Centre (*f 0951 6735 488*) at the bus station, open every day 08.00–18.00, although their English is limited. They can organise your travel arrangements to anywhere within the province and beyond.

Buses travelling west, such as to Bayun, Zhenbeitai Film City and to Xixia Wangling Tombs, usually stop at the train station to pick up passengers, and following the trend in China now to separate bus stations by destination, it is likely that westbound buses may soon no longer run from Nanmen at all, but only go from the train station in the west of the city.

A number of **city buses** serve the old town and run between the old town and the new town. Minimum fare is ¥1. Bus 20 travels in a circular fashion essentially

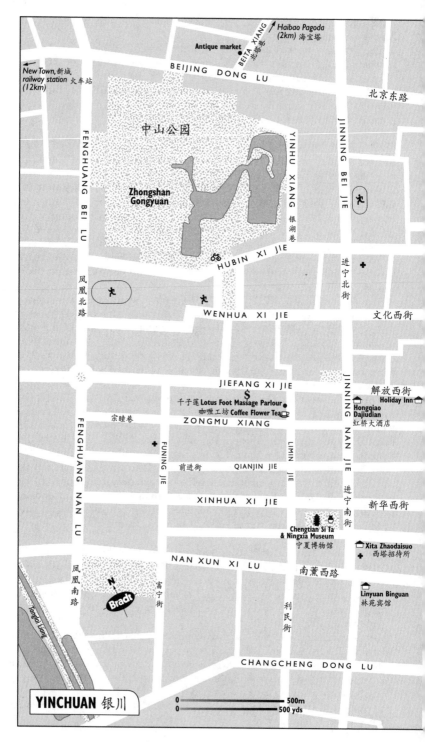

Haibao Pagoda
(2km) 海宝塔

Antique market

BEITA XIANG
北塔巷

BEIJING DONG LU

北京东路

New Town, 新城
railway station 火车站
(12km)

中山公园

JINNING BEI JIE

进宁北街

YINHU XIANG

Zhongshan
Gongyuan

银湖巷

FENGHUANG BEI LU

凤凰北路

HUBIN XI JIE

WENHUA XI JIE

文化西街

JIEFANG XI JIE

解放西街
Holiday Inn

千子莲 Lotus Foot Massage Parlour
咖喱工坊 Coffee Flower Tea

Hongqiao
Dajiudian
红桥大酒店

ZONGMU XIANG

JINNING NAN JIE

进宁南街

宗睦巷

FUNING JIE

前进街   QIANJIN JIE

LIMIN JIE

XINHUA XI JIE

新华西街

Chengtian Si Ta
& Ningxia Museum
宁夏博物馆

Xita Zhaodaisuo
西塔招待所

NAN XUN XI LU

FENGHUANG NAN LU

凤凰南路

南薰西路

利民街

Linyuan Binguan
林苑宾馆

富宁街

Tongtai Liang

CHANGCHENG DONG LU

长城东路

YINCHUAN 银川

0 ————— 500m
0 ————— 500 yds

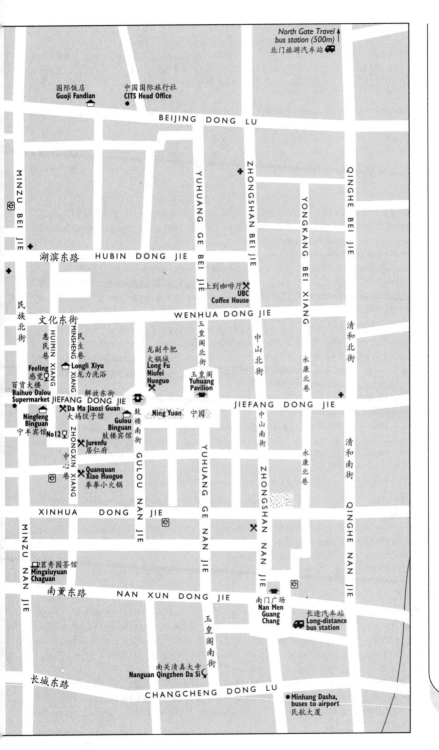

North Gate Travel
bus station (500m)
北门旅游汽车站

国际饭店
Guoji Fandian

中国国际旅行社
CITS Head Office

BEIJING DONG LU

MINZU BEI JIE

YUHUANG GE BEI JIE

ZHONGSHAN BEI JIE

YONGKANG BEI XIANG

QINGHE BEI JIE

湖滨东路 HUBIN DONG JIE

民族北街
MINZU BEI JIE

上到咖啡厅
UBC Coffee House

WENHUA DONG JIE

文化东街

中山北街

清和北街

惠民巷
HUIMIN XIANG

民生巷
MINSHENG XIANG

龙副牛肥火锅城
Long Fu Niufei Huoguo

玉皇阁北街

永康北巷

Feeling
感觉

Longli Xiyu
龙力洗浴

玉皇阁
Yuhuang Pavilion

百货大楼
Baihuo Dalou
Supermarket

解放东街

JIEFANG DONG JIE

JIEFANG DONG JIE

Da Ma Jiaozi Guan
大妈饺子馆

Ning Yuan 宁园

中山南街

清和南街

Ningfeng
Binguan
宁丰宾馆 No12号

Gulou Binguan
鼓楼宾馆

鼓楼南街

ZHONGXIN XIANG
中心巷

Jurenfu
居仁府

GULOU NAN JIE

YUHUANG GE NAN JIE

ZHONGSHAN NAN JIE

永康北巷

QINGHE NAN JIE

Quanquan
Xiao Huoguo
拳拳小火锅

XINHUA DONG JIE

MINZU NAN JIE

茗秀园茶馆
Mingxiuyuan
Chaguan

南薰东路 NAN XUN DONG JIE

南门广场
Nan Men Guang Chang

长途汽车站
Long-distance bus station

玉皇阁南街

南关清真大寺
Nanguan Qingzhen Da Si

长城东路 CHANGCHENG DONG LU

Minhang Dasha,
buses to airport
民航大厦

around along the old city walls, connecting Nanmen and Beimen bus stations. Buses 1 and 2 run between Nanmen and the train station for ¥2.

Flag fall for metered **taxis** is ¥5. A taxi to Gunzhong Pass National Park costs ¥60. A taxi between the old town and the new town is ¥12–17. A taxi to Shuidong Gou and Hongshanbao Great Wall is ¥80 A taxi to Wudaokou's Great Wall costs ¥120.

Bicycles can be rented for ¥20 per day at the south gate to Zhongshan Park Zhōngshān Gōngyuán 中山公园.

A useful **map** of Yinchuan new and old town and of the province is available (in Chinese only) at the bus stations and most kiosks for ¥5. City bus lines are on the map as well as advertising for a number of local sites, services and more upmarket hotels.

There are several useful **travel agents** in town:

CITS Ningxia Tourism Building Níngxià Lǚyóu Dàshà 宁夏旅游大厦 Beijing Dong Lu; *ℓ* 0951 6719 771. Has a large team of English-speaking staff who can sort most travel plans out, including hiking along the Ningxia Great Wall. Located next to the expensive International Hotel.

Cultural International Travel Service 60 Wenhua Dong Jie; *ℓ* 0951 6013 559. Mr Shen Zizhong speaks excellent English and can arrange most trips within the province as well as secure discounted hotel rooms for hotels over ¥200.

North Gate Travel Service Běi Mén Lǚyóu Qìchē Zhàn 北门旅游汽车站 580 Qinghe Bei Lu; *ℓ* 0951 6735 488; *e* lxs@nxtb.com; www.nxtb.com. Very good local knowledge and some excellent combination tours around Ningxia, but limited English spoken.

A useful place for picking up food, toiletries and other sundry items is Lǎodàlóu 老大楼, the multi-storey shopping centre at 2 Jiefang Xi Jie, on the corner with Minzu Nan Jie. The entire second floor is an excellent **supermarket**. Bags should be deposited at the bag counter on the east side of the building before entering the supermarket.

The main Public Security Bureau (**PSB)** is at Yuhuangge Bei Jie (*ℓ* 0951 6915 080).

MONEY AND COMMUNICATION In the old town, the main branch of the Bank of China on Jiefang Xi Lu exchanges travellers' cheques and currency; open Monday–Friday 08.00–18.00, Saturday and Sunday 09.30–16.30. There are many ATMs accepting foreign credit and debit cards scattered around town.

The usual flurry of internet bars are scattered around the town. Try:

Long Wangba 龙网吧 Xinhua Dong Jie. On the south side of this popular shopping street just west of Gulou pedestrian zone. ¥3 per hour.

Tianlong Wangba 天龙网吧 East side of Nanmen Guangchang. Big comfy armchairs in front of modern terminals with Windows XP. Bad toilets. Deposit required. ¥2 per hour.

Aichong Wangba 爱虫网吧 Minzu Bei Jie. ¥2 per hour.

Yi Mei'er Wangba 溢美而网吧 26 Ju An Xiang. Windows XP. Sells drinks and yoghurts. ¥2 per hour.

WHERE TO STAY

⌂ **Longli Xiyu** 龙力洗浴 (20 rooms) 18 Minsheng Xiang; *ℓ* 0951 6033 885. This brand-new bathhouse is a step above the rest, with clean modern rooms and bathing standards comparable to Europe or North America. Down a quiet alley, all the hotel rooms are en suite, but the cheaper rooms on the third floor come without showers. See box below for more on the bathing and massage services. Room service available, but breakfast is not included in the price. *Standard twin or double ¥138; discounted rooms can come down to ¥98. Suite with jacuzzi ¥388.*

⌂ **Gulou Fandian** 鼓楼饭店 (74 rooms) 98 Jiefang Dong Jie; *ℓ* 0951 6024 331; *f* 0951 6022 573. Very conveniently located near the Drum Tower right in the centre of the old town, with quiet rooms at the back. Clean and serviced. Well worth it if you can get a discount. *One five-bed dorm without bathroom ¥125. Standard twin en suite ¥135; common twin en suite ¥115.*

🛏 **Holiday Inn** (230 rooms) 4 Jiefang Dong Jie; ☎ 0951 6011 366. Opening June 2006, this brand-new hotel from the familiar Holiday Inn chain will be the first familiar Western hotel branch in Yinchuan.

🛏 **Guoji Fandian** 国际饭店 (97 rooms) 365 Beijing Dong Lu; ☎ 0951 6728 688; 🖷 0951 6728 788. The 'International Hotel' in English is a pricey high-end hotel with all the trimmings and Western food in the restaurant. Sometimes they have 30–40% discounts so it is worth inquiring. All rooms have free ethernet connection. *Business-standard twin, double or sgl ¥888.*

🛏 **Hongqiao Dajiudian** 红桥大酒店 (192 rooms) 38 Jiefang Xi Jie; ☎ 0951 6918 888; 🖷 0951 6918 788; 🖃 hongqiao@public.yc.nx.cn. Also known as the Rainbow Bridge Hotel in English, this meticulous Chinese-run four-star hotel has all the trimmings: several Chinese and a Western restaurant, saunas, massage, golf simulator, fitness centre, business centre, ethernet in each room, buffet breakfast included. *Standard twin ¥339; sgl (double bed) ¥382.*

🛏 **Linyuan Binguan** 林苑宾馆 (72 rooms) 88 Nanxun Xi Lu; ☎ 0951 4122 288; 🖷 0951 4118 179. A Chinese three star from the 1980s. Not the best value for money, but it is very quiet facing a big tree-lined garden courtyard from which it gets its name 'Hunting Park Hotel'. No internet. ¥10 for breakfast. *Standard twin ¥268; three-person room ¥218; extra bed 20% of room rate.*

🛏 **Ningfeng Binguan** 宁丰宾馆 (50 rooms) 6 Jiefang Dong Jie; ☎ 0951 6028 898. A Chinese-run three star, a bit on the dark side, but relatively good rooms and a good if noisy location. Will accept outsiders for their Chinese buffet breakfast for ¥5 per person. *Standard twin ¥280; three-person room ¥380.*

🛏 **Xita Zhaodaisuo** 西塔招待所 (40 rooms) 101 Liqun Xi Jie; ☎ 0951 6041 050. A clean, bright hostel with big rooms and communal baths, very close to the Western Pagoda and Ningxia Museum. *Standard twin ¥100; common twin ¥60; three-person room ¥90; four-person room ¥100; room by the hour ¥10.*

✘ **WHERE TO EAT AND DRINK** Yinchuan has a number of great places to eat, and if you are craving a bit of Western food, some of that is available, too. The usual street stalls can be found around the town for breakfast. **Ning Park** Nìng Yuán 宁园 is a great place early in the mornings for getting sweet black sesame seed doughnuts, hot tofu drinks and a variety of other goodies. The road south of the park is also a clothes and vegetable market, and a great place to sit out in the evening and drink a beer and eat lamb skewers on the street. The busy main street of Xinhua Dong Jie is also good for lots of cheap restaurants, including KFC, as well as a number of bars. Zhongshan Nan Jie down to the South Gate has many small restaurants often serving eight-treasure tea (bābǎochá 八宝茶) or where you can see the cooks making jiaozi. The smaller street of Limin Jie is also good for small cheap restaurants, good tea and coffee houses and the well worthwhile Lotus foot massage parlour.

✘ **Da Ma Jiaozi Guani** 大妈饺子馆 32 Jiefang Dong Jie (on the corner with Zhongxin Xiang); ☎ 0951 6072 378. Serves lots of delicious boiled dumplings (jiaozi) as well as an array of other traditional and speciality dishes for very good prices. No lamb. Try their fried vegetable dumplings (sān shū guō tiē 三蔬锅贴).

✘ **Long Fu Niu Fei** 龙副牛肥 93 Jiefang Dong Jie (on the northeast corner of Gulou); ☎ 0951 6024 249. A very good hotpot (huoguo) place, serving three types of soup bases and some very good fried vegetable jiaozi as well as all the usual hotpot ingredients (see page 264 for the huoguo ingredient guide).

✘ **Napoli** 195 Xinhua Dong Jie; ☎ 0951 6035 111. Serves all the pizza, salad, other Chinese fried foods you can eat for ¥39. Drinks including beer and coffee also included. Open 11.00–14.30 and 17.00–21.30.

✘ **Quanquan Xiao Huoguo** 拳拳小火锅 57–59 Zhongxin Xiang; ☎ 0951 8100 282. A cheap and cheerful little hotpot place. Hotpot for four with beer for under ¥60.

✘ **Jurenfu** 居仁府 21 Zhongxin Xiang; ☎ 0951 6026 417. Advertising itself as a Han cuisine restaurant, this very good restaurant serves no lamb dishes. You can order almost anything else you might get in Beijing though. Try their broccoli and sweet tofu balls (lánhuā sàozi dòufu 兰花臊子豆腐) and their ground pork in Beijing sauce (jīngjiàng ròusi 京酱肉丝) where you put strands of delicious pork, thinly sliced cucumber and onions into a lightly steamed bun pocket.

11

DRAGON POWER BATHHOUSE AND MASSAGE PARLOUR Lónglì Xǐyù 龙力洗浴

After a long walk on the Great Wall, whether you stay at the hotel side of the bathhouse or not, it is worth coming here for a sauna, scrub and massage. Dragon Power Bathhouse has a nice big airy reception, where like most upscale bathhouses in China now, you will need to change your shoes for plastic sandals (¥10). You will then be given an electronic locker chip and a number of tokens depending on what you order in advance for the afternoon (services can also be added afterwards).

You will then be ushered up to the changing and shower rooms. For the women this is where the steam room, scrubs, rubs and masks take place; for the men a Roman bath awaits as well as the scrubs, rubs and masks. Toiletries are available en masse. On finishing up in this room, you can don a pair of free (miǎnfèi 免费) panties and freshly laundered soft cotton pyjamas. You may also choose an unused, less soft, and patterned pair (to take home) for ¥26. Appropriately clothed, you may then enter the top floors of the bathhouse and hotel, along with guests of the opposite sex, to relax, eat or sleep. DVDs are available in the lounge, or mahjong and card rooms are on site. Food can be ordered to your room, table or the DVD lounge.

A variety of different massage services are available, including ànmó 按摩, tuīná 推拿, zúliáo 足疗 (foot massage and pedicure) and cǎibèi 踩背 (back massage by treading on your back). Be prepared to spend several hours in here if you want the full bath, scrub and massage treatment. It is well worth it.

Bargain package deals are available (steam room for women, Roman bath for men, scrub and foot massage ¥68) or you can pay for services individually: small towel ¥3; baths ¥48; milk and honey body rub ¥10; egg mask ¥18; face massage and back massage by foot ¥50. All payments are made at the end on checkout.

✗ **UBC Coffee House** Shàngdǎo Kāfēi Tīng 上岛咖啡厅 84 Zhongshan Bei Jie; ✆ 0951 3971 777. When you have tired of Chinese food, or just want a comfy place to hang out on a rainy day, this is the place to come. Big soft armchairs, wide-ranging Western and Chinese menu, including good French fries, salad bar, (medium-weak and small) coffees and plenty of teas. Slightly pricey, but worth it.

Cafés, teahouses and bars Aside from the coffee and teahouses above, the following are also of note:

Coffee Flower Tea Gāli Gōngfáng 咖喱工坊 12-1 Limin Jie; ✆ 0951 6032 870. A spotlessly clean, and very comfortable tea and coffee house, serving nice long freshly brewed coffees and big pots of tea (with or without milk, ¥15 and upwards). For something different, try the southeast Asian favourite Yuǎnyáng Kāfēi 远洋咖啡 , a sweet black tea and milky coffee mix! Has one of the cleanest toilets in China. New store opening in the centre in 2006.

Feeling Gǎnjué 感觉 4 Huimin Xiang; ✆ 0951 6023 989. Sandwiched between Der Rosenkavalier and F8, this bar is much bigger on the inside that it looks on the outside. Plays good alternative music, serves the usual drinks as well as a good gin and tonic (jīn tānglǐ 金汤里), and a variety of other lesser-known cocktails, such as Bull/Public Cow Gōngniú 公牛 (beer with a shot of something) and Western Lake Xīhú 西湖 (crème de menthe and another shot of something). Lots of teas and coffees also available.

Mingxiuyuan Chaguan 茗秀园茶馆 35 Minzu Nan Jie; ✆ 0951 6025 192. This basement teahouse was opened in 1996 and was the first in Yinchuan, prompting a spate of other lesser teahouses. This one has lots of character and is spacious enough for drinking tea in the public spaces, as well as in the well-decorated private rooms. The halls are decorated with teacups, pots and sets, all available for sale, ranging from ¥10 for a cup and snifter set, to ¥1,000 plus for a cast-iron teapot. Open around the clock, the teahouse also serves snacks and meals, and the *guzheng* (a type of sitar) is played live from 19.00–21.00. Ceremony teas are available from ¥100 upwards for one-tenth of a pound (yì liǎng 一两), and a tea lady to perform the ceremony and serve you tea is an additional ¥100.

No 12 12 Zhongxin Xiang; ☎ 0951 6012 822. Immaculate waiters with bow ties usher you to this upstairs bar, where comfy sofas and relaxing 1980s music await you. The manager, unused to serving cocktails, might take a while to put one together for you, but it will be good. Long Island ice tea (cháng dǎo bīng chá 长岛冰茶), margarita (mǎ gé lì tè 玛格丽特), a variety of whisky blends (and a Glenfiddich single malt) and more are available.

WHAT TO SEE AND DO It is old-town Yinchuan that is the more interesting side of the city, with several noteworthy sites. For anyone (most people) arriving by bus to the old town, the first of such sites is the **South Gate** (Nanmen), which looks like a small replica of Tian An Gate in Beijing, complete with a small portrait of Mao Zedong over the gateway. Behind South Gate is the terraced street of Zhongshan Nan Jie.

Southwest of South Gate is **Nanguan Mosque** Yuhuangge Nan Jie (☎ 0951 410 6714). Its claim to fame is that it was originally built in the early 17th century under the Ming dynasty and razed to the ground during the 'so-called Culture Revolution' (according to its own literature). Unfortunately, this replacement built in 1981 is a sorry concrete and white-tile apology for the original, and is hardly worth the ¥8 entry fee, although the small bird- and plant-festooned courtyard is nice. Good Xinjiang Bābāgāo (粑粑糕 — like a Snickers chocolate bar without the chocolate) is sold outside at ¥2 per yi liang (45 grams). *(Open 07.00–20.00.)*

The main street bisecting the old town east to west is Jiefang Lu. Forming the centre of the old town on this street are the **Drum Tower** and the Yuhuan Pavilion. Neither is open to the public but both are useful landmarks.

The **Ningxia Museum** Níngxià Bówùguǎn 宁夏博物馆 and **Western Pagoda** on Jiangning Nan Jie have excellent permanent and travelling exhibitions on the region with English translations. Three permanent exhibition rooms present the history of Ningxia, the rock carvings of the region, and the culture of the Hui Muslim people. A fourth travelling exhibition covers other interesting areas of Ningxia history, such as the excavation of artefacts from the Han and Tang dynasties found around the Guyuan Great Wall. If you don't get a chance to see the rock carvings at Suyukou, then it is well worth going to the museum to see what they are all about. The museum has a few of the 2,000–3,000-year-old smaller rock pieces on display, as well as lots of rubbings and photos. A couple of good books on the province in English can also be bought at the museum. The museum is housed in the courtyard buildings of the Western Pagoda, whose 191 steps you can climb to the top to get a view of the city. Open daily 09.00–17.00. *(Entry ¥22.)*

Zhongshan Gongyuan 中山公园 in the northwest of the old town is a medium-sized park, good for whiling away a couple of hours on a hot afternoon, catching melodies of èrhú 二胡 players. Just northeast of the park's north entrance is a small **antiques market** on Beita Lu. The market, open every day, is not very big, but you'll find a nice range of old Chinese paraphernalia at reasonable prices. Bargain hard. Outside the south gate of the park, you can **rent bicycles** at ¥20 for the day.

Taking Beita Lu another 2km further northeast past the big five-way intersection on Beijing Lu, you will come to **Haibao Pagoda**. It is not really worth the trek out this far, considering the Western Pagoda (see above) is more conveniently located and affords a more interesting view of the city. The view of the desert from Haibao Pagoda is poor. *(Entry ¥10.)*

A good **foot massage parlour** in town is **Lotus** Qiānzi Lián 千子莲 at 2 Limin Jie (☎ 0951 5123 801). This new and fancy foot parlour is clean, comfortable and friendly. Maps of the various pressure points of the feet and hands greet you in the lobby. Rooms for three or more people are available so you can have your

11

Ningxia is renowned throughout China for its wines. The semi-alpine desert combination of the region allows for hot days and cool nights – perfect for grape growing. Bottled under the label Xixia (western Xia), the Ningxia plains produce some good reds, whilst the Helan Mountains produce some quaffable whites. They might not yet be of worldwide award-winning standards, but you can get something very decent for under ¥40 a bottle, which most restaurants will let you drink at your table if you bring it with you. Here is a short list of some of the wines you might sample along the Great Wall:

NINGXIA WINES

Imperial Horse A Sauvignon grape producing a full fruity wine. ¥33.

Xixia This is the wine that models itself on a Bordeaux. Of course, it's not a Bordeaux; it's a bit lighter, very quaffable and good value for money. ¥19.

GANSU WINES

Mogao Ice Wine A very pleasant white wine at the sweet end of Riesling or a Pinot Noir. ¥58. The Mogao red is fruity and Merlot-ish. Gansu wines are generally tarter than their Ningxia-equivalent grapes.

SHANDONG WINES

Castle Estates Wine coming from a little further south than the Great Wall are generally good, with some heart and not too dry. ¥55.

HEBEI WINES

Great Wall Despite its grand name, this is not a good wine, perhaps because the Great Wall does not get sufficient sun for long enough to produce a consistently sweet grape. The cheap bottles (under ¥50) are not a pleasant drink. Over ¥100, the wine is slightly better, but hardly worth the money.

Chang Yu Established since 1892, produces markedly better wine than Great Wall. A good reliable white is their Changyu Riesling for ¥55. Visit www.changyu.com.cn to find out more about their Wine Culture Museum and how to visit their Castel Chateau for a wine tour.

massage at the same time as all your friends. TV available, and drinks are extra. Basic 90-minute foot massage costs ¥68; extra for individual senior and expert masseurs (their names and prices in Chinese are up on the wall behind the counter).

AROUND YINCHUAN Zhenbeibu Film City Zhènběibǔ Yíng Chéng 镇北堡影城 is a half-hour drive away (see page 231).

Rock art dating back as early as some 10,000 years and as late as 2,000–3,000 years ago can be found scattered all over the Helan mountain range. The most prolific concentration of these carvings of animals and people can be found at Helankou Rock Art Park Helankou Yanhua (*(' 0951 602 1641)*. A taxi there costs ¥40. *(Entry ¥20.)* If you don't have time to get out to see the real thing, then visit the Ningxia Museum in Yinchuan for a good display of what the rock art is about.

Mount Helan National Park offers a range of hiking trails with minimal Chinese kitsch. A number of trails wander around the park, and fitter hikers can attempt Mount Helan (3,554m) if they arrive early. There are two main entrances to the national park. Gunzhong Guan at 1,536m (✆ 0951 8930 100) is the closest entrance from Yinchuan. It is a 13km hike in from the main road, or get a taxi to take you from Yinchuan for ¥30. (Entry ¥20.) Suyukou entrance (✆ 0951 2079 103) is a little further north and more developed. *(Entry ¥30.)* You can stay here at the Sūyùkǒu Shānzhuāng 苏峪口山庄 *(35 rooms; ✆ 0951 2085 007).* Good serviced accommodation with restaurant. *(Standard twin en suite with 24hr hot water ¥260; triple without bathroom ¥160.)*

Baisikou Shuang Ta (✆ 0951 6022 706) stand out in the landscape between the two entrances to the national park. These twin pagodas are somewhat unusual in China, but they are nothing special to write home about. *(Entry ¥10.)*

The **Xixia Lingmu Tombs** to the west of Yinchuan house eight emperors from the western Xia dynasty of 1038 to 1227. Scattered over 40km^2, the imperial tombs stand out like giant cones surrounded by over 70 tombs of their followers and servants. After two centuries of ruling the northwest of China, the Xia were all but exterminated by Genghis Khan in 1227. It is from their extermination that Ningxia gains its name 'Pacification of the Xia'. Unless you are a real tomb fan, these can be a bit dry, and anyway you get a glimpse of them from the bus to Sanguankou if you go to visit there. *(Entry ¥40.)*

Qingtongxia National Park is another site worth a visit if you have the time, and want a day out hiking along the shores of the gorge. Buses run to the gorge every half-hour from Nanmen bus station (one hour, ¥13). Nearby is also the site of **108 dagobas**, a Tibetan-styled stupa. These 108 (the number of beads on a monk's rosary) are unusually situated up the side of a small hill in the shape of a triangle. A hike in the gorge is more rewarding.

THE EASTERN NINGXIA WALL

This section of the Ningxia wall extends in a double layer from the border with Shaanxi province, through Yanchi town and joins together again just outside Caijialiang. The layers range between 30km and 100km apart but is now so worn down that some of it is less than 2m high. Nevertheless, this is some of the most continuous section of mud wall in China, and Ningxia has recognised the need to preserve it. From Caijialiang, the wall then proceeds northwest past Hongshan and the Water Cave Gully Shuǐ Dòng Gōu 水洞沟 river encampment, after which it heads north along the eastern bank of the Yellow River. The wall here is now completely destroyed.

The eastern Ningxia wall is mostly on flat ground and can make for monotonous hiking. Biking along the back roads would be more sustainable if you can get a decent bicycle. The bus from Yanchi to Yinchuan (three hours) essentially follows the route of the Great Wall and this, therefore, also makes for a good and easy option for viewing the wall.

From Yinchuan, the now-ruined castle of Hongshan and the river encampment of Shui Dong Gou, are an easy 40-minute bus or taxi ride away. The wall here stretches all the way to Yanchi, and makes for a good day hike or several in sunny weather. In less favourable conditions it can look rather bleak. On the north side of the wall is Inner Mongolia and a few untidy Mongolian hut resorts offering accommodation (with very unserviced-looking bathroom ¥100, without bathroom ¥40) and food. At the time of writing Hongshan Castle and Water Cave Gully were about to be renovated, with a completion date of 2008.

The northern Ningxia wall also had a double layer formation, extending east from the cities of Shizuishan and Dawukou to the west bank of the Yellow River, and extending west to the Helan mountain range. Now very little of this wall remains, except for a few bits of mud wall in the northwest of town, and a couple of more interesting sections in the foothills of the Helan range by Wudang Monastery. Within the town of Dawukou, the short section of mud wall remaining was part of the walled village of Zhenda. Unfortunately, it is particularly dilapidated, in a poor industrial part of town and not worth the visit. A number of signs forbid walking on the wall, yet it is clear that the section is basically beyond saving at this point. At Wudang Monastery, some of the stone facing on the Great Wall is still intact (just), and while the sections are not long enough for a day hike, approaching them from the monastery makes for a good day trip.

Wudang Monastery Wǔdāng Miào 武当庙 is a full working monastery with an impressive number of adherents from the local Buddhist community in this Hui Muslim province. At the weekend you can see locals pay the monks ¥10 for the privilege of partaking in Buddhist rites, including crawling under the table to the sound of a monk chanting and tapping a wooden gong. The monastery is set in the foothills of the Helan mountain range, away from the main town of Dawukou, where you can find peace and quiet and several paths leading into the mountains. Cold noodle lunch, snacks, drinks and a few camel souvenirs are available without the usual oppressive haranguing. *(Entry to the monastery ¥2. Fee to climb the pagoda ¥1.)* Taxi to the monastery from Dawukou ¥10. Taxis are also available to take people back from the monastery at the end of the day.

From the monastery, you can see a section of the western Great Wall called **Chive Gully** Jiucai Gou. It is a half-hour hike to the wall from the monastery along the old riverbed and up the gully. This section has mostly been robbed of stone, and the shale mud interior is deteriorating with frequent molestation. Like a number of sections along the Helan range, this piece is only a short plug over the saddle of the gully, comprising at least three beacon towers and a 50m section of wall. It is unclear how some of the beacons, hidden within the foothills, would communicate by line of sight. The ascent up the gully and to the top beacon tower is shaley and steep.

A few metres from the marked start of the gully is another marked sign indicating the presence of ancient rock carvings at Chive Gully.

Further southwest on the Helan range is another section of the western Great Wall. This is visible on the approach to the monastery from the road, but is hidden by mountains once there. To get there, hike for a half-hour down the road at the foothills of the range (or take a taxi for ¥5) until you see the wall to your west. It is a good hour's hike in from there.

THE WESTERN NINGXIA WALL

The western Ningxia wall runs north to south from the southern end of the Helan Mountains, using the mountain range as an extension of the Middle Kingdom's frontier defensive line. It is by far the best-preserved and worthwhile of the Ningxia walls, in part because of its continuous length, and also by the number of heavily fortified passes and gateways regulating passage through the Helan Mountains. Now the hills above the wall are within a good two–three-hour hike from an outlying village or the Gunzhong Pass entrance to the Mount Helan National Park.

Some 20km from Gunzhong Pass and 30km northwest of Yinchuan town is Suppress the North Castle, Zhenbeibu (not to be confused with Zhenbeitaibu near Yulin, see page 231). Two forts in fact grace this site, a circular one built in 1500 by Yinchuan garrison troops in the Ming period and a later square one built by the Qing. Now only the mud walls are left but the entire site, having been used by Zhang Yimou in his movie *Red Sorghum*, has been turned into a **film set:** Zhènběibǔ Yǐng Chéng 镇北堡影城. Although a bit kitsch, the site is worth a visit for an insight into what it might have been like to live inside a fortified town in Ming and Qing times. *(Entry ¥40.)* To get there, take the Yǐng Chéng 影城 bus from Nanmen (¥5) or the train station (¥4).

Two important defensive structures punctuate the western wall, regulating passage through it. The northernmost is Sānguānkǒu 三关口, or 'three link gateway', located at the southern tip of the Helan Mountains, right on the border with Inner Mongolia. A stretch of the wall climbs up the mountain range, partially still faced with stone, but mostly revealing its mud and stone interior. By far the most impressive piece, however, is the almost continuous mud wall stretching south as far as the eye can see and worthy of several days' hiking if you can carry the water and food. Inner Mongolia lies to the west of this wall, Ningxia to the east. To get to Sanguankou, take the bus bound for Bayun (in Inner Mongolia), which leaves from Nanmen and the train station every 20 minutes for ¥10. It takes 60–90 minutes to get to Sanguankou depending on the state of the roads. You will know when you get there by the massive stretch of mud Great Wall appearing in the desert on your left. The last bus back to Yinchuan is at 18.00.

The southernmost pass controlling the western Great Wall before it heads west and into Gansu province is **Shengjing Pass**. Located halfway between Zhongning and Zhongwei on the south bank of the Yellow River, very little of it is left now. Skirting the north of Zhongwei town, through the Tengger Desert, the wall crosses the Yellow River at the village of Xiaheyan and then follows the southern bank into Gansu province at Heishan Gorge.

ZHONGWEI 中卫

Zhongwei is a compact little town, easy to navigate around its central Drum Tower, with good hotels and a number of things to do in the surrounding area. Many of the things Zhongwei has to offer are at its Yellow River 'beachfront' at Shapatou. Here you can take boats or sheepskin rafts along the river, ride camels for several days into the Tengger Desert, find out about desert reclamation at the Desert Research Centre, as well as many other sand-related amusements at Shapatou Park. Within the town itself is Gaomiao Temple, which has a long multi-chambered house of horrors in its basement depicting the Chinese version of Hell. And, of course, the Ming Great Wall is ever nearby, with a 5km stretch heading west from Xiaheyan village.

GETTING THERE AND AROUND There are four **trains** a day leaving from Yinchuan to Zhongwei, but, especially if you are staying in the old town, they are none too convenient for getting to Zhongwei, taking two-and-a-half hours with no guarantee of a seat.

Much more convenient from the old town are the fast **coaches** from Yinchuan's Nanmen long-distance bus station. These leave every 50 minutes

07.40–16.20, blissfully on time, whether full or not, for the 160km journey by motorway on clean spacious coaches (two hours, ¥36).

Once in Zhongwei, it really is small enough to walk around, taking about 15 minutes from the bus station at the end of Gulou Dong Jie or the train station at the end of Gulou Bei Jie to the hotels around the Drum Tower. Flag fall for **taxis** is ¥5.

A map of the town (in Chinese) can be bought for ¥5 at the Zhongwei Peace Travel Service at the entrance to the Zhongwei Binguan at 33 Gulou Xi Jie. Another excellent, friendly travel service for the Zhongwei region is:

Ningxia Desert Travel Service Co Ltd Zhongwei Dajiudian, 53 Gulou Bei Jie; ✆ 0955 7011 206 or 0955 8533 023; 📠 0955 7018 841; 📧 billyh1978@hotmail.com; www.nxtour.com.cn. Managing director, Billy Huang, and his staff speak very good English and offer desert safaris by camel and jeep as well as river trips to Chengtan ancient waterwheel or Shapatou to Zhongwei by sheepskin raft. Safaris cost ¥250 per day per person all inclusive; river trips cost ¥150–250 depending on length of the trip and number of people.

WHERE TO STAY AND EAT Zhongwei has lots of good, cheap, new hotels, which can easily be bargained down midweek and off-season.

⌂ **Yixing Binguan** 逸兴宾馆 (197 rooms) 2 Gulou Bei Jie; ✆ 0955 7017 666; 📠 0955 7019 993. A centrally located hotel with clean serviced rooms in three buildings. The south building is the cheapest of the three, while the north building has views of the Drum Tower. None of the buildings, views or not, is able to cut out the noise from the traffic circle around the tower. All rooms en suite and include a Chinese buffet breakfast. *Standard twin, double or sgl ¥150–368.*

⌂ **Zhongwei Binguan** 中卫宾馆 (250 rooms) 33 Gulou Xi Jie; ✆ 0953 7012 609; 📠 0953 7012 350. This massive state-run hotel, slightly set back from the road, is typically worn down and full of party cadres shouting at each other down the corridors. *Standard twin ¥168; sgl/double ¥238; deluxe twin ¥218.*

⌂ **Zhongwei Dajiudian** 中卫大酒店 (110 rooms) 53 Gulou Bei Jie; ✆ 0955 7025 555; 📠 0955 7028 829. Not to be confused with the hotel above, this four-star hotel is opposite the Gaomiao entrance on Guluo Bei Jie. Spick-and-span with friendly staff and a counter for the even more useful Ningxia Desert Travel Service (see above). All rooms en suite, 24hr hot water, free ethernet connection and free breakfast. *Standard twin ¥290; sgl or double ¥255; room by the hour ¥80.*

⌂ **Zhongying Jiudian** 中影酒店 (40 rooms) 100m down Gulou Nan Jie; ✆ 0953 7091 518; 📠 0953 7091 550. A nice clean hotel, although the rooms are small. All rooms en suite. Restaurant serves buffet breakfast (not included in the room price). *Standard twin ¥130; sgl/double ¥90; trpl ¥160; deluxe twin ¥180; by the hour ¥20.*

⌂ **Zhuoyue Dajiudian** 卓越大酒店 (56 rooms) Gulou Dong Jie; ✆ 0955 7037 999; 📠 0955 7022 628. Opened in 2004, this very clean hotel is halfway between the bus station and the Drum Tower. Friendly staff. *Standard twin ¥268; common twin ¥228; sgl ¥188.*

Zhongwei is hardly the centre of fine dining, but you can still eat well and cheaply here. A number of small restaurants, teahouses, and fruit stalls line the busy little street of Shangye north and south. There is also a lively night market running between Shangye Nan Jie and Gulou Nan Jie, where you can get the usual bowls of noodles, skewers of lamb and fried anything. Two recommended restaurants ares:

✗ **Laomao Shouzhua Mei Shi Lou** 老毛手抓美食楼 Gulou Dong Jie; ✆ 0955 7012 207. Established in 1915, this Muslim restaurant is cheap, cheerful and busy: a sign of good food.

✗ **Jinwei Minzu Fandian** 金味民族饭店 Shangye Nan Xiang. Pleasant little Muslim restaurant with great Yellow River fish, with meat and aubergines (qiézi shāo niányú 茄子烧鲇鱼) for ¥28.

WHAT TO SEE AND DO Shāpōtóu 沙坡头 Most Chinese come to Zhongwei to go to nearby **Shapatou Yellow River Entertainment Park.** The brochures claim that it is Ningxia's version of a seaside resort. It definitely has the feel of a resort or

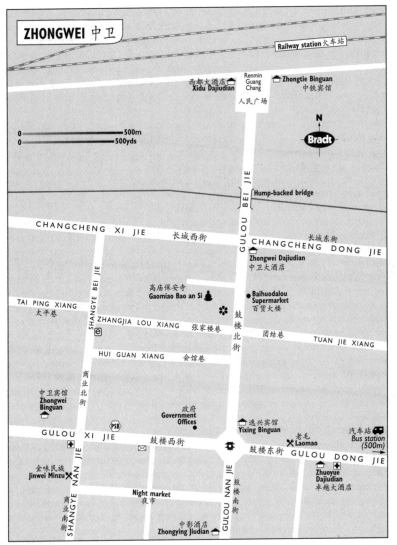

amusement park, but the only place to swim is in the outdoor pool (which doesn't always look much cleaner than the Yellow River). The park is divided into the north and south sides of the river. The north side is the more engaging, although the south side, accessible by a footbridge over the river, is more peaceful and there isn't really anything there except a small pagoda above the dunes. A small gate two-thirds of the way down the bridge is sometimes locked, but for the nimble is easy enough to get over.

The main gate to the north side is at the top of the road, where there is a big map of the area and a few small shops. From the top you can either slide down the river bank dune on a tray for ¥20 or just walk down the sand. The zip line might start at the top of the riverbank but you in fact have to buy your ticket (¥60) at the bottom of the riverbank and then you can take the chairlift back up.

Other amusements include a camel ride for ¥15 from the bottom of the riverbank to the top, where you are left to buy a slide tray back down, or walk. Motorboat rides are available for a variety of prices depending on numbers in the boat and length of the ride, while jetskis and parasailing cost ¥100 each. Sheepskin rafts down the river to Zhongwei (2½ hours) cost ¥100, or a full-day ride can cost up to ¥480. The sheepskin rafts are approximately 4m², made of a wooden platform tied to some 16 inflated sheepskins, which do look just like sheep without the head and legs!

Accommodation is available inside the park on the north bank at **Shapo Shanzhuang** 沙坡山庄 (11 rooms) (*(' 0955 7689 073; f 0955 7689 380)*. There are basic two- and three-bed rooms en suite with TV, but only two hours of hot water per day, according to when most guests might want it.

Next to the Shapo Shanzhuang is a small outdoor covered restaurant called **Small Eat Street** Xiao Chi Jie where you can get bowls of soup noodles as well as the usual slew of basic dishes. Also sells cold drinks.

Further north of the main entrance, the road and the railway, is the entrance to the Tengger Desert side of the park. The main path into the desert has a number of explanation boards (in Chinese) on the reclamation work on the desert. The path passes a camel ranch, dune buggy park, another dune slide and a mud mock-up of a Great Wall fire beacon decorated with camel skulls. Beyond this is the Tengger Desert itself and Inner Mongolia. Camel rides can be taken further into the desert. For a good view of the desert and across the Yellow River, climb up the steps of the small lookout tower to the east of the amusements. During peak periods, there is also a small restaurant on the Tengger side of the park.

To get to Shapatou, minibuses leave Zhongwei bus station regularly for ¥3.5, or take a taxi for ¥30. Returning taxis cost ¥40 if the stalls at the north entrance need to call one for you. Entry to the north and south sides of the park costs ¥35 separately, or ¥65 together. If you stay at Shapo Shanzhuang, you will need to pay the entry fee once to get in, but not again the next day.

Desert Research Field Centre (Shāmò Yánjiū Zhōngxīn 沙漠研究中心) Exiting the gateway at the bottom of the riverbank is the Chinese Academy of Sciences Desert Research Centre *(' 0955 7093 456)*. This small centre is the field branch of its headquarters in Lanzhou. There are a couple of exhibits of desert reclamation and cabinets full of moth-eaten, stuffed local birds and mammals. At the time of writing, the exhibitions were all in Chinese, but if you are really interested in the work of the centre, then you may find an English-speaking researcher inside who might be able to answer some of your questions.

Changtan Village Waterwheel (Chángtān Shuǐchē 长滩水车) West of Shapatou at the village of Changtan on the south bank of the Yellow River is a working waterwheel from the 18th century. The village itself is one of the few left in China that still has no electricity, a sign of the enormous work which still needs to be done in so much of the country (it would take about ¥10,000 to bring electricity to the village). As a local attraction, the waterwheel is helping to boost the local economy through tourism. A sheepskin raft journey from the village to Shapatou through the white water rapids of the Yellow River takes about three hours and can be arranged through Ningxia Desert Travel Services for ¥200–250 per person for between two and five people.

Xiàhéyán 下河沿 This section of the Great Wall runs south of the Yellow River. It is thoroughly abandoned and families who used to live in cave huts within the wall

up to about ten years ago have been moved out after explosives use in the nearby coal mines made their living quarters unsafe. This stretch of wall runs for about 5km starting in Xiaheyan village and running southwest, crossing the Xin–Shang natural gas pipeline just west of the village. The Xin–Shang gas pipeline pipes natural gas all the way from Xinjiang to Shanghai in one of those amazing Chinese engineering feats of modern times. (Two more from the past few decades are the Three Gorges Dam and the Yangtze to Yellow River canal.) At the point where the Xin–Shang pipeline crosses the Great Wall (kilometre 1,996 of the pipeline) the builders simply bulldozed through the six-century-old rammed earth wall leaving a large gap for all to see. On the hill at the western end of the village is a semi-abandoned Buddhist temple with skeletal formations of what were to become Boddhisattvas. Villagers were also trying to erect a giant Buddha in front of the temple, but this too has been abandoned. To get to Xiayehan take a bus from Zhongwei bus station or a taxi for ¥70. Ningxia Desert Travel Service (see page 232) can also arrange transport and guiding.

Tengger Desert (Ténggélǐ Shāmò 滕格里沙漠) One-day or multi-day trips into the Tengger Desert can be arranged by any of the travel services on page 232. Costs start at ¥230 per person per day including camel, all food and drink and overnight accommodation in tents.

11

12

Gansu 甘肃

Jiayuguan is an ancient place, and for China a significant one. In the desert to the west lies the Last Gate Under Heaven, marking the end of the Great Wall and the beginning of the barbarian lands beyond.

Stanley Stewart

Gansu province is a long piece of land sandwiched between the Qinghai Plateau and the Inner Mongolian deserts. More commonly known as the Gansu Corridor (or Héxi 河西 in Chinese, meaning region west of the Yellow River), it links Shaanxi and Ningxia in the east with Xinjiang in the west. Through this corridor ran the trading route known today as the Silk Road. Silk, teas and fine bone china exited the Middle Kingdom via this route to the barbarian western regions, and tributes of or trade in spice, glass and other goods entered along the same route. Owing to the importance of the Gansu Corridor for trade, a Great Wall has protected the Silk Road from as early as 3BC. The furthest extension of the Great Wall was built on the orders of Emperor Wu of the western Han dynasty, when the wall was extended from Lanzhou, now the capital of Gansu, to Lop Nor in Xinjiang. The Ming emperors rebuilt the Gansu Corridor Great Wall only as far as Jiayuguan, where the wall ends at the famous Jiayu Gate, also known as the Last Gate Under Heaven. Very little remains of the inner wall extension from Ningxia autonomous region into Gansu province. Lanzhou city, which the inner wall originally incorporated in its defences, is now a sprawling industrial metropolis, and any remains of the Great Wall have been destroyed to make way for the expansion of the city. Most visitors to the Gansu wall fly or train straight into Jiayuguan, which, while not exactly picturesque, is quaint enough and very manageable.

THE GANSU OUTER WALL

The Gansu Ming outer wall emerges from Heishan Gorge into Gansu province and continues southwest to Jingtai (also known as Yitiaoshan) before heading northwest to Wuwei, Minqin, Zhangye, Jinta, Jiuquan and finally the last outpost of Jiayuguan. These towns were originally the garrison towns that were built up with elements of government in order to protect the Silk Road and provide soldiers to combat invaders beyond the Great Wall.

WUWEI 武威

Originally called Liangzhou, the town of Wuwei, meaning 'powerful' was developed by General Huo Qubing of the Han dynasty after conquering the Gansu Corridor in 2BC.

Hami,
Urumqi
哈密,乌鲁木齐

XINJIANG
新疆

额济纳旗
EJI NAQI

LIUYUAN
柳园

ANXI 安西

悬壁
Xuanbi

嘉峪关
Jiayu Guan

Yumen Guan
玉门关

DUNHUANG
敦煌

玉门 YUMEN

Di Yi Lou
第一楼

JIAYUGUAN 嘉峪关
JIUQUAN
酒泉

AKEZHAI
阿克寨

Sanchakou
三岔口

Qilian Shan
5,564m
祁连山

ZHANGYE
张掖

Yaisha Shan,
Kashgar

Tuanjie Feng
5826m
团结峰

岗格尔肖合力
Gang Ge'er
Xiao Heli
5174m

5020m

天峻
TIANJUN

青海湖
Qinghai Lake
3266m

都兰
DULAN

格尔木
GE'ERMU (GOLMUD)

QINGHAI
青海

黄河
Huang He

Wudaoliang
五道梁

黄河

N

Bradt

Kunlun Pass,
Tanggula Pass,
Lhasa

Huang He

0 — 200km
0 — 150 miles

GANSU PROVINCE 甘肃省

四川
SICHUAN

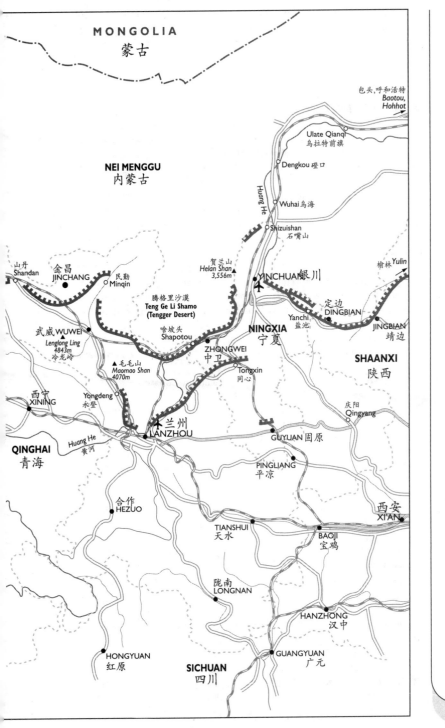

Today, Wuwei is a pleasant enough little town, although it doesn't really live up to its cultural heritage. The symbol of Gansu, the flying horse, was found in Leitai Temple just north of the town, but this significant historical fact is not enough to hold the attention in this otherwise very average temple.

Nevertheless, Wuwei is a fine stopping point in the long journey to Jiayuguan if you have the luxury of time to do so.

GETTING THERE AND AROUND Wuwei is served by a train station and plenty of buses. There is one Wuwei–Zhongwei **train** for which you could get seats, leaving Zhongwei at 15.45 and arriving in Wuwei at 22.30, leaving Wuwei at 07.15 and arriving in Zhongwei at 13.45. All other trains passing through these towns are difficult if not impossible to get tickets for, but if you go through a travel agent you might get lucky.

Buses to and from Yinchuan are three a day (ten hours, ¥86). Buses to Zhangye leave every half-hour 07.00–17.00 (three to four hours, ¥43). Buses to Lanzhou leave every hour, and to Zhongwei or Jiayuguan every two hours. There is one bus a day to Dunhuan and Urumqi. If you are asked for travel and or life **insurance** (lǚyóu bǎoxiǎn 旅游保险) when buying tickets, then you will need to go to the China Life Insurance Company Zhōngguó Rénshòu Bǎoxiǎn Gōngsī 中国人寿保险公司 on Nan Da Jie, or (preferably) try to buy it at the travel office/business centre in your hotel if you are staying in one of the bigger establishments. China Life, open daily, is generally very busy in the mornings, and it can take up to two hours to purchase the required insurance. This is likely to be abolished soon in line with other provinces in China.

A **map** of Wuwei town (in Chinese) with a map of Wuwei county and scenic spots on the back is available at street kiosks for ¥5.

The **PSB** is on Dong Da Jie, just east of Wenhua Square.

MONEY AND COMMUNICATION The main branch of the Bank of China is conveniently located at the western end of the pedestrian zone. It changes travellers' cheques and foreign currency and has an **ATM**; open daily 08.30–18.00. Other branches of the Bank of China also change currency.

Two **internet** bars, Xiàntōng Wǎngshàng Shìjiè 线通网上世界 and Zhǐménshā Wǎngba 指门沙网吧, are at the western end of Minsheng Xiang.

🏠 **WHERE TO STAY AND EAT** Wuwei is not renowned for its quality cheap hotels, but now that foreigners can stay almost anywhere, many cheaper places are available. Lots of places of different prices can be found on the pedestrian zone, which has the advantage of being relatively quiet, especially at night. See the *Accommodation* section (pages 90–92) for the Chinese characters to look out for, or try the following:

🏠 **Tianma Binguan** 天马宾馆 (260 rooms) Xixiao Shizi; ☎ 0935 2212 355; 📠 0935 2212 356. Big but friendly three-star hotel, even open when you come in on the late-night bus. Located at the west end of the pedestrian zone, it is close to shops and amenities, and rooms are not too noisy. Clean and serviced, with cheaper rooms in the north tower than in the main tower. All rooms en suite with 24-hour hot water. Sauna, steam baths and massage parlour on site. A good Chinese buffet breakfast serving coffee is included in the room price. *Standard twin ¥168–488; dbl ¥288; quadruple ¥80.*

🏠 **Lantian Fandian** 蓝天饭店 (40 rooms) Nan Da Jie; ☎ 0935 2258 981. Clean, cheap and cheerful. All rooms are en suite with TV and AC. *dbl suite ¥120; standard twin ¥100; sgl ¥60; common twin ¥40; trpl ¥45.*

🏠 **Tianyuan Zhaodaisuo** 天源招待所 (27 rooms) Buxing Shangye Jie; ☎ 0935 6978 342. This tiny friendly little guesthouse is just off the pedestrian zone. Clean quiet rooms, all en suite. *Dbl suite ¥160; standard twin ¥60; common twin ¥40; trpl ¥100.*

⌂ **Huafeng Fandian** 华丰饭店 (60 rooms) Western end of Buxing Shangye Jie pedestrian zone; ☏ 0935 6978 008. Basic rooms and dorms with 24-hour hot water around a courtyard car park. *Standard twin en suite ¥88. All other rooms use communal bathrooms: twin ¥17; trpl ¥51; quadruple ¥52.*

Fine dining is not exactly Wuwei's forte (yet). Lots of places to eat as well as coffeebars on Shengli Jie are upstairs and not at all obvious from the street level. Minsheng Xiang has a number of cheap places selling the usual noodles and basic fare. More upmarket places can be found on Nan Dajie. Try **Yining Zhai** *(109 Nan Da Jie; ☏ 0935 2212 498)*. Has good hotpot as well as other dishes.

WHAT TO SEE AND DO Wuwei's centre revolves around Culture Square Wénhuà Guǎngchǎng 文化广场, from which a pedestrian zone Bùxíng Shāngyè 步行商业 heads off west. The square is the centre of shops and strolling, has a massive bath and sauna centre, but not much in the way of eating. Within the town there are the usual pagodas (Luoshi, north of Culture Square) and museums (Wenmiao 文庙, Chinese artefacts housed in an old temple). North of the town is Leitai Temple, where the flying horse of Gansu was found in 1969 (now on display in Lanzhou Provincial Museum). To get there take bus 2 from anywhere on Nan or Bei Da Jie, but there's not much to visit without the horse. Entry to the impressively restored Nanmen 南门 southern gate costs ¥10. The remainder of the old town wall is non-existent, and unusually the **bell tower** is located to the northeast of the centre of the town. Its grounds alone are worth the ¥10 entry fee just for a bit of tranquillity and the flowers.

THE GREAT WALL AROUND WUWEI About an hour east of Wuwei the minor road from Zhongwei affords glimpses of a very neglected Ming wall north of the road. The main road west to Zhangye picks up the Ming wall again about an hour out of town, where it can be seen for over an hour of the journey. Several kilometres east of **Shandan** town, the road cuts through the wall, which then runs south of the road until Shandan, after which hardly any of it remains until the reconstructed sections at Jiayuguan. About half an hour east of Wuwei, a section of the wall can be seen at the aptly named town of **Changcheng** 长城 (meaning 'Great Wall' in case you have forgotten by now). A taxi to Changcheng costs ¥100 return.

Minqin 民勤 This former border outpost does not boast much as a town, but beyond the town are a number of fortified mansions from the former local warlords who were charged with keeping the border with Inner Mongolia under control. Although the Great Wall was built to encompass the small oasis town of Minqin, hardly any of it remains today. A small section can be seen outside the village of Xuebai, but it is not really worth the stop. An 80m section of the old town wall could still be seen outside the bus station at the time of writing, but new buildings are also planned for the site. Taxis to Rui An Bao 瑞安堡 fortified mansion cost ¥10 and entry is also ¥10. Buses to Minqin from Wuwei leave every 20 minutes (three hours, ¥11.50). Last bus back from Minqin is at 19.30.

If you get stuck in Minqin for the night or want to explore further, there are several hotels and guesthouses. Try the small friendly **Youpeng Binguan** 友鹏宾馆 (20 rooms) (☏ 0935 4121 686), a ten-minute walk south of the bus station on the southeast corner of the crossroads with Dong Da Jie. Suite with bathroom and 24-hour hot water ¥160; doubles and twins ¥60; single ¥48.

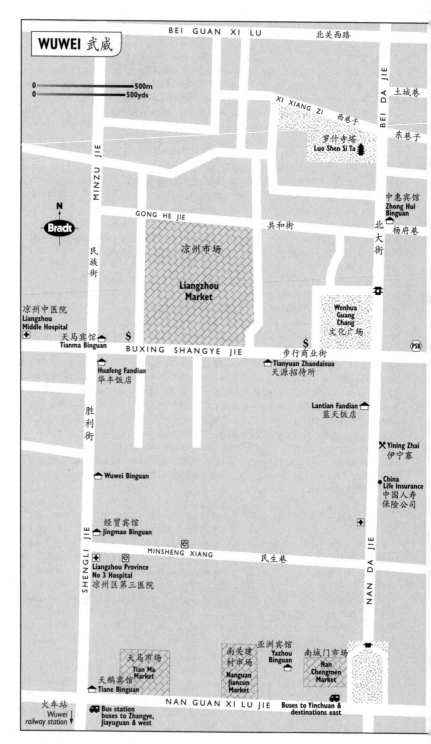

WUWEI 武威

0 ——————— 500m
0 ——————— 500yds

Bradt

N

BEI GUAN XI LU   北关西路

BEI DA JIE 北大街

土城巷

XI XIANG ZI   西巷子

东巷子

罗什寺塔
Luo Shen Si Ta

中惠宾馆
Zhong Hui
Binguan

MINZU JIE
民族街

GONG HE JIE   共和街

杨府巷

凉州市场

Liangzhou
Market

北大街

凉州中医院
Liangzhou
Middle Hospital

天马宾馆
Tianma Binguan

$

Wenhua
Guang
Chang
文化广场

(PSB)

BUXING SHANGYE JIE   步行商业街

$

Tianyuan Zhaodaisuo
天源招待所

Huafeng Fandian
华丰饭店

Lantian Fandian
蓝天饭店

胜
利
街

Yining Zhai
伊宁寨

Wuwei Binguan

China
Life Insurance
中国人寿
保险公司

经贸宾馆
Jingmao Binguan

SHENGLI JIE

MINSHENG XIANG   民生巷

Liangzhou Province
No 3 Hospital
凉州区第三医院

NAN DA JIE

天马市场
Tian Ma
Market

南关建
村市场
Nanguan
Jiancun
Market

亚洲宾馆
Yazhou
Binguan

南城门市场
Nan
Chengmen
Market

天鹅宾馆
Tiane Binguan

火车站
Wuwei
railway station

Bus station
buses to Zhangye,
Jiayuguan & west

NAN GUAN XI LU JIE

Buses to Yinchuan &
destinations east

242

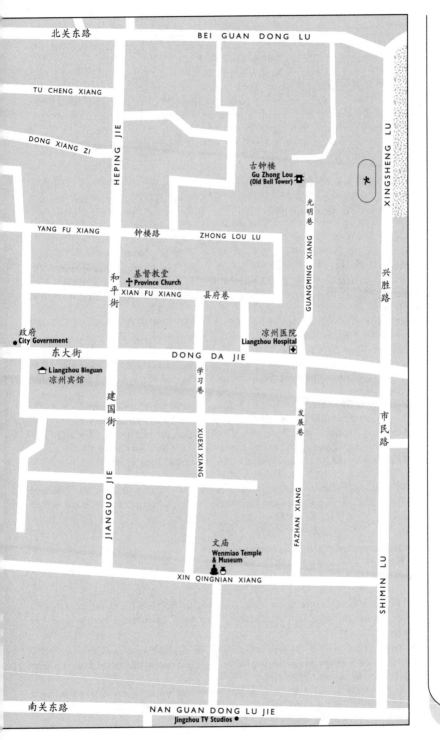

北关东路 BEI GUAN DONG LU

TU CHENG XIANG

DONG XIANG ZI

HE PING JIE

古钟楼
Gu Zhong Lou
(Old Bell Tower)

光明巷
GUANGMING XIANG

XINGSHENG LU

兴胜路

YANG FU XIANG

钟楼路 ZHONG LOU LU

基督教堂
† Province Church

和平街

XIAN FU XIANG 县府巷

政府
● City Government

凉州医院
Liangzhou Hospital

东大街 DONG DA JIE

Liangzhou Binguan
凉州宾馆

建国街

学习巷

XUEXI XIANG

发展巷

FAZHAN XIANG

市民路

JIANGUO JIE

文庙
Wenmiao Temple
& Museum

SHIMIN LU JIE

XIN QINGNIAN XIANG

南关东路 NAN GUAN DONG LU JIE
Jingzhou TV Studios ●

Originally named Ganzhou back in the centuries BC, Zhangye became the garrison headquarters after General Huo established control of the corridor. The town was part of the western Xia dynasty from 1098 until Kublai Khan conquered it in 1227. Shortly after that Marco Polo visited. Leafy and cool, the town is a joyful break in the journey west towards Jiayuguan or beyond. Today the town has a lively, can-do feel about it, graced with a number of temples, parks, outdoor eateries, good-value hotels and some attractive Ming-/Qing-imitation streets. The town is also the connection point for a trip to the Tibetan monastery of Mati in the Qilian Mountain foothills.

GETTING THERE AND AROUND Zhangye has three **bus** stations:
East bus station on Huai Cheng Dong Lu (*℡ 0936 8214 073)*, serves buses to and from Wuwei, Yinchuan and other places east. Buses to and from Wuwei leave every hour (three hours, ¥43). Wuwei is the last stop of the overnight bus from Yinchuan (three per day, ¥106).
South bus station on Huai Cheng Nan Jie (*℡ 0936 8240 019)*, serves buses to Lanzhou, Jiayuguan, Matisi and other places south. There are three sleeper buses to Lanzhou, leaving at 19.30, 20.00 and 20.30 (ten hours, ¥108). Four buses a day make the journey to Jiayuguan, leaving at 07.30, 09.30, 10.30 and 11.30 (four hours, ¥46). For buses to Matisi see page 249.
West bus station on Huai Cheng Xi Lu (*℡ 0936 8204 573)* serves buses to and from the west. Buses from the east travelling further west will also stop here.

As with Wuwei, travelling here by **train** is, sadly, not very convenient, but nevertheless possible. The train station at the end of Zhanghuo Gonglu (*℡ 0936 5972 222)* is 8km northeast of the town, and at the end of bus lines 1 and 2 serving the town centre.

Zhangye is just about small enough to walk to all the main sites and stations if you are staying around the bell tower. Or **taxis** cost ¥3 and **rickshaws** ¥2.

Maps of Zhangye (in Chinese) with other local towns on the back (Minle, Gaotai, Shandan, Linfeng and Lunan) are available in local kiosks for ¥3.

The **PSB** is on Qingnian Xi Jie, just east of Central Square.

MONEY AND COMMUNICATION The Bank of China on Xianfu Jie near the Zhangye Binguan 张掖宾馆 changes travellers' cheques and foreign currency and has an **ATM**. Open daily 08.30–18.00.

Internet bars are many, all for ¥2 per hour:

Rendezvous Internet Café 相约网吧 Xi Jie, opposite the post office.
Xijie Wangba 西街网吧 Xi Jie, near the west bus station.
Xingyun Wangba 幸运网吧 Minsheng Dong Jie, just west of the town market.

WHERE TO STAY Zhangye has a lot of good-value hotels around the central bell tower, although as usual these suffer from a lot of noise if rooms face the streets.

🏠 **Honghao Binguan** 泓昊宾馆 (90 rooms) 11 Xianfu Jie; ℡ 0936 8250 588. A very new hotel between the lively Central Square and the eating pedestrian zone, Qing Ming Jie. Bright, clean rooms and friendly staff. All rooms en suite, but no breakfast. *Standard twin ¥188; trpl ¥168.*

🏠 **Huayi Binguan** 华谊宾馆 (57 rooms) Dong Jie, 200m from the Drum Tower on the north side of the street, east of Little Eat Market Xiao Chi Chang; ℡ 0936 8242 118. A new, if bijou hotel, conveniently centrally located. All rooms en suite, no breakfast. *Standard twin ¥98; common twin ¥68.*

🏠 **Jindu Binguan** 金都宾馆 (139 rooms) 19 Dong Jie; ☎ 0936 8245 088; 📠 0936 8245 122. Bright clean hotel opposite Little Eat Market Xiao Chi Chang. All rooms have AC, en suite and 24hr hot water. Sauna, steam bath andmassage parlour on site. Breakfast included. *Suite: dbl or twin ¥200; standard twin or sgl ¥148; trpl ¥155.*

🏠 **Jinxin Binguan** 金鑫宾馆 (45 rooms) Bei Jie, 100m north of the Drum Tower; ☎ 0936 8210 178. Another very nice new hotel. Opposite the lively Bei Jie Square. All rooms en suite with 24hr hot water. No breakfast. *Standard twin ¥128; standard sgls and common twins ¥118; trpl ¥108.*

🏠 **Yingbinlou Binguan** 迎宾楼宾馆 (26 rooms) 11 Nan Da Jie; ☎ 0936 8230 140. This small hotel is the front building of a large communist courtyard hotel, the remainder of which is still the cheaper but less attractive Ganzhou Binguan. Under new management, the hotel is bright, cheerful and welcoming. Rooms facing the road have a small enclosed balcony/tea room with sliding doors which do help to block out some of the noise from the road. Rock-hard mattresses. All rooms have AC and en suite, but hot water only 17.00–22.00. Breakfast (standard Chinese) and lunch included in the price of your room. *Deluxe twin (with balcony area) ¥148; standard twin ¥108; trpls ¥125; quadruples ¥160.*

🏠 **Zhangye Binguan** 张掖宾馆 (220 rooms) 56 Xianfu Jie; ☎ 0936 8212 601; 📠 0936 8213 806. By far the largest hotel in town and popular with tour groups. A three-star Chinese hotel with intriguing concrete and tile ornamental garden in the centre of the hotel complex. Conveniently close to the Sleeping Buddha Temple and Central Park. *Standard twin or sgl ¥380.*

🏠 **Zhongguang Zhaodaisuo** 中广招待所 (40 rooms) Xianfu Jie, on the south corner with Minsheng Xi Jie; ☎ 0936 5985 449. Very simple guesthouse on the second floor. Friendly and clean. All rooms share communal showering facilities with 24-hour hot water. *Twin room ¥30.*

WHERE TO EAT Zhangye has the usual abundance of eating places, but two areas stand out: Qing Ming Jie 明清街 and Little Eat Market Xiǎo Chǐ Chǎng 小吃厂. Qing Ming Jie is a pedestrian street built in imitation Ming and Qing style. Extending all the way up to Zhongshan Park, the shops along the street are a mix of restaurants, clothes' boutiques and little supermarkets. Busy until late in the evening, the street is popular just for a stroll or as a place to go out to eat. Xiao Chi Chang is a small covered market with stalls selling different foods from around China. Very popular are the sand pots (shā guō 沙锅), a mix of clear broth with mung bean noodles (fěntiáo 粉条), tofu skin strips (yóupí 油皮), seaweed, vegetables and your choice of meat all cooked over a gas flame in the same pot it is served to you in. There are also bowls of 'rubbed fish noodles' (cūoyúmiàn 搓鱼面), a tasty bowl of inch-long noodle strips alongside a plate of fish-flavoured pork and vegetables. Many of the other usual favourites are also sold at Little Eat Market, including water dumplings (shuǐjiǎo 水饺), beef noodles (niúròu miàn 牛肉面) and wonton soup (húntun 馄饨).

There are also several up-and-coming tea and coffee houses which make pleasant bars in the evening. A good centrally located one is **Haagen Coffee Shop** (☎ 0936 8212 899) on the southwest corner of the Gulou roundabout. Doesn't serve HäagenDazs ice cream, but many other delights beside, including a decent coffee and a well-stocked bar. Big red sofas look out of this second-floor curved café onto the Drum Tower. *(Open 09.30–02.00.)*

Other tea/coffee houses/bars can be found on Minsheng Xi Jie.

WHAT TO SEE AND DO Zhangye is a great town just to walk around and hang out in. The centre of town is marked by the large **Drum Tower** Gulou; unfortunately none of the town gates has survived. North of the Drum Tower along the length of Bei Jie is a park and marketplace selling all sorts of wares and clothes. Several streets (Minsheng Xi Jie, Dafo Jie and Qing Ming Jie) have successfully recreated the old Chinese style of red-columned covered walkways, making

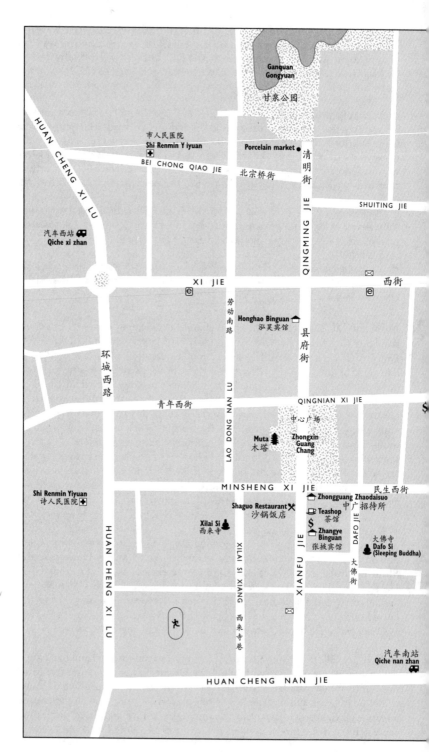

Ganquan
Gongyuan
甘泉公园

市人民医院
Shi Renmin Y iyuan

Porcelain market ●

清明街
QINGMING JIE

BEI CHONG QIAO JIE
北宗桥街

SHUITING JIE

汽车西站
Qiche xi zhan

环城西路

HUAN CHENG XI LU

XI JIE

西街

劳动南路
LAO DONG NAN LU

Honghao Binguan
泓昊宾馆

县府街

QINGNIAN XI JIE

青年西街

中心广场

Muta
木塔

Zhongxin
Guang
Chang

$

MINSHENG XI JIE

民生西街

Shi Renmin Yiyuan
诗人民医院

Shaguo Restaurant
沙锅饭店

Zhongguang Zhaodaisuo
中广招待所

Teashop
茶馆

Xilai Si
西来寺

$ Zhangye
Binguan
张掖宾馆

DAFO JIE

大佛寺
Dafo Si
(Sleeping Buddha)

大佛街

XILAI SI XIANG

西来寺巷

XIANFU JIE

汽车南站
Qiche nan zhan

HUAN CHENG XI LU

HUAN CHENG NAN JIE

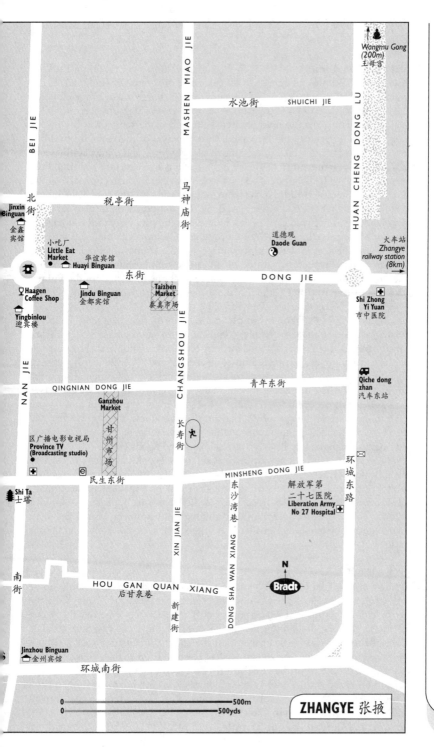

BEI JIE
北街

马神庙街
MASHEN MIAO JIE

水池街 SHUICHI JIE

HUAN CHENG DONG LU

Wangmu Gong
(200m)
王母宫

税亭街

Jinxin
Binguan
金鑫
宾馆

小吃厂
Little Eat
Market

华谊宾馆
Huayi Binguan

道德观
Daode Guan

火车站
Zhangye
railway station
(8km)

东街 DONG JIE

Haagen
Coffee Shop

Jindu Binguan
金都宾馆

Taizhen
Market
泰真市场

Shi Zhong
Yi Yuan
市中医院

Yingbinlou
迎宾楼

NAN JIE

QINGNIAN DONG JIE

CHANGSHOU JIE

青年东街

Qiche dong
zhan
汽车东站

Ganzhou
Market

甘州市场

长寿街

区广播电影电视局
Province TV
(Broadcasting studio)

民生东街 MINSHENG DONG JIE

环城东路

Shi Ta
土塔

XIN JIAN JIE

东沙湾巷
DONG SHA WAN XIANG

解放军第
二十七医院
Liberation Army
No 27 Hospital

N

南街

HOU GAN QUAN XIANG
后甘泉巷

新建街

Bradt

Jinzhou Binguan
金州宾馆

环城南街

0 ———————— 500m
0 ———————— 500yds

ZHANGYE 张掖

Gansu 甘肃 ZHANGYE 张掖

12

247

them very pleasant to walk through. A number of other squares and parks also grace the town.

Great Buddha Temple Dàfósì 大佛寺 contains the largest reclining Buddha in Asia. At 34.5m long and almost 1,000 years old, this statue of Buddha is really quite unique. The temple was originally built in 1098, the first year of the emperor of the western Xia dynasty (see page 26). After the western Xia were overthrown by Kublai Khan of the Yuan dynasty, Marco Polo visited the temple on his travels through China to Beijing, and remarked on the marvel of the reclining Buddha. The temple also contains some interesting displays of Ming and Qing paintings and scrolls, as well as the most complete set of Ming dynasty imperial Buddhist scripture. Of the 6,000 volumes of text padlocked away in wooden cupboards at the back of the **Palace of Buddhist Scriptures**, only a few are on display, including one of the gold copies of 600 of the scriptures. The scriptures on display are quite underwhelming even if you can speak Chinese, but the simplicity of the storage of such great historical relics defies Western thinking. Other palaces take you through the history of the region with pictures, maps and the scantest of English. At the back of the temple is the earth stupa, which can be seen prominently from South Boulevard Nan Jie. Visit late in the afternoon to catch the full length of the **Palace of the Reclining Buddha** bathed in the evening sun. *(Open 07.30–18.30 in the summer, 08.00–18.00 in the winter. Entry ¥30.)*

Dàodéguàn 道德观 **Daoist temple** on the north side of Dong Jie is an exquisite example of a Daoist temple, complete with Dao teachers. Set back from the main street down a short hútòng, this tiny temple was completely renovated in 2005. Its usual courtyard structure houses an array of gods (heaven, earth and sea), the god of mercy Guanyin, teacher Lao Zi, and the temple to women around the central incense burner displaying the Yin, Yang and eight-diagram revelations (see pages 44–45 for more on Daoism). Entry is free, and if you slip a bit of money into the red money box by the side of your favourite god/goddess, the Dao teacher will gong a bell for you. The temple is open when the door is open.

Zhongxin Guangchang 中心广场 and the **Wooden Pagoda** (Mùtǎ 木塔) opposite each other on Shengfu Jie is a lively place at all hours. People come here to exercise in the mornings, fly fantastic kites during the day, and dance and sing in the evening.

North of the pedestrian Qing Ming Jie is the **porcelain market** at the entrance to the town park Gānquán Gōngyuán 甘泉公园. Here you can pick up a couple of enormous china vases for under ¥4,000, although just how you would get them home is another matter. Many smaller beautiful bowls, teapots, tea mugs and plates are also available.

AROUND ZHANGYE

Horse Hoof Temple (Mǎtí Sì 马蹄寺) **and the Qilian Mountains** In the foothills of the permanently snowcapped Qilian Mountains, some 60km south of Zhangye, are the Tibetan hanging temples of Mati (horse hoof). The temples received this name after the large horse hoof imprints in the floor of the main cave/temple. The temples themselves rival those of the original Hanging Temple (see page 201), but were closed to visitors during 2005 for safety reasons. Even so the site is a wonder to see from the bottom of the cliffs and they are due to reopen in 2006. Over 70 grottoes, stupas and shrines adorn almost 2km of cliff walls, and many more hide in the forests and hills of the Qilian Mountains. The Daoist temple of **Lower, Middle and Upper Guanyin Caves** (Xià, Zhōng, Shàng Guānyīn Dòng 下，中，上观音洞) and **Golden Pagoda Temple** (Jīntǎ Sì 金塔寺) can be reached within a few hours, but Tibetan ponies are also available to speed you effortlessly up the mountain paths (saddle sore aside). A ten-minute ride to **Sword Split Stone** (which stands up in a field not far from the Tibetan restaurant tents) costs ¥20. Half an hour to the waterfall or Orchid Garden holiday village costs ¥50. One hour to Guanyin Dong costs ¥150 and 75 minutes to Golden Pagoda Temple costs ¥200. Remember to account for the time you stay at the site and of your return journey when planning to go up into the hills by horse.

The path up the hill to the mountain sites goes past a dozen or so large and small Tibetan-style tents, complete with Tibetan-clothed attendants, serving food and beverages; TV and karaoke are also available. For a more standard experience, try the tiny restaurant between the roundabout/car park and Crouching Dragon Mountain Lodge. Serves good cumin lamb (zīrán yángròu 孜然羊肉), fried noodles (chǎo miàn 炒面) with vegetables, and salt tea (well, perhaps the tea is not so good; it tastes soft, like it has soap in it).

Although the site can be visited in a day from Zhangye, an overnight stay or several in the wòlóngshānzhuāng 卧龙山庄 Crouching Dragon Mountain Lodge (20 rooms) (✆ 0936 8891 694 or 135 1936 9728) is worth it if you really want to explore the mountain range at some length. Limited hot water. *(Suite ¥200; standard twin ¥120; triple ¥100; quadruple ¥20 per bed.)*

Mati Si lies at almost 2,500m above sea level and the air and water descending from the 5,000m+ mountains can be cold, so wrap up warm for the evenings, even in the summer, and especially as the hotel is not heated in the summer. Like all high mountains, the Qilian are typical afternoon cloud creators, so get your hiking done early in the day, or go out prepared if you are staying out late or overnight.

To travel the 60km to Mati, there are only two direct buses a day from Zhangye South bus station, leaving at 08.00 and 15.00 (up to three hours, ¥9) This is only in part because of the 1,500m elevation between the two sites, and mostly because of the number of stops made in between. Direct return buses leave at 07.00 and 16.00. Almost every half an hour in between these times buses run to Nángǔ 南古 from Zhangye and stop at Mǎtíhé 马蹄河 , from where you can take a taxi for ¥10 to the temple hamlet. A return motorbike coast back down to Matihe (engine off!) can be bargained down to ¥8 per person. The last bus from Matihe is at 16.00.

JIAYUGUAN 嘉峪关

Jiayuguan, the final frontier of the Ming dynasty wall, is where the Ming built their 'Last Gate Under Heaven'.

GETTING THERE AND AROUND There is a small airport 13km northeast of Jiayuguan. At the time of writing it no longer served **flights** in and out of Beijing. Its only daily flight was to Xian via Lanzhou, which arrives too late in Lanzhou to be able to connect with a flight to Beijing. Flight to or from Lanzhou costs ¥560, to Xian ¥780. It is worth checking with a CAAC office to see whether there have been any changes to this limiting schedule. As usual, most hotels can arrange plane and train tickets for you, and the local CAAC office (✆ 0937 6226 237) is at 4-3 Xinhua Nan Lu, just south of the roundabout.

Trains to and from Jiayuguan are fairly regular, but it's almost impossible to get soft sleeper tickets owing to the pre-booking of tickets months in advance by travel agents serving foreign tour groups. There are two overnight trains to Lanzhou from Xian leaving at 17.00 and 20.15, both arriving around 06.30 the next day. It is easier to get tickets for the earlier slower train. The train station is in the southwest of the town.

The long-distance **bus** station is on Lanhua Xi Lu. Buses to and from Zhangye are hourly in the morning.

Although Jiayuguan's population is relatively small, the town itself is spread out over a large area. There is no heart to the city, having a small compact centre, but all the streets are wide and long. As a result walking around town can become tiring and boring quite quickly. **City buses** are not many, however, in this sparsely populated large town. Most usefully to foreign travellers, bus 1 goes to and from the train station via Xiongguan Square and along Xinhua Lu. There is no city bus to any of the Great Wall sites. Flag fall for taxis is ¥6. A taxi to Jiayuguan fort is ¥10.

A **map** of the town (in Chinese and without bus routes) is available at street kiosks for ¥5.

The **PSB** is at Xinhua Nanlu where it cross Highway 312. If you find you are still in need of Gansu life insurance by the time you use this guidebook, then the PICC **insurance office** is on Xinhua Zhong Lu.

MONEY AND COMMUNICATION There are several ATMs in Jiayuguan and many of the big hotels will accept credit cards and exchange travellers' cheques. The main branch of the Bank of China, on Xinhua Zhonglu, also exchanges travellers' cheques and can provide you with cash from your credit card (but not debit card).

The main post office is on Xinhua Bei Lu, opposite the Jiayuguan Hotel. There is also a 24-hour China Telecom internet café in the same building. Some of the many other internet cafés in town include:

Judian Wangba 聚典网吧 Lanxin Xi Lu, next to the bus station. ¥3 per hour.

Hongfei Wangba 宏飞网吧 Xinhua Bei Lu. Big comfy chairs for spending lots of time on in front of your terminal. ¥3 per hour.

Yalong Wangcheng 轧龙网城 Xinhua Zhonglu. Head downstairs towards the snooker bar. ¥3 per hour.

WHERE TO STAY AND EAT Jiayuguan has long been developed as one of China's best tourist spots in the west of the country. Despite this, the town lags far behind most other provinces and even other cities in Gansu in opening up (or approving) budget accommodation for foreigners. This is largely because most tourists visit as part of a tour group and stay in luxurious four-star hotels. At the time of writing most hotels and guesthouses still refuse ('are not permitted to house') foreigners. This is likely to change by the Olympics and Gansu is bound to eventually follow the suit of other leading provinces in allowing foreigners to stay anywhere. In the mean time try the following:

Great Wall Hotel Chángchéng Bīnguǎn 长城宾馆 (166 rooms) 6 Jianshe Xi Lu; ☎ 0937 6225 288; 🖷 0937 6226 016; 🖃 info@cchotel.com; www.cchotel.com. This mock fort of a hotel looks more like it should belong in Las Vegas or Disneyland rather than on a very plain street in China. Supposedly a four star, it is not nearly as plush as a Las Vegas casino, however. Deterioration in hotel standards and the lack of travellers to this far-flung part of China mean that room prices in the hotel are often posted as half that of the brochure price. All rooms are en suite and include breakfast. Bike rental at ¥3 per hour just inside the hotel gates. Room prices listed here are the more expensive brochure prices. Accepts credit cards. Standard twin ¥560; deluxe ¥760.

Jiayuguan Binguan 嘉峪关宾馆 (180 rooms) 1 Xinhua Bei Lu; ☎ 0937 6226 983; 🖷 0937 6227 174; 🖃 jiayuguanbinguan@jiugang.com; www.jiayuguanhotel.com. This well-kept four star is very popular among tour groups. Western and Chinese restaurants available. All rooms en suite, with wireless internet (¥20 per day) available in rooms in the main building. Standard twin, dbl or sgl ¥568; trpl ¥600.

Xiongguan Binguan 雄关宾馆 (88 rooms) 31 Xinhua Zhong Lu; ☎ 0937 6201 116; 🖷 0937 6225 399. A two-star hotel

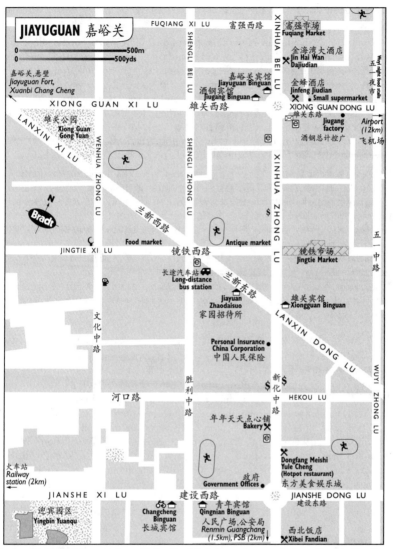

in what might be called the centre of town. The hotel is a little dark even after renovation but staff are friendly and rooms are well serviced. *Standard twin ¥140; trpl ¥100; quadruple ¥120. Dbl beds in the suite only, can be bargained down to ¥300.*

🏠 **Qingnian Binguan** 青年宾馆 (88 rooms) 4 Jianshe Xi Lu; ☎ 0937 6201 088. Despite its misleading-sounding name this hotel is not particularly oriented towards young people, especially not the backpack-toting-independent-traveller type. Nevertheless, a much cheaper alternative than the Great Wall Hotel next door. *Standard twins and sgls are en suite with breakfast ¥300; common twin en suite ¥190; trpl without bath ¥90.*

🏠 **Jiayuan Zhaodaisuo** 家园招待所 (17 rooms) 7 Lanxin Xi Lu, 50m east of the long-distance bus station; ☎ 0937 6284 130. Clean, friendly and cheap, on the fourth floor (no lift). Communal showers only. No breakfast. *Dbl or twin ¥40; trpl ¥60; quadruple ¥80.*

🏠 **Taihe Shan Zhuang** 太和山庄 (6 rooms) inside the grounds of the park around Jiayuguan fort, 100m west of the museum; ☎ 0937 6396 616. This beautiful little courtyard hotel and restaurant is well worth staying out of town for.

Aside from the tranquillity and beauty of the location, you also get to be the first and last during the day to visit the fort and its surroundings. Rooms are bijou, all en suite with 24-hr on-demand hot water. *Dbls/sgls ¥60; twins ¥80–100.*

Eating out in Jiayuguan is nothing exceptional. The usual noodle shops and restaurants can be found along Xinhua Lu, and a good **night market** on Wuyi Bei Lu with stalls selling Xinjiang style 'pulled' noodles lā miàn 拉面 (pulled from a round of noodles looking rather like an oversized white liquorice wheel) and lots of lamb skewers yáng ròu chuàn'r 羊肉串儿 and roasted buns. During 2005, the night market at Wuyi Bei Lu was a replacement for the Fuqiang market while construction work took place there. The intention is for the night market to return there once construction is complete, but it is not certain when that will be.

A few suggestions for restaurants and snacks on Xinhua Zhong Lu include:

✗ **Dongfang Meishi Yule Cheng** 东方美食娱乐城 Southern end of Xinhua Zhong Lu on the east side of the road, 100m from the roundabout; ☏ 0937 6717 076. This small plain restaurant with private rooms (bāoxiāng 包厢) offering karaoke upstairs has the standard choice of dishes and excellent hotpot (huǒguō 火锅 – see hotpot guide on page 264 for help with the menu).

✗ **Jinfeng Jiudian** 金峰酒店 2-2 Xinhua Bei Lu, on the northeast corner opposite the Jiayuguan Hotel; ☏ 0937 6231 888. Wide selection of dishes and especially fish.

✗ **Niannian Tiantian Bakery** 年年天天点心铺 26–4 Xinhua Zhong Lu; ☏ 0937 6280 257. Has a good selection of cookies, buns and biscuits – good for a day out along the wall.

✗ **Xibei Jiudian** 西北酒店 Xinhua Nan Lu, 100m south of the Xinhua supermarket; ☏ 0937 6233 208. Ignore the mistranslation of the restaurant as 'Northwest Hotel'; there is no accommodation in this establishment. Small but good dishes of the standard Chinese variety.

WHAT TO SEE AND DO IN AND AROUND JIAYUGUAN

On the western edge of town, 5km from the town centre is the westernmost fort of the Ming wall, Jiayuguan. Standing out prominently in the splendid isolation of the valley floor between the impressive snowy mountaintops of the Qilian range (5,564m above sea level) to the south and the smaller Jiayu range to the north. The fort is almost square in shape, each of the four walls being just over 150m in length. The fort is then surrounded by a second wall that hugs three sides and on the east side opens out to a larger yard area. Interestingly, the western gate, Rouyuanmen, means 'Gate of Conciliation with the Remote Ones', referring to the barbarians west of the Middle Kingdom, while the eastern gate, Guanghuamen, means 'Gate of Enlightenment', referring to the passage into the cultured and civilised Middle Kingdom. The fort was built over a period of some 80 years between 1449 and 1530. It deteriorated gradually over the centuries despite some attempts at maintenance, and was in bad need of repair by the 20th century. Now it and various other sections of the wall near the fort have been completely renovated.

Within the grounds of the fort park is the Jiayuguan **Great Wall Museum**. Relocated here from its town location in 1998, the museum is encompassing and informative, with almost 90% of displays translated into English. Displays cover the history of the Great Wall, its construction, its use as a defensive structure, life at the wall as a soldier as well as many other details. The museum shop (as well as other shops throughout the grounds) has an interesting selection of Chinese souvenirs and old Chinese artefacts, although you may find some of them cheaper at the very small antiques market opposite Jìngtiě Shìchǎng 镜铁市场. *(Entry to the fort, museum and surrounding grounds is ¥60.)*

Two arms of the wall spread out north and south from Jiayu fort. The southern arm extends 5km to the banks of the Beida River, where **Number One beacon tower** Dìyī fēnghuǒ tái 第一烽火台 sits on the edge of the 60m-high riverbank. At the time of writing it is possible to walk alongside the wall from Jiayuguan fort to Number One beacon tower, although you have to cross two roads and the rail tracks in order to get there. The tower itself is fenced off, but your ¥21 entry fee allows you to access the underground viewing platform where you pop out onto an overhanging glass floor. From here you can view the beacon tower above, the river below, the mock military camp on the other side of the river as well as the zip slide (¥35) to the camp. There is also a small restaurant in the underground section as well as a bar overlooking the river.

Following the wall north from the fort, you come to the **Overhanging Castle** Xuánbìlóu 悬臂楼. Within the grounds the wall has been completely reconstructed, mostly with concrete and covered with a flimsy mud veneer. Still, the 110m ascent to the Mazong ridge and pagodas affords a great view of the surrounding countryside and you may even catch a show of the local army practising tank manoeuvres along the nearby firing range. At the time of writing another castle very near Xuanbilou was in the process of reconstruction so it may not be long before the ¥21 entry fee to Xuanbilou is increased. Taxis to Xuangbilou cost ¥15, although catching a taxi back is more difficult unless you ask for it to wait.

From Xuanbilou the wall heads east and back to Shanhaiguan and North Korea. If you have the time and inclination, you may also be interested in taking in a little of the unrestored wall in the vicinity of Jiayuguan. Some 20km northeast of the town are the remains of the small walled fort of **Yemabi** 野马壁. The wall leading up to the old fort is fairly continuous, although east of Yemabi the wall is mostly destroyed. Today Yemabi is used to grow local vegetables. A small plaque makes note of the fort as a historical site. There is no entry fee. A few kilometres southeast of Yemabi are the remains of another very small walled fort, which now houses a brick pagoda and is otherwise surrounded by the small village of **Xincheng** 新城.

LANZHOU 兰州

HISTORY After the long and arduous journey through the Gansu corridor from the barbarian lands, Lanzhou was a welcome stop and marked the transition into China proper. It remained a mere travellers' pit-stop for centuries until the turn of the 7th century when the progressive Emperor Wen of the Sui dynasty developed it into a sizeable town named Jincheng, or Golden City. The name referred to the gold mining near the town. The amount of trade traversing the city by then was significant and it was renowned as a magnificent travellers' trading bazaar writ large, with its larger-than-life accompanying entertainment and bargains. By the 14th century, Lanzhou was sufficiently strategically important that the Ming emperors had the town fortified with a 17m-high, 13m-wide city wall with a circumference of 1.5km. It was further defended by a 15m-deep moat on all but the north side of the city.

Sadly, Lanzhou's development under communism and now a thriving 21st-century economy has swept away all of the old town, city wall and moat. Nevertheless, as the provincial capital it is lively and fun, and remains the welcome stop it always used to be after a period of time in the hinterland of Gansu and beyond. One of the town's main attractions is the Yellow River, which meanders through the narrow valley of Lanzhou. Hemmed in by steep mountains rising up visibly to the north and south, the city has been forced to spread out along some 30km of the river.

Although the outer Great Wall is far from here and only a very small portion of the inner wall remains at Wushaoling, you may find yourself in Lanzhou merely because the provincial capital remains the fastest way to get in and out of the region.

GETTING THERE Lanzhou airport is 73km north of the city. An airport shuttle bus meets arriving **flights** and takes passengers into the airline offices on Dongming Xi Lu in the city centre for ¥30. A taxi into town costs ¥80. Going to the airport, a shuttle bus leaves from outside the airline offices on 488–512 Donggang Xi Lu every hour on the hour between the first and last flights from the airport. There are four flights to Beijing a day with Air China and Hainan Air, ¥1,340; one flight a day to Jiayuguan, ¥560; two flights a day to Guangzhou, ¥1,320. There are also other flights to Chengdu, Xian, Taiyuan, Urumqi, Nanjing, Hangzhou and many other cities in China.

Lanzhou **train** station is in the east side of town. There are two overnight trains from Yumen via Jiayuguan, both arriving at around 06.45. Trains from the east include: Beijing (30+ hours), ¥569; Shanghai (28 hours), ¥548; and Xi'an (20+ hours), ¥207.

Lanzhou has two long-distance **bus** stations. The east bus station is 500m north of the train station on Tianshui Lu. The west bus station is, as you would expect, over in the west town at the end of city bus 1.

City buses are numerous in Lanzhou. Lines 1 and 127 run from the train station through the east town and to the west bus station in the west town. Both go past the Xiguan roundabout and the provincial museum.

Several **maps** of Lanzhou are touted outside the train station. Unless you specifically find the information on the older maps of use to you, make sure you get the most recent map (date, publication information and price are always printed somewhere on the map). The 2005 map is a long, folded map covering the east and west towns, showing the bus lines.

The **PSB** is at 310 Wudu Lu (✆ *0931 8462 851*).

MONEY AND COMMUNICATION As the provincial capital, the city has a number of ATMs both at Bank of China branches and at branches of Industrial and Commercial Bank of China (ICBC). The main branch of the Bank of China is at 589 Tianshui Lu and changes both travellers' cheques and foreign currency. *(Open daily 08.30–18.00.)*

The streets around Lanzhou University on Tianshui Lu house many an **internet café**. As this busy road between the train station and the Xiguan roundabout was undergoing a facelift at the time of writing, the shelf life of many of the cafés appears to be limited, so ask around when you get there or look for the familiar 网吧 sign.

The main **post office** is on the corner of Pingliang Lu and Minzhu Dong Lu. Open daily 08.00–19.00, with the telecommunications section open even later until 23.00 every day.

WHERE TO STAY There are plenty of places of all price ranges in the city. Again consult the *Accommodation* section on pages 90–92 for the characters to look out for if you want to find a hotel of your own. The suggestions below aim to be close to onward travel stations, central locations and to offer some peace and quiet. There are also plenty of big hotels directly opposite the noisy train station.

⌂ **White Dagoba Tea Lodge** Báitǎ Cházhuāng 白塔茶庄 (16 rooms) ✆ 0931 8364 007. Located in the centre of Baita Gardens on the north side of the Yellow River. The rooms are mostly used as resting rooms in the heat of the summer, but have heating in the winter. Other hotels were in the process of being built in the park at the time of writing. Communal bathrooms. *Standard twin room ¥80.*

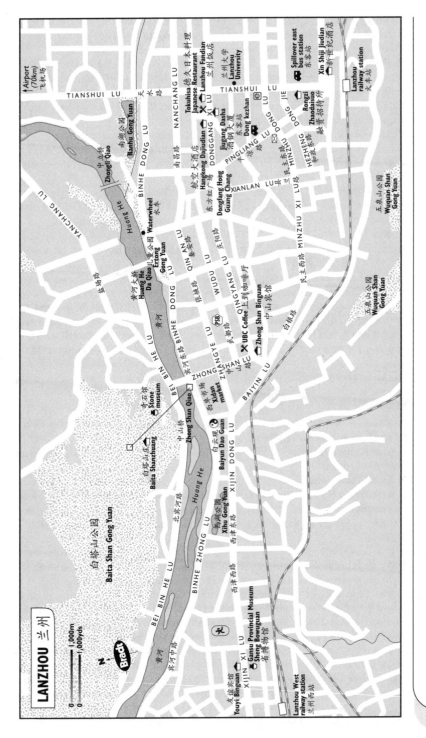

LANZHOU 兰州

0 —— 1,000m
0 —— 1,000yds

Brad†

N

Airport (70km) 飞机场

TIANSHUI LU 天水路

南湖公园
Nanhu Gong Yuan

Zhonghi Qiao 中立桥

Huang He 黄河

BINHE DONG LU

Waterwheel 水车

BINHE DONG 滨河东路

Ertong Gong Yuan 儿童公园

QIN AN LU 秦安路

WUDU 武都路

张掖路

ZHANGYE LU

ZHAN-HAN LU 山-汉路

UBC Coffee 上岛咖啡厅

Zhong Shan Binguan 中山宾馆

白银路

BAIYIN LU

QINGYANG 庆阳路

NANCHANG LU 南昌路

Tokuhisa 德久日本料理 Japanese Restaurant
Hangtong Dajiudian 航空大酒店
东方红广场
Lanzhou Fandian 兰州饭店

Dongfang Hong Guang Chang 东方红广场

XIANLAN LU 西兰路

Jiugang Dasha 酒钢大厦
DONGGANG 东岗路
东客站

Lanzhou University 兰州大学

TIANSHUI 天水
LU

Dong kezhan 东客站

PINGLIANG LU 平凉路

MINZHU XI LU 民主西路

MINZHU DONG 民主东路

HEZHENG 和政路

藏货招待所

Rongzi Zhaodaisuo

Dong JIE 东街

Spillower east bus station 东客站
Xin Shiji Jiudian 新世纪酒店

Lanzhou railway station 兰州火车站

五泉山公园
Wuquan Shan Gong Yuan

YANCHANG LU 盐昌路

盐场路

Huang He 黄河

BEI BIN HE LU 北滨河路

Stone museum 寿石馆

Zhong Shan Qiao 中山桥

Baita Shanzhuang 白塔山庄

白云观
Baiyun Dao Guan

白塔山公园
Baita Shan Gong Yuan

Xidan market 西单市场

中山桥

Huang He 黄河

Xihu Gong Yuan 西湖公园
马滩公园

XIJIN DONG LU 西津东路

BINHE ZHONG LU 滨河中路

BEI BIN HE LU 北滨河路

西津东路
西津西路

Gansu Provincial Museum 甘肃省博物馆
Sheng Bowuguan 省博物馆

友谊宾馆
Youyi Binguan
XIJIN XI 西津西

Lanzhou West railway station 兰州西站

255

兰州 Gansu 甘肃 LANZHOU

12

🏠 **Hangkong Dajiudian** 航空大酒店 (110 rooms) 582 Donggang Xi Lu; 📞 0931 8844 888. Run by CAAC, this hotel is convenient if you arrive late by plane, or need to catch an early plane, but it is a bit too functional if cheap. *Standard twins at ¥180 are often offered at almost half price.*

🏠 **Jiugang Dasha** 酒钢大厦 (72 rooms) 469 Donggang Xi Lu, down a small alleyway with an archway sign on the main street saying 'Dong Ming Lou' in Roman letters; 📞 0931 888 1911; 📠 0931 886 4672. This smart two star with friendly staff is very good value for money. Set back in a large courtyard (head for the red lanterns at the end of the short alley) it is also fairly quiet. Opposite the shuttle buses for the airport. All rooms en suite with 24hr hot water, but no breakfast. *Very nice dbl suite for ¥388; standard twin ¥260.*

🏠 **Lanzhou Fandian** 兰州饭店 (493 rooms) 434 Donggang Xi Lu, on the northwest corner of the Xiguan roundabout. An enormous three star, but set back from the road with smart serviced rooms which are fairly quiet. Staff are not renowned as the friendliest. *Standard twin in the middle building ¥398; standard twin in the east or west buildings ¥230 (both after discount).*

🏠 **Ruizi Zhadaisuo** 融资招待所 (17 rooms) Tianshui Lu, down an alleyway directly opposite the east bus station and sandwiched between a brand-new building and the restaurant at 163 Tianshui Lu; 📞 0931 8734 316. Super cheap rooms and quiet. Communal baths, hot water 20.00–midnight only. No breakfast. *Dbl or sgl ¥50; twin ¥40.*

🏠 **Victory Hotel** Shènglì Bīnguǎn 胜利宾馆 (697 rooms) 📞 0931 846 5221. Located right in the thick of Xidan shopping area and at the end of Zhongshan Bridge Road, you can't get more central or more noisy than this. *Standard twin ¥350; trpls without bath ¥180.*

🏠 **Yingbin Fandian** 迎宾饭店 (80 rooms) 35 Tianshi Lu; 📞 0931 8886 552; 📠 0931 8886 776. A two star 100m north of the train station. Clean and serviced but noisy rooms facing the street. *Standard twin en suite ¥158.*

🏠 **Youyi Binguan** 友谊宾馆 (630 rooms) 16 Xijin Xi Lu; 📞 0931 2333 051; 📠 0931 2330 304. The advantage to this hotel is its enormous variety of rooms and its proximity to the provincial museum (opposite). The disadvantage is that it is far from where the heart of the town is in the east. Nevertheless it is well connected via buses 1 and 127 as well as many others. *Executive deluxe at ¥1,060; deluxe dbl ¥380; standard twin ¥198; trpl suite ¥168; economic twin ¥60.*

✖ WHERE TO EAT As the provincial capital, Lanzhou abounds with good places to eat of all price ranges. Zhongshan Lu has plenty of restaurants, plush coffee shops and a food stall market on the south side of Xidan shopping plaza.

✖ **UBC Coffee House** Zhongshan Lu, opposite the Victory Hotel. Like the other UBC Coffee Houses throughout China, this one is comfy and bright with a broad menu.

✖ **Juyuan Zhai Muslim Restaurant** 聚源斋清真餐厅 71 Tianshui Lu; 📞 0931 8871 082. Friendly with good food and close to the train station.

✖ **Tokuhisa Japanese Restaurant** Déjiǔ Rìběn Liàolǐ 德久日本料理 518 Donggang Xi Lu, on the third floor; 📞 0931 8849 666; 📠 0931 8856 487. When you have tired of the usual Chinese dishes but still want something oriental, this reasonably priced (by Japanese standards) Japanese restaurant with all the aesthetic trimmings is a pleasurable alternative. Can be a little slow when full. Menu with pictures also offers spaghetti bolognese and a few other Western dishes.

WHAT TO SEE AND DO Whether you are stuck in Lanzhou for a day or several, the town has plenty of pleasant enough attractions to while away some time.

The **Yellow River** Huáng Hé 黄河 , so named because of the precipitous load of yellow loess sand (see page 55) which it carries, marks the northern edge of this elongated town. For a Chinese river it smells remarkably OK, and the southern riverbank makes for several kilometres of pleasant walking or bike riding. Although several city buses run parts of their journeys along the riverside road, you can't really see much of the river from the bus, and so if you want to experience the willows and roses and the myriad walkers and people out for a riverside drink then you need to join them personally. Around the pedestrian Zhongshan Bridge, which joins the centre of east town with the White Dagoba Park north of the river, are a number of activities. Down on the river you can take a **sheepskin raft** (a sturdy wooden lattice lashed to inflated sheepskins without the heads and legs) or a high-speed boat cruise. Further east along the river is an old waterwheel, now mostly just a tourist attraction.

Just west of the bridge is the cable car, which takes you up to the top of the **White Dagoba Park** (Báitǎ Gōngyuán 白塔公园). The ride up costs ¥15, the ride down ¥10 and a return trip costs ¥20. The park itself was quite barren and uninviting at the time of writing while a number of new constructions were underway. When finished the park should boast new temples, restaurants and pleasant riverside accommodation. In the mean time, a walk back down the hillside starts up the small hill behind the cable car and winds through a number of cheap teahouses, where people while away the day playing cards, mahjong, Chinese chess and other drinking games. Midway down the hill is the White Pagoda Tea Lodge Báitǎ cházhuāng 白塔茶庄 which also offers basic accommodation (see above). One of the more interesting items in the park is the **Stone Museum**. Housed in an old temple building, the museum is a jumbled mix of stone exhibits and curio sales. The Chinese have long been fascinated with finding pictures, usually of landscapes and animals, in rocks and stones. This museum, one of the few of its kind, has an excellent collection of amazing stones, rocks and tree branches or roots, where different strains of rock sediment entwined together really do look like forest scenes, wild animals, the moon rising and people undertaking various activities. There are also excellent petrified flowers and animals set in stone, some of which are for sale. Beware the false picture stones for sale on the street: the clearer the picture the more likely it is to be a veneer of permanent ink. The museum also sells a variety of carved húlu 葫芦, **carved gourds**. Growing and carving gourds used to be the pastime of kept ladies and palace concubines. Some of the scenes depicted are exquisite, and some of the gourds on sale go into several thousand yuan. Smaller cheaper gourds for ¥10–25 are also on sale inside and outside the museum. If you enter the park from the north end of Zhongshan Bridge, then entry costs ¥5. From the cable car the entry fee is included in the fare.

South of Zhongshan Bridge is Zhongshan Street, lined with cafés and restaurants, leading to **Xidan**, one of the main shopping districts in Lanzhou (for expensive 'exclusivity' go to the west town). Yingxing road leads from Xidan to **The East Is Red Square**, which is also lined with more shops and people taking a stroll. West of Xidan is **Zhongshan Park**, a marvellously green and lush park where old and young practise taiqi in the morning, mothers take their children in the afternoon, and lovers meet in the evening. Entry ¥5 on the east side of the park.

On the border of the west town is **Culture Court** Wénhuà Gōng 文化宫 A converted old monastery, the front courtyard and temples sell scrolls of calligraphy and painting, whilst the back courtyards and pavilions have become a veritable tea garden, packed with Lanzhouers. Deckchairs covered in towels line every space possible, while people sup tea and eat snacks, either playing games or simply chatting. Some of the side pavilions are dedicated to the serious mahjong players, whilst the very back pavilion screens live Beijing Opera amateurs. Shaded and cool, this is a wonderfully atmospheric place to while away the afternoon reading a book or simply soaking in the Chinese atmosphere. Eight-treasure tea (bābǎo chá 八宝茶) costs ¥6 per person and you are left with a large thermos to refill the plastic cup yourself. Hawkers sell ¥1–5 snacks of nuts, raisins and seeds, whilst more substantial dishes, beer and the Chinese liquor baijiu can be bought from the tea ladies.

Near Culture Court at the corner of Heyan and Baiyin roads is a large **Daoist temple**, White Cloud Court Báiyún Dàoguàn 白云道观, complete with Daoist teachers and many visiting adherents. Still under significant renovation at the time of writing, the court should be complete sometime in 2006.

In the heart of the west town, opposite the enormous Friendship Hotel complex, is the **Gansu Provincial Museum** Gānsù Shěng Bówùguǎn 甘肃省博物馆. This museum is renowned for its outstanding displays of over 3,000 years of Chinese life in the province, and includes the exhibition of the famous Wuwei flying horse (see page 240) that now symbolises Chinese tourism. After years of extensive renovation, the museum reopened in October 2005 with renewed displays and more extensive English translations. *(Entry ¥60.)*

A1

Appendix

LANGUAGE Yǔyǎn 语言

The Chinese language is made up of seven mutually unintelligible tongues (see *Language*, page 43) and a further 40 dialects. Despite the stark variations in pronunciation and use of considerably different words, grammar remains largely the same throughout and the written form of the language is the same for all tongues and dialects. This is because the Chinese written language consists of pictograms rather than an alphabet. Most pictograms are made up of two parts, a radical (or root) on the top, left or bottom of the character, which gives it the basic category of meaning, and then a second part providing sound and additional definition. Each character represents one syllable and is also one word. Several characters or words can be combined to create other words. Because of the difficulty in pronouncing Chinese (see below), Chinese characters are provided throughout this book so that it is easy to point to them when trying to communicate.

PRONUNCIATION AND TRANSLITERATION OF MANDARIN Pǔtōnghuà 普通话 This guidebook uses the national language of China, which is Mandarin Pǔtōnghuà 普通话 .

Everybody in mainland China is taught Putonghua at school, even though a lot of China in fact speaks another language at home. In other words, no matter where you are in China along the Great Wall, you should be able to communicate in Putonghua. Putonghua is transliterated today into the Roman alphabet using the pinyin system. Formerly, Chinese was transliterated using the Wade–Giles system, which was much less straightforward. This guide transliterates Putonghua using the pinyin system except for the names of a few well-known individuals who are better known under their Wade–Giles spelling. This applies for instance to individuals such as Sun Yatsen and Chiang Kai Shek. An example of the difference between pinyin and Wade–Giles is the difference between Beijing and Peking. In fact they are pronounced the same using both systems, but those who are not used to Wade–Giles would pronounce 'p' and 'k' as we normally do.

Chinese languages are tonal, so each syllable can be pronounced in different tones. Putonghua is one of the easier tonal languages as it has only four tones and a mute tone (Cantonese has nine!) The four tones are essentially high (first tone), rising (second tone), falling-rising (third tone) and falling (fourth tone).

WORDS AND PHRASES
Courtesies

hello/good day	nǐ hǎo	你好
goodbye	zàijiàn	再见
please	qǐng	请
thank you	xièxie	谢谢

goodnight	wǎn ān	晚安
how are you?	nǐ hǎo ma	你好吗?
I'm fine	hěn hǎo	很好
pleased to meet you	rènshi nǐ hěn gāoxìng	认识你很高兴
my pleasure/it's nothing	nǎ li / bù kèqi	哪里 / 不客气
excuse me/sorry	duì bu qǐ	对不起
welcome!	huānyíng	欢迎

Basics

yes/no	shì de/bù shì	是的 / 不是
OK	hǎode	好的
maybe	hǎo kěnéng	好可能
large/small	dà/xiǎo	大 / 小
more/less	gèng duō/gèng xiǎo	更多 / 更小
good/bad	hǎo/bù hǎo	好 / 不好
excellent/terrible	fēicháng hǎo/ hěn bù hǎo	非常好 / 很不好
hot/cold	rè/lěng	热 / 冷
toilet	cèsuǒ	厕所
men/women	nánde/nǚde	男的 / 女的

Basic questions

How/What?	Zěnme?/ Shénme?	怎么? / 什么?
How do you say in Chinese?	Yòng hànyǔ zěnme shuō?	用汉语怎么说?
What is that?	Zhè shì shénme?	这是什么?
When?	Shénme shíhou?	什么时候?
When does the shop open/close?	Shāngdiàn shénme shíhou kāimén/guān mén?	商店什么时候 开门 / 关门?
Where?	Zài nǎr?	在哪儿?
Where is there a telephone?	Gōng yòng diànhuà zài nǎr?	共用电话在哪儿?
Who?	Shéi?	谁?
Why?	Wèi shénme?	为什么?
Do you speak English?	Nǐ huì shuō yīngyǔ ma?	你会说英语吗?
Do you understand French/ German?	Nǐ huì shuō fǎyǔ/déyǔ ma?	你会说法语 / 德语吗?
I do not understand Chinese	Wǒ bù huì shuō hànyǔ	我不会说汉语。
How much does it cost?	Duō shao qián?	多少钱?
What time is it?	Jǐ diǎn?	几点?

Nationalities 国籍 Guójí

American	měiguórén	美国人
Australian	àodàlìyàrén	澳大利亚人
British	yīngguórén	英国人
Canadian	jiānádàrén	加拿大人
Chinese	zhōngguórén	中国人
Dutch	hélánrén	荷兰人
French	fǎguórén	法国人
German	déguórén	德国人
New Zealander	xīnxīlánrén	薪西兰人
Spanish	xībānyárén	西班牙人

Getting around

| How do you get to the…? | Dào…zěnme zǒu? | 到 ... 怎么走? |
| Great Wall/hotel | chángchéng/lǚguǎn | 长城 / 旅馆 |

fortress/museum	chéngbǎo/bówùguǎn	城堡 / 博物馆
palace/drum tower	gōngdiàn/gǔlóu	宫殿 / 鼓楼
tomb/cave	fénmù/shāndòng	坟墓 / 山洞
temple/monastery	sìmiào/xiūdàoyuàn	寺庙 / 修道院
mosque/church	qīngzhēnsì/jiàotáng	清真寺 / 教堂
here/there	zhèr/nàr	这儿 / 哪儿
on the left/right	zài zuǒbiande/zài yòubiande	在左边的 / 在右边的
Where is...?	...zài nǎr?	…在那儿？
taxi rank/train station	chūzūchē/huǒchē zhàn	出租车 / 火车站
bus station	gōnggòng qìchē zhàn	公共汽车站
long distance bus station	Chángtú Qìchē Zhàn	长途汽车站
underground/metro	dì tiě	地铁
doctor/hospital	yīshēng/yīyuàn	医生 / 医院
police station/bank	jīngchájú/yínháng	警察局 / 银行
restaurant/shop	fàndiàn/shāngdiàn	饭店 / 商店
town/village	zhèn/xiāngcūn	镇 / 乡村
house/dormitory	fángzi/sùshè	房子 / 宿舍
cinema/theatre	diànyǐngyuàn/jùchǎng	电影院 / 剧场
When does the train arrive/ leave?	Huǒchē jǐdiǎn dào/líkāi?	火车几点到 / 离开？
I need a telephone	Wǒ yào dǎ diànhuà	我要打电话

Hotels and money

Where is the hotel?	Bīnguǎn zài nǎ?	宾馆在哪？
What is the address?	Shénme dìzhǐ?	什么地址？
What is your telephone number?	Nǐde diànhuàhàomǎ shì shénme?	你的电话号码是什么？
Do you have any vacancies?	Yǒu kòng fángjiān ma?	有空房间吗？
I'd like a...	Wǒ xiǎngyào yīgè	我想要一个…
single/double room	dānrén fáng/shuāngrén fáng	单人房 / 双人房
bed in a dormitory	tōng pù	通铺
Where can I change money?	Zài nǎr kěyǐ huàn qián?	在哪儿可以换钱？
I want to change dollars to yuan	Wǒ yào bǎ měiyuán huàn chéng rénmínbì	我要把美元换成人民币
How many yuan will you give me for $1?	Yīgè měiyuán gěi duō shao rénmínbì?	一个美元给多少人民币？

Eating and drinking

What do you have to drink?	Nǐ yǒu shénme hē de?	你有什么喝的？
I would like to drink ...	wǒ xiǎng hē	我想喝…
water/juice	shuǐ/guǒzhī	水 / 果汁
tea/coffee	chá/kāfēi	茶 / 咖啡
red/green tea	hóng / lǜchá	红 / 绿茶
jasmine tea	mòli huāchá	茉莉花茶
chrysanthemum tea	júhuāchá	菊花茶
eight-treasure tea	bābǎochá	八宝茶
hot doufu milk	rè dòufu nǎi	热豆腐奶
milk pearl tea	zhēnzhū nǎichá	珍珠奶茶
milk/yoghurt	niūnǎi/suānnǎi	牛奶 / 酸奶
wine/beer	pútaojiǔ/píjiǔ	葡萄酒 / 啤酒
(Chinese) liquor	báijiǔ	白酒
What do you have to eat?	Nǐ yǒu shénme chī de?	你有什么吃的？
I want (to eat)···	Wǒ xiǎng chī ···	我想吃…

chicken/pork	jīròu/zhūròu	鸡肉 / 猪肉
beef/lamb	niúròu/yángròu	牛肉 / 羊肉
fish/tofu	yú/dòufu	鱼 / 豆腐
vegetables/fruit	shūcài/shuǐguǒ	蔬菜 / 水果
sweet and sour (literally 'sugar vinegar')	tángcù	糖醋
plain rice/fried rice	báifàn/chǎofàn	白饭 / 炒饭
noodles/fried noodles	miàntiáo/ chǎo miàn	面条 / 炒面
bread/cake	miànbāo/dàngāo	面包 / 蛋糕
steamed buns/dumplings	mántou/shuǐjiǎo	馒头 / 水饺
dough twists	yóutiáo	油条
pancaked dough twists	jiānbing guǒzi	煎饼果子
apples/oranges	píngguǒ/chéngzi	苹果 / 橙子
pears/grapes	lízi/pútao	梨子 / 葡萄
pineapple/banana	bōluó/xiāngjiāo	菠萝 / 香蕉
watermelon/persimmon	xīguā/shìzi	西瓜 / 柿子
peanuts/eggs	huāshēng/jīdàn	花生 / 鸡蛋
I don't eat meat/fish	Wǒ bù chī ròu/yú	我不吃肉 / 鱼
The bill please	Fùqián, kěyǐ ma?	付钱，可以吗？

NUMBERS

0	líng	零
1	yī	一
2	èr	二
3	sān	三
4	sì	四
5	wǔ	五
6	liù	六
7	qī	七
8	bā	八
9	jiǔ	九
10	shí	十
11	shíyī	十一
12	shí'èr	十二
13	shísān	十三
14	shísì	十四
15	shíwǔ	十五
16	shíliù	十六
17	shíqī	十七
18	shíbā	十八
19	shíjiǔ	十九
20	èrshí	二十
21	èrshíyī	二十一
30	sānshí	三十
40	sìshí	四十
50	wǔshí	五十
60	liùshí	六十
70	qīshí	七十
80	bāshí	八十
90	jiǔshí	九十
100	bǎi	百
200	liǎngbǎi	两百
300	sānbǎi	三百

Here is a list of dishes commonly found on a menu in northern China. There are many other dishes, but these are some of the most popular:

Aubergine with catfish	qiézi shāo niányú	茄子烧鲇鱼
Beijing duck	běijīng kǎoyā	北京烤鸭
Boiled dumplings	shuǐjiǎo	水饺
Broccoli and doufu pockets	lánhuā sàozi dòfu	兰花臊子豆腐
Cabbage in cream of chicken	jīyóu wáwacài	鸡油娃娃菜
Chicken and sweetcorn soup	yùmǐ jīsī tāng	玉米鸡丝汤
Chicken with cashew nuts	jiānguǒ jīpiàn	坚果鸡片
Clear lamb soup	qīngtāng yángròu	清汤羊肉
Crispy aromatic duck	xiāng sū yā	香酥鸭
Cumin fried spicy lamb	zīrán yángròu	孜然羊肉
Double cooked pork	huí guō ròu	回锅肉
Egg and tomato soup	fānqié dàntāng	番茄蛋汤
Egg fried rice	dàn chǎo fàn	蛋炒饭
Fish-flavoured chicken	yúxiāng jīdīng	鱼香鸡丁
Fish-flavoured aubergine	yúxiāng qiézi	鱼香茄子
Hot and sour soup	suān là tāng	酸辣汤
Hot spicy beancurd	mápó dòufu	麻婆豆腐
Kale in oyster sauce	háoyóu báicài	蚝油白菜
Kung Pao chicken	gōngbào jīdīng	宫爆鸡丁
Meat fried mountain mushrooms	ròuchǎo shān mógu	肉炒山磨菇
Minced meat pockets	jīngjiàng ròusī	京酱肉丝
Mongolian fried lamb	ménggǔ kǎo yángròu	蒙古烤羊肉
Noodle soup	tāng miàn	汤面
Pan-fried vegetable dumplings	sānsù guōtiē	三素锅贴
Red braised fish	hóng shāo yú	红烧鱼
Salt and pepper shrimp	yánjiāo chǎoxiā	盐椒炒虾
Sand pot	shā guō	沙锅
Skewers of meat	chuànròu	串肉
Shredded potato with capsicum	tǔdòusī	土豆丝
Steamed dumplings	bāozi	包子
Steamed sea bass/perch	qīngzhēnglúyú	清蒸鲈鱼
Steamed rice packets	héyè zhēngfàn	荷叶蒸饭
Sweet and sour spare ribs	tángcù páigǔ	糖醋排骨
Tomatoes fried with egg	fānqié chǎodàn	番茄炒蛋
Wonton soup	húntun tāngshuǐ	馄饨汤水

400	sìbǎi	四百
500	wǔbǎi	五百
1,000	qiān	千
2,000	liǎngqiān	两千
10,000	wàn	万
1,000,000	bǎiwàn	百万
2,000,000	liǎngbǎiwàn	两百万
quarter	sìfēn zhīyī	四分之一
half	bàn	半
three-quarters	sìfēn zhīsān	四分之三

Appendix I LANGUAGE 语言

AI

263

The following represents a typical *huoguo* sheet so you can just point and hopefully order a delicious hotpot. This meal is also commonly called shuànyángròu 涮羊肉 in northern China. Drinks are ordered separately.

HOTPOT BROTHS

鱼锅	yú guō	fish pot
狗肉锅	gǒuròu guō	dog meat pot
驴肉锅	lǘròu guō	donkey meat pot
鸡锅	jī guō	chicken pot
兔肉锅	tùròu guō	rabbit pot
高汤锅	gāotāng guō	starch soup pot

SAUCES liàolèi 料类

山釜料	shānfǔ liào	mountain pot sauce
豆花料	dòuhuā liào	peanut sauce
麻酱料	májiàng liào	sesame seed sauce
香油料	xiāngyóu liào	sesame oil sauce

INGREDIENTS
Fish

活基围虾	huójī wéi xiā	live local shrimp
冰鲜大虾	bīngxiān dà xiā	fresh prawns on ice
虾丸	xiā wán	prawn balls
蟹肉	xiè ròu	crab meat
黄鳝	huángshàn	eel
泥鳅	níqiu	loach
墨鱼	mòyú	cuttlefish
鱼块	yú kuài	pieces of fish
鱼丸	yú wán	fish balls
鲜鱼头	xiān yú tóu	fresh fish head
鱿鱼	yóuyú	squid

Offal

鲜牛鞭	xiān niúbiān	fresh ox tail
鸡腰	jīyāo	chicken kidney
鸭血	yā xuè	duck's blood
牛脊髓	niú jǐsuǐ	ox bone marrow
牛肚	niúdǔ	tripe
牛柏叶	niú bǎiyè	ox third stomach
水牛毛肚	shuǐniú máodǔ	buffalo third stomach
牛蹄筋	niú tíjīn	ox tendon
羊肚	yang dǔ	sheep stomach
牛肝	niú gān	cow liver
血旺	xuè wàng	blood pudding

TIME

hour/minute	xiǎoshí/fēnzhōng	小时 / 分钟
week/day	xīngqī/tiān	星期 / 天
year/month	nián/yuè	年 / 月
today/tonight	jīntiān/jīnwǎn	今天 / 今晚
tomorrow/yesterday	míngtiān/zuótiān	明天 / 昨天
morning/afternoon	shàngwǔ/xiàwǔ	上午 / 下午
evening/night	wǎnshàng/yè	晚上 / 夜

| 腰花 | yāohuā | kidney |
| 猪肚 | zhū dǔ | pork stomach |

Vegetables

菠菜	bō cài	spinach
贡菜	gòng cài	bak choi
娃娃菜	wáwa cài	baby bak choi
鸡毛菜	jīmáo cài	kale
油菜	yóucài	rapeseed plant
生菜	shēng cài	lettuce
茼蒿	tónghāo	dandelion leaf
莜麦菜	yóumài cài	oat sprouts
白菜	báicài	Chinese cabbage
豆苗	dòu miáo	bean sprouts
黄花 / 百合	huánghuā / bǎihé	lily
木耳	mú'ěr	wood ear mushrooms
油皮 / 豆皮	yóupí / dòupí	tofu skin
鲜海带	xiān hǎidài	fresh seaweed
冬瓜	dōng guā	winter melon
粉丝	fěn sī	mung bean vermicelli
土豆粉	tǔdòu fěn	potato starch
土豆片	tǔdòu	potato slices
红薯	hóng shǔ	sweet potato
香菜	xiāng cài	coriander
冻豆腐	dòng dòufu	frozen tofu
鲜豆腐	xiān dòufu	fresh tofu
全蛋面	quán dàn miàn	pickled egg
小麻花	xiǎo máhuā	fried dough
麻酱饼	májiàng bǐng	sesame paste bun

Mushrooms

金针菇	jīnzhēn gū	enoki (golden needle) mushrooms
鲜香菇	xiānxiāng gū	shiitake mushrooms
鸡腿菇	jītuǐ gū	oyster mushrooms
猴头菇	hóutóu gū	hedgehog mushrooms
茶叶菇	cháyègū	tealeaf mushrooms
草菇	cǎo gū	straw mushrooms
百灵菇	bǎilíng gū	lark mushrooms

Meat

猪肉片	zhūròu piàn	pork slices
鸡肉片	Jīròu piàn	chicken slices
羔羊肉	gāoyángròu	first-class lamb
精选羊肉	jīngxuǎn yángròu	select mutton
肥牛王	féi niú wáng	super fat marbled beef
特级肥牛	tèjí féi niú	very fat beef

| this/next week | zhège/ xiàgè xīngqī | 这个 / 下个星期 |
| now/soon | xiànzài/kuài | 现在 / 快 |

Days

Monday	xīngqī yī	星期一
Tuesday	xīngqī èr	星期二
Wednesday	xīngqī sān	星期三

Thursday	xīngqī sì	星期四
Friday	xīngqī wǔ	星期五
Saturday	xīngqī liù	星期六
Sunday	xīngqī tiān	星期天

Months

January	yī yuè	一月
February	èr yuè	二月
March	sān yuè	三月
April	sì yuè	四月
May	wǔ yuè	五月
June	liù yuè	六月
July	qī yuè	七月
August	bā yuè	八月
September	jiǔ yuè	九月
October	shí yuè	十月
November	shíyī yuè	十一月
December	shí'èr yuè	十二月

Seasons

spring	chūntiān	春天
summer	xiàtiān	夏天
autumn	qiūtiān	秋天
winter	dōngtiān	冬天

A2

Appendix

GLOSSARY

armillary sphere		a mechanical astronomical instrument made up of interlocking rings and circles representing celestial spheres
arrow loop		see *crenellation*
adobe		a sun-dried, unburned brick of clay and straw
bǎolěi	堡垒	castle
bǎozi	堡子	walled village enclosed by earth wall
battlement		ramparts, parapets, balustrades, or other forms of protective structures built on top of a wall
beacon tower		a tower, usually at a high point, on which fires are lit to send signals to another beacon tower
crenellation		evenly spaced gaps in a defence wall on top of a castle or barrier wall, through which arrows or guns are fired
cūn	村	village
dagoba	塔	or stupa, a dome shaped structure containing the relics of a Buddha or one of his disciples
defence in depth		multiple layers of defence and/or security
diagram		eight combinations of three whole or broken lines used to divine the future
dūntái	墩台	earth mound
embrasure		opening in a building from which missiles, usually arrows, could be fired
empress dowager		title given to the mother of a Chinese emperor
èrhú	二胡	alto fiddle consisting of only two strings and a small drum played with a bow
faith		the body or dogma of a religion
gōu	沟	gully
guān	关	pass, junction, enclosure
gǔzhēng	古筝	a flat-lying several-stringed instrument played with the fingers, similar to a sitar
horseway		a stone wall built wide enough for mounted horses to ride along (predecessor of the motorway)
hútòng	胡同	a narrow alley way lined with courtyard residences
junk		a Chinese flatbottom ship with a high poop and battened sails
kiln		a large oven for firing, burning or drying pottery, porcelain or bricks
kǒu	口	Great Wall gateway
lǐ	里	a unit of measurement equivalent to 500m
lǐng	岭	mountain range or ridge
lunar calendar		In the lunar calendar, the months are determined by the rotation of the moon around the earth. In general this is

29.53 days. It does not, therefore, necessarily correspond to the Gregorian calendar currently in use by most of the world (including China today), and so the date for Chinese New Year changes every year. In the Chinese lunar calendar, most years have 12 lunar or synodic months, and every now and again a leap year of 13 months.

luòchéng	摞城	a wide circular defensive wall beyond the wèngchén
pepper pot		to move as two teams alternately: one team moving ahead of the other while the other gives covering/protective fire
philosophy		a system of values by which one lives, usually grounded in critical analysis and the sciences or empirical data
potsticker		a minced mixture of meat and/or vegetables wrapped in a very thin egg-noodle skin and steamed in a steam basket
pushe		small barrack for lodging soldiers and food
rammed earth		a mixture of earth, a bonding agent such as reeds, rice or cement, and water which is compacted into forms. Layers of 8cm of mixture can be compacted down to 5cm. When the forms are then removed, a solid durable earth wall remains.
regent		an acting ruler or governor ruling in the minority, absence or disability of a ruler
religion		a set of beliefs, values and practices based on the reverence or worship for a supernatural power regarded as the creator or governor of the universe — usually associated with an institutionalised system; also based on the teachings of a prophet sent by the creator and on the teachings of the disciples of the prophet; can also be based on the teachings of a mortal spiritual leader without adherence to belief in a creator or governor of the universe
shàng	上	upper
signal tower		see *beacon tower*
stele		a tall marker usually made of stone or metal bearing an inscription
stupa		see dagoba
tamped earth		see *rammed earth*
treasure ship		a Chinese sailing ship up to 140m long with up to nine sails
trigram		see *diagram*
Turkistan(s)		a historical/geographical region extending east from the Caspian Sea across west-central Asia and into western China
wèngchéng	瓮城	a high protective wall immediately in front of the exit or passageway through the Great Wall. Entrances through the wèngchéng were through side gates.
xià	下	lower
xiàn	县	county
yíng	营	camp, trading post
yù	峪	valley or ravine
yurt		a circular domed portable tent used by nomads in the Turkistans
zhài	寨	camp, stockade, garrison
zhèn	镇	town

A3

Appendix

FURTHER INFORMATION

BOOKS There is a lot of literature in a number of languages on the Great Wall of China. There are also some beautiful coffee-table books. All those listed can be ordered through most bookstores or amazon.com / amazon.co.uk, or can be loaned from a good university library.

History/politics

Cheng Dalin *The Great Wall of China* South China Morning Post, Hong Kong, 1984. A hefty hardback of a bible on all the Chinese great walls. Informative with good illustrative maps.

Dong Yaohui *The Eternal Great Wall* China Nationality Art Photograph Publishing House, Beijing, 2005. This is an excellent new book on the wall by the secretary general of the Great Wall Society (for website details see below). Aside from more great photos, it also has an easy-to-read summary of the best parts of the wall, as well as a useful guide at the back on the different architectural styles and fortification and defence structures of the wall. Hardback.

Hoff, Benjamin *The Tao of Pooh and the Te of Piglet* Methuen, London, 1994. An irresistible book making easy access to the philosophical tenets of Daoism.

Johnson, Ian *Wild Grass* Pantheon Books, New York, 2004. A real eye-opener into the rise of civil society in China, incidentally along parts of the Great Wall. One is left wondering how long the Chinese Communist Party can last before it tumbles.

Nathan, Andrew and Ross, Robert *Great Wall and Empty Fortress* W W Norton & Company, 1998. Contains nothing about the Great Wall itself, but the concept of barrier building and defence in China's foreign policy. As the *Wall Street Journal* describes it 'A strong antidote to the growing sinophobia in the US'. Nathan has written many very good history and political science books on China.

Polo, Marco *The Travels of Marco Polo* Everyman, London, 1983. The travels of Marco Polo, who travelled to China at age 17, spent 17 years in the court of Kublai Khan, and returned to Venice after 24 years of travel, is encyclopaedic for the time (1271–95), but hardly a page-turning cliffhanger of a novel. Many editions exist of the translation of the original. The Everyman editions have extensive footnotes by the editors of 1818 and 1854. The Orion Press edition of 1958 also contains 25 colour illustrations.

Waldron, Arthur *The Great Wall of China: From History to Myth* Cambridge University Press, Cambridge, 1992. Waldron traces how Chinese defensive walls went from mere regulations of trade and defence to becoming the very identity of the Chinese. Dense, but with an excellent section on how the myth was built around how the wall could be seen from the moon. Paperback.

Wilkinson, Robert *Sun Tzu: The Art of War, Shang Yang: The Book of Lord Shang* Wordsworth, Ware, 1998. For those interested in China and especially Chinese thought, leadership and war-fighting, Sun Tzu's *The Art of War* is seminal. This book also includes other works which bring *The Art of War* to life and delve into a number of military campaigns which led to the construction of the Great Wall.

Xinran *The Good Women of China: Hidden Voices* Vintage, London, 2003. A mind-opening and at times disturbing book of real-life tales of women in China. Well written and reveals the helter-skelter ride of change in China through the past half a century.

Yan Qiubai *The Great Wall: History and Pictures* Foreign Languages Press, Beijing, 1995. More pictures than history. Informative coffee-table book with insights from China's leading Great Wall expert Luo Zhewen. Hardback.

Travel reading and fictional history

Lindesay, William *Alone on the Great Wall* Fulcrum Publishing, 1991. Lindesay's account of his journey through China at a time when the Great Wall was not so accessible is awe-inspiring. Based in Beijing, Lindesay now dedicates his energy to preserving the Great Wall.

Menzies, Gavin *1421: The Year China Discovered the World* Bantam, London, 2002. Absolutely fascinating book about China's heyday of exploration in the very early Ming years that completely blows a hole in misconceptions of our world discovered by the Portuguese. Sets the scene for the frenzy of wall building that took place later in the Ming dynasty.

Min, Anchee *Empress Orchid* Bloomsbury, London, 2004. An excellent and very readable rendition of the last effective Qing ruler of China, the Empress Dowager Cixi. Based on the true story of Cixi's life, Anchee Min writes this novel through the eyes of Cixi. An easy way to understand some of the history of the fall of China around the end of the 19th and beginning of the 20th century.

Stewart, Stanley *Frontier of Heaven: A Journey beyond the Great Wall* Flamingo, London, 1996. Light reading, very little on the wall, but some good cameos on the meaning of the wall to those living around it.

Thubron, Colin *Behind the Wall* Vintage, 2004. A difficult read, wrapped up in long descriptive passages of minutiae and personal feelings. Some of it, however, offers interesting insights into China in the 1980s.

Natural history

Chapman, G and Wang, Y *The Plant Life of China: Distribution and Diversity* Springer Verlag, Heidleberg, 2002. Hardback and fascinating.

Cheng Xuke *Wild Flowers of China* Shanghai Culture Publishing House, 1998.

Mackinnon, John *A Field Guide to the Birds of China: Ornithology* Oxford University Press, 2004. Great for the birdwatcher – 600 pages in paperback.

Sheng Helin and Lu Houji *Mammalians of China* University of Columbia Press, 2000. A hardback pictorial guide to large and medium-sized animals in China.

Walters, Martin *Chinese Wildlife* Bradt Travel Guides. The first handy wildlife book that you can take with you on holiday to China will be published by Bradt in 2007. If only I had had it for mine.

Business

Bucknall, Kevin *Chinese Business, Etiquette and Culture* C&M Online, 2002. An extremely useful paperback. Although Beijing may have moved on in some of the lifestyle aspects, it is still relevant and especially for the interior of China.

Clissold, Tim *Mr China* Robinson, 2004. A cautionary tale of a Wall Street banker who lost millions in the 1990s doing business in China. Easy novel-like reading of all the many pitfalls that can befall the eager and unaware.

Lieberthal, Kenneth and Yan, Rick (eds) *Harvard Business Review on Doing Business in China* Harvard Business School Press, 2004. Authoritative and compact high-level stuff.

WEB RESOURCES

Websites for tour operators and embassies can be found in the respective sections of *Chapter 5, Practical information*.

General Northern China

www.news.bbc.co.uk/1/hi/world/asia-pacific/1184306.stm An excellent source of news, facts and figures on China.

www.ebeijing.gov.cn Official site of Beijing city. Packed with useful information, including all the necessaries for expats, this site is a model of China's leap into 21st-century communications and information sharing.

www.friesian.com/sangoku.htm#china-era For a comprehensive history of China including timelines, tables of emperors and maps of Chinese-conquered lands throughout the dynasties.

www.scuttlebuttsmallchow.com/northchina.html A record of US marine entry into China at the end of World War II in order to repatriate the Japanese. They then went on to provide 'advice' to the nationalists to try to win the ensuing civil war against the communists.

www.rotten.com/library/bio/dictators/mao A very interesting comparison of Mao Zedong with other famous dictators around the world.

www.mindground.net/loess.html For very good information on the loess plateau in China and how loess came about. Extracts are used in this guide.

www.chinatoday.com An informative site covering a huge array of topics on China – from business, to travel, to news and more.

www.orientaltravel.com/people.htm Describes all 55 ethnicities in China.

General Great Wall

whc.unesco.org/pg.cfm?cid=31 For all you might want to know about the Great Wall as a UNESCO World Heritage Site.

www.friendsofgreatwall.org William Lindesay, one of the first to walk considerable lengths of the wall, now heads up the NGO International Friends of the Great Wall. They aim to educate the public, prevent the further deterioration of the wall and promote sustainable tourism. They also organise various clean-up days along the wall.

www.great-wall-marathon.com For details of all the past marathons on the wall at Huangyaguan and the schedule for the next one. Marathons are usually only 10km in length, but are nevertheless very steep! Half marathons available.

www.greatwallsociety.org This small organisation does considerable work to protect the wall, research its origins, development and construction, and works with the government to try to manage it better. Chinese-only at the time of writing.

http://www.studenttraveler.com/mag/01-01/china.php The account of two US students who walked 1,800 miles of the Great Wall in the summer of 1997.

www.china.org.cn Another informative site on all matters Chinese. Lots of very good articles on the Great Wall.

Travel and accommodation

www.seat61.com/Trans-Siberian.htm All about how to book a ticket and travel on the Great Siberian/ Mongolian/Manchurian.

www.chinadiscounthotel.com/beijing/hao_yuan_hotel/index.html An easy way to book from abroad if you want to guarantee your first nights in Beijing.

www.commune.com.cn If you can't afford to stay at The Commune by The Great Wall, then at least have a look at what you are missing.

www.travelchinaguide.com Aside from being the portal for the tour operator, China Travel Service, this site offers a lot of background information on places to visit in China.

www.chinahighlights.com/travelguide.html Another very useful site for background information on places to visit in China.

Government and media

www.gov.cn The government's official site, and interesting for a glimpse of where transparency in governance and sophistication in progaganda are these days in China.

www.chinaview.cn English portal of the Xinhua news agency, China's largest state-run media outlet.

www.chinadaily.com.cn The daily English-language newspaper available in China (state run).

WIN £100 CASH!

READER QUESTIONNAIRE

**Complete and return this questionnaire for the chance to win
£100 cash in our regular draw**

(Entries may be posted or faxed to us, or scanned and emailed.)

Your feedback is important. To help us plan future guides please answer all the questions below. All completed questionnaires will qualify for entry in the draw.

Have you used any other Bradt Guides? If so, which titles?. . . . .

. . . .

Where did you buy this guidebook? . . . .

Your age   16–25 ☐   26–45 ☐   46–60 ☐   60+ ☐

Please send us any comments about this guide or other Bradt Travel Guides. . . . .

. . . .

. . . .

. . . .

. . . .

CLAIM YOUR HALF-PRICE BRADT GUIDE!

Order Form

Please send me one copy of the following guide at half the UK retail price

Title   *Retail price   Half price*

. . .   .

Post & packing (£1/book UK; £2/book Europe; £3/book rest of world)   . . . .

Total   . . . .

Name . . . .

Address. . . . .

Tel . . . .   Email . . . .

☐ I enclose a cheque for £. . . . . . . made payable to Bradt Travel Guides Ltd

☐ I would like to pay by credit card. Number: . . . .

Expiry date . . . . /. . . . 3-digit security code (on reverse of card) . . . .

☐ Please add my name to your mailing/e-newsletter list. (For Bradt use only.)

☐ I would be happy for you to use my name and comments in Bradt

marketing material.

Send your order on this form, with the completed questionnaire, to:

Bradt Travel Guides/GWOC
23 High Street, Chalfont St Peter, Bucks SL9 9QE
☎ +44 (0)1753 893444   f +44 (0)1753 892333
e info@bradtguides.com   www.bradtguides.com

Bradt Travel Guides

www.bradtguides.com

Africa

Africa Overland	£15.99
Benin	£14.99
Botswana: Okavango, Chobe, Northern Kalahari	£14.95
Burkina Faso	£14.99
Cape Verde Islands	£13.99
Canary Islands	£13.95
Cameroon	£13.95
Eritrea	£12.95
Ethiopia	£15.99
Gabon, São Tomé, Príncipe	£13.95
Gambia, The	£12.95
Georgia	£13.95
Ghana	£13.95
Kenya	£14.95
Madagascar	£14.95
Malawi	£12.95
Mali	£13.95
Mauritius, Rodrigues & Réunion	£12.95
Mozambique	£12.95
Namibia	£14.95
Niger	£14.99
Nigeria	£15.99
Rwanda	£13.95
Seychelles	£14.99
Sudan	£13.95
Tanzania, Northern	£13.99
Tanzania	£14.95
Uganda	£13.95
Zambia	£15.95
Zanzibar	£12.95

Britain and Europe

Albania	£13.99
Armenia, Nagorno Karabagh	£13.95
Azores	£12.95
Baltic Capitals: Tallinn, Riga, Vilnius, Kaliningrad	£12.99
Belgrade	£6.99
Bosnia & Herzegovina	£13.95
Bratislava	£6.99
Budapest	£7.95
Cork	£6.95
Croatia	£12.95
Cyprus see North Cyprus	
Czech Republic	£13.99
Dubrovnik	£6.95
Eccentric Britain	£13.99
Eccentric Edinburgh	£5.95
Eccentric France	£12.95
Eccentric London	£12.95
Eccentric Oxford	£5.95
Estonia	£12.95
Faroe Islands	£13.95
Hungary	£14.99
Kiev	£7.95
Latvia	£13.99
Lille	£6.99

Lithuania	£13.99
Ljubljana	£6.99
Macedonia	£13.95
Montenegro	£13.99
North Cyprus	£12.95
Paris, Lille & Brussels	£11.95
Riga	£6.95
River Thames, In the Footsteps of the Famous	£10.95
Serbia	£13.99
Slovenia	£12.99
Spitsbergen	£14.99
Switzerland: Rail, Road, Lake	£13.99
Tallinn	£6.95
Ukraine	£13.95
Vilnius	£6.99

Middle East, Asia and Australasia

Great Wall of China	£13.99
Iran	£14.99
Iraq	£14.95
Kabul	£9.95
Maldives	£13.99
Mongolia	£14.95
North Korea	£13.95
Palestine, Jerusalem	£12.95
Sri Lanka	£13.99
Syria	£13.99
Tasmania	£12.95
Tibet	£12.95
Turkmenistan	£14.99

The Americas and the Caribbean

Amazon, The	£14.95
Argentina	£15.99
Cayman Islands	£12.95
Costa Rica	£13.99
Chile	£16.95
Chile & Argentina: Trekking	£12.95
Eccentric America	£13.95
Eccentric California	£13.99
Falkland Islands	£13.95
Peru & Bolivia: Backpacking and Trekking	£12.95
Panama	£13.95
St Helena, Ascension, Tristan da Cunha	£14.95
USA by Rail	£13.99

Wildlife

Antarctica: Guide to the Wildlife	£14.95
Arctic: Guide to the Wildlife	£14.95
British Isles: Wildlife of Coastal Waters	£14.95
Galápagos Wildlife	£15.99
Madagascar Wildlife	£14.95
South African Wildlife	£18.95

Health

Your Child Abroad: A Travel Health Guide	£10.95

274

Index

Page numbers in bold indicate major entries; those in italic indicate maps